D1736217

# THE KING'S ROAD

# The King's Road

## DIPLOMACY AND THE REMAKING OF THE SILK ROAD

XIN WEN

PRINCETON UNIVERSITY PRESS

PRINCETON & OXFORD

Published by Princeton University Press
41 William Street, Princeton, New Jersey 08540
99 Banbury Road, Oxford OX2 6JX

press.princeton.edu

All Rights Reserved

ISBN: 978-0-691-23783-1
ISBN (e-book): 978-0-691-24320-7

British Library Cataloging-in-Publication Data is available

Editorial: Priya Nelson, Barbara Shi and Emma Wagh
Production Editorial: Jenny Wolkowicki
Jacket design: Katie Osborne
Production: Lauren Reese
Publicity: Alyssa Sanford and Charlotte Coyne

Jacket art: *Mogao Cave 61*. Courtesy of Dunhuang Research Academy.

This book has been composed in Arno

10 9 8 7 6 5 4 3 2 1

To my parents, Wen Shuzhen 文樹禎 and Sun Shiyuan 孫時媛

# CONTENTS

# ACKNOWLEDGMENTS

This book grew out of my 2017 dissertation for the Committee on Inner Asian and Altaic Studies at Harvard University, but its origins go all the way back to 2005, when I entered the Department of History at Peking University as a master's student. Rong Xinjiang, my academic advisor, taught me how to read excavated manuscripts and introduced me to the world of Dunhuang and medieval China. These skills allowed me to conceive the project even before I arrived in the United States to pursue further study. After entering Harvard, I was fortunate to enjoy the mentorship of two exemplary advisors: Prods Oktor Skjærvø taught me what I know about Iranian languages, particularly Khotanese, and the art of reading slowly and carefully; Mark C. Elliott, the primary advisor for both my MA thesis (2011) on ethnicity in Dunhuang and my PhD dissertation, helped me go beyond philological details and place the story of Dunhuang in the broader contexts of Chinese, Inner Asian, and global histories. This book certainly would not have been written without their generous support and patient guidance.

In addition to these advisors, other mentors have guided my research, imparted language skills, and provided other kinds of support: Duan Qing, Valerie Hansen, Peter K. Bol, Leonard van der Kuijp, Janet Gyatso, Luo Xin, Meng Xianshi, Zhu Yuqi, Shi Rui, and Yao Chongxin. My friends and fellow graduate students Chen Liu, Ziqing Zhao, Zhang Zhan, Heng Du, Joshua Freeman, Eric Schluessel, Nathan Vedal, Andrew Campana, Sakura Christmas, Huijun Mai, David Porter, Lincoln Tsui, Miya Qiong Xie, Ying Qian, Yin Hang, Conrad Lawson, Natalie Koehler, Rian Thum, Wen Yu, Lei Lin, Hanung Kim, and Wang Hongsu all gave me helpful suggestions that strengthened the dissertation.

The revision of the dissertation into a monograph began after I joined the faculty of Princeton University in 2017. Since then, I have enjoyed the company of many engaging and encouraging colleagues, all of whom have enriched my professional life while challenging me to reconceptualize the dissertation as a monograph. He Bian, Anna Shields, Stephen Teiser, Tom Conlan, Martin Kern, Marina Rustow, Sue Naquin, Helmut Reimitz, Wendy Belcher, and Peter Brown each provided insightful suggestions that much improved the manuscript. In the meantime, although I intentionally avoided talking to them too much about "the book," my friends Guangchen Chen, Peter Wirzbicki, Meg Rooney, Gavin Steingo, Helen Kim, Laura Kalin, Dan Beckman, Johannes Wankhammer, Harvey Lederman, Natasha Wheatley, Michael Blaakman, Ksenia Chizhova, Brian Steininger, Erin Huang, Franz Prichard, Cheng-hua Wang, Xin Zou, Bryan Lowe, Iryna Vushko, Dan Sheffield, and Chao-hui Jenny Liu have all helped to make Princeton feel like home.

During the 2019–20 academic year, I received a visiting scholarship from the Institute for the Study of the Ancient World (ISAW) at New York University. This opportunity provided me with the time and space to conduct additional writing and research. Even though my time spent at ISAW was shortened by the Covid-19 pandemic, I am grateful for the camaraderie of the other fellows—Fokelien Kootstra, Mitra Panahipour, Ann Macy Roth, Daniela Wolin, Odette Boivin, and Cicek Tascioglu Beeby—and the guidance that I received from other ISAW colleagues, including Sören Stark, Lillian Lan-ying Tseng, Judith A. Lerner, and Ethan Harkness.

On several occasions, I presented the research contained in this book and developed my thinking in conversation with colleagues at various institutions. For their invitations, questions, comments, and generous help in various ways, I thank Michelle C. Wang, Anne Feng, Hyunhee Park, Naomi Standen, Shao-yun Yang, Chen Boyi, Armin Selbitschka, James Pickett, Patrick Geary, Joshua Van Lieu, Jonathan Skaff, Dorothy C. Wong, Tansen Sen, and Ma Weihua.

The conversations, suggestions, and occasionally ruthless criticism I have received from colleagues and friends at Princeton, ISAW, and elsewhere completely transformed this book. As a result, I removed more than half of the content of the dissertation from the book manuscript, substantially reworked the rest of the dissertation into three chapters (5, 6, and 10), and wrote six new chapters (2, 3, 4, 7, 8, 9). I hope the result is a more focused book.

After finishing the first draft of *The King's Road* in 2020, I convened a manuscript workshop at Princeton University that included Robert Hymes, Ellen Cong Zhang, Susan Whitfield, and Christopher Atwood as my readers. The suggestions that came out of this meeting were a tremendous boost to the manuscript, as they helped me broaden its scope and sharpen the arguments I have put forward. I also added what is now chapter 1 thanks to the suggestions from these readers.

In the course of writing *The King's Road*, I had the good fortune to visit the many libraries and research institutes around the world that store Dunhuang documents. These invaluable research trips would not have been possible without the assistance and generosity of Susan Whitfield, Nathalie Monnet, Étienne de la Vaissière, Desmond Durkin-Meisterernst, Nicholas Sims-Williams, Ursula Sims-Williams, Sam van Schaik, Imre Galambos, Chen Juxia, and Zhang Xiaogang. They introduced me to the Dunhuang and other Central Asian manuscripts, artifacts, paintings, and murals now preserved in London, Paris, Berlin, and Dunhuang. Being able to directly observe, study, and even touch these objects, all of which are over one thousand years old, is one of the main reasons that the study of Dunhuang continues to fascinate me.

After submitting the manuscript to Princeton University Press, I received comments from two anonymous readers, which helped me reshape the arguments of the book and avoid many errors. I thank them for their work.

My partner, Ben, offers the best combination of a caring companion and an insightful reader. He gave me crucial lessons on how to make my writing more engaging, and his presence was indispensable as I finished the manuscript while being locked down during the pandemic.

In 2004, when I told my parents that I wanted to be a historian, they were surprised, and more than a little alarmed. Since then, however, they have never wavered in their support, even as I have ended up further and further away from home. As a small token of my enormous gratitude, I dedicate this book to them.

# Introduction

## A Song of Diplomacy
## on the Silk Road

IN MEDIEVAL DUNHUANG, New Year's Eve was usually cold and rowdy. At dusk, in a widely practiced ritual of exorcism, dozens of teenage boys would dress up as Buddhist, Daoist, and Zoroastrian deities, and local gods—the ghostbuster Zhongkui, the Nine-Tailed Fox, or the "Poisonous Dragon of the Golden Mountain." Their leader might wear a bronze mask and a leopard-skin robe draped over his body, painted red with cinnabar. With chants like "I am Zhongkui the god!" he would lead this motley procession of deities, beating drums and singing songs, and marching through the streets of the city. These noisy gods would try to expel the many spirits that had been haunting the streets, farms, pastures, and homes of Dunhuang during the previous year. People of all ranks, from commoners to the governor and his family, would witness or even join the carnival as the boys danced from the city gates to their houses and government offices.[1] It would have been difficult to sleep on these festive nights.

Many centuries later, we can almost experience what it felt like to be present during these raucous festivities, because many of the songs that would have been heard on the streets of Dunhuang were recorded in manuscripts that were stored in a small cave southeast of the city and sealed for nine centuries. The rediscovery of these manuscripts in 1900 allowed the buried voices to be heard once again: the boy-exorcists sang for a prosperous new year, with "cows and sheep filling the pastures; wheat and barley piling like hills"; they also prayed that their families would be fortunate and healthy in the new year and behave in a manner appropriate to their social status. Although our contemporary end-of-year rituals are boisterous in rather different ways, we can relate to these sentiments. But in other songs, we find a perspective more distinctive to medieval Dunhuang. One in particular includes the following stanzas:

> The ten thousand commoners sing songs with full bellies like drums,
> [living in] a time like that under [the sage kings] Shun and Yao.
> Do not worry about the eastern road being blocked.
> In the spring, the heavenly envoys will arrive,
> and they will contribute large *jin*-silks with coiled dragons,
> and different kinds of damask, gauze, plain silk, colored silk.
>
> . . . . . . . . . . . . . . . . . . . . . . . . . . . . . . . . . . . . . . . . . . . . . . . . . . . . . . . . . . . . . . . . . . . .
>
> To the west all the way until Khotan
> the road is smoother than those covered in cotton cloth.
> [The Khotanese] will offer precious artifacts and white jade,
> as well as a thousand rolls of cotton, damask, and miscellaneous
>    fabrics.
> All within the border [of Dunhuang] chant the song of happiness
> and enjoy a long life like Ancestor Peng![2]

Here, the crowd in Dunhuang wished for a world of happiness and long life, where kings ruled in the manner of ancient sages such as Yao and Shun and commoners prospered like "Ancestor Peng," who famously lived for eight hundred years. In the context of this song, these better times will not come about through the establishment of any new social institution, the realization of any moral or religious obligations, or the dissemination of any school of thought. Instead, the key to this ideal world is the network of roads that connect Dunhuang to its neighbors, conveying a perpetual influx of diplomatic travelers, such as the "heavenly envoys," and luxury goods into Dunhuang. Singers of this song reassured their audience that the road leading eastward to North China would remain open, allowing Chinese envoys to bring silk the following spring. Meanwhile, the road to the west to Khotan would be smoother than cotton cloth, and Khotanese envoys would offer jade as tribute. Put another way, to these singers, the operation of diplomacy was crucial to the happiness of the Dunhuang people.

In our time, diplomatic matters are generally far removed from the minds of New Year's revelers while they wait for the clock to strike midnight. Why were they so critical to the hopes and wishes of the people living in medieval Dunhuang? What social, cultural, and economic circumstances gave rise to the ecstatic vision presented in these lyrics? Looking beyond Dunhuang, what does this ceremonial song reveal about the history of long-distance travel and connection in medieval Eurasia more broadly?

This book is an investigation into the world envisioned within this song. Key to that world are the actions of diplomatic travelers, the very people that the singers eagerly anticipated. By following the emergence, activities, and impact of these travelers, we can begin to understand the world the Dunhuang singers wished for at the dawn of a New Year.

## From the Age of Empire to the Age of Kings

The oasis city of Dunhuang sits at the intersection of three main roads in the eastern half of the Eurasian continent (see map i.1). These roads lead to East Asia by way of the Hexi Corridor, to North Asia via the valleys in the Tianshan mountains, and to Central Asia through the oases and deserts north of the Tibetan Plateau. Because of its strategic location, Dunhuang was embroiled in the political drama of the broader Eastern Eurasian world from the moment that it first entered recorded history with the Han emperor Wudi (156–87 BCE) wrangling control of the region from the Xiongnu Empire. This dynamic of survival at the margins of empires persisted into the medieval period, as Eastern Eurasia was dominated, starting in the late sixth century, by three empires: the Tibetan, the Tang, and the Turco-Uyghur.

The power of these empires fluctuated over time: The First Turkic Empire (552–630) achieved regional supremacy in the late sixth and early seventh centuries and subjected the first Tang emperor to political vassalage.[3] In the 620s, the Tang Empire (618–907) gained the upper hand, achieving military supremacy and consolidating its rule in the region. The Tang all but eradicated the Turkic Empire as a political power in the mid-seventh century, but the Turkic elites' dissatisfaction with the Tang mounted until they reclaimed their status and established the Second Turkic Empire (681–742).[4] This new state was less powerful than its earlier incarnation and lasted only a few decades before it was overthrown by an alliance of Tang and nomadic groups. One group of these nomadic rebels, the Uyghurs, succeeded the Turks as rulers of the steppe; their empire (744–840) maintained friendly relations with the Tang, whose empire was greatly weakened by the An Lushan Rebellion (755–63).

Just as the First Turkic Empire was disintegrating, Songtsen Gampo (?–650) expanded the domain of the Yarlung dynasty to cover the entire Tibetan Plateau. He established formal diplomatic relations with the Tang in 634 and consolidated this relationship in 641 by marrying Princess

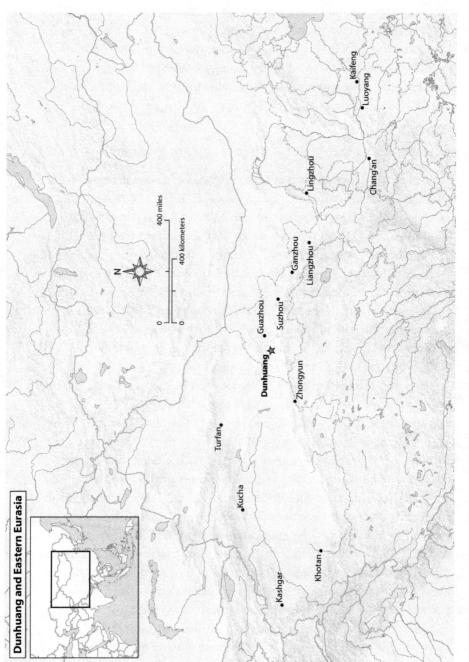

MAP I.1 Dunhuang and Eastern Eurasia

Wencheng (623–80). Under the next several *btsan-po* (Tibetan for "emperor"), the Tibetan Empire (618–842) grew to be a formidable military force and expanded its influence far into modern Afghanistan, Central Asia, and Nanzhao in southwestern China.[5]

The oasis region in the Central Asian deserts between Dunhuang and Kashgar—an area central to the events discussed in this book—was located among these three imperial powers, making it the coveted prize of this medieval "Great Game."[6] All three empires attempted, at times successfully, to conquer this region.[7] Beginning in the middle of the sixth century, it was ruled by the First Turkic Empire. The Tang, however, expanded westward into the Hexi Corridor (including Dunhuang) in 619, and then Turfan in 640. In 648, they established "four garrisons to pacify the west" (*anxi sizhen*) in four Central Asian oasis-towns: Kucha, Khotan, Shule (modern Kashgar), and Suyab (Ak-Beshim, near Tokmok in what is now Kyrgyzstan). Then, in 662, Tibetan forces began their incursion into the region. The oases changed hands between Tibetan and Tang forces several times until 692, when Empress Wu (624–705) recaptured them from the Tibetans and stationed thirty thousand troops at the four garrisons.[8]

The significant military presence in the region secured Tang rule until the An Lushan Rebellion in the mid-eighth century. After the retreat of the Tang forces, the Tibetan Empire regained control of the area, imposing a similar military occupation and conquering Dunhuang in 781.[9] At the same time, the Uyghur Empire invaded, challenging Tibetan forces on the northern frontier. In the 790s and 800s, the Uyghurs successfully captured such important oasis kingdoms as Beshbalik, Kucha, and Turfan from the Tibetans.[10] During the first half of the ninth century, the region between Dunhuang and Kashgar was divided between these two powers, with the Uyghur Empire ruling its northern half and the Tibetan Empire ruling the south.

Then, in the middle of the ninth century, all three imperial powers simultaneously went into decline. The assassination of the last *btsan-po*, Langdarma (799–841), in 841 initiated a long process of disintegration within the Tibetan Empire. Seven years later, in 848, the Kyrgyz drove the Uyghur Empire out of the steppe, leading to the dispersal of Uyghurs across Central Asia. With the rebellion of Huang Chao, lasting from 874 to 884, the Tang dynasty was decisively wounded. Its eventual overthrow would come two decades later.

While we cannot determine whether there was an overarching cause of the near-simultaneous demise of all three empires, we can say unequivocally that the result was the intense territorial division of Eastern Eurasia. Many smaller states arose in the late ninth and early tenth centuries, including the "Five Dynasties and Ten Kingdoms" in China, the Guge kingdom in western Tibet, the independent oasis states along the Hexi Corridor from Liangzhou to Dunhuang, and such Central Asian states as Khotan and Turfan. Although many kings of these states clung to imperial titles and rhetoric (the king of Dunhuang, for instance, called himself "emperor" for a few years after the fall of the Tang), none were territorially expansionist in the way that rulers of the three old empires had been.[11] In the ruins of these empires, then, we can witness the emergence of a new epoch of political fragmentation—an age of many kings.

It is to this period, when Dunhuang was a de facto independent state (848–1036), that the song about diplomacy, silk, and jade, with which we began, belongs.[12] The "heavenly envoys" from the east, of which it speaks, came from either one of the Five Dynasties (907–60) in North China or the early Song state (960–1127), while the envoys from the west came from the newly independent Central Asian kingdom of Khotan, located at the southern edge of the Taklamakan Desert.[13] The existence of these long-distance connections running from North China through Dunhuang to Central Asia contradicts how some scholars have previously assessed this age of political fragmentation in Eastern Eurasia. The historian Morris Rossabi, for instance, comments that "starting around 845, the [Tang] court, as well as rebels, targeted and attacked Buddhism and other foreign religions. Most foreigners reacted by avoiding China, leading to four centuries of limited intercultural contact along the Silk Roads."[14] Others have written, in similar terms, about how political disunity hindered long-distance connection during this time.[15] The idea that the decline of the Tang brought about centuries of reduced trans-Eurasian connection is widely shared, especially in the field of global history. According to this view, long-distance, intercultural contact was either lost entirely or severely reduced in the absence of large, unified empires, and it would not fully recover until the rise of the Mongol empire in the thirteenth century.[16]

If long-distance trans-Eurasian travel was indeed as rare at this time as many believe, why would the people of Dunhuang sing about their connections with North China and Central Asia? One possibility is that these references to foreign envoys and luxury goods convey an unrealistic and idealized set of hopes, much like the lyric about Ancestor Peng's octocentennial lifespan. Or, does this exorcist song performed in Dunhuang disclose a highly interconnected world, the existence of which has gone largely unnoticed by historians?

## A Bottom-Up History of Diplomacy

These questions would be impossible to answer—indeed, impossible to raise—if not for an accidental discovery made in 1900. On a hot summer night, a Daoist monk named Wang Yuanlu (1851–1931) was cleaning the sand from the front of the complex of caves known as "The Grottoes of Unparalleled Height" (Mogao ku), located southwest of the city of Dunhuang. These caves housed Buddhist statues and mural paintings created from the fourth to the fourteenth centuries. By the late nineteenth century, however, this former center of Buddhism had lost its luster, and few visitors came to see its medieval caves anymore. Perhaps its lone resident at the time, Wang wished to rebuild parts of the cave complex as a Daoist "Palace of Celestial Purity." On this particular evening, as he channeled running water before the entrance to one of the caves, an opening suddenly appeared in the wall, "giving out a flickering light."[17] Intrigued by the light, Wang dug through the opening, inside which he found a small hidden chamber of about thirteen square meters.[18] As scholars would eventually realize, this chamber had been sealed in the early eleventh century and remained undisturbed for almost nine hundred years. It contained sixty thousand manuscripts.

The large number of secular documents found in this cave makes it possible to reconstruct, in microscopic detail, the social lives of residents in Dunhuang, including the experiences of travelers who passed through this hub of exchange in the Eurasian heartland. In a remarkable study, Sam van Schaik and Imre Galambos have used a single Sino-Tibetan manuscript to show how a traveling monk navigated his life on the road.[19] In this book, I follow their example and expand the lens outward to the entire Dunhuang corpus.[20] Many hundreds of unique long-distance journeys are recorded in the Dunhuang archive in different formats: contracts show how travelers financed their journeys; royal edicts include the information that they communicated; maps and road guides reveal how they navigated the difficult terrain of Central Eurasia; personal correspondence and notebooks offer a window into their minds and sentiments while on the road; petitions demonstrate their need for assistance in times of distress; messages of greeting and gratitude bear witness to the relationships that they enjoyed with their hosts. Their stories attest to the persistence of long-distance travel in the "age of kings," between roughly 850 and 1000.

As the New Year's Eve song would suggest, the overwhelming majority of long-distance travelers described in the Dunhuang documents undertook their journeys for diplomatic purposes. The centrality of diplomacy to these documents is unmistakable: an official report details the gifts delivered and received by Dunhuang envoys after they went to the Tang capital; a wine expenditure record from the Dunhuang government describes the reception of Turfan envoys at arrival and departure; two lists of places a group of Khotanese envoys would visit are scribbled on a notebook; a set of poems by a Chinese envoy laments the damage of guesthouses on the Silk Road. Time and again, travelers describe themselves, and are described by others, as envoys, dispatched on their long journeys on behalf of the state. Each year, dozens, perhaps even hundreds, of foreign envoys came to Dunhuang, and dozens of Dunhuang envoys were dispatched to neighboring states. In comparison, commercial travelers are almost entirely absent in the Dunhuang documents.[21] The examples I collect in this book show that the images presented in the New Year's song are not the fanciful concoction of a dreaming poet. Instead, they reflect the actual experience of the people of Dunhuang in the context of the city's relations with its neighbors in the ninth and tenth centuries.

This book is a social history of the lives of these diplomatic travelers. By tracing their steps, observing their actions, and assessing their impact, the book investigates the organization and mechanisms of Eastern Eurasian international relations in the age of kings. Unlike earlier works of diplomatic history, I am not primarily concerned with military strategies and decision-making in court.[22] Instead, my interest lies with more mundane matters: What did the envoys eat and drink? Where did they stay? How did they organize the logistics of transporting goods across the difficult terrain of Eastern Eurasia? How did they communicate, both orally and in writing, with people who spoke a different language? What diplomatic protocols did they follow? These matters open onto a set of larger questions about the political dimensions of this time. What motivated kings to engage in diplomacy? Was diplomacy critical to their idea of kingship, and if so, why? What motivated envoys to participate in diplomacy? The documents discovered in the Dunhuang cave provide the answers to these questions, and many others.

It might be tempting to see these envoys as operating in a "tributary system," a set of diplomatic practices and rhetoric that recognize the superiority of the Chinese emperor in his dealings with neighboring vassal states.[23] This would not be entirely wrong, because the hierarchies typical of such a system are everywhere visible in their lives on the road. But the bottom-up view taken by this book reveals the messy and contradictory way that this "tributary system" actually played out on the ground, and thus challenges the official accounts in sources produced in Chinese courts. One example appears in the

New Year's song with which we began. Here, on the one hand, envoys from North China are described as "heavenly envoys," which seems to suggest their state's elevated status in comparison to Dunhuang. But, on the other hand, the lyrics characterize these Chinese envoys as "contributing" (*jinfeng*) gifts, a close synonym of the more familiar verb *gong* ("to pay tribute"), which implies inferior status of the person performing the action. The assumed hierarchy in the tributary system begins to dissolve when we see "heavenly envoys" from the Chinese emperor "paying tribute" to the lord of the small oasis kingdom of Dunhuang.

Attending to such contradictions allows me to dissect this system and examine its inner workings. As we follow the movement of envoys along the road and their interactions with different states, the Tang and the Song, the two major Chinese empires at the time, move to the margins of our field of vision. Looking closely at the kings of smaller states, we see that they sometimes accommodated the tributary system when dealing with the states based in North China. But, just as often, they rejected the hierarchies that it implied and actually regarded themselves as superior. Certain cases—such as when the Chinese-speaking rulers of Dunhuang acknowledged the superiority of the Iranian-speaking kings of Khotan and addressed them as "emperor" (*huangdi*)—completely subvert our conventional understandings of the tributary system. Meanwhile, envoys had their own economic and religious motives that sometimes caused them to disagree with, or even disparage, the kings who dispatched them. Furthermore, all of these actions taken by kings and envoys can be observed not only in Chinese sources but also in documents written in Khotanese, Tibetan, Uyghur, and Sogdian. Taken together, these sources reveal the interaction between a North China–dominated tributary system and an equally well-established, though much less well-known, Inner Asian tradition of diplomacy. Although widely assumed to have occurred, this process has never before been examined in detail owing to a lack of available sources.[24] The world of diplomacy viewed from this peripheral, envoy-centered, and multilingual perspective differs drastically from the tributary system that appears throughout sources from the Chinese court.

## Another Silk Road

In addition to diplomacy, this book is also about the Silk Road, a mythical term that is almost universally invoked but rarely defined with precision. A product of the nineteenth century, the concept was introduced by the German geologist and geographer Ferdinand von Richthofen (1833–1905), who drew scholarly attention to the long-neglected Central Asian interior just as Prussian industrialists were drawing up plans for a trans-Eurasian railroad.[25] Richthofen relied on ancient geography: from the works of Marinus of Tyre (ca. 70–130) and Ptolemy (ca. 100–170), and from the Chinese annals of Sima Qian (ca. 145–86 BCE) and Ban Gu (32–92), he advanced the idea that luxury goods like silk might have traveled from workshops in Han-dynasty China to the markets of the Roman Empire via a single route, the "Silk Road."[26]

Since Richthofen, scholars have expanded the use of this term. It is now common to increase the lifespan of the Silk Road beyond the Han-Roman period to other premodern eras, such as the Tang-Abbasid period and the Mongol Empire.[27] Some have further extended it both backward and forward in time, covering the prehistoric as well as the modern era.[28] Others have widened it geographically to encompass not only latitudinal, transcivilization routes but also longitudinal, transclimatic routes.[29] The recent advent of the term "maritime Silk Road" has further broadened the term to include the entire Afro-Eurasian world.[30] For some historians, the term "Silk Road" has come to serve as a metonym for "global," despite its longstanding association with the region of Central Eurasia in particular.[31]

At the same time, metaphorical uses of the "Silk Road" remove the term from history and tether it to certain qualities and tropes, as in novels and travelogues that rely on its exotic appeal.[32] The name of cellist Yo-Yo Ma's "Silk Road Ensemble" alludes to the amicable coexistence presumably practiced by different neighboring cultures.[33] China's ambitious "Belt and Road Initiative" of infrastructure development in nearly seventy countries, on the other hand, conjures the trans-Eurasian economic prosperity that the Silk Road seemingly once made possible.[34]

Given its origin in nineteenth-century imperial politics and the casual ways in which writers of different stripes use it, scholars have grown skeptical that "the Silk Road" is a productive term to use when referring to premodern Eurasian connections.[35] Many reject it altogether as an anachronism. One historian argues that Richthofen's original concept is a fantasy unsupported by "a single ancient historical record."[36] Another suggests that it "is a purely modern intellectual construct, one that would have been utterly unfamiliar and likely incomprehensible to those historical agents it purports to describe."[37] Even those who continue to refer to a "Silk Road" appear to do so only reluctantly, cautioning their readers that its literal components ("silk" and "road") do not constitute the full dimensions of premodern trans-Eurasian cultural exchange.[38] It seems that the more popular the idea of the "Silk Road" becomes, the less confident scholars are that it can usefully describe premodern transregional connections.

And yet, the song heard in medieval Dunhuang on New Year's Eve poses a challenge to such skepticism. By tying luxury goods—both silk and other textiles—directly to an "eastern road" to North China and a road leading west to Khotan, it seems to approximate Richthofen's historical thesis. To those who sang it, the network of roads that brought luxury goods like silk into Dunhuang was not a myth but a structuring fact of everyday life. People in Dunhuang, of course, did not exactly call the roads that connected them with their neighbors the "Silk Road." Nevertheless, had they been asked about it, they likely would have found the phrase entirely intelligible, even meaningful.

My investigation in this book shows that both elements of this concept—the "silk" and the "road"—are key to understanding the transregional connections found in the Dunhuang documents. "Silk Road" is not just a convenient shorthand with which we are saddled, but a historically accurate term that we should embrace. Silk, along with other precious textiles such as cotton, is representative of the things that traveled with Eurasian envoys in this period. These envoys carried and exchanged high-value, low-weight goods such as jade, medicines, and aromatics, rather than grain, livestock, and other items for everyday use. But silk and textiles were more central to diplomatic exchange than any other luxury goods. The quantity of silk that traveled was enormous—in large part, because of its versatility: silk was used to create clothing, decorations, paintings, book covers, and other luxurious objects, and, crucially, it served as a medium of exchange.[39] It is not an exaggeration to say that silk and other luxury textiles were *the* most important items that these travelers carried with them.

As the New Year's song makes clear, the people of Dunhuang, from kings and officials to monks and commoners, were keenly aware of the fact that they lived along roads that connected places hundreds, sometimes thousands of kilometers away. These roads brought them political intelligence, news of their families, luxury goods, and foreign guests. Kings and officials relied on the roads to sustain their legitimacy, while commoners depended on them for material necessities. Dunhuang and its neighboring states often swore in diplomatic treaties to protect "the road that made us a family."[40] It was clear to the people of the Eurasian heartland that a network of transregional roads bound them together, and that keeping these roads open was critical to their collective political survival and economic well-being.

How might this study change the way we understand the Silk Road? Aside from validating the term's utility, the most important revision may have to do with *who* set the travelers in motion along it, and for what reasons. Throughout its existence, the Silk Road has been a concept primarily associated with merchants.[41] Even though scholars point out the cultural, religious, and diplomatic dimensions of the Silk Road, many believe that it was fundamentally a commercial network.[42] Because of the close association between merchants and the Silk Road, the breakdown of the Sogdian merchant network in the late eighth and ninth centuries that followed the Arabic conquest of Sogdiana is often regarded as the end of the Silk Road's golden age.[43]

This book uncovers another Silk Road that formed in the wake of the imperial decline and the retreat of the Sogdians. I show that, in the late ninth and tenth centuries, states between Kaifeng and Kashgar attempted, but ultimately refrained from, territorial expansion, and recognized, if sometimes begrudgingly, the existence of their neighbors on a shared road. The many long-distance journeys chronicled in this book demonstrate that political fragmentation did not simply hinder connections on the Silk Road. If anything, the existence of a large number of independent states further incentivized diplomatic travel, as each state needed to acquire diplomatic information and validate its own status through the exchange of gifts, investiture from a more powerful state, or the tribute from a smaller state. This collection of smaller states was capable of generating and maintaining the physical infrastructure and the systems of knowledge that allowed the Silk Road to flourish. The history of the post-Sogdian Silk Road is not one of precipitous decline. Rather, it involves a long process of remaking by kings and their envoys. By the early tenth century, a network of envoys crisscrossed Eastern Eurasia with evident frequency and regularity along what I call the "King's Road," marking a new phase in the history of the Silk Road.[44]

## The Structure of the Book

To describe the "King's Road," the three parts of the book are structured around the three aspects of a diplomatic journey on the Silk Road:

1. Who became diplomatic travelers?
2. How did they travel?
3. What was the world that the travelers created like?

Part I, "Travelers," consisting of three chapters, offers a profile of the diplomatic travelers found in the Dunhuang documents. Chapter 1, "An Archive for an Age of Kings," provides the context for the rest of the book in two ways. It introduces the Dunhuang manuscript collection and the social and political world of this collection and the travelers it recorded. I first survey the content of the Dunhuang manuscripts, analyze its use for understanding long-distance travel, and assess its inherent limits and biases. Since most of the travelers I discuss were active between 850 and 1000, I then offer a political history of Eastern Eurasia by following the record of a diplomatic traveler. I argue that, even though this era was one of political fragmentation, the history of Dunhuang and the making of the Dunhuang manuscripts were both deeply rooted in a network of diplomatic connection that reached from the Tang and Song capitals in the east to Khotan and Kashgar in the west. Chapter 2, "People," shows that, instead of a small coterie of trained bureaucrats, envoys traveling through Dunhuang included Buddhist monks and laypeople, kings and slaves, men and women, and people of diverse (Han Chinese, Tibetan, Sogdian, Uyghur, and Khotanese) cultural backgrounds. When on the road, these individuals banded into diplomatic missions, often with envoys from other states, thus creating a complicated social world of diplomatic travelers. While there is no accounting of how many people in Dunhuang traveled as envoys, evidence suggests that serving as an envoy of the state was a common profession, practiced with routinized regularity and involving a significant percentage of the population in Dunhuang. Chapter 3, "Things," turns to the nonhuman members of the diplomatic missions. I divide these "things" into five categories: food, clothes, texts, animals, and luxury items, and discuss the relationships they formed with their human companions. These things differed in their functionality, weight, and expected travel time (food items were often consumed after a few days on the road, while luxury items regularly traveled for longer, and lived longer, than envoys themselves), forming a transient companionship that human travelers had to negotiate with care. While envoys directed things to travel with them, particularly potent things, like a large and precious piece of jade, also drove envoys into action. This chapter positions the human-thing symbiosis, rather than envoys alone, as the protagonists of the Silk Road.

Part II, "Traveling," consisting of four chapters, dissects the diplomatic traveler's life on the road. Chapter 4, "Facing the Road," argues that the roads that diplomatic travelers encountered were neither well-maintained highways nor merely unidentifiable, shifting paths. Depending on the existence of postal systems, military establishments, and sources of water, one can broadly distinguish four types of stops that lent different degrees of navigability to the roads they served. Without comprehensive maps, medieval travelers nonetheless navigated these often-challenging roads through geographical treatises, lists of place names, place-centered poems, and travelogues, as well as with the assistance of local guides and host states. In this way, travelers were able to connect fragments of information about diverse areas into an intelligible whole. Chapter 5, "Praising the Host," lays out a program of common practices during envoys' encounters with foreign states in medieval Eastern Eurasia. Envoys met and dined with their hosts, performed official duties, and conducted personal affairs; they did these things in the suburbs, by the city gate, at the polo field, and in palaces. In the process, they often formed a reciprocal relation with their host state. The host state was responsible for their accommodation and honorable treatment as guests; the envoys in turn were expected to praise the host for their generosity and spread their "good name." Envoys failing to properly conform to this program were reprimanded or even treated as "bandits." Kings and emperors, and occasionally queens, of host states desired the good name that they could acquire through their generous treatment of envoys, thus perpetuating further diplomatic exchange. Chapter 6, "Exchanging Gifts," continues this line of investigation and shows the central importance of gift exchange for diplomatic travelers. Gifts accompanied every aspect of the life on the road, from gifts sent along with letters to those exchanged in meetings, and those left after departure. Like cash for a modern traveler, gifts served as the medium that smoothed interpersonal and interstate negotiations and made long-distance travel possible. The exchange of gifts differed from commercial exchanges in that, instead of attempting to gain profit, the parties involved often tried to outspend, and thus to out-gift, one another. This chapter shows how this dynamic of competitive gifting organized not only the relations between kings, but also the daily life of diplomatic travelers on the road. Chapter 7, "Switching Languages," turns to the question of linguistic negotiation. By analyzing envoy reports, diplomatic letters, and bilingual phrasebooks, this chapter argues that multilingualism on the Silk Road existed, not only because some travelers spoke more than one language, but also through the multilingual diplomatic missions that consisted of monolingual travelers who spoke different languages. Regardless of the language(s) they spoke, the diplomatic travelers shifted their ways of communicating through translations of official documents, interpretations of key conversations, and exchanges on mundane topics on the road. In all of these cases, shifts occurred not only among different languages, but also between different registers—imperial, bureaucratic, or colloquial—of the same language.

Part III, "The King's Road," in three chapters, assesses the economic, political, and cultural consequences of this network of diplomatic travelers in Eastern Eurasia. Chapter 8, "The Economics of Diplomacy," examines the ways that transregional travel invigorated the local economy in Dunhuang. Using pretravel contracts, stipulations of the Society for Long-Distance Travel, and private and official records of gift redistribution after the return of the travelers, I show that diplomatic travel was an essential part of the Dunhuang economy. Travelers took great financial risks in borrowing camels and silk to fund their trips; such risks were worth taking because the travelers were often able to acquire large numbers of gifts and goods to sell from their journeys. Residents who did not travel themselves pooled resources to support other residents as envoys and were rewarded accordingly after the trips had concluded. In this way, diplomatic travel injected luxury goods into an agrarian economy and offered residents economic opportunities otherwise unavailable in the arid heartland of Eurasia. Chapter 9, "The Kingly Exchange," considers the kings of Eastern Eurasia whose desires animated this network. I show that these kings made personal gains through gift exchanges and used these exotic and rare gifts, in particular jade and silk, to decorate their bodies. Through the exchange of diplomatic travelers, these kings also kept abreast of the news about other kings and states, and learned about the manner of rulership in other states. It was in this context of intense exchange among the Eurasian courts that we find extraordinary expressions of kingly power, such as the Dunhuang kings' claim to be "emperors" and the Khotanese kings' claims to be "kings of kings of China." This chapter argues that it was this pursuit of kingly glory, expressed in the acquisition of exotic goods, cultural capital, and political information, that motivated the kings of medieval Eastern Eurasia to participate in the diplomatic network described in this book. Chapter 10, "The Politics of the Road," turns to regional politics in and around Dunhuang. By analyzing the letters exchanged between sovereigns of Dunhuang, Turfan, Ganzhou, and Khotan, I show the central role a shared "road" played in the diplomatic rhetoric and practice among states around Dunhuang. Not only did diplomatic treaties use the idea of a shared road as the rationale for negotiation, rulers and commoners in Dunhuang also regularly prayed for peace on the road in devotional texts. On certain occasions, states even went to war over the blockage of roads or the disruption of travel. Despite their sometimes adversarial relations, sovereigns of these Central Eurasian states were keenly aware of their states being "on the road," and reached a political consensus about the need to keep these roads open.

This book represents an attempt to reconstruct the world of diplomatic travelers in medieval Eastern Eurasia between 850 and 1000. In the conclusion, I reflect on how knowledge about this world changes the way we tell the history of the Silk Road and of diplomacy in China and the Eastern Eurasian world.

# PART I

# Travelers

# 1

# An Archive for an Age of Kings

## An Accidental Archive

What was hidden in the "library cave" in Dunhuang? It took decades of cataloging, publication, transcription, translation, dating, and interpretation of these manuscripts before a clear overall picture of this collection began to emerge. Among the most spectacular finds in these sixty thousand manuscripts are medieval Nestorian Christian and Manichean manuscripts in Chinese, the earliest Zen Buddhist manuscripts, the first Tibetan written history, a Hebrew prayer book, actual copies of edicts issued by the Tang emperor, and the earliest-dated printed book in the world.[1] The research into these manuscripts forms the backbone of a new field of research called Dunhuang studies.

These unique items, however, are the exceptions. In fact, Chinese Buddhist texts like the Prajñāpāramitā Sūtra account for the overwhelming majority of the manuscripts in the collection.[2] Buddhist texts in Tibetan are also well represented.[3] The library cave, in which the manuscripts were found, once served as a mortuary chamber for a renowned local Buddhist monk.[4] Both socially and in terms of its contents, the Dunhuang manuscript collection is first and foremost a collection of Buddhist texts.

Therefore, when considering the nature of the collection, scholars have sought answers in the social context of Buddhist institutions. Broadly speaking, there are two schools of thought. The collection is viewed either as a Buddhist library (most likely for the nearby Sanjie Monastery)[5] or as a repository of "sacred waste," Buddhist sutras and paintings that were no longer in use but could not be simply discarded or burned.[6] The debate is not yet resolved because neither theory explains the presence of all the different types of Buddhist manuscripts. Recently, a compromise has been proposed between the two theories, which suggests that the "library cave" functioned both as a Buddhist repository and as a storage room for the library of the Sanjie Monastery.[7] This view better addresses some of the inconsistencies in both theories, but one might still ask about the nature of the *documents* in the collection: If the Dunhuang manuscript collection is primarily a deposit, be it a repository or a library, of Buddhist texts, why did so many secular documents end up in this cave?

By "documents," I mean noncanonical and nonliterary texts produced and used for personal and governmental purposes.[8] Therefore, a contract made by a monk would be a document rather than a Buddhist text. The Dunhuang manuscript collection includes a wide variety of documents, such as contracts, letters, account books, official reports, and governmental orders. In this book, I call this part of the Dunhuang manuscript collection, which accounts for around 5 percent of the entire collection, the "Dunhuang documents." These documents are all part of the larger collection of "Dunhuang manuscripts." But as a subgroup, they also have distinguishing features. Some of them clearly originated from the bureaucracy of the Dunhuang government; some relate to family life and the daily functioning of monasteries; others were brought to Dunhuang by non-Chinese-speaking travelers. The eclectic nature of this subgroup of the Dunhuang manuscript collection makes it harder to characterize than the manuscript collection as a whole.

The clues to understanding the genesis of the Dunhuang document collection are, in fact, buried in these documents themselves. A tenth-century inventory of the possessions of a Buddhist monastery lists items like sutra tables, Buddha statues, and "one bronze bell decorating the corner of the Buddha Hall."[9] Among these entries we find "the house-selling contracts from various households as well as documents about buying water mill: one file."[10] Another similar inventory includes "one file of official documents along with other related documents."[11] From these records we know that monasteries in Dunhuang collected used documents from private and official channels. The Dunhuang document collection in fact includes many contracts dealing with the sale of houses and water mills, as well as the paperwork produced by the government.[12] Evidently, after these documents fulfilled their social roles, they were recycled as used paper and collected by Buddhist monasteries, often in the form of paper donation.

A spectacular example that helps illustrate this process of recycling is an edict issued by Emperor Ruizong (r. 684–90, 710–12) in 711 (figure 1.1). The fluid aesthetics of the emperor's signature led the International Dunhuang

FIGURE 1.1 Imperial edict from the Tang emperor.
*Credit*: The British Library.

Project, an interlibrary collaboration that reassembles Dunhuang manuscripts and publishes their images online (http://idp.bl.uk/), to use this document as its official emblem. Emperor Ruizong issued this edict to Neng Changren, the prefect of Shazhou (Dunhuang), and the edict duly reached the prefectural government in Dunhuang. It is impossible to precisely reconstruct the subsequent life of this document in the three centuries between its issuance and its burial in the library cave, but we can make a few educated guesses. Edicts from the Tang emperors were often preserved well after they no longer served as a means of communication because of the political prestige they held for their recipients. When, in 982, a Song dynasty envoy visited Yizhou (modern Hami) and Turfan, two cities to the west of Dunhuang, he was shown the edicts from Tang emperors that both states had preserved. Turfan even constructed a "house of edicts, where the imperial letters and edicts from emperor Taizong of the Tang as well as the Luminous Emperor [i.e., emperor Xuanzong, 685–762] [were] securely kept."[13]

The 711 edict from Emperor Ruizong might have been just as symbolically potent, which would explain why, although pieces of paper were intentionally cut off the document (see the upper left corner), the cuts avoided the large

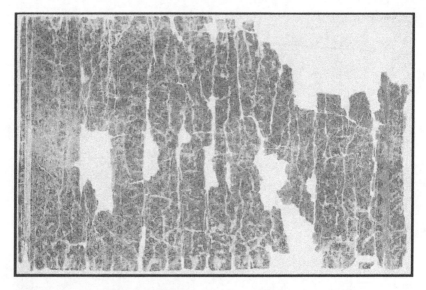

FIGURE 1.2 Cover of a Buddhist sutra. The imperial edict shown in figure 1.1 was used, along with fifteen other documents, to patch up this fragmentary cover. *Credit*: The British Library.

character *chi* (敕), which means "edict." The quality of the paper bearing this edict made it an excellent choice as restoration material. Presumably, after being stored by the government of Dunhuang for some time, the edict was donated to a Buddhist monastery. The monks then used the edict, along with fifteen other documents, most of which are records of military mobilization in Dunhuang in the decades before it was conquered by the Tibetan Empire, to restore and strengthen the tattered silk cover of a Buddhist text.[14] We know this last step for certain because when the silk cover was discovered, these documents were still attached to it and were keeping it in one piece; modern conservators disassembled the cover, confirming that it had indeed been in dire need of repair (figure 1.2).

Many more Dunhuang documents survived because they had been pasted to the back of Buddhist texts for reinforcement.[15] Documents used in this way were brought into the collection more or less arbitrarily, as Buddhist monks most likely collected and used whatever pieces of paper they could get their hands on. These scraps, pasting papers, and other complete manuscripts waiting to be used for these purposes form a significant portion of the Dunhuang documents. Many may have originally belonged to state archives, as local governments of the Tang dynasty typically kept official documents only for a certain period of time.[16] When their owners donated them to the monastery, the documents lost their original social function, and became useful only as paper. Other types of documents, such as contracts, letters, writing exercises, and doodles, originated from other places in Dunhuang, including local mutual-aid communities, foreign diplomatic missions, and private households. After they were placed in what eventually became the Dunhuang manuscript collection, however, they too were used merely as paper. If we consider only the *documents* in the Dunhuang manuscript collection, it is evident that there was no clear curatorial standard regarding what was collected. As such, these documents make up an *accidental* archive.[17]

However, the "accidental" character of the Dunhuang document collection does not mean that it is a perfectly unbiased and representative sample of all the documents used in Dunhuang society. Because these documents were donated to Buddhist monasteries and eventually survived in a Buddhist library/repository, institutions with social and geographical proximity to those Buddhist monasteries are better represented. Unsurprisingly, the institutions that are best represented in the Dunhuang documents are the Buddhist monasteries themselves, which produced large quantities of administrative and personal documents.[18] The Dunhuang government, with its close connection to these monasteries, is also well represented. Private residents, including both elites and commoners, and community organizations such as the mutual-aid groups known as *she* (社) similarly donated documents to Buddhist monasteries and left traces in the archive. Foreign visitors paid homage to the Buddhist sites in Dunhuang and interacted with the Dunhuang government; texts about and by them likely entered the archive indirectly. As a result, this haphazardly assembled collection of documents opens up an uneven yet broad view of Dunhuang society.

This collection of diverse documents allows scholars to pursue a wide array of research topics concerning everything from the institutional presence of the Tang dynasty in Central Asia to the intricacies of monastic life to the transmission of Nestorian Christianity, Zoroastrianism, and Manichaeism from Central Asia to China—and much more.[19] Moreover, its location at the crossroads of Eastern Eurasia means that this archive has much to tell us about the trans-Eurasian network of connections commonly known as the "Silk Road." Indeed, the historian Valerie Hansen has characterized the Dunhuang library cave as a "time capsule for the history of the Silk Road," sealed at a moment of intense trans-Eurasian exchange.[20] In this book, I reopen this time capsule and mine its contents for insights into the history of the Silk Road.

In addition to the Dunhuang document collection, my examination of the Silk Road is drawn from two other related groups of archaeological sources. First, numerous mural paintings, many with colophons, are found in the Mogao Buddhist caves complex, where the library cave is only one among hundreds of other, mostly much larger, caves. These paintings, created at roughly the same time as the Dunhuang documents, provide information that complements and corroborates the documents.[21] Second, Dunhuang is not the only place where a substantial number of documents were discovered: areas further west in Central Asia, such as Turfan and Khotan, have yielded many equally significant findings.[22] While most of these documents were produced earlier (in the sixth through eighth centuries), they are often similar in nature to the Dunhuang documents, and thus useful in lending a comparative lens.

Even further afield, courts in more distant regions also produced records about Dunhuang and adjacent areas. Documents generated and kept by the Tang (618–907) and the Northern Song (960–1127) courts are particularly informative, given their abundance and accuracy.[23] Song texts such as the *Recovered Draft of the Collected Essential Documents of the Song* (*Song huiyao jigao*) and *Long Draft Continuation of the Comprehensive Mirror That Aids Governance* (*Xu zizhi tongjian changbian*) preserve extensive records about envoys from the west, including those from Dunhuang, to the Song court in Kaifeng.[24] These records can be put in profitable dialogue with the Dunhuang manuscripts, not least because they often depict the same events. To a lesser extent, Islamic sources such as Mahmud al-Kashgari's eleventh-century dictionary of Turkic languages and Aḥmad ibn Faḍlān's (877–960) account of an Abbasid diplomatic mission also include intriguing information about travelers on the Silk Road at roughly the same time.[25]

An especially fortuitous case where these different types of sources converge concerns a failed Tang diplomatic mission to Turfan in 856. The contour of this mission and the subsequent demotion of all the major officials who took part in it entered the Tang court records, and are preserved in the *Old Tang History* (*Jiu tangshu*).[26] The epitaph of the deputy head of this mission, one of the officials demoted for the failure, was recently discovered in his tomb, and it offers a forceful defense of his supposedly virtuous behavior during the incident.[27] Then, a Dunhuang document (Pelliot chinois 2962), a panegyric for the lord of Dunhuang, tells the story of a low-level member of this mission (who is otherwise unknown), who got lost amid the chaos following the failed mission, accidentally wandered into the domain of Dunhuang, and delivered the news about the mission.[28] These three sources allow us to examine the diplomatic mission from the various perspectives of the Tang government, one of its leaders, and one of its low-level participants. Their agreements are as interesting as their inconsistencies.

In spite of this vast trove of additional source material, this book is primarily based on research into the Dunhuang documents, and the scope of my analysis is determined by their geographical and temporal bounds. While India, Persia, Korea, and South China all show up in the documents, the diplomatic connections between these places and Dunhuang were much thinner than those connecting Dunhuang to the Tang and Song courts in the east and Turfan and Khotan to the west. Thus, I have chosen to focus on the region between Khotan and Kaifeng (the Song capital), a vast area amounting to about half of the Eurasian continent. (For a sense of the geography, envoys traveling from Khotan to the Song capital of Kaifeng—a path well trodden by many of the travelers discussed in this book—would reach the Black Sea if they covered the same distance traveling in the opposite direction.) Throughout the book, I use the shorthand term "Eastern Eurasia" to refer to the world of the Dunhuang envoys, while fully aware that not every region in Eastern Eurasia is discussed in equal measure.[29]

The temporal coverage of this book is also determined by the sources. The cave rediscovered by Wang Yuanlu was sealed in the first decades of the eleventh century. Even though the earliest-dated Dunhuang manuscript was written in 406,[30] the vast majority of documents were written centuries later, particularly after 848, when Zhang Yichao (799–872) rebelled against the Tibetan overlords and established a de facto independent state in the region. The century and a half between 850 and 1000 is the best-documented period in the history of Dunhuang, and the focus of this book.[31]

## A Journey through a World of Kings

It is a coincidence that the period from the mid-ninth century to the early eleventh century was also the most intense era of political regionalism in Eastern Eurasia. I call this era an "age of kings." To get to know the kings of Eastern Eurasia in this period, many of whom are obscure even to scholars of Chinese history, let us trace the footsteps of Gao Juhui, an envoy of the short-lived Later Jin (936–47) dynasty, on his journey from Kaifeng to Khotan in 938 (see map 1.1). Gao kept a record of this trip, which is included in the section on Khotan in Ouyang Xiu's *New History of the Five Dynasties*.[32] Because the region

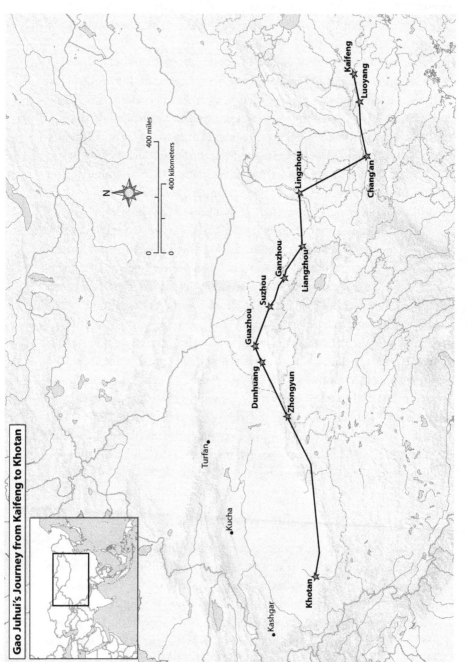

MAP 1.1 Gao Juhui's journey through Eastern Eurasia

covered by Gao—from Kaifeng to Khotan—is roughly coterminous with the geographical boundaries of this study, his succinct narrative serves as a fitting introduction to this world.

Nothing else is known about Gao beyond his record of this journey. We learn that, at the time of his journey, Gao was serving in the regional government of Zhangwu Garrison centered in Yanzhou (modern Yan'an in northern Shaanxi). Perhaps his familiarity with the northwestern border made him a suitable person to serve in this diplomatic mission. The exact dates of Gao's journey are also impossible to reconstruct; the only concrete information is that his mission left in 938. From contemporary records, we may speculate that he could have been on the road for at least a year, but likely much longer.[33]

Gao begins his account as he was leaving his home state, the Later Jin:

> From Lingzhou we crossed the Yellow River. After traveling for thirty *li* [1 *li* equals roughly 540 meters], we reached the border of the Dangxiang [the Tanguts].

Gao was dispatched by Shi Jingtang (892–942), Emperor Gaozu of the Later Jin dynasty. In 907, Zhu Wen (852–912), the warlord in control of the ailing Tang court, deposed (and then killed) the last Tang emperor and assumed the throne as the emperor of a new state known as the Later Liang. In so doing, he initiated a series of five brief dynasties—the Later Liang, Later Tang (923–36), Later Jin, Later Han (947–51), and Later Zhou (951–60)—which would rule North China until 960.[34] Grouping them into a unit of "Five Dynasties," as traditional historians have often done, masks important differences among them: the three middle kingdoms, the Tang, the Jin, and the Han, were established by strongmen of Shatuo Turkic origins, while the founders of other two were "Han" people;[35] the Later Tang also fashioned itself as a continuation of the Tang dynasty, and harbored territorial ambitions exceeding those of the other states.[36]

In 960, a Later Zhou general, Zhao Kuangyin (927–76), launched a coup against the sitting emperor, a seven-year-old boy, and founded a new dynasty later known as the Northern Song (960–1127). Zhao Kuangyin, the emperor Taizu of the Song, pursued a series of successful military campaigns and eliminated several independent southern states. His efforts were followed by those of his brother (and possibly also his murderer), Zhao Guangyi (939–97, Emperor Taizong), who conquered more regional states in the south and the north.[37] Even though this Song "reunification" fell far short of recovering the landmass of the Tang dynasty at its height—an achievement that would have required conquering territories in the northeast, around modern Beijing, and the entire northwest—the first two Song emperors did succeed in establishing a stable and large state.

Another change that occurred in these states was the movement of the capital. In the Tang, Chang'an and Luoyang were the two capitals, with the former being the primary capital. This arrangement persisted until 904, three years before the fall of the Tang state, when Zhu Wen forced the puppet Tang emperor to relocate to Luoyang, abandoning the old capital of Chang'an. When Zhu finally took the throne in 907, he made Kaifeng, his old power base to the east of Luoyang, the new capital. Thereafter, with the exception of the Later Tang, which saw itself as a continuation of Tang rule and therefore placed its capital in Luoyang, Kaifeng remained the capital until the end of the Northern Song dynasty. The changes of capital are important to my story because the travelers I discuss, when they visited these states, often made China's capital city their final destination.

After Gao left the capital, Kaifeng, he and his companions must have taken postal roads within the Later Jin state, possibly passing the old capitals of Luoyang and Chang'an, until they reached Lingzhou, the place where his travelogue begins. Lingzhou, modern Lingwu in Ningxia Province, was a town at the border of the Later Jin along the Yellow River. This same border persisted from the late Tang through the "Five Dynasties" and into the Song dynasty. The history of this area is symptomatic of the forces of fragmentation and recentralization that characterized Eastern Eurasia more broadly. After a warlord—we know only his surname, Han—took control of the area no later than 887, the Han family ruled the region until 929, a period spanning three "dynasties" (the Tang, the Later Liang, and the Later Tang), at which point it was reincorporated into the Later Tang state. Throughout its four decades of semi-independence, Lingzhou recognized the sovereignty of the regimes in North China and functioned as a conduit for travelers from the west.[38]

Once Gao and his entourage crossed the Yellow River, they encountered the rising power of the Tangut (Dangxiang) people. The Tanguts were a group of nomadic people living in the vast area between the northern bend of the Yellow River and the edge of the Tibetan Plateau who spoke a Tibeto-Burmese language.[39] The most famous branch of the Tangut people would consolidate its power in northern Shaanxi in the late ninth century and found the Xia state (1038–1227).[40] The branch that Gao encountered, however, resided to the west of the Yellow River and was known as the "Hexi" Tangut. The Hexi Tangut would eventually succumb to the Kitan state of the Liao (907–1125) and become a vassal state.[41]

Having described the locations of the royal camps of the Hexi Tangut people, Gao continued with his journey west:

> Crossing the Baiting [White Pavilion] River, traveling west of Liangzhou for 500 *li*, we reached Ganzhou. Ganzhou was the military camp of the Uyghurs.

After leaving the domain of the Hexi Tangut people, Gao and his mission officially entered the strings of cities along the Hexi Corridor, a narrow land bridge between two mountain ranges in modern Gansu that connects North China with Central Asia. The Hexi Corridor was incorporated into the domain of the Han dynasty in 121 BCE under emperor Wudi (r. 141–87 BCE), who in 111 BCE instituted four commanderies in this region: Wuwei, Zhangye, Jiuquan, and Dunhuang.[42] These four commanderies, running from the east to the west through the Hexi Corridor, were all located in natural oases. They remain major cities of the Gansu province to this day.

In the Tang dynasty, these four towns were known as Liangzhou, Ganzhou, Suzhou, and Shazhou. All were official prefectures (*zhou*) of the Tang Empire until the late eighth century, when they were conquered by the Tibetan Empire. In 848, following the collapse of the Tibetan Empire, Zhang Yichao, a local strongman in Dunhuang (Shazhou), rebelled against the remnants of the Tibetan government. After years of military campaigns, he extended his domain to include all four prefectures in 861.[43] But Zhang's rule did not last long. By the time Gao Juhui traveled past Liangzhou, it was most likely ruled by a group of Tibetan people known in Chinese sources as "Wenmo."[44]

Ganzhou is the next major town to the west of Liangzhou in the Hexi Corridor, and its history followed a rather different trajectory. The kings of Ganzhou claimed to be direct descendants of the Uyghurs, one of the three empires of the previous age. After the Kyrgyz Rebellion overthrew their empire, Uyghur elites began a process of western migration. In 884, a group of Uyghurs took control of the Ganzhou region, previously under the successive control of Zhang Yichao and various Tibetan peoples, and established a new kingdom.[45] Generations of Uyghur khans ruled this area until 1028, when it was conquered by the Western Xia. At times, Ganzhou was so powerful that it posed a military threat to Dunhuang, and may have directly ruled places like Liangzhou. When Gao passed Ganzhou in 938 or 939, the Uyghur khan in Ganzhou was named Renyu (r. ca. 927–60).[46] As a major power to the east of Dunhuang, Ganzhou maintained close ties to states in North China and facilitated, but also occasionally interfered with, Dunhuang's connections with these states. Thus, Ganzhou was a crucial player in the world of the travelers found in Dunhuang, and will appear frequently in the stories of travelers in this book.

After leaving Ganzhou, Gao and his diplomatic mission proceeded to the next oasis:

> Traveling northwestwards for 500 *li*, we reached Suzhou. After crossing the Gold River, [we proceeded] to the west for 100 *li* to go through the Tianmen Pass, and another 100 *li* to go through the Yumen Pass. Then we crossed the border of Tufan [Tibet]. Tufan men wore hats of the Central Country, while women braided their hair and wore *sese* beads. A good bead was worth as much as a quality horse.

Suzhou, another old prefecture of the Tang dynasty, was also under the Tibetan rule until 849, when Zhang Yichao took control of the area from his base in Dunhuang.[47] However, the control of the Zhang regime over Suzhou was lost in the mid-880s to a group called Longjia (龍家, "Dragon clan," Tibetan Lung, Khotanese Dūṃ) who originated from Yanqi (also known as Agni, Kharashar in eastern Xinjiang) to the west of Dunhuang.[48] Thereafter, Suzhou maintained diplomatic relations with Dunhuang. Between 924 and 926, it was one of the main battlefields of a military conflict between Ganzhou and Dunhuang.[49] After this conflict, Suzhou slowly lost its independence to Ganzhou. In 1010, when the Liao army invaded Ganzhou, Suzhou was listed as a prefecture under the control of Ganzhou.[50]

Unlike the people of Suzhou, who maintained a recognizable state, the next group that Gao met, the Tufan, was more amorphous in its structure. The name of this group is the same as that of the old Tibetan Empire, but in the late 930s no such empire existed any longer. The group that still assumed the name "Tufan" may have been descendants of the military officers of the Tibetan Empire, but did not possess any real political or military power in the tenth century.[51] From the evidence found in the Dunhuang documents, it is clear that it was under the control of the Dunhuang government.

> Further to the west we reached Guazhou and Shazhou. There were many people of the Central Country [Zhongguo ren] in these two places. Upon hearing the arrival of the Jin envoys, the prefect [*cishi*] Cao Yuanshen and others welcomed us in the suburbs and inquired into the health of the Son of Heaven [of Later Jin].

Finally, Gao arrived at Dunhuang, the central nodal point of the events discussed in this book. As an envoy from North China, Gao would have been greeted in Dunhuang as a "heavenly envoy." Guazhou (Prefecture of Melons) and Shazhou (Prefecture of Sands) in Gao's record are the names of the next two oases under the Tang administration. Guazhou is located about 120 kilometers to the east of Shazhou, whose earlier name was Dunhuang. In this book, for the sake of consistency, I use the more familiar name Dunhuang, but it is worth noting that many of the primary sources, in both Chinese and non-Chinese languages, continued to call this place Shazhou.

In Dunhuang, the one and a half centuries between 850 and 1000 can be divided into two eras. From 848 to 914, Dunhuang was ruled by Zhang Yichao and his descendants, with occasional periods when power was seized by families that were related to the Zhangs through marriage. During much of this period, the Zhang rulers maintained Dunhuang's status as a nominal vassal state of the Tang, sending envoys on continuous and mostly unsuccessful quests for the imperial bestowal of official titles. The fifth and last of the Zhang rulers, Zhang Chengfeng (r. 894–910, birth and death dates unknown), briefly rebranded Dunhuang as an independent "Golden Mountain Kingdom of the Western Han" and claimed the title of emperor after the fall of the Tang.[52] This political experiment was quickly thwarted by a combined force of Uyghurs from Ganzhou and rebels within Dunhuang, and Zhang was soon replaced by a local strongman named Cao Yijin (?–935). The Cao family rulers adopted a more pragmatic approach to diplomacy, establishing political marriages with neighboring states of Khotan and Ganzhou. This new strategy allowed for regional peace and stability, and the Cao family ruled for over a century until 1036, when the state of Dunhuang was conquered from the east by the expanding Western Xia state. The vast majority of the diplomatic travelers I describe in this book were dispatched by these states. Because of the centrality of the rulers of Dunhuang to this book, I list their names and the dates of their reigns in table 1.1.[53]

After leaving Dunhuang, Gao Juhui's mission entered the treacherous, arid terrain along the eastern edge of the Taklamakan Desert. Here, they encountered a mysterious group of people known as the Zhongyun.

> To the west of Shazhou there are a people called Zhongyun, and their military camp is located in the Hulu Desert. It is said that the Zhongyun are descendants of the Minor Yuezhi people.

This group of people is also recorded in Tibetan (as Jingul), Khotanese (Cūmūḍa), and Uyghur (Čungul) sources.[54] Its origin has been passionately debated, and modern scholars are perhaps as confused as Gao Juhui, who

TABLE 1.1. Rulers of Dunhuang

| Ruling Family | Ruler | Reign |
|---|---|---|
| Zhang | Zhang Yichao | 848–67 |
| | Zhang Huaishen | 867–90 |
| | Zhang Huaiding | 890–92 |
| [Usurpation] | Suo Xun | 892–94 |
| | Zhang Chengfeng | 894–914 |
| Cao | Cao Yijin | 914–35 |
| | Cao Yuande | 935–39 |
| | Cao Yuanshen | 939–44 |
| | Cao Yuanzhong | 944–74 |
| | Cao Yangong | 974–76 |
| | Cao Yanlu | 976–1002 |
| | Cao Zongshou | 1002–14 |
| | Cao Xianshun | 1014–35 |

attributes it to the "Minor Yuezhi" people, a notoriously enigmatic group difficult to locate in Chinese sources.[55] This is not the place to try to solve the famous Yuezhi question—suffice it to say that the Zhongyun people constituted an independent state with its own bureaucracy. Zhongyun envoys traveled to Dunhuang and mediated the passage of other travelers through the region, and they appear in the Dunhuang documents. For instance, in 1081, when a group of Fulin (Byzantine) envoys traveled to the Song court, they reported that between Khotan and Dunhuang they passed a group of people called Zhong-wen, evidently a different transcription of "Zhongyun."[56]

After leaving the domain of Zhongyun, Gao reached the destination of his journey: Khotan.

> Further to the west we arrive at Ganzhou [紺州, different from the Uyghur kingdom in Ganzhou 甘州 discussed earlier]. Ganzhou is established by Khotan and is located to the southwest of Shazhou. It is said that [Ganzhou] is 9,500 *li* from the capital [Kaifeng]. Then we traveled for two more days and arrived at Anjunzhou; here we have arrived at Khotan.

Khotan was an oasis state situated on the southern edge of the Taklamakan Desert.[57] Before its conquest by the Qarakhanids in the early eleventh century, Khotan was a largely Buddhist kingdom where Khotanese, a middle Iranian language, was used. The history of pre-Islamic Khotan can be roughly divided into three periods. During the first period, from its earliest recorded history in the second century BCE to the early seventh century CE, despite Kushan, Han, and Rouran influences, the kingdom of Khotan seems to have retained a high level of autonomy, with no discernable trace of direct foreign occupation.[58] This autonomy was lost in the second period, from the late seventh to late ninth centuries. As Khotan became a battleground for the great powers of Central Asia, both the Tang and the Tibetan Empires occupied the region for long periods of time.[59] With the fall of these imperial powers, however, Khotan regained independence from the late ninth century to the early eleventh century.[60] When Gao Juhui visited, the kingdom of Khotan was at the height of its power.

———

From Kaifeng to Khotan, Gao's journey took him through the heart of the eastern half of the Eurasian continent. Following Gao's steps, I have introduced nine states: the Tang–Five Dynasties–Song states in North China, Lingzhou, the Tangut state in Hexi, Liangzhou, Ganzhou, Suzhou, Dunhuang, Zhongyun, and Khotan. Eight of the nine—the only exception is Lingzhou—were independent at the time of his journey. But even Gao's long journey does not cover the territories of all the states that are part of this book's story. To finish familiarizing ourselves with the political world of Eastern Eurasia, we will need to mention a few other states that Gao did not visit.

After passing Dunhuang, Gao traveled southwest to Khotan. Had he taken the northwestern path, he would have reached the kingdom of Turfan (also known as Gaochang, "Everlasting prosperity," and Xizhou, "Prefecture of the west"), another oasis state ruled by Uyghur khans and an important neighbor of Dunhuang. Located in an arid depression south of the Tianshan mountains, Turfan's political history, like that of Khotan, fluctuated between a frontier town of expansionist empires of the Han and the Tang and an independent kingdom from the fifth to the seventh centuries.[61] In the late eight century, the Tibetan and Uyghur Empires fought prolonged battles over Turfan, with the latter eventually taking possession of the area. After the fall of both empires, a group of the Uyghurs took control of Turfan in the mid-ninth century and established a kingdom known as Xizhou Uyghur, or Gaochang Uyghur. In this book, I will simply refer to this kingdom using its best-known name, Turfan.

Looming to the north of most of the states Gao visited, the most powerful state in this part of the world was arguably that of the Kitan Liao dynasty.[62] The Kitans were a group of people in modern Northeast China who spoke a language related to Mongolian. Yelü Abaoji (872–926) disrupted the term-limited succession pattern and established the patrilineal rule of the Yelü family.[63] In 916, Abaoji claimed the title of emperor and founded his state, the "Great Central State of the Kitan." After the conquest of the Sixteen Prefectures, which includes modern Beijing, from the Later Jin, the newly acquired, Han Chinese–majority region was known as "the Liao."[64] The Kitan state did not (or was not able to) follow the expansionist policy of the past empires: when the second emperor, Yelü Deguang (902–47, Emperor Taizong), conquered the Later Jin capital, Kaifeng, his rule of the city lasted for only three months. There was also no attempt, like the one the Uyghur Empire had made, at conquering Central Asia. Nonetheless, the Kitan rulers could stake a more credible claim to the title of "emperor" than any other sovereigns in tenth-century Eastern Eurasia, and the Kitan court rivaled the Song court as a magnet for exotic goods and diplomatic travelers.

South of the North China Plain, there existed nine independent states in the tenth century. These nine states, along with the Northern Han (951–79), a successor state to the Later Han located in modern northern Shanxi, are known in traditional Chinese historiography as the "Ten Kingdoms." A detailed description of each of these states is unnecessary for our purposes, the only exception being the Shu kingdom. This kingdom, located in modern Sichuan, had access to Dunhuang and Central Asia via routes through the Qinghai–Tibet Plateau independent of the states in North China.[65] When Gao Juhui went on his journey to the west in 938, eight of these nine southern states were ruling various economic centers in South China. Their conquest by the Song in the 960s and 970s was an important part of the process of recentralization of Eastern Eurasia in the tenth and the early eleventh centuries.[66]

Another state that contributed to this process of recentralization was the Western Xia (1038–1227). Even though historians generally date the beginning of the Western Xia state to 1038, when Li Yuanhao (1003–48) declared himself emperor, the Xia dynasty was already a regional political power by the late tenth century.[67] After strengthening relations with the Song between 1028 and 1036, the Xia conquered the string of states including Ganzhou, Guazhou, and Dunhuang, thus incorporating the entire Hexi Corridor into its domain. In the time span covered by this book, however, the Xia was not yet a major player.

Finally, the Qarakhanid state to the west of Khotan also appears in this book, primarily as a military foe of Khotan. The Qarakhanid people were of Turkic origin and lived in southern Central Asia, with their capitals in

Balāsāghūn (modern Kyrgyzstan) and Kashgar (modern Xinjiang). After their third khan converted to Islam in 934, the Qarakhanids became the first Turkic Islamic state, and were at the forefront of the dual processes of Islamization and turkicization that were to transform Central Asia in the next two centuries. One of the first steps in this dual transformation was the 1006 conquest of Khotan, which spelled the end of this Iranian Buddhist kingdom in southern Central Asia and contributed to a general fear for the demise of Buddhism that, according to Rong Xinjiang, may explain the closure of the Dunhuang library cave.[68] After the conquest of Khotan, the Qarakhanid state had more direct contacts with its eastern neighbors, including the Song court. In Song sources, both the preconquest Khotanese state and the postconquest Qara-khanid state were recorded as "Yutian" (于闐).

Gao's brief travelogue offers a broad view of Eastern Eurasia at the height of political fragmentation. Among the rulers of the eight independent states he recorded, at least three claimed the status of emperor (*huangdi*) or "Son of Heaven" (*tianzi*). Gao was dispatched by Shi Jingtang, the emperor of the Later Jin. When he met the Tangut people after crossing the Yellow River, he noted that their ruler claimed to be the "Son of Heaven of Nianya."[69] The sovereign at his destination, the Khotanese king Li Shengtian, also claimed to be an emperor (*huangdi*) in the Chinese documents produced by Khotan.[70] Gao's observation that Li Shengtian's "clothes and hats were like those of the Central Country [*yiguan ru Zhongguo* 衣冠如中國]"[71] is directly borne out by Dunhuang materials: Li Shengtian, whose Khotanese name (we learn from the Dunhuang documents) is Viśa' Saṃbhava (r. 912–66), is depicted in Dunhuang mural paintings like a Chinese emperor.[72]

The existence of so many "emperors" is the surest sign that none was in fact imperial. We know nothing about the "Son of Heaven of Nianya," but judging from the obscurity of his people, who were unrelated to the founders of the Western Xia state, it is easy to surmise that few outsiders would have treated this title seriously. The kings of Khotan were more prominent, and indeed might have occasionally (at least diplomatically) subjugated the kings of Dun-huang in the late tenth century; but they never ruled anywhere beyond the southern half of the Taklamakan Desert. The emperor who dispatched Gao to Khotan, Shi Jingtang, is best known in Chinese history as the "son emperor" because of his self-professed inferior status to the Liao ruler, the "father emperor," Yelü Deguang.[73] Thus, the defining feature of the political world that Gao traveled through was a *lack* of imperial power—a fact that is under-scored in the remarks of Liu Yan (889–942), the sovereign of the Southern

Han kingdom in modern Guangzhou: "now that the Central Country [Zhongguo] is disordered, who can claim to be the Son of Heaven?"[74] Perhaps not surprisingly, Liu Yan himself also claimed the title of emperor shortly after making these comments.

Therefore, starting around the middle of the ninth century, from the Taklamakan Desert to the South China Sea, we see the emergence of a large number of independent political entities, many of which claimed to be descendants of the old empires. With the possible exception of the Liao, none of these new states had the kind of transregional political prestige attained by the three old empires: the Tang, the Uyghur, and the Tibetan Empire. Even the Liao, the only real contender for imperial status in tenth-century Eastern Eurasia, was never territorially expansionist in the way that all three empires had been. This absence of widely recognized transregional political power means that the period after 850 should be regarded as a new age of kings.[75]

I use the word "king" because of its syntactic flexibility. The term is the generally accepted translation of the Chinese term wang, which is to be distinguished from the more elevated universal ruler of huangdi (august emperor—or simply "emperor") and tianzi (Son of Heaven).[76] After the first emperor of the Qin (259–210 BCE) coined the term huangdi, the older term wang lost its cachet.[77] By the Tang dynasty, wang generally referred to either client kings beyond the Tang border, or sons of the emperor who were not selected as the heir. In the latter case, it is often translated as "prince." This relation between client kings and the universal ruler, or emperor, is a common feature of both the early Chinese and Roman empires.[78] In both empires, a king was a ruler lower in status than a universal ruler (emperor). It is in this sense that the word "king" should be understood throughout this book.

During Gao Juhui's journey, as we have seen, this age of kings was at its zenith. But the Song and the Xia gradually reconsolidated power, with the Song conquering states in North and South China in the late tenth century and the Xia expanding into the Hexi region and Central Asia early in the eleventh century. This age of kings in Eastern Eurasia came to an end with the Chanyuan Covenant (signed between the Song and the Liao) in 1004 and the subsequent conquest of Dunhuang by the Xia in 1036. Therefore, one may date this age of kings roughly between 850 and 1000. During this century-and-a-half period, the eastern half of the Eurasian continent experienced a degree of political fragmentation that it had not seen since the fourth century—in the age of the "Five Barbarians and Sixteen Kingdoms" (304–439)—and would never see again.

The head-spinning number of political players in this period quite naturally gives a chaotic impression.[79] But it is important to recognize the longevity of many of the states introduced above, especially those located between Ling-zhou and Khotan. For instance, the Dunhuang state maintained its independence for 188 years, from 848 to 1036, making it a more enduring state than the Northern Song (167 years, 960–1127) or the Jin (109 years, 1125–1234). The Turfan kingdom survived for more than three centuries (848–1209), longer than the Tang, the Ming, or the Qing. The coexistence of oasis kingdoms between Kashgar and Dunhuang was remarkably stable between the late ninth and early eleventh centuries, a more than century-long period in which the territorial possessions of Dunhuang, Khotan, Ganzhou, and Turfan, as well as those of the Liao and the Song, hardly changed. Evidently, political fragmentation did not necessarily lead to territorial instability, much less constant chaos. And, as the journeys of Gao Juhui and many others show, diplomatic travelers routinely passed through this politically fragmented landscape.

This age of kings, roughly dating from 850 to 1000, coincides almost completely with the best-documented period in the Dunhuang archive. But more than just temporal coincidence, many Dunhuang documents also reveal dynamics of international relations not found in transmitted Chinese sources from this period. The collection preserves many original and close copies of documents used in diplomatic dealings, revealing how Dunhuang formed relations with its neighbors; it also includes testimonies to the broader world of Eastern Eurasia, such as letters between the Later Jin emperor (the grandson of the emperor who dispatched Gao Juhui) and the Kitan emperor.[80] Many of the documents and literary works produced during the decline of the Tang also made their way into the Dunhuang library cave.[81] Several of the kings Gao encountered, such as Cao Yuanshen of Dunhuang and Li Shengtian of Khotan, figure prominently in the Dunhuang documents. And, most importantly for this book, the routes and experiences of many travelers in the Dunhuang documents mirror that of Gao Juhui. By exploring these cases, I hope to show that the archive of Dunhuang documents is not only useful for reconstructing the local history of Dunhuang but is an invaluable, and largely untapped, source base for understanding the world of many kings in Eastern Eurasia.

## Conclusion

This chapter serves as a dual introduction to the rest of the book. It has given an overview of the main source base that I use: the Dunhuang manuscript collection. In particular, I have shown that the secular subset of this collection—the Dunhuang *document* collection—was assembled not on the basis of the documents' content, but as used paper. Even though these documents were not

simply a random selection of all texts produced in the social world of Dunhuang, the apparent lack of any curatorial agenda in the process of their collection sets them apart from governmental or personal archives at the time.
They constitute an accidental, but not unbiased, archive of secular documents
from a diverse array of social and governmental institutions in Dunhuang.

The majority of documents in this accidental archive were produced between
850 and 1000, an era of political fragmentation in Eastern Eurasia. Using the
travelogue of Gao Juhui, this chapter has also introduced the various states
that coexisted in this world. I have argued that the lack of widely recognized
imperial power makes this period an age of kings rather than of empires and
emperors. The rest of the book represents my attempt at understanding this
world.

In this chapter, we met the group of travelers recorded by Gao Juhui from
Kaifeng to Khotan. They help me explain the geotemporal scope of this study,
but the faces of those who traveled in this mission, including Gao himself,
remain murky. For a more intimate, and sometimes surprising, picture of who
these diplomatic travelers were, let us now dive deeper into the Dunhuang
documents.

# 2

# People

IN THE LATE SUMMER OF 982, an envoy named Zhang Jinshan left Khotan and came to Dunhuang in a 115-member diplomatic mission.[1] During his stay in Dunhuang, Zhang produced a scroll of bilingual texts that eventually ended up in the Dunhuang library cave (figure 2.1). On one side, Zhang wrote a brief note in Chinese at the top and a text in Khotanese below. The Chinese text runs vertically in accordance with the standard Chinese writing practice at the time, but instead of starting from the left the way Chinese was conventionally written, Zhang started his text from the right, similar to the Khotanese text.[2] This note in Chinese relates Zhang's personal experience in Dunhuang: He lit ceremonial lamps at the Buddhist caves, burned incense to honor the Buddha, turned the sutra wheels, and initiated the project of constructing a stupa (mound forming a memorial shrine of the Buddha), all with the wish for safe journeys in the future.[3] The Khotanese text is a panegyric that compares the Khotanese king to the legendary Indian king Aśoka (r. 268–232 BCE) and describes Zhang's diplomatic mission, whose purpose was to ask, for the Khotanese king, the hand of a "queen, pure, born among the Chinese" in Dunhuang.[4]

In addition to this manuscript, Zhang left several other texts in the Dunhuang archive. His predilection for text production—and the incredible good fortune of these texts' survival in the library cave—makes him one of the best documented travelers in the Dunhuang archive. In the colophon of a collection of stories of the Buddha's previous lives (*Jātakastava*), Zhang (whose name is written as Cā Kīmä Śąnä in Khotanese) lists the names of his parents, wife, siblings, and two daughters as benefactors of the writing of this Buddhist text. Some of them have names transcribed from Chinese just like Zhang Jinshan (Jinshan means "golden mountain"), while others had a Chinese surname (Zhang, or Cā in Khotanese) with Khotanese given names.[5] Zhang's

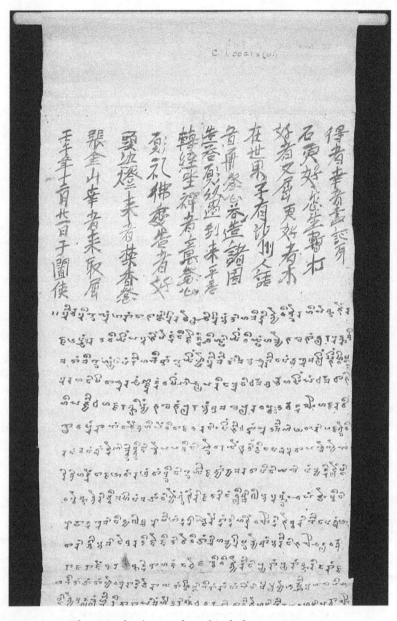

FIGURE 2.1 Zhang Jinshan's note about his diplomatic trip.
*Credit*: The British Library.

Sino-Khotanese family may have been descendants of Chinese soldiers and officials posted in Khotan during the height of Tang rule two centuries earlier.[6] By Zhang's time, however, his world was much broader. He produced texts in the Vajrayāna tradition of Buddhism, which had gained wide popularity in Tang China and Tibet.[7] He was also interested in Indian medicine, and commissioned a copy of *Siddhasāra* on palm-leaf manuscripts.[8] These texts likely traveled with Zhang to Dunhuang on his diplomatic trip, and were then donated to a Buddhist monastery, disseminating new knowledge from Khotan to Dunhuang.

It is possible that Zhang did not travel only from Khotan eastward to Dunhuang, but also further westward. On the verso side of the bilingual scroll, Zhang copied an itinerary from Khotan to India, with reference to a king named Abhimanyugupta, who ruled from 958 to 972.[9] At the end of his copies of the *Jātakastava* and *Siddhasāra*, both texts of Sanskrit origin that were translated into Khotanese, Zhang Jinshan signed his name, in a cheeky manner, in Sogdian script as "Kymš'n" and "Čw Kymš'n." All stored in the small library cave, Zhang's documents reveal the life of a Sino-Khotanese diplomatic traveler who had broad interests in Indian medicine, geography, contemporary politics, Vajrayāna Buddhism, and Sogdian writing. Zhang was the product of a tightly integrated Eastern Eurasian world.

We know Zhang Jinshan was a diplomatic traveler because the sources describe him as such. In Chinese, he characterizes himself as a "Khotanese envoy" (*yutian shi* 于闐使), whereas in Khotanese he was counted among the 115 "envoys" (*haḍa*) the Khotanese king had dispatched.[10] The title *shi*, which is short for *shizhe* (使者), is the most common term used for envoys in Chinese. Its basic meaning is "to depute," "to dispatch," or "the one who is dispatched."[11] Not everyone bearing this title was a diplomatic traveler: a *shi* of a garrison (*zhenshi* 鎮使), for instance, meant a military official stationed at a garrison.[12] Only when the term *shi* is combined with the designation of the state of origin, as is the case in Zhang Jinshan's document, or with the place of destination, can we be sure that we are looking at a diplomatic traveler. Certain verbal phrases such as "traveling out (of the country) as an envoy [*chu shi*]" or "serving as an envoy [*chong shi*]" also typically refer to diplomatic journeys. Similarly, in Khotanese the word *haḍa* is the most common for "envoy." Its basic meaning is that of a messenger, but it is frequently used for "envoy" or "ambassador" in official documents.[13] This meaning of "envoy" is particularly well attested among the Dunhuang documents.[14] In Tibetan, we have the well-established term *pho-nya*, already used to mean "emissary" or "envoy" in the famous Sino-Tibetan treaty inscription of 821.[15] In diplomatic documents in Dunhuang, it continues to carry the meaning of "envoy."[16] In Uyghur, the word *yala:vaç* is used for "envoy" or "ambassador." In Manichean and Islamic sources, it was adopted to mean "Prophet" in the sense of God's envoy.[17] In the two Uyghur documents where this term appears, it denotes, respectively, envoys who just came to Dunhuang and envoys from the "Golden Kingdom [Altun El]," meaning Khotan.[18] Therefore, in the vast majority of the sources I use, the identity of envoys is clearly expressed. Wherever there is ambiguity, I pay close attention to the context in which these terms occur to determine their meaning.

There are hundreds of other diplomatic travelers like Zhang recorded in the Dunhuang documents. Unlike Zhang, most of these travelers appear like lightning bolts, revealed briefly in one document and then vanishing back into darkness. This chapter collects these moments of illumination and paints a group portrayal of long-distance travelers. Put in this context, Zhang Jinshan's case looks more exceptional in many ways, but also commonplace in others.

## Travelers for the State

Many people appear in the various documents from the Dunhuang archive: they are Buddhist monastic figures or secular householders;[19] they are wealthy and powerful like the kings of Dunhuang or khans of Ganzhou, or destitute, even desperate, like the slaves sold in contracts; they are men or women; they are governmental officials or commoners, known in Chinese as the "hundred surnames"; they are Han Chinese, Tibetan, Uyghur, Sogdian, Khotanese, Indian, or, like Zhang Jinshan, from culturally mixed backgrounds. Compared with transmitted histories in Chinese, which tend to vastly overrepresent nonmonastic, elite Han Chinese men, the Dunhuang archive contains records by and about a much wider assemblage of humanity.[20]

The job of traveling for the state, instead of being limited to a small group of trained bureaucrats, cut through all these social groups. Unsurprisingly, being an envoy was a natural job for government officials. Both military officers and administrative bureaucrats, as is the case for Zhang Jinshan, traveled as envoys.[21] The experience of serving as an envoy was crucial in advancing one's official career. An official in Dunhuang named Zhang Baoshan (unrelated to Jinshan) had his first important post as commissioner at a military garrison in 901.[22] According to his biography, Zhang visited the Chinese court five times in the first three decades of the tenth century. Among these trips, two were described in some detail. After each trip, Zhang gained a higher military post because of his accomplishment as an envoy. Even a scandal of the murder of an accompanying Uyghur envoy during Zhang's last diplomatic mission did little to derail his illustrious career.[23] The only other occasions on which he advanced in the bureaucracy were through success on the battlefield. For an official like Zhang Baoshan, diplomacy was as important as warfare as a means to career advancement.

But envoys in the Dunhuang documents are by no means limited to the class of generals and bureaucrats. People of both higher and lower social status also served as envoys. At one end of the spectrum are heads of state: Cao Yijin (r. 914–35), the lord of Dunhuang, "personally visited Ganzhou" and discussed matters of state with the Uyghur khan in order to secure the future passage of envoys between Dunhuang and North China.[24] Other members of the ruling family, such the brothers, sons, and daughters of the ruler, also frequently traveled as envoys. In 964, a Khotanese prince visited the Song court as an envoy.[25] He also appears in the Dunhuang documents and mural paintings and had a significant presence in Dunhuang.[26] The most famous case in this regard is Zhang Yichao, the founder of the semi-independent state of Dunhuang in 848. After the death of his older brother, who lived in the Tang capital Chang'an as a hostage, Zhang traveled to the capital and offered himself as the new hostage.[27] This trip, which would be Zhang's last—he eventually died in Chang'an—is not a typical diplomatic journey. Yet it accomplished the goal of solidifying relations between Dunhuang and the Tang court. The precarious political situations of small Central Eurasian states meant that, in unusual circumstances, both the Zhang and the Cao lords of Dunhuang needed to conduct long-distance travel themselves to deal with matters of state.[28]

At the other end of the social spectrum, people of much humbler backgrounds also served as envoys. Because of their limited economic means, many had to borrow money (often in the form of silk) and rent horses, donkeys, and camels to travel as envoys.[29] In 946, a man in Dunhuang borrowed an eight-year-old camel from another man for his trip as an envoy to Turfan. Both men engaged in the transaction are clearly designated as "commoner" (*baixing*), indicating a lack of official status.[30] In a petition to the lord of Dunhuang, another commoner explained that he was poor and unable to repay his debt, and this destitution motivated him to travel as an envoy; unfortunately, his diplomatic mission was ambushed by bandits and he himself rendered a captive.[31] Such a desire to pursue diplomacy as a means to change one's fortune is also clear from a Khotanese letter about a certain "prime minister" who captured a slave. This slave submitted a petition, stating "I shall go to the land of China, so that I shall not be a slave."[32] Indeed, such upward social mobility through diplomatic travel did occur: according to a Chinese contract, a man previously sold into slavery was able to redeem himself after a trip as an envoy to Ganzhou.[33] For enterprising individuals in Dunhuang and neighboring states, diplomatic travel provided a rare opportunity to dramatically elevate their social standing.

One major revelation from the Dunhuang documents is that serving as an envoy was by no means the prerogative of secular people. Monks also frequently traveled for the states where they lived. For example, Haiyin was the leader of the Buddhist monastic community in Dunhuang in the late ninth and early tenth centuries, and answered to the lords of Dunhuang from both the Zhang and the Cao families.[34] According to his posthumous biography, Haiyin once traveled to North China as an envoy of Dunhuang. On this trip, he made a pilgrimage to the Buddhist Mount Wutai, the dwelling place of Bodhisattva Mañjuśrī, and composed a travelogue.[35] Then, as the route between Dunhuang and its western neighbors, such as Khotan, was blocked, Haiyin was tasked with a journey to the west in order to reopen the road. On his return from Khotan, in 931, he succumbed to an illness and soon died. In his diplomatic trips, Haiyin was both a monk and an envoy, and traveled for diplomacy and for pilgrimage. These dual roles were mutually reinforcing: serving as an envoy allowed him the opportunity to visit, on his official trips to China, famed Buddhist sites such as Mount Wutai, while his status as a renowned monk must have also facilitated his journeys as an envoy.[36]

Like their secular counterparts, many monk-envoys were humbler members of the monastic community. For instance, Fabao was an ordinary monk in the Sanjie Monastery, the library of which constituted much of the holdings of the library cave. In the spring of 956, he borrowed one *pi* (about twelve meters) of raw yellow silk from a fellow monk of higher status in the same monastery in order to fund his journey to Turfan as an envoy.[37] According to the contract, he was to pay back the original *pi* of silk with an additional *pi* of cotton cloth as interest on the day of his safe return from Turfan; any further delay in repayment would have incurred more interest. If "inauspiciousness occurs on the road," and Fabao failed to return, his guarantors would be required to repay the original amount with interest as collateral. This contract is among the several dozen drafted by envoys prior to their trips.[38] In this case, Fabao's monastic affiliation was significant for his journey as an envoy, as it made it easier for him to borrow silk from a fellow monk. Like Haiyin, Fabao's dual identities of monk and envoy were mutually facilitatory.

Another way that the social role of an envoy transcended conventional boundaries has to do with cultural identity.[39] A culturally hybrid background suited the tasks of an envoy, whose job often entailed negotiation between people from different backgrounds. Hun Ziying was a person of Tuyuhun (or Azha in Tibetan, a Xianbei confederacy from North Asia) origin, which is made clear through his adoption of the Chinese surname Hun, one character taken from the name Tuyu-*hun*. Hun served as a military officer in the early tenth century in Dunhuang. In 924, during a campaign against the Uyghur kingdom of Ganzhou, he died in a battle in Jiuquan, just to the east of Dunhuang.[40] His life is memorialized in a posthumous biographical account written to accompany his portrait.[41] Before this final battle, Hun Ziying frequently worked as an envoy. According to the biography, Hun "was well versed in the ritual instructions, and when conveying the situations of the barbarians he always followed the sentiment of the sovereign. His tongue is refined and his lips are sweet, and in translating the barbarian languages, the barbarian Hun [Tuyuhun] people marvel at the beauty [of his words]."[42] Having someone of Tuyuhun origin was clearly important to the lord of Dunhuang in communicating with the Tuyuhun people. But Hun's talent was not limited to dealing with one group of people. The biographical account goes on to celebrate his diplomatic trips to the Uyghurs and the Southern Mountain tribes. In the case of Hun Ziying, a Tuyuhun native living in the Han Chinese–majority state of Dunhuang, the in-betweenness of his cultural background allowed him to function more effectively as an envoy.

The most surprising, and also rarest, case in which traveling as an envoy unsettled social division appears in a record from the Song court in Kaifeng. In 1007, a nun named Faxian visited the Song court. She was dispatched by the Uyghur khan of Ganzhou and traveled with one other unnamed person. In this smallest of diplomatic missions, the nun Faxian was the leader. She offered the Song court ten horses as gifts. The manpower necessary to manage these horses implies that she must have had an entourage under her command. After delivering the horses, Faxian requested permission to visit Mount Wutai, like the renowned monk Haiyin discussed above. Her wish was granted by the Song emperor.[43] This brief yet tantalizing record is the only one that I can find of a female envoy. The fact that Faxian was a Buddhist nun might have opened up a social space for long-distance travel that would have been closed to laywomen.

However, the paucity of information about female envoys does not mean that women did not travel for the state.[44] In a letter to the lord of Dunhuang dated to 884, a border officer reported about a mission led by Zhang Huaiquan, the brother of the lord of Dunhuang, which included Zhang Huaiquan's "wife and family members" (*niangzi jialei* 娘子家累).[45] A Song source that describes the New Year's Day celebration in the late Northern Song reveals that Khotanese envoys often traveled with their wives and sons (*bing qinan tonglai* 並妻男同來) to the Song capital.[46] From these records, we know that male envoys, particularly high-ranking ones such as the head envoy, sometimes brought their wives and children along on the journey.

Like officials and monks, women of varying social status participated in diplomatic missions. The ties between Dunhuang and its neighbors were created and cemented through diplomatic marriages, particularly among the rulers of Dunhuang, Guazhou, Khotan, and Ganzhou.[47] One result of this extensive network of diplomatic marriages is that dignitaries such as Khotanese princesses went to and often lived permanently in Dunhuang.[48] Their presence is seen, among other things, in the numerous donor paintings of royal women in the Dunhuang caves.[49] The journeying of princesses also introduced whole retinues of attendants and servants, many no doubt also women, into the world of diplomatic travel. In a letter written in 962, two female attendants of a Khotanese princess in Dunhuang made a few requests to the princess, who was back in Khotan at the time.[50] They must have accompanied the Khotanese princess to Dunhuang, but continued to function as an outpost of the Khotanese government even when the princess was not present. Although the writers of the letter called themselves, according to convention, "feeble female servants," the role they played in diplomacy was not insignificant.

Then, even lower in the social pecking order, female slaves also appeared in diplomatic missions. In 866, Zhang Yichao, the lord of Dunhuang, submitted to the Tang court "four pairs of Qingjiao eagles from Ganjun mountain, two horses from Yanqing, and two Tibetan women."[51] The Tibetan women were offered to the Tang emperor in the same way as eagles and horses. They certainly were not free members of the diplomatic mission and cannot be called envoys. But they traveled for the purpose of diplomatic relations between Dunhuang and the Tang, albeit not of their own volition. In this sense, they should also be considered diplomatic travelers.

A final group of diplomatic travelers that appears often in the Dunhuang documents is artisans of different trades. The king of Khotan, for instance, once demanded in a letter that accompanied a large piece of jade as a gift to Dunhuang that the lord of Dunhuang deliver him a carpenter surnamed Yang.[52] The lord of Dunhuang, in turn, begged the Song court to send "bell makers as well as Chinese pearl connoisseurs" in order to impart their skills to the people of Dunhuang.[53] In the diplomatic mission recorded in the Staël-Holstein manuscript (discussed in detail in the next section), we find "Paḍä Dūsa the drummer, Kharuṣai the goldsmith, and Khrrī-rttanä the barber" among the members of the mission. Their standing in the diplomatic missions is ambiguous. The fact that they were requested and exchanged implies an unfree status not unlike that of the Tibetan women given to the Tang court. Indeed, the appeal from the lord of Dunhuang for the artisans from the Song court follows his request for golden leaves for constructing Buddha statues, suggesting that the artisans were similarly treated as gifts. But the fact that, in the Khotanese king's request, a *specific* carpenter was asked for seems to indicate the carpenter's transregional fame. As is often the case, the specialized skills of these artisans both constrained and elevated them in diplomatic missions.

These examples from the Dunhuang documents show that diplomatic travel was not a job performed exclusively by governmental officials. Such officials were certainly an important part of diplomatic missions, and often led as the head envoys. But many other people of varying social status and cultural background—from secular and monastic communities, free and bounded, of both genders—participated in long-distance travel on behalf of the state. This broad representation has cultural, economic, and political implications that will be explored in the rest of the book.

## Diplomatic Missions

So far in this chapter, I have described envoys as individuals. In reality, these individuals almost never traveled alone. The only time an envoy was alone was when, for some reason, he or she was separated from the diplomatic mission and put in danger. For instance, an envoy from Dunhuang was on his way to Ganzhou when his diplomatic mission was "broken" by bandits. He was captured and taken to Yizhou (modern Hami, Kumul), four hundred kilometers north of Dunhuang, where he was sold into slavery.[54] He was later redeemed by a countryman from Dunhuang, who then tried to further extort him. We meet him in a petition to the lord of Dunhuang, where the ex-envoy pleaded for justice against the scam. This unhappy odyssey shows the fate of an envoy when he was isolated. In most cases, envoys, as with other travelers, sought safety in numbers in a diplomatic mission.[55]

A diplomatic mission could have as few as half a dozen or as many as over one hundred members. Zhang Jinshan's Khotanese marriage alliance mission, with 115 members, is representative of these larger missions, whereas the mission led by the nun Faxian is among the smallest ones. In large and small missions alike, there was a hierarchy among different envoys and other diplomatic travelers. At the top of the hierarchy was usually a clearly identified leader. For instance, in the ninth month of 1004, a diplomatic mission from Ganzhou consisting of 129 members arrived at the Song court in Kaifeng.[56] According to the Song record about this mission, the three leaders were the head envoy, a monk named Baozang, the deputy Li Xu, and another deputy, Jiexu. These three leaders were the only people the Song government deemed worthy of documentation. Such status distinction ran through entire missions. In an 878 mission from Dunhuang to the Tang court, of the twenty-nine envoys who arrived at the Tang border, thirteen of higher status were allowed to proceed to the Tang capital, while the rest were requested to remain at the border. When the emperor offered gifts to these envoys, the envoys were also divided into three groups according to their rank and were offered gifts of differing values.[57] Similarly, when the Dunhuang government hosted envoys from other states, even the food they were offered was divided into "fine supply, medium supply, coarse supply," presumably according to the official rank of these envoys.[58] The diplomatic missions were as hierarchical as the states that sent them.

The difference among members of a mission was often also cultural.[59] Of the three head envoys in Zhang Jinshan's mission, two had Chinese names (Yang and Zhang) and one a Khotanese one (Sera).[60] In the 1004 mission from Ganzhou to the Song, the head bore a monastic name; one of his two deputies had a Chinese name, the other a non-Chinese, possibly Uyghur name. Among eighteen named envoys from Dunhuang in 878, at least six have typical Sogdian surnames, while others had typical Chinese surnames.[61] Hence, the cultural complexity a diplomatic mission exhibited consisted not only in envoys of mixed backgrounds, such as the Tuyuhun-Chinese envoy Hun Ziying or the Sino-Khotanese envoy Zhang Jinshan, but also in the way members with different backgrounds banded together in a single mission.

Therefore, a diplomatic mission was not a monolithic entity that simply performed tasks assigned by the sovereign, but was itself a complicated social space in which members of different status, cultural background, and interests interacted. Such interactions sometimes produced strong disagreements.

A report about a mission from Dunhuang to the Tang capital in 887 exposes a fierce dispute between different factions within the same diplomatic mission. One faction insisted that the goal of the mission, the acquisition of the title of "governor" (*jiedu shi*) for the lord of Dunhuang from the Tang emperor, should be followed through despite the many setbacks they had encountered. But the other faction was convinced that this task was doomed to fail. The head of this second faction uttered some unruly words about the lord of Dunhuang: "What accomplishment did the lord [of Dunhuang] have to ask for the governorship? In the past twenty years, how many minions have tried to come here [to ask for governorship]?" He then ridiculed the other faction: "If you can get the governorship, the four of us [in the dissenting faction] will walk backwards on our heads [*yitou daoxing* 以頭倒行]!"[62] As it turned out, his assessment of the situation was correct, and the mission failed to get the title, again. The frustration these envoys encountered was the reason for this internal strife. As long-distance travel was an inherently demanding affair that involved tough decisions, such internal disagreements must have been quite common.

This internal complexity of diplomatic missions was further compounded by the fact that missions from different states often voyaged together. From the Song sources, we see that the envoys from small states beyond its western border frequently reached the Song court as a group.[63] In particular, envoys from the states near Dunhuang, such as Turfan, Khotan, and Ganzhou, regularly traveled with Dunhuang envoys. In 968, for instance, a group of envoys from Dunhuang, Khotan, and Ganzhou visited the Song court together.[64] As a result, they were sometimes confused with one another in Song sources.[65] Less often, envoys would also join ranks with fellow envoys from countries further away: Dunhuang envoys visited the Song court with Tajik Arab envoys,[66] while envoys from Turfan traveled along with those from Persia.[67] In these cases, it is not difficult to imagine a scenario in which envoys from further west (Tajik Arabs and Persia) passed through states in eastern Central Asia (Turfan and Dunhuang), and were joined by envoys from these states in their journey to North China. There is unfortunately no record about the internal working of these missions. But one cannot help but wonder the kind of relations that developed in these composite missions.

In one case, at least, we do not have to wonder. In 925 one such composite mission, with envoys from Ganzhou and Dunhuang, returned from the Later Tang court in Luoyang to their home kingdoms. The mission, it is reported, went smoothly at first, and the head of the Uyghur mission made it to the

Chinese court and was even recorded in a Chinese court document.[68] Yet on their return, this Uyghur envoy was mysteriously murdered. During the investigation, it became clear that a young, low-level envoy from Dunhuang had played some role in the murder. He was significant in this matter because, despite his low status, he became sworn brothers with the deputy head of the Uyghur mission and concealed information from the lord of Dunhuang. The letter that detailed this incident chides this young envoy as "not having any experience of difficult travels and therefore being unfamiliar with the rituals of the state."[69] The way he acted was considered inappropriate, and he was subsequently jailed. The creation of this personal bond and the young envoy's access to sensitive information that was unavailable even to the lord of Dunhuang were possible only in the context of the close association between the Ganzhou and the Dunhuang missions. Therefore, being on a diplomatic mission could put one in a socially fluid (and perilous) state, when recognized hierarchies were unsettled and new relations formed.

The single most revealing document about the internal working of a diplomatic mission is the manuscript commonly known as the "Staël-Holstein Miscellany" (figure 2.2). This manuscript is one of the most enigmatic among the Dunhuang manuscripts. It acquired its name from Baron Alexander von Staël-Holstein (1877–1937), an exiled Russian scholar who taught Sanskrit at Peking University in the 1910s and 1920s. During his long academic tenure in Beijing, because of his knowledge of Indic languages and religions, Staël-Holstein earned the respect and friendship of many leading Chinese scholars of the time, such as Hu Shih (1891–1962) and Chen Yique (1890–1969).[70] In the process, he was also able to acquire a personal collection of precious texts, among which the most famous is this eponymous manuscript. Between the initial discovery of the Dunhuang "library cave" in 1900 and its acquisition by Staël-Holstein, the manuscript must have traveled through the hands of Qing officials, collectors, and scholars, but the exact route is irrecoverable. The first appearance of this manuscript is in the publication of "Two Medieval Documents from Tun-Huang," jointly written by the Tibetologist F. W. Thomas and the Iranist Sten Konow, in which they state that "Among the treasures collected by Baron A. von Staël-Holstein in Peking is a scroll which is stated to have been from Tun-huang. . . . In 1927 the Baron sent photographs of the two documents to us, the Tibetan section to Thomas and the Iranian portion to Konow."[71] The original manuscript was in Staël-Holstein's possession and reportedly made its way to the Harvard-Yenching Institute because of his visit and appointment there. But the whereabouts of the manuscript is now unknown,

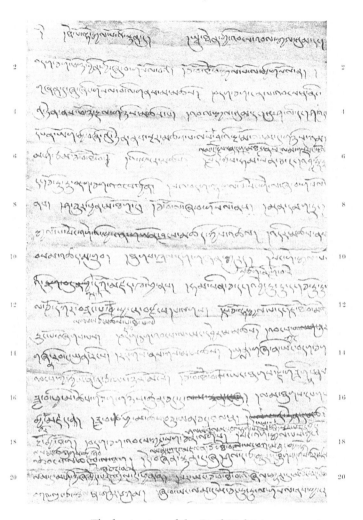

FIGURE 2.2 The beginning of the Staël-Holstein manuscript.

and my reading, like all existing research on it, is based on the photographs published in the Thomas-Konow article.[72]

Because of the Thomas-Konow article and many subsequent works, the basic contour of the manuscript is clear.[73] On one side of the manuscript is supposedly a Buddhist sutra in Chinese, which has not been published. On the other side, we find both Tibetan texts (a draft envoy report, a revised envoy report, and a list of ten numerated topics) and Khotanese texts (an economic document, an envoy report with two extensive lists of place names, a list of

TABLE 2.1. The Content of the Staël-Holstein Manuscript

| Section | Content | Envoys Mentioned |
|---|---|---|
| Tibetan 1 | Draft envoy report | 'Bal Rgyal-sum, Su Sha-li, Sha-'du (= Khotanese Ṣaṃdū), Ham Sin-ca, 'Bye Tutu, Cong Tutu |
| Tibetan 2 | Envoy report | 'Bal Rgyal-sum, Ham Sin-ca, 'Bye Tutu, Co Tutu |
| Tibetan 3 | Ten topics | None |
| Khotanese 1 | Economic document | Śvāṃnakai |
| Khotanese 2 | Survey document | Rrgyaḍä-sūmä (Rgyal-sum), Ṣarrnädatta, Ṣaṃdū, Śvāṃnakai |
| Khotanese 3 | List of place names 1 | None |
| Khotanese 4 | List of place names 2 | None |
| Khotanese 5 | List of Chinese personal names | None |
| Khotanese 6 | List of Turkic personal names | None |
| Khotanese 7 | Envoy report | Rrgyaḍä-sūmä (Rgyal-sum), Ṣarrnädatta, Cām Ttūttū, Ṣaṃdū, Śvāṃnakai, Paḍä Dūsa (drummer), Kharuṣai (goldsmith), Khrrī-rttanä (barber) |
| Khotanese 8 | Love poem | None |

Chinese personal names, a list of Turkic personal names, a more extensive envoy report, and a love poem). In table 2.1, I list the texts sequentially as they appear in the manuscript and the envoys explicitly mentioned in these texts.

This manuscript has long been considered a "miscellany" because of the complex series of texts written on it.[74] Yet, if we consider the *user* rather than just the content of these texts, it is clear that every section of this complex text has to do with a diplomatic mission from Khotan. Both envoy reports in Tibetan (Tibetan 1 and 2) were submitted to the lord of Dunhuang by the envoys of Khotan.[75] Many of the same envoys appear in these Tibetan reports and the Khotanese report sent to the king of Khotan (Khotanese 7). Four of the envoys also appear in the survey document (Khotanese 2), which lists those who had geographical knowledge of different places in the region. Two lists of these places are recorded in Khotanese 3 and 4. Khotanese 1 is a document about the amount of cloth and money owed; Śvāṃnakai, the sole debtor, appears in Khotanese 7 as an envoy.

The texts not explicitly mentioning envoys are nonetheless also related to this diplomatic mission. The brief list of "ten topics" (Tibetan 3) is a guide to epistolary etiquette in diplomatic letter writing, which includes, for instance, the words one should use in addressing a royal lady. It would undoubtedly be handy as the diplomats compose official letters during their trips. Khotanese 5 and 6 contain two lists of personal names of officials, one in Chinese and the other Turkic. Just as the places listed in Khotanese 3 and 4 are the ones the envoys had to know to travel in the area, these two additional lists represent officials with whom the envoys should also be familiar. The poem (Khotanese 8) describes the longing for a distant lover. When read in the context of all the other texts relating to the work of envoys, it is clear that this poem, though distinct in genre, also deals with a key aspect of life on the road.

Therefore, instead of referring to the Staël-Holstein manuscript as a miscellany, it is more accurate to see it as an "envoy's notebook." The idea of a "notebook" conveys the fact that these texts were kept by one person or a group of people, but also allows that the origins of the various parts of the manuscript may be diverse. It is difficult to be certain who composed the reports, copied them, and made the corrections. As the official head of the mission, 'Bal Rgyal-sum should have been in charge of the drafting of the report. Judging from the handwriting, which is consistent in both the first draft, the second draft, and, crucially, the corrections on the first draft (see figure 2.2), it is clear that the act of copying these texts was conducted by the same hand.[76] Whether this is the hand of 'Bal Rgyal-sum, another envoy, or some other unnamed member of the mission is impossible to know for sure. This envoy's notebook, with its diverse content, provides an unparalleled window into the internal structure of a small diplomatic mission from Khotan to Dunhuang in the early tenth century.

The first thing the notebook reveals is the composition of the mission. The two Tibetan reports (Tibetan 1 and 2) show that it included two subgroups. Each group had at least three members, 'Bal Rgyal-sum, Su Sha-li, and Sha-'du in group one, and Ham Sin-ca, 'Bye Tutu, and Cong Tutu in group two.[77] From the Khotanese report (Khotanese 7) we know that, in addition to Rgyal-sum (written in the Khotanese part as Rrgyaḍä-sūmä), Sha-'du (from the Khotanese name Ṣaṃdū), and *Zhang Dudu (whose name is spelled Cong Tutu in Tibetan and Cäm Ttūttū in Khotanese), who are mentioned in the Tibetan reports, there are at least five more diplomatic travelers (Ṣarrnädatta, Śväṃnakai, Paḍä Dūsa the drummer, Kharuṣai the goldsmith, and Khrrī-rttanä the barber). Altogether, the reports mention eleven names. Compared with some missions, such as Zhang Jinshan's, this diplomatic mission is relatively small.

Like Zhang Jinshan's mission, however, there was clear hierarchy among the envoys in this modest mission. Rgyal-sum was its head and is described as the Khotanese king's "right-hand man."[78] His name in the Tibetan reports always appears first on the list of names. In the second report, his group is shortened to "Rgyal-sum and others." Aside from Rgyal-sum, three envoys with Khotanese names (Saṃdū, Ṣarrnädatta, and Śvāṃnakai) are described as ṣau, a Khotanese official title.[79] The envoys with Chinese names (Su Sha-li, Ham Sin-ca, 'Bye Tutu, Cong Tutu) also have official titles, and these titles are incorporated into their names. For instance, in the case of Cong Tutu, the name is a combination of his surname (Chinese Zhang > Tibetan Cong) and his title, "general" (Chinese Dudu > Tibetan Tutu). The other three people did not bear official titles but are identified by their profession (drummer, goldsmith, and barber). Like many of the groups I have mentioned above, this small mission was both culturally hybrid and bureaucratically hierarchical.

As the three diplomatic reports make clear, these envoys conducted matters of state. The Tibetan letters tell us that the envoys, after a difficult trip where they had to kill their camels to survive, arrived in Dunhuang intact. The first thing they did upon arrival was to submit a letter from the Khotanese king to the lord of Dunhuang to report that the gifts from the lord of Dunhuang from a previous mission had been duly received. Then, the envoys from Khotan laid out gifts from the Khotanese king in front of the lord of Dunhuang. From the Khotanese report we know that all these envoys were then given gifts by the lord of Dunhuang.[80] After this exchange of letters and gifts, the envoys asked permission to leave "by the first or the second day of next month."[81] They then delivered the lord of Dunhuang a minor threat: If the letters from the Khotanese king were not listened to, they claimed, "we [the envoys] will not have the heart to come in the spring of next year."[82] What is clear from these reports is that this small mission was tasked with no grave matter, and the only significant activity was the gift and letter exchange. It was a routine mission, and, as the Tibetan reports imply, they would come again the following year if things went well. In fact, the Khotanese report says explicitly that this trip was the seventh time that Rgyal-sum and Saṃdū traveled to Dunhuang. The intensity of connection between these two places is quite evident.

The notebook also reveals the kind of information the envoys possessed. The four lists (Khotanese 3–6) include the names of Chinese and Turkic officials that the envoys presumably would meet on their trips. Many of them are identified by their names and titles. Because these names are not found in other sources, not much more can be said about them. But this is not the case with the two lists of geographical names. Based on our knowledge of the geography of this region in the tenth century, we have a good sense of what these two lists are about. The first list includes places one would have to pass going from Khotan to Shuofang/Lingzhou, while the second includes "cities of Xizhou [Turfan]." The places that have been identified by previous scholars are shown on map 2.1. We can see from the map that the two sections are internally meaningful, and do not intersect with each other. For the Khotanese envoys from Central Asia, the area between Shuofang/Lingzhou and Khotan formed a unit of geographical knowledge, while the area between Yizhou/Hami and Kucha formed another. These two units correspond to the two routes that circumvented the Taklamakan Desert in the Tarim Basin. Historically, they were known as the "northern route" and the "southern route" between China and Central Asia. Such organization of geographical knowledge into regional units was a feature of the way envoys made sense of the world in which they traveled.[83]

Like the envoys discussed earlier, the ones we find in this notebook also conducted more than just state business. The fragmentary economic document (Khotanese 1) shows the exchange of money and cloth; the fact that one of the envoys (Śvāṃnakai) owed cloth indicates that the envoys were engaging in commercial activities. Similarly, they also acted as devout Buddhists. Taking the opportunity of their stay in Dunhuang, Zhang Dudu ("General Zhang") commissioned the construction of a stupa; Ṣarrnädatta read Buddhist texts and visited various shrines; Śvāṃnakai went to shrines and offered donations. But none were as industrious as Ṣaṃdū, who "went around the city to 121 shrines," and "sent 502 liters of oil for use in all the temples situated around the city."[84] The goal of these activities was, according to the Khotanese report, to accrue merit for the two kings: the king of Khotan and the lord of Dunhuang. But, presumably, the envoys also accumulated a handsome amount of merit for themselves in the process.

Finally, the most intriguing part of the Khotanese text is the lyrical poem at the end. Continuing in the same hand, this part switches the tone of the entire manuscript to describe the longing for a beloved man: "If I should not see you, yet should get news of you, in my limbs rises the immortal elixir, the pores separately opening rise."[85] One is tempted to read these lines alongside the first envoy report in Tibetan, which expresses the urgent wish of the envoys to get back to Khotan, where "the families of us servants are in distress at

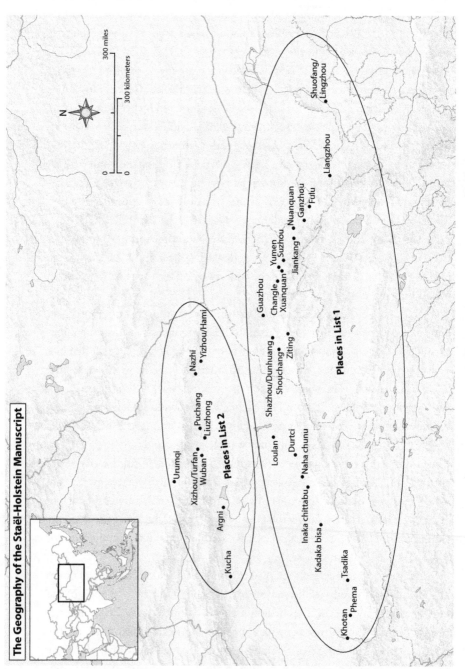

MAP 2.1 The geography of the Staël-Holstein manuscript

home."[86] It is impossible to know whether one of the envoys composed this love poem himself, was the recipient of the poem, or copied it into the notebook to console his fellow travelers while away from home. But its content is understandable in the context of an envoy toiling in a distant country and longing to get back home to his loved ones.

Taken as a whole, this envoy's notebook reveals the multifaceted life in a diplomatic mission from Khotan to Dunhuang. The mission consisted of a multicultural and multilingual group of envoys. These envoys wrote letters to the lord of Dunhuang in Tibetan in order to be granted a speedy return home and compiled a report to the king of Khotan in Khotanese about their activities in Dunhuang. They bought and sold things, and recorded cloth owed by one envoy. They familiarized themselves with the cities along the way between Dunhuang and Khotan as well as the names of officials they dealt with in Dunhuang and Ganzhou. And they included a poem that expressed passion for a distant lover. This notebook was produced by a small, routine mission that covered a relatively short distance. Yet it already reveals the multicultural makeup and the intricate internal workings of this mission, and the diverse activities conducted within it. Such complexity of identities and actions must have been infinitely greater in other, larger diplomatic missions that covered longer distances.

## How Many Envoys Traveled?

In the final section of this chapter, I approach a question that I will not be able to fully answer: How many people traveled for diplomatic purposes in the world of medieval Dunhuang?

While the real number of transregional journeys is impossible to know because of the lack of comprehensive accounting, many Dunhuang documents hint at an impressive frequency of such diplomatic travel. For instance, the official Zhang Baoshan discussed earlier traveled five times as an envoy, and visited the Chinese emperor more than 1700 kilometers away. In 923, Zhang Xiuzao, a commoner of much lower status, rented camels twice in three months to aid his official trip to Turfan, about 900 kilometers northwest of Dunhuang.[87] Similarly, a monk named Huide traveled to three major neighbors of Dunhuang: Ganzhou (about 600 kilometers away), Turfan (800 kilometers), and Khotan (1600 kilometers) within one year.[88] In the Staël-Holstein manuscript the envoy 'Bal Rgyal-sum talks about his seventh trip to Dunhuang. A Turfan envoy, writing in Uyghur, states that "I have been to the Divine State of Yaglaqar [Ganzhou] once and have been to the blessed state

of Shazhou [Dunhuang] four times."[89] These examples show envoys from different states on trips of different lengths. Collectively, they suggest busy and
routinized diplomatic journeys unhindered by political fragmentation.

While these cases show how many times a single person traveled as an
envoy, another document reveals how many diplomatic missions from the
same state were on the road at the same time.[90] In 884, the officials in charge
of the military garrison in Suzhou on Dunhuang's eastern border delivered a
letter to the lord of Dunhuang Zhang Huaishen. In the letter, they explained
that a messenger had recently returned from the east, delivering a report about
some Dunhuang envoys who had been sent to the east, presumably to the
Tang court. The most important information in this report was that the rebel
Huang Chao (835–84) had been killed and the Tang emperor Xizong (862–88)
had returned to the capital. But along with this blockbuster news (which I
shall explore further in chapter 9), the messenger also informed the lord of
Dunhuang of the whereabouts of four Dunhuang diplomatic missions.

The first mission, headed by Song Shulue, included seven people who, presumably after a successful journey, returned to Liangzhou along with a group
of Uyghur envoys; earlier on their return journey in Binzhou, a town 150 kilometers to the northwest of Chang'an, Song Shulue had met Zhang Huaiquan,
the cousin of the lord of Dunhuang and the head of another twenty-member
mission, which was unable to return just yet because traveling clothes and equipment were still being prepared. A third mission, led by Bai Yongji and Yin
Qing'er, also on the way back from the east, was stalled in Jialin just outside
Liangzhou because of the military chaos in the latter. Finally, according to the
report, a fourth mission, headed by Song Runying, was similarly stalled in
Liangzhou. From this document we know that, at that very moment, there
were at least four Dunhuang missions to the east, all 800 kilometers or further
from Dunhuang.

The frequency of diplomatic trips gleaned from individual testimonies in
the Dunhuang documents is corroborated by the records kept by the Chinese
courts about envoys from the west. Between 850 and 1050, for instance, at least
forty missions from Dunhuang to Chinese courts are recorded.[91] Between 870
and 1030, the Uyghur kingdom of Ganzhou, an important neighbor to the east
of Dunhuang, sent diplomatic missions to the Chinese courts no less than
seventy-nine times.[92] The "Chinese court" during this period shifted from the
late Tang (618–907) through the "Five Dynasties" (907–60) to the Song
(960–1127), yet Dunhuang, Ganzhou, and their many neighbors unwaver-
ingly sent envoys to the east without regard to the political shifts. To a lesser
extent, these states also maintained connections with the northern rival of

the Song, the Kitan Liao state; the Uyghur kingdom in Ganzhou, for instance, sent thirty-one missions to the Liao between the early tenth and early twelfth centuries.[93] In the world of the Dunhuang envoys between 850 and 1000, dynamic, large-scale transregional travel occurred with demonstrable regularity.

However, for three reasons, these numbers from the Tang/Song/Kitan court records likely represent only a fraction of actual diplomatic journeys in the region between Kaifeng and Khotan. First, these records do not reflect all diplomatic missions sent from Dunhuang and other Central Eurasian states to North China. In the Dunhuang manuscripts we find many missions from Dunhuang to the Tang/Song court that left no trace in the official Chinese record: neither the 878 mission that clearly reached Chang'an,[94] nor the four missions on the road in 884 were recorded in the documents produced by the Tang court. The same must have been true about other Central Eurasian states as well.

Second, these trips to the Tang/Song capitals were among the most arduous ones for diplomatic travelers between North China and Central Asia. The more frequent trips were likely shorter ones, such as the one between Khotan and Dunhuang recorded in the Staël-Holstein manuscript, that were of little importance to observers in the Tang/Song capitals.

The third reason for this undercount requires more explanation. The Tang/Song courts closely monitored visits from foreign envoys, and therefore produced this vast, though incomplete, record. But they generally did not describe the reciprocal trips that they themselves no doubt sent in response to the envoys from the west. Therefore, each entry in the Chinese official account often represents two or more actual trips, in both directions. This point is illustrated in the case of Wang Yande's mission. In the early months of 981, a mission from the Uyghur kingdom of Xizhou (Turfan) visited Kaifeng. It informed the Song emperor that the head of the Uyghur kingdom had adopted a new title: "the nephew [from] Xizhou, the Lion King Arslan Khan."[95] As a response to this envoy, the Song court dispatched a group of envoys headed by Wang Yande and Bai Xun in the fifth month of 981. It took them close to a year on the road before they arrived at Turfan in the fourth month of the following year. They stayed for almost another year in the Uyghur kingdom and returned only in the spring of 983. This time, more than a hundred envoys from the Uyghur kingdom accompanied them on their way back, with the task of "expressing gratitude for the favor" (xie'en). This larger group of travelers spent yet another year on the road and arrived at Kaifeng in the fourth month of 984.[96] We do not know when this second group of Uyghur envoys left Kaifeng. But it is clear that the initial Uyghur embassy in 981 triggered a chain reaction of at least two more large-scale diplomatic missions lasting until at least 984.

This kind of multiround diplomatic exchange also existed among the smaller kingdoms around Dunhuang. On Pelliot 3016, two official documents are copied one after the other.[97] The first document is a petition by a "Commissioner for the Return of Gifts" from Dunhuang to Khotan, named Suo Ziquan, written in the eleventh month of 956; the second is another petition to Khotan by a Dunhuang "messenger" named Fuzhu, written in the sixth month of 958.[98] The official title of the first writer indicates that the mission from Dunhuang was not the initiator of this round of diplomatic exchange; the king of Khotan must have first dispatched envoys that gave gifts to Dunhuang. It is unclear if, as Suo Ziquan returned to Dunhuang, another Khotanese embassy traveled with him. But from the second document, we know that Fuzhu, a lower level official in Dunhuang, traveled to Khotan again in 958 to simply *report* the safe return of Suo Ziquan. This round of diplomatic exchanges also involved many individual journeys.

These three missing categories—(1) missions to the Tang/Song/Liao courts not recorded in official histories, (2) the equally (if not more) robust regional diplomatic networks among Dunhuang, Khotan, Ganzhou, and Turfan that are entirely missing in Tang and Song sources, and (3) the many follow-up missions and return missions—attest to the frequency and scale of the exchange of envoys over long distances in Eastern Eurasia.

Such regularity of diplomatic traveling is reflected in other, sometimes surprising, social settings in Dunhuang. In 887, two Dunhuang residents wrote to the lord of Dunhuang to ask for a reduction in the amount of wine they had promised to provide to the government.[99] These two, one of whom was clearly a woman, belonged to the wine households (*jiuhu*), artisans specifically tasked with producing alcohol for the Dunhuang government. But, according to this complaint, their limited supply could not keep up with the "envoys going to Xi[zhou] [Turfan], Ting[zhou] [Jimsar], and Canwei, and the numerous foreign diplomats from Liangzhou and Suzhou [to Dunhuang]."[100] Here, these artisans made clear that they were supposed to provide alcohol to both outgoing and incoming envoys, and at a busy time of a year—this complaint was made about the activities of envoys in the spring—they needed support from the government.

In another document that lists people who were late in tax payment of firewood, the creator of the document carefully explains the reasons for the delay.[101] Of the forty-six residents in the neighborhood of "Suo Liuzhu Alley" in the city of Dunhuang who were yet to pay, the document shows that some were serving as winemakers for the government, others worked at the military garrison and city and governmental gates, while still others were sick. Twelve out of the forty-six, furthermore, are recorded as "having traveled to Khotan." As the other reasons for delayed payment were tasks sanctioned and required by the government, it is reasonable to assume that these trips to Khotan were also governmental affairs that could legitimately be cited as a reason for delaying tax payment. Therefore, at this particular moment, more than a quarter of the residents who owed tax in this small neighborhood were serving as envoys. While there is no way to know if this entry is representative of broader Dunhuang society, it does show the scale of the involvement in diplomacy among residents in Dunhuang.

The prevalence of diplomatic travel is further evident in a letter from two disgruntled parents. This older couple lived in Ganzhou and wrote to their daughter and son-in-law who lived in Suzhou, a town between Ganzhou and Dunhuang. The daughter and son-in-law had not written to their parents for about half a year. This lack of attention and communication drew sharp reproach from the parents: "Were you [the daughter] not related to us by blood, you should at least have some fond memories of our acquaintance, not to mention the fact that we are your parents; [how can] there be no message for half a year?" As a part of the accusation, the parents' letter brought up the fact that Ganzhou and Suzhou were "[as close] as being both under our eyes, and the envoys are traveling like the running of rivers. Yet not a single word was relayed to care for us." Further on, the letter writers reiterated that "even with envoys running like rivers, there is not a single word."[102] Evidently, it was common practice to convey personal information between commoners in the area through the traveling envoys (I will discuss this more in the next chapter). The frequency of the envoys "traveling like the running of rivers" made the two places, Ganzhou and Suzhou, 208 kilometers apart on the modern road, "[as close] as being both under our eyes" to the anxious parents waiting for a letter from their daughter. The parents' complaint would not have been effective unless the regularity of envoys between these two places was a well-established and accepted fact.

Therefore, while it is impossible to answer the question of how many people were traveling as envoys with specific numbers, the anecdotal pieces of evidence presented here do suggest a frequent, routinized network of diplomatic travelers around Dunhuang. The large number of envoys who must have been involved in these frequent journeys help explain why, as I showed in the first section of this chapter, in Dunhuang people from a diverse array of social and religious backgrounds, rather than a few trained bureaucrats, participated in diplomatic travel. It is possible, perhaps even likely, that diplomacy had become a common (likely also part-time) profession that employed a significant percentage of the population in Dunhuang.

Data from other oasis states on the Silk Road in earlier times substantiate the central role of diplomacy in demanding government manpower. For instance, a document from Turfan tells us that in 474 and 475, within the span of less than eleven months, the independent Turfan kingdom dispatched over 1400 people, with one horse for each person, to escort diplomatic missions from as far away as southern China and northern India to the Rouran Empire on the Mongolian steppe.[103] The population of Turfan at the time was likely less than thirty thousand, which means that, assuming 30 percent of the population were adult males (and that the work was tasked to men only), more than 15 percent of adult men engaged in the work of escorting and supporting foreign envoys in this year in Turfan. While such documentation does not exist for Dunhuang, a similar scale of involvement in diplomatic travel among its population is at least conceivable.

## Conclusion

This chapter has painted a portrait of the people who, according to the Dunhuang documents, traveled long distances for the state. These travelers were not just trained bureaucrats, but included kings and slaves, monks and laypeople, men and (occasionally) women. They were from diverse (Han Chinese, Tibetan, Sogdian, Uyghur, Khotanese, etc.) and mixed (Sino-Khotanese, Sino-Uyghur, Tibeto-Khotanese, etc.) cultural backgrounds. They almost never journeyed alone, but banded into diplomatic missions of from a dozen to more than a hundred members. These diplomatic missions were frequent and routinized, and involved a significant percentage of the population of Central Eurasian states like Dunhuang and Turfan. These travelers, through their numerous journeys, integrated the states and people of medieval Eastern Eurasia into a tight-knit network.

But these people, diverse as they were, were not the only members of the diplomatic missions. They traveled also with other, nonhuman entities, including food and clothing, camels and horses, texts and luxury items. The Staël-Holstein manuscript is so instructive because it does not simply record activities of envoys, but was a notebook taken with and used by envoys on their travels—in this sense, it was a diplomatic traveler in its own right. These "things" often traveled further and lived longer than the human travelers, and resisted their control. To complete my portrayal of diplomatic travelers on the Silk Road, I turn to these nonhuman travelers in the next chapter.

# 3

# Things

IN 971, A MONK named Jixiang visited the Song court in Kaifeng as an envoy from Khotan. He brought a letter from the Khotanese king, stating that the king had "crushed the kingdom of Shule [Kashgar] and acquired a dancing elephant."[1] Jixiang conveyed the king's intention to offer this elephant to the Song as tribute, and the Song emperor Taizu (927–76, r. 960–76) agreed to accept the elephant. In medieval China, elephant dances were performed on ceremonial occasions such as the birthday of the emperor.[2] That an elephant might dance in front of an emperor served to boost his claim of legitimacy, as elephants were known to have refused to perform for illegitimate rulers.[3] Emperor Taizu was expecting such a spectacle at his court in the near future.

This brief account of the "dancing elephant" from the official record of the Song government is not the only cameo this elephant makes in our sources. In a letter to the lord of Dunhuang in 970 that is preserved in the Dunhuang archive (P. 5538), the king of Khotan Viśa' Śūra (r. 967–77) announced that his army had recently defeated Turkic Qarakhanid invaders from Kashgar who had been aided by a Khotanese turncoat prince and taken captive "his wife, sons, elephant(s), and *vālāhä* [thoroughbred?] *mūlī* [pricy?] horse."[4] The timing of this letter strongly suggests that it is related to the record in the Song source: the king of Khotan likely sent envoys to deliver the news of his military success to the lord of Dunhuang and dispatched the monk Jixiang to the Song court around the same time. Between these two missions, the elephant that the Khotanese king bragged of as war booty to the lord of Dunhuang transformed into a "dancing elephant" offered to the Song emperor as tribute. Both transmitted and excavated sources are silent about whether this elephant traveled to and indeed danced at the Song court. Had the Khotanese king followed through with the promise, this elephant, who likely originated from India, would have trudged a greater distance than most of the human travelers we met in the previous chapter.

Regardless of its eventual fate, this elephant teaches us two important lessons about diplomatic travelers on the Silk Road. First is the obvious but often overlooked fact that humans did not travel all by themselves.[5] The elephant is a most spectacular case among all the nonhuman travelers that accompanied humans on the road. Food and drink, clothes and documents, gifts and animals all belonged to this category. The diversity of human travelers I described in the previous chapter pales in comparison to the diversity of things that traveled with them. To complement the group portrait of diplomatic travelers offered in chapter 2, this chapter paints a portrait of these nonhuman travelers or, to put it simply, "things."

The second lesson from the dancing elephant is that humans did not always control things. The goal of monk Jixiang's trip to the Song court was to report the recent acquisition of an elephant. The trip to actually deliver the elephant, if it indeed occurred, would have involved many human companions to care for and ensure the safe passage of the mammalian giant. In such a trip, the desire to deliver the elephant would be the main motivation that moved human travelers for thousands of kilometers. These people were transporting the elephant; but, in a more fundamental sense, the elephant was also moving the people. Instead of being simply carried along by humans, things formed entangled relations with people and with other things.[6] These things "take meaning in space and time, they change as human thoughts about them change, and it is in the human–object relationship that history is written."[7]

To disentangle this complex relationship, I divide the things that traveled with people in the Dunhuang archive into five categories: food, clothing, texts, animals, and luxury items. These categories are devised on the basis of how things behaved on the road, and are admittedly artificial. For instance, the elephant, a luxurious gift when it reached the court of the sovereign, must have behaved *on the road* more like other animals—it would have needed water, food, and physical care—than like other luxury items. Thus, I group the elephant with the other animals, such as camels and horses. The distinctions between categories are also fluid: an object, like the tail of a yak, that was mundane at the start of a journey might have transformed into something exotic and highly valued by the journey's end. But, as I will show, such grouping helps reveal distinct features in the life cycle, transportability, weight, and value of each category of things that shaped the travel experiences of both the things and their human companions.

In discussing these five categories of "things," I perform two tasks. First, I offer brief biographies of the traveling things, which I hope will result in a more comprehensive portrayal of diplomatic travelers on the Silk Road. At the same time, I also analyze how particular qualities of the things motivated and compelled, but also conditioned and constrained, the human travelers in their transient symbiosis on the road. More than merely "people," this entangled human-thing symbiosis was the real agent of diplomacy on the Silk Road.

## Food

Dunhuang, like its immediate neighbors Khotan, Turfan, and Ganzhou, was an oasis state. Its agriculture was powered by an extensive canal system that channeled water from the Dang River, a tributary of the Shule River, as well as melted snow from the Southern Mountains.[8] Together, these water sources nourished "ten-thousand *qing* of flat farmland surrounded by deserts on four sides."[9] The limited supply of water meant that the staple foodstuff in Dunhuang and the surrounding areas derived primarily from wheat, millet, and barley; rice, the cultivation of which demands more water than an oasis could afford, was likely grown in small quantities, but not widely available.[10] In areas beyond the reach of the canals, people in Dunhuang herded sheep, goats, and horses to further exploit sources of energy that humans cannot directly consume. Therefore, lamb and cheese were also important components of the local diet. These grain, meat, and dairy products were processed in conjunction with one another, and supplemented by vegetables, fruit, condiments, and alcoholic drinks, producing a diverse menu.[11]

As a result of the local climate, the most common food for travelers mentioned in the Dunhuang documents was based on wheat and millet, the two staple crops in the area.[12] These grains were made into different kinds of bread, known as *bing*. The semantic range of this term has shrunk in modern Chinese to mean any type of flatbread, but in Dunhuang, the term could mean steamed buns (steamed *bing*), noodles in soup (soupy *bing*), cheesed bread (milk *bing*), or pancakes (thin *bing*).[13] The typical food for travelers, termed "road food" in the Dunhuang documents, was a kind of bread known as "barbarian bread" (*hu bing*; *hu* meaning "Central Asian").[14] This was made with a fermented dough of flour mixed with oil, which was baked and then dried. The process produces a kind of bread similar the *naan* popular in modern Xinjiang, which can keep for months after initial production. Such bread has been in production for over a millennium, as attested by a carbonized specimen found in a seventh-century tomb in Turfan.[15] It was commonly consumed in China at this time: when the Tang monk Jianzhen (688–763) traveled to Japan, he carried with him "two carts of dried barbarian bread."[16]

According to the expenditure accounts of the Dunhuang government, when foreign envoys came to Dunhuang, they were often provided with "oiled barbarian bread."[17] An expenditure account from a monastery tells us that one *sheng* of oil was mixed with two *dou* (twenty *sheng*) of wheat flour to be used for Khotanese envoys, while two *sheng* of oil was used along with five *dou* of wheat flour for two traveling Vinaya monks.[18] Thus, the weight ratio of oil to flour in such bread is around 4%–5%, similar to most modern recipes for *naan*. In some cases, the bread had fillings, as oil was recorded to have been used to make "vegetable bread as road food."[19] The filling could grow well beyond simple vegetables: rich families in Chang'an produced a kind of deluxe version of the otherwise mundane "barbarian bread" using one *jin* (around 650 grams) of lamb stuffed layer by layer in the bread and mixed with peppered black bean sauce and butter.[20] The addition of fillings certainly improved the taste, and gave the dry bread a boost in moisture and fat. But most of our envoys likely did not travel with such a sumptuous variety of the bread. As with the airplane dinners that invite scorn from modern travelers, portability was often the enemy of taste.

Other food items traveled with envoys, but were often not meant for them to consume. An eminent monk from Turfan sent three watermelons through traveling envoys to several high-ranking monks in Dunhuang.[21] An exchange by letter between two family members tells us that a bag of dried chili was delivered by envoys.[22] These food items resembled other luxury items, such as textiles and aromatics, that were often used as gifts. In the idealized images of travelers produced in the Tang dynasty in the form of porcelain figurines, camels often carried a few food items, such as dead rabbits and birds. The ewers that hung over the camels' backs might also be imagined as containing drink for travelers.[23] While it is possible that diplomatic travelers hunted and consumed wild animals—they did carry bows and arrows with them—wildlife could not have been the main source of food on the road. Most likely, envoys ate quite modestly when traveling.

While it is more than probable that the envoys prepared some of their own food, much of what they ate on the road was provided for them. The need for food mediated the relation between diplomatic travelers and other groups of people, both at home and while traveling. Prior to departure, a banquet was often held, where wine and fine food items were consumed.[24] Upon their return from a trip, envoys would receive another banquet from the government and their relatives to welcome them home. In Dunhuang, if these diplomatic travelers were members of the Society for Long-Distance Travel, they would also be welcomed by a banquet to "soften their feet" (*ruanjiao* 軟腳).[25] On each of these occasions, the chance to eat together allowed envoys to exchange information and form new relations.

In addition to banquets, travelers also received food as gifts upon departure. This is known in the Dunhuang documents as food "to send one off on the road" (*song lu wu* 送路物) or "road food" (*chengliang* or *daoliang* 程糧/道糧).[26] Records of provisions offered to travelers are found in the many expenditure accounts. In particular, many accounts exist from the Jingtu Monastery, located within the city walls of Dunhuang. One of the longest such accounts, running for 474 lines, details numerous instances when the monastery offered food as "goods for a send-off on the road" for people including monastic officials, military officials, and even the lord of Dunhuang himself.[27] On two separate occasions, the Jingtu Monastery gave two *sheng* of oil to "cook food for General Gao's trip to the Southern Mountains,"[28] and 3.5 *shi* of wheat flour to be processed into food "as a send-off on the road" for the lord of Dunhuang and his retinue. By my estimation of the oil to flour ratio mentioned earlier for barbarian bread, the oil given to General Gao would have been used with 4–5 *dou* of flour, whereas the flour offered to the lord of Dunhuang would have been mixed with 1.4–1.75 *dou* of oil. As an adult male consumes about two *sheng* of food each day,[29] General Gao could have made 20 to 25 days' worth of bread out of the amount of oil given to him, whereas the amount of food the lord of Dunhuang received from the Jingtu Monastery could sustain a person for 175 days on the road, enough for a trip all the way to North China.

But of course, this 175 days of provisions was not consumed by one person, not only because the lord of Dunhuang did not travel all by himself, but also because the 3.5 *shi* of grain would have weighed around 220 kilograms, more than a camel could carry.[30] For our long-distance travelers, it was impractical, not to mention unappetizing, to prepare in one go all the food one would need for the entire journey. As I will show later in this chapter, pack animals such as camels and horses carried much more than just food. It was in the interest of human travelers to maximize the amount of luxury items carried, which would accrue economic and/or social capital at their destination. Even though barbarian bread could last for a few months, many other food items would perish long before the end of a journey, which might take months or sometimes over a year. Therefore, the weight of provisions and the length of their journeys presented our envoys a structural problem: for all the farewell banquets and "road food," they simply would not have been able to take enough food for their trips when they departed.

This structural problem was usually solved by the provisions given to travelers by their hosts during the trip. When envoys arrived at a major stop on the road, their hosts would often entertain them with a banquet, where they enjoyed finer meals than the food they carried on the road.[31] The banquets that the government of Dunhuang held for foreign envoys offered wine, meat,[32] and delicacies like "intestine noodles."[33] While envoys stayed with their hosts, they were provided food on a daily basis. The Office of Banquets and Hospitality in Dunhuang kept records of the provision of food to envoys from as far away as China, India, and Persia.[34] According to an account of wine expenditure in 964, the Dunhuang government supplied wine to a group of Ganzhou envoys continuously for 143 days.[35] The need for food compelled envoys to form and maintain amicable relations with their host states. For their long-distance journeys to succeed, virtually all diplomatic missions required both preparation of food at home and the replenishment of provisions on the road. The longer the journey, the more important the latter source of food becomes. When the places envoys reached on the road could not offer them proper accommodation, one immediate consequence was a lack of food. A Khotanese envoy complained about the dire situation he encountered in Ganzhou, which then was ravaged by internecine fighting following the death of its khan: "On one hand there is chaos, on the other hand there is no food there."[36]

This problem with food is seen in other contemporary envoy reports too. Tamīm ibn Baḥr, a Samanid envoy who traveled to the land of the Uyghurs in the early ninth century, reported that "he was carrying with him twenty days' provision" because he knew that the journey on the steppe with "wells and grass" would take twenty days. But this was not the end of his journey. After leaving the steppe, he traveled twenty more days "among villages lying closely together and cultivated tracts" before arriving at the "king's town."[37] How did he sustain himself in the second twenty-day period? The report is silent on this issue. With the help of Dunhuang materials, however, we can see that Tamīm must have relied on provisions from the townspeople in the agricultural region after his exited the steppe, where such supplies were difficult to find. The fact that he intentionally brought only provisions enough for half of the journey implies an *expectation* that he would be provided for during the journey's second half. The structural shortage of food and the routinized provision by hosts were a central feature of diplomatic travel both in Dunhuang and further west in Central Asia.

Water was as crucial to travelers as food, and its weight posed a greater problem than pieces of bread. If travelers had to load large quantities of water, it would severely impede their ability to carry other things. Fortunately, in postal stations and other governmental establishments, along with food, wine, and other amenities, hot water would have presumably been provided by the hosts. When on the road, the travelers could often easily locate natural water sources; in fact, the stops that envoys chose, when they were not halting at a governmental facility, were generally places close to lakes and rivers.[38] For more barren regions where water sources were not easily identifiable, road guides that envoys used often helpfully report the number of water sources suitable for humans and animals. A geography of Dunhuang, for example, explains that the 1500-*li* road between Dunhuang and the Stone City Garrison to its southwest has "eight locations with a spring, all of which with pasture [near the spring]."[39]

Only in the most punishing deserts did travelers have to carry water themselves. Gao Juhui, the Later Jin envoy to Khotan in 938, noted in his travelogue that: "We first encountered rocky desert [*qi*] to the west of Ganzhou. There is no water in the rocky desert, and we had to carry water in order to proceed."[40] On the spans of desert between Dunhuang and Turfan, one geographical text tells us that "there are springs and wells, but [the water from them] is salty and bitter. There is no grass, and travelers have to carry water and load food."[41] As the geography notes, having to transport water through the desert made travelers' lives much more challenging.

When travelers could access natural bodies of water, the water would need to be boiled before it could be consumed or used for cooking other food items. This perennial need was no doubt behind the intriguing story of the "magical cauldron" from Khotan witnessed by Song officials. According to this story, some Khotanese envoys' journey took them through a great desert, where, for over three days, "no water or fire can be found." By this line the envoys meant that not only were there no sources of water, which forced them to carry water into the desert, there was also no firewood or other sources of fire. The "magical cauldron" was useful in this scenario because, according to the story, when you pour water into it and wait for a few seconds, the water would start to boil on its own.[42] People in Dunhuang did indeed use cauldrons to cook: in an account of the possessions of a monastery, we find a "large cauldron with wheels" that is big enough to cook one *shi* of grain.[43] The wheels improved the portability of the otherwise unwieldy cauldron. Such cauldrons, even without the self-boiling magic, must have been crucial to hygienic water and food consumption for our travelers.

Compared with virtually everything else that the envoys carried, food items such as plain bread and drinkable water were both low in value and relatively high in weight. Therefore, it did not make economic sense, given the limited carrying capacity of a diplomatic mission, to travel with a huge quantity of food and water. Their low-value, high-weight nature, combined with the fact that they would have to be consumed daily, means that they were the most transient things that accompanied envoys on the Silk Road. It is unlikely that a piece of bread would travel with envoys for a very long time, and they needed to replenish their food and water supplies regularly while on the road. This central demand necessitated a constant relation with hosts along the road that profoundly shaped the social lives of diplomatic travelers on their journeys.

## Clothes

Clothes were as indispensable as food for our diplomatic travelers. While food was consumed daily, clothes lasted for much longer. The key rhythm of change in clothing was that of the alternating seasons. Not unlike in modern fashion shows, the clothes worn by medieval travelers can be broadly divided into two categories: summer clothes and winter clothes. Because many of the trips lasted for months, even years, envoys had to have both types of clothing with them. According to a registry of soldiers' clothes from the eighth century, a set of summer clothing included a jacket, an inner shirt, a set of loose pants, a half-sleeve shirt, a headscarf, and a pair of socks and of shoes, while a set of winter clothing comprised a coat, a pair of pants with cotton padding, a headscarf, a pair of socks and of shoes, and a sleeping bag.[44] These clothes were likely also used by envoys in the ninth and tenth centuries.

While it is conceivable that many diplomatic travelers might have worn their daily clothes on the road, long-distance trips do sometimes require special clothing. In an account of expenditure from a monastery, a monk used wheat to purchase the following items for his trip to the east: a leather jacket, full-crotch pants, and draped carpet.[45] The first two items were common ones for travelers and Dunhuang residents alike, showing that in terms of basic clothing, that used by travelers did not differ drastically from that in sedentary daily use. But the last item, draped carpet, is more unique to travelers. A Song source explains its use in detail: "carpets from the north are thick and firm. The length of carpets from the south reaches more than three *zhang*, and the width is about one *zhang* [around 3 meters] and six to seven *chi* [one *chi* is around 0.3 meters]. When folded along the width and sewn, the width [of the folded carpet] is still eight to nine *chi*. One uses a long carpet belt to go through the folded part, and puts the carpet on and fastens the belt around one's waist. The carpet thus drapes luxuriantly. During the day, one wears the carpet; at night one uses it to sleep on. Rain or shine, winter or summer, it does not depart from one's body."[46] Thus, the large carpet served not only as clothing but also as shelter. One might imagine that the monk could have depended on it to endure through the cold night when more comfortable facilities were not readily available.

Clothes are more durable than food, but they do eventually wear out, and would need to be replaced. The provision of clothing, like that of food, came primarily from the host state on the road rather than by additional packages carried by the travelers themselves. In a letter to the lord of Dunhuang written in late October of an unspecified year, a monk from Khotan states that "since I came to Shazhou [Dunhuang], my food has been provided by the magnanimity and graciousness of the lord. Now it is approaching autumn and the weather is getting colder, my clothing will also depend on the lord."[47] Here, the monk clearly connected the provision of food and that of clothing as two similar cases of the magnanimity of the lord of Dunhuang. He then asked for clothes for a monkey that accompanied him, saying that the monkey's clothes "will also depend on the lord." For both the monk and his monkey, the coming winter brought a need for new, thicker clothes, which the monk had not brought when he traveled to Dunhuang in the warmer months earlier in the year.

Such requests were not always successful. As another group of Khotanese monk-envoys in Dunhuang wrote to the king of Khotan: "It pleases us to do service [and] to go to the China land," but they "had only one overcoat [and] it has become old." They then lamented that the lord of Dunhuang would not give them a single coat, and as a result "there is no longer any draft horse [left] here nor any overcoats" to support their trip further eastward.[48] In another Khotanese letter, the envoy also complained that "all the animals our men had are lost. Our clothes are lost. . . . there is [text missing] for the animals, nor for clothes."[49] Similarly, the Dunhuang envoy Zhang Huaiquan and his twenty-person retinue, who were stuck in Binzhou and planning to come back to Dunhuang along with another group of envoys, "were not able to go because they could not prepare their clothes and equipment."[50] Since this group included Zhang Huaiquan's wife and children as well as other officials, providing clothing for them must have been a significant investment that Zhang, a recently freed prisoner at the time, was unable to raise.

The Khotanese envoys' complaint about the lack of clothing from their Dunhuang host suggests that normally the host would provide clothes to envoys. This practice is found in accounts of the Dunhuang government, though not with the same regularity that they provided food and paper. Cao Yuande, the lord of Dunhuang, respectfully gave the following pieces of clothing documented in a letter to the unnamed recipient: a robe of purple cotton and circular patterns, a pair of pants made of fine cotton, a pair of dark leather shoes, and socks made of fine cotton cloth.[51] The extreme respect seen in the formatting of the document shows that the recipient must have been of considerable social status. Because this set of items was to be used by a male, nonmonastic figure, it is likely that the intended recipient was the sovereign or a prominent representative of a foreign state. Perhaps this text represents a response to a desperate request like the one from the previously mentioned Khotanese envoy?

In this and many other cases, the dividing line between normal clothing for travelers and luxury gifts is blurred. Clothes were regularly used as gifts between sovereigns and from sovereigns to subjects. In these cases, they fulfilled the function of investiture in a very literal sense. In a mission to the Tang capital Chang'an in 878, each of the twenty-nine envoys from Dunhuang received a set of clothing made of cotton of varying degrees of fineness.[52] The lord of Dunhuang and twelve other officials, none of whom traveled to Chang'an, were also each given one set of cotton clothing. Instead of immediately wearing it, the envoys likely carried their gifted cotton clothing along with clothing intended for Dunhuang luminaries on their way back. The relation that the travelers formed with the clothing in this case resembles the one that they had with other luxury items. The biography of an envoy killed on the road mentions the "immeasurable amount of gifted clothing and hats" that he carried with him.[53] These clothes were likely traveling in a manner similar to other luxury items.

After an item of clothing was worn out, it ceased to be used as clothing. But this did not always mark the end of its life. "Torn" silk skirts were still donated to and accounted in Dunhuang monasteries, suggesting a continued value of the textile even after its form as a piece of clothing disintegrated.[54] These fragments of cloth, many of which certainly were once parts of clothes that people wore, might have then been made into banners, paintings, or bags. Many silk banners were found in the Dunhuang library cave. It is possible, indeed almost inevitable, that some of the pieces of fabric used to make these banners would have originally belonged to some traveler.[55]

While both were necessities on the road, clothes differed from food in their relative longevity, lighter weight, and higher value. Medieval envoys on the Silk Road certainly did not change their clothes daily, so two sets of clothes that could be easily packed into a bag would have sufficed for journeys of a long distance. Yet once they were worn or damaged beyond repair, envoys needed to either purchase new sets of clothes or request them from their hosts. The relatively high value of clothes meant that such requests were not as routinely granted as those for food. Clothes were less burdensome to carry than food and water, but the need for new supplies could potentially create more fraught relations. Neither were easy companions for the envoys.

## Texts

Food, drink, and clothes sustained diplomatic travelers physically, while texts organized their life on the road socially. Paintings of long-distance traveling monks in Dunhuang always have them stuffing their packages with rolls of texts, as one of the main goals of such trips was the acquisition and dissemination of religious knowledge, most of which manifested physically in the form of scrolls of texts.[56] In comparison, diplomatic travelers interacted with texts of greater diversity in genre and functionality.

Diplomatic letters were to envoys what Buddhist sutras were to monks. The physical copy of the diplomatic order or edict—official communication between heads of state—was the most important object that traveled in a diplomatic mission. The lack of such letters could break an entire mission. An embassy from Khotan bearing tributes arrived at the Song border in 1079, but was ordered to leave by a Song official because the envoys were found "without royal letter or petition." As such, their identity could not be substantiated and their mission was in danger of being expelled. In this case, the Song emperor eventually overruled his official and allowed the envoys to enter, but the emperor's decision was an exception to the established rule.[57] Conversely, the issuance of a diplomatic letter could change the nature of a mission. In 1009, the king of Khotan dispatched an envoy to the Song court, who briefed the Song emperor about conditions on the road and asked for Song envoys to travel to Khotan. The emperor's response was that "the road is distant, and sending envoys there will cost a great deal of your country."[58] Then the Song emperor suggested "now I will deign to issue the edict, and you can carry it to go [back to Khotan]. This will be no different than sending envoys [from the Song]."[59] The Khotanese envoy, because of the newly acquired edict from the Song emperor, *became* a Song envoy. To diplomatic travelers, the edict from a sovereign had a socially transformative power.

Because of the potency of edicts and royal orders in the lives of envoys, the physical treatment of these texts was crucial. A Khotanese envoy report describes how official orders were to be cared for on the road: "In the hand of each and every one [were] yellow orders. Under each and every red coat the envoys wear a . . . on the shoulder. Wherever they dismount, if there is no tree there, there he must tie on a . . . and place the orders on top of it. And they rise very early. All must be . . . and their orders must be . . . The first horse must be employed for the orders. The others must watch until the order-bearer mounts. And above all you must travel quickly and deliver the order as soon as possible."[60] The text prescribes how the order was to be placed at different junctures of a trip: when resting, the imperial edict, or the "yellow order," should be securely placed first; when traveling, the edict was to be placed on the first horse, with a rider as "order-bearer." In this way, the edict was treated with the same kind of respect given to the one who issued the order. This is likely the reason why, in a Sogdian document, the person who traveled with the edict was designated an "edict bearer" (*cwn ywzy*).[61] In both cases (order bearer/edict bearer), the text commanded the traveler to its service.

But the royal/imperial edict was by no means the only type of letter that the envoys were carrying. A diplomatic mission dealt not only with sovereigns but also governmental and social elites, so it often also carried letters for them. In the 878 mission to Chang'an, Dunhuang envoys delivered not only a letter to the Tang emperor but also letters to four ministers.[62] When the lord of Dunhuang wrote to ministers of the Uyghur kingdom of Ganzhou, his letters were also relayed by envoys.[63] Moreover, the transmission of private correspondence at the hand of envoys is a common practice found in the Dunhuang documents. For instance, S. 361 and S. 329, both collections of letter models in Chinese, mention that the letters were exchanged by envoys on at least fifty occasions. As for examples of real letters: A Chinese monk traveling to India sent his letter back to China through an envoy.[64] Two family members living in Yizhou and Dunhuang exchanged a series of miscellaneous items, including a bag of dried chili, a piece of green silk, two (unit unknown) of fermented beans, two *chi* of cloth, and three pieces of paper, all through envoys traveling between these two places.[65] The head of the monastic community in Turfan sent a letter, along with three watermelons, through an envoy to a monk and two officials in Dunhuang.[66] The frequency and efficiency of the these envoys resembled a mail-delivery service for all kinds of people with means.

There is one rare case where a letter is preserved along with its envelope. This letter was written by a monk in Suzhou to a few eminent monks in Dunhuang. It mentions no particular event, and seems to be a routine message of greetings and well-wishes. The writer states that "previously the envoys came and brought a letter," to which the current letter was a response.[67] It is very likely that this current letter was also delivered by an envoy. A similar envelope from the Khotanese queen was also brought to Dunhuang: the content of the letter has not been found, but the envelope was pasted onto the back of a printed Diamond Sutra as supporting material and thus survived. After the original message from the queen was written, it was folded or rolled up, and a smaller piece of paper was then wrapped around it as an envelope, with the characters "the envelope of the Heavenly Queen" written on the outside and a royal seal applied (see figure 3.1).[68] These letters and envelopes must have constituted a small part of the total weight that envoys had to carry on the road. But the preserving power of the library cave means that they are among the only things once accompanying these envoys on the Silk Road that are still with us.

In addition to diplomatic, governmental, and private letters, envoys also transported books. For instance, in 866, when Zhang Yichao submitted to the Tang court "four pairs of Qingjiao eagles from Ganjun mountain, two horses from Yanqing, [and] two Tibetan women," the monk who accompanied him delivered a Buddhist text entitled *Discourse on the Hundred Characteristics of Purpose in the Great Vehicle Doctrine* (*Dacheng baifa mingmen lun*).[69] But the overwhelming majority of the texts transmitted by envoys seem to be going in the other direction, from the courts in North China to Central Asia. According to a tantalizing record from the Song court, a monk from Dunhuang visited the Song capital in 1007 and conveyed the request from the lord of Dunhuang, Cao Yanlu, for a whole set of the Tripiṭaka ("Three baskets") Buddhist texts written in gold. The Song emperor "ordered a set of the Tripiṭaka written in gold and silver from Yizhou [Sichuan] and bestowed it [to Dunhuang]."[70] The text leaves little ambiguity as to what was asked and what was bestowed: a complete set of the Buddhist canon, as understood at the time, in Chinese. The whole Tripiṭaka in the early Song would have constituted hundreds of thousands of sheets of paper—their transportation to Dunhuang would have been an accomplishment in and of itself.

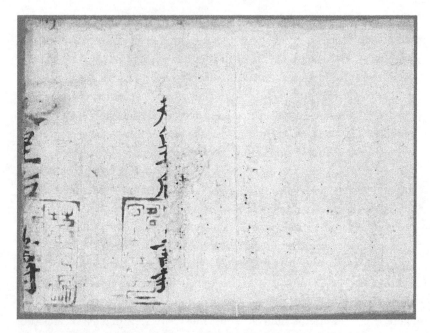

FIGURE 3.1 The envelope of a letter from the "Heavenly Queen"
(Khotanese queen), with the royal seal.
*Credit*: Bibliothèque nationale de France.

But envoys were not just transporters of texts, but also users and producers
of them. In fact, texts permeated all aspects of envoys' lives on the road. Before they began their trips, they would likely have consulted the prophecy
books that guided their fortunes. One such book advises that, on a certain
day, "there will be wine and meat if you go east; it will be auspicious to go
south; you will be delayed if you go west and north."[71] The fact that envoys
used this type of text while on the road is clear from a Tibetan letter from the
Khotanese envoys to the lord of Dunhuang, where they claimed that a group
of envoys "having seen signs of disaster [*rjes ngan dag*] on the road, diverted
to a new road."[72] To fulfill their official duty, envoys constantly wrote back to
their home countries to report on their conditions and the news they acquired.
Many Khotanese official reports preserved in Dunhuang were written by envoys to the Khotanese king.[73] But this practice was not limited to Khotan: In
884, an official in Suzhou to the east of Dunhuang wrote a message to the lord
of Dunhuang in which he reported the news from the east (we have already
encountered this report in chapter 2). Attached to this message, he indicated,

were three letters from three different envoys as well as a petition by a camel herder.[74]

When they were on the road, envoys often also kept notes about their experiences. The travelogues by Gao Juhui and Wang Yande were likely not composed in one sitting after the end of the trip, but compiled on the basis of notes made during the trip.[75] They also composed various kinds of texts on the road: an envoy from China in the ninth century wrote a series of poems about the places he visited traveling into Central Asia.[76] Other pieces of paper were used to write phrasebooks that helped translingual negotiation,[77] as well as to copy geographical treatises for current and future trips.[78] Certain envoys were even tasked with delivering papers over long distances.[79]

Because of envoys' considerable need for text production, their hosts provided them with paper in the same way that they offered them food, clothes, and shelter. The Dunhuang government gave paper extensively to both envoys coming from other states and its own envoys traveling elsewhere.[80] For instance, in 901, the envoy from the Tang received one *shu* (five hundred sheets) of fine paper from the Dunhuang government, whereas an envoy from Khotan received one *shu* and eight *tie* (nine hundred sheets; one *tie* of paper = fifty sheets).[81] On the other hand, the envoys from Dunhuang were each given fifteen or thirty sheets of "drawing paper," presumably of coarser quality. In providing paper to both incoming and departing envoys, the Dunhuang government was expecting significant textual use for these envoys.

Therefore, the medieval diplomatic mission as seen in the Dunhuang documents was an operation of enormous textual exchange, production, and consumption. Through their engagements with texts, envoys exchanged information and knowledge, mediated their relations with their sovereigns and their hosts, while creating and substantiating their own identities. Without food and clothing, the envoys would not have been able to travel, but without texts their journeys would have been meaningless.

## Animals

Animals traveled alongside humans on the Silk Road. Camels, horses, and donkeys carried goods, while other animals, like monkeys, provided a different kind of companionship. An elephant could be used as a pack animal, but in the context of the Silk Road, it more frequently functioned as a luxury gift not unlike silk or jade. Then there were animals such as birds, lions, and tigers that did not exist physically in the lives of travelers on the road, but loomed large in their imaginations. The stories of these animals reveal the physical and psychological needs of travelers. To begin a trip on the Silk Road was to initiate an interspecies relationship that in the end often transformed both the animals and the humans.

Camels are the quintessential symbol of the Silk Road.[82] In medieval Eastern Eurasia, camels were widely raised and kept for transportation.[83] There are good reasons for this status. The predomestication life of camels played out in an area even broader than Eurasia: wild camels originated in North America and migrated over the frozen Bering Strait to the Eurasian continent. Since its domestication in the third millennium BCE, this sturdy, cantankerous beast gradually swept across the Eurasian continent because of its unique ability to both carry heavy loads—a camel can carry about four hundred kilograms; humans only about one twentieth of that weight—and subsist with such load for up to ten days without water. Certain camels can even reach a running speed comparable to the best horses.[84]

What did the camels carry? The richest source of evidence on this issue is the tomb statuettes of camels in medieval China. A camel's load in these representations includes two wood/bamboo packboards (one on each side of the animal), loads of large bags that hung over the packboards, and skeins of silk, rolls of cloth, as well as other items such as vessels, meat, and dead animals (birds and rabbits), all dangling over the packboards on both sides of the large bags.[85] Elfriede Knauer suggests that the bags or leather satchels often depicted as carried by porcelain camels likely contained "industrial minerals, pigments, aromatics, drugs and condiments."[86] The last part of load—the vessels, meat, and animals—should be considered more the load of the dead in whose tomb the camels' statuettes were buried rather than the load of actual long-distance travelers. But the packboards and the large bags seem to represent how camels were loaded, given modern parallels.[87] The pictorial depictions of camels in Chinese paintings, such as the ones in *Along the River during the Qingming Festival* (figure 3.2), broadly corroborate the observations made on the basis of porcelain camels.

Camels did not only serve as pack animals but were also frequently exchanged as gifts. There are many reports of camels being delivered as gifts to the Song court.[88] In these records, one can distinguish two kinds of camels. The camels that were employed as pack animals were likely double-humped Bactrian camels (*Camelus bactrianus*). The other type of camel, the single-humped Arabian camel, or dromedary (*Camelus dromedarius*), was less common in Central Eurasia, and its rarity meant that, whenever one traveled with

FIGURE 3.2 Camels carrying loads in the painting *Along the River during the Qingming Festival* by Zhang Zeduan (1085–1145), held at the Palace Museum in Beijing.

envoys, it was considered a luxury item rather than a pack animal. In Song records, Western and Central Asian states often sent envoys to offer what they called "single-humped camels" to the Song court.[89]

Horses cannot carry nearly as much weight as camels,[90] and certain terrain, like deep, sandy desert, is not suitable for horses.[91] But for travelers on the Silk Road, horses complemented camels in important ways. They can travel much faster than most camels, so when travelers needed to transmit information or goods quickly, they often would use horses. Culturally, horses also assumed a more significant place: rare horses often were given unique and individual identities closely associated with their owner,[92] whereas camels only rarely acquired such status.[93] As a result, horses were among the most common gifts exchanged on the Silk Road that arrived at the Song and the Kitan Liao courts. But less rare horses were often used as pack animals too. In the Sanskrit-Khotanese bilingual phrasebook, the imaginary interlocutor asks a traveling monk: "Have you equipment for the road or not?" The answers suggested include "A horse or two and I shall go."[94] The "equipment for the road" here evidently meant the means of transportation. The least-valued horses were sometimes consumed as food.[95]

Camels and horses are among the most essential of the "things" that accompanied envoys, because their carrying capacity vastly exceeded that of human beings and allowed envoys to transport other things. Therefore, the acquisition and protection of camels and horses were central to the success of diplomatic journeys. The Dunhuang government owned camels and horses. In an accounting of its livestock made in 968, two camel herders were in charge of forty and thirty-three camels each.[96] These numbers represent part of the Dunhuang government's total reserve of camels. The Dunhuang government's horse ranch was located in the Ziting Garrison to the south of Dunhuang, in the foothills of the Qilian Mountains. According to one estimate, the Dunhuang government kept more than seven hundred horses.[97]

The government dispatched these camels and horses for their envoys, as well as for envoys from other states. In one instance, an official in charge of the management of government camels in Dunhuang reported that a camel was given to an envoy to Turfan.[98] But the government was not always capable of providing sufficient supply of pack animals. A certain Lü Fuding, in a complaint, wrote about a horse that he contributed to another envoy to the "land of the Tatars." Lü stated that the horse died on the way back from the Tatars, but a replacement was not issued. Therefore, he wrote to the lord of Dunhuang to ask for compensation.[99] In this letter, Lü indicated that he had provided the horse to the envoy "according to the official stipulations." Evidently, the Dunhuang government was not only herding its own horses but also requested horses from its residents, to whom it promised compensation but could not always deliver. In other cases, the government provided animals to envoys who visited Dunhuang. A tenth-century account enumerates camels that were used for an envoy to Turfan, as well as for Khotanese envoys visiting the Tatars.[100] Another account shows that the Dunhuang government gave a male camel from the Southern Mountains to the head envoy of a Khotanese mission.[101] In all these cases, the state functioned as a major source of pack animals for envoys.

In many other cases, however, envoys needed to provide their own pack animals. In a letter dated to 904, a group of military officials described a desperate situation: "ever since we started working in the government, we have needed to supply our own camels and horses." This included not only the camels and horses themselves but also their saddles and other equipment, to the point that "a needle and a piece of grass have to be prepared on our own." These camels and horses thus prepared were used for their "earlier and future [trips as] envoys." The officers requested that the lord of Dunhuang consider their contribution and destitution, and spare them from the "[tax in] state-sanctioned clothes, land tax, work as beacon-tower watchmen, [tax in] governmental firewood, and other miscellaneous labors."[102] It is unclear if the request was granted. But judging from this document, it seems that it was a common practice of the Dunhuang government to have envoys provide their own camels and horses.

To acquire these pack animals on their own, envoys-to-be drew up contracts to hire them. In 995, A certain general (*yaya*) in Dunhuang named Suo Shengquan borrowed a horse from another general for his diplomatic journey to Khotan. The contract stipulates that, after his return from a successful trip, Suo was to repay one *pi* of raw silk, one *pi* of processed silk, and one *pi* of crimson cotton cloth. If, on the other hand, the journey was not successful, the repayment would have to be made by the cosignatories of the contract, which in this case included Suo's wife and two sons.[103] If officials like generals had to borrow horses to travel, then it is no surprise that other envoys also had to resort to this practice to fund their trips. There are many examples in the Dunhuang documents. A commoner named Shi Xisu, likely of Sogdian descent, purchased a horse from a military official so that he could join a diplomatic mission.[104] In 923, an envoy named Zhang Xiuzao hired a camel twice for two separate trips to Turfan within three months,[105] while in 931, two commoners named Dong Shantong and Zhang Shanbao together hired one camel for their journey to North China.[106] The price of hiring a camel for a trip to Turfan was around one *pi* of raw silk,[107] whereas hiring a camel to the Chinese capital could cost as much as five to seven *pi* of raw silk.[108] In contrast, *buying* a cow cost only about one *pi* of raw silk.[109] In a Sogdian letter, a desperate traveler spent two *rayzi* (pieces of woolen cloth) to hire a camel. In this case the trip must have been quite short because he also offered five *rayzi* to buy one sheep and half a sheep's carcass, an indication of the relatively low value of the *rayzi*.[110] In most cases, hiring a camel or a horse was a significant investment, and one that envoys often had to shoulder themselves. In taking these loans, both the envoys' family members and neighbors, who often served as guarantors of the transaction, and the people who lent the animals out were implicated in this risky endeavor.

The contracts often list the risks these hired animals could encounter on the road. Dong and Zhang's contract, for instance, distinguished three such scenarios: if there were "danger on the road" that prevented the envoys from returning, with the clear implication that the camel would not have returned either, both parties would follow the "established Grand Precedence"; if the camel went missing on the road but the envoys returned, the envoys were required to provide a replacement within one year; if the camel died on the road of natural causes, then a written corroboration from the envoys' companions had to be provided to alleviate them from liability.

We do not know what happened to this particular camel. But from other documents, we know that the risk to camels and horses was not hypothetical. A Khotanese envoy report accounts the condition of camels and horses that certain elite envoys traveled with from Khotan to Dunhuang: "As for the prince from Gūmattīra, he had three camels—not a single one had gotten away—and he made it to Shazhou [Dunhuang] with only one *va'stairma* [meaning unclear] horse. . . . As for Prince Yiṃnakä, he had six camels. Three of them and one horse made it to Shazhou. As for Prince Śvakala, only one of his camels made it to Shazhou."[111] The loss of the animals in these cases may have been the result of the harsh conditions in the desert between Khotan and Dunhuang. To ensure the health of pack animals, they have to be fed regularly. These animals mostly eat plants, which were abundant in most places along the road where there was water. But because naturally growing plants were not available everywhere, envoys must have also brought with them hay to feed the animals.[112] But even with care, illness and death were unavoidable. In some cases, after death, these animals continued to travel with envoys: among the gifts sent to the late Tang court from the Uyghur kingdom of Ganzhou was an unspecified number of "green wild horsehides."[113]

Camels and horses were the two most important pack animals for long-distance travelers, so much so that they as a group became a symbol for long-distance travel. For instance, the travel costs that the Tang government reimbursed to the Dunhuang envoys was called "the value of camels and horses."[114] In Dunhuang, a local deity called the "God of Camels and Horses" likely protected the welfare of travelers.[115] When travelers departed from Dunhuang heading east, they would encounter the site of an old shrine to a Han dynasty general who, legend has it, cleaved the mountain to create a spring. The shrine was no longer extant, but as a local geography tells us, "the stone camels and horses are where travelers pray for good fortune."[116] Such close association of these two animals explains why, when artists of Dunhuang had to produce images of official travelers, they painted a horse and a camel together (see figure 3.3; the hats of the travelers indicate their status as governmental officials).

Because of the prominence of camels and horses, knowledge about these animals was also key information exchanged on the Silk Road. When the Jin

FIGURE 3.3 Dunhuang painting of a horse, a camel, and their riders. *Credit*: The British Library.

envoys including Gao Juhui arrived at Ganzhou, the people of Ganzhou taught them how to treat the hooves of pack animals in order to prepare them for the desert. "Wooden feet should be made for horse hooves. Carve four openings on the wooden feet and four openings on the horse hooves, and then latch them [together]. As for camel hooves, simply cover them with yak hide and they can walk."[117] As the Jin envoys learned, camels were more adept than horses at trudging the sandy paths of Central Asia.

Donkeys and mules are only rarely mentioned in our sources. Their carrying capacity is, according to a Song source, one-third that of camels.[118] They were also less apt at adapting to difficult environmental conditions. Therefore, they were only occasionally used as pack animals for our long-distance travelers. An envoy from Dunhuang to Ganzhou hired a donkey from a monk for the price of nine pieces of fine sheepskin.[119] The relatively easy road between Dunhuang and Ganzhou might have been the reason why this envoy hired a donkey rather than a camel. It might also explain another record in which an official used a donkey on his trip to Guazhou to deliver fruit.[120] When they did accompany humans, however, the connection they formed was no less enduring. In a much-discussed eulogy preserved in Dunhuang, the writer mourns his deceased donkey. He recounts the difficulties he shared with the donkey in the Taihang Mountains and on the Yangtze River, which produced an unusually strong bond that compelled the writer to say, "even when I can afford a good horse, I will not sell you!"[121] In this case, the donkey formed a personal relationship with its rider. Many of our envoys must have had similar relations with their pack animals.

Beyond camels, horses, and donkeys, other kinds of animals participated in envoys' journeys in one way or another. Sheep did not usually travel with envoys, but their prevalence in areas that the envoys passed through meant that they served as good source of food. The Song envoy Wang Yande observed in Turfan a kind of sheep with a large tail that was particularly succulent.[122] This type of "large-tailed sheep" is also recorded among the gifts given by the kingdom of Kucha to the Song court in 984.[123] Occasionally, sheep also served a different purpose: when crossing the Yellow River, Jin dynasty envoys were taught to turn sheepskins into airbags and fix them together into rafts.[124]

Other animals were mostly on the road as luxury gifts. The elephant I mentioned at the beginning of this chapter was one spectacular case. Having an elephant in the diplomatic mission must have drastically changed the pace of movement, the need to acquire fodder, and the relations with other animals. Less disruptive than an elephant but similar in nature were smaller mammals such as the monkey that traveled with Khotanese envoys as a gift.[125] In that case, the existence of the animal demanded care, but likely also provided comfort and companionship on the road.

Like the best horses, certain birds were among the gifts that traveled with envoys. In 933, a Uyghur mission brought a white eagle to China, which was ordered to be released by the Chinese emperor.[126] But arguably more important was the psychological impact birds and their swift and unobstructed movements had on envoys. When describing the political chaos that disrupted the road, a Khotanese envoy stated that "now, apart from a bird in the air the envoy of another man has no passage one to another."[127] The association of birds with free movement can explain why in pictorial and physical depictions of horses and camels, they are often seen together with, or even transformed into birds.[128] If camels and horses allowed envoys a kind of mobility beyond human capacities, birds served as a symbol of an even greater freedom that the envoys could only envy.

This host of animals that traveled with envoys can be broadly divided into two groups: pack animals, such as camels, horses, and donkeys, and prestige animals, such as elephants, monkeys, and sheep, that were often exchanged as gifts. The former group was structurally crucial to the diplomatic mission, because it defined the carrying capacity of the mission. The acquisition, in-journey care, and eventual return of these pack animals were central events in a diplomatic mission that affected all other aspects of the life on the road of both envoys and the "things" that went with them. On the other hand, the role of the luxury animal was less crucial, and many missions operated without luxury animals. But when they did appear, like the elephant from Central Asia, their rarity commanded attention and drove envoys into action. It is to the power of these luxury goods that I turn in the next section.

## Luxury Items

The category of luxury items differs from the four previous categories because of its porosity. Certain things in each of the four previous categories could be regarded as "luxury items." While most food items were certainly mundane, things like the "wild camel's hump" that traveled with Uyghur diplomats in 935 were luxury items.[129] In a letter from Cao Yijin, the lord of Dunhuang, to the Uyghur khan in Ganzhou, Cao describes the arrival of diplomats from China as "bringing clothes, endowing gifts, and elevating the official title."[130] Traveling envoys did not wear these clothes, but transported them as gifts for others. The complete set of Buddhist Tripiṭaka and the dancing elephant are both also luxury items, which distinguishes them from other texts and animals that accompanied diplomatic travelers.

In 951, a group of envoys from Turfan reached the Later Zhou (951–60) court in Kaifeng. A particularly detailed record is preserved of the things that accompanied this mission.

> Six large and small lumps of jade, . . . one lump, nine *jin* of green amber, 1329 pieces of white cotton, 280 pieces of white plain cloth, six branches of coral, 2632 pieces of white sable skin, 250 pieces of black sable skin, 503 pieces of blue sable skin, four used jackets [made of] sable skin, one white jade ring and one green ring band, two iron mirrors, 69 harnesses with jade band, one jade band, along with appropriate amount of aromatics and medicine.[131]

Another mission in the same year also recorded as from "the Uyghurs," which could mean either Turfan or Ganzhou, immediately follows this entry in *Cefu yuangui*, a Song-era compilation of earlier sources. From this second mission the court received:

> 77 lumps of jade, 350 pieces of white cotton, 28 pieces of blue and black sable skin, one pair of jade belts, jade harness, and [illegible], 420 strings of yak tails, 20 large pieces of amber, 300 *jin* of red salt, 390 *jin* of tears of barbarian tong tree, and 2100 *jin* of sal ammoniac.[132]

The sundry items in these two lists fall into several subcategories: natural products (sable skin, yak tail, and tears of barbarian tong tree), precious stones and minerals (jade, amber, coral, red salt, and sal ammoniac), and manufactured goods, including jade objects and cotton cloth. These categories, along with rare animals such as purebred horses and single-humped camels, accounted for the majority of luxury items that came from Central Asia to North China.

In the other direction, the courts of North China gave out to the returning envoys a rather different group of items that consisted mostly of manufactured goods. According to the record of a group of envoys from Dunhuang in 878, the Tang court gave rolls of silk, clothes made of silk and cotton, and silverware as return gifts.[133] In an undated letter to the lord of Dunhuang, the emperor stated that "The Heavenly Court values the borderland [i.e., Dunhuang]. Considering that its land does not produce silkworm, I specifically bestow you with silk, as well as *jin* silk."[134] Even though we know that Central Asian countries had been producing silk long before this time,[135] the good quality of silk from North China was still highly appreciated. In a Song record, in reciprocation to the jade, jade seal, frankincense (*ruxiang*), sal ammoniac, camels, and horses given by the lord of Dunhuang, the Song court offered a "brocade robe, golden belt and other ritual objects" as well as "medicine and golden leaves."[136] The superior manufacturing technology in silk and gold in North China was thus compensated by an abundance of natural products from as far away as the Arabian Peninsula. An especially direct reciprocal relation existed in this exchange between the sal ammoniac from Dunhuang and the golden belts and golden leaves from the Tang. As sal ammoniac was used in China as "a flux for soldering gold and silver,"[137] it was instrumental in the production of golden objects. Conceivably, the sal ammoniac that came from Dunhuang on this trip could potentially have be used to make the golden belts that flowed back westward in a later exchange.

The exchange of luxury items did not occur only between regimes of North China, such as the Tang and the Song, and Central Asian states, but also among different Central Asian states themselves. In a well-preserved letter, a female attendant named Youding in Dunhuang made a few requests to a Khotanese princess, who was in Khotan at the time.[138] After stating that she had served the princess for a long while, Youding asked the princess to petition the Khotanese king to send her a Sogdian-brocade skirt, and suggested that the princess discuss with ministers about other materials needed, including silk, pigment, iron, and colored brocade, "for the construction of caves" in Dunhuang. She also suggested that fine medicine should be delivered to an unidentified elderly lady, and further asked for a large amount of fine silk from Gancheng (a town in Khotan) as well as red copper. At the end of the letter,

Youding conveyed the request from the prime minister in Dunhuang for jade belts and thirty to forty arrows. In this brief correspondence between two women, we see a whole range of materials being exchanged between Dunhuang and Khotan, none of which would have been possible without the diplomatic connection created by the marriage of the Khotanese princess. The goods included in this letter, from a silk skirt and brocade to jade belts and arrows, show that Central Eurasian states were not sending out merely natural produce; much of what they exported was also manufactured goods.

The central feature that united these diverse items mentioned above is their relatively high value compared with their weight. As the carrying capacity of camels and horses was limited, one can imagine that the following calculation went on in the minds of those preparing for gifts and goods to bring on the road:

*Relative value = perceived value of item at destination / weight*

This metric is a useful heuristic because it emphasizes the *relative* nature of these considerations. One would hardly characterize an elephant as "lightweight." But the value of the elephant was understood, by both the Khotanese king and the Song emperor, as so exceptionally high that it was worthwhile to transport it over thousands of kilometers—of course it didn't hurt that this particular luxury item could walk on its own. Similarly, over a hundred thousand *jin* (sixty-four thousand kilograms) of frankincense and other miscellaneous items were reportedly transported by Khotanese envoys to the Song border in 1080.[139] This amount of goods would have required somewhere between 120 and 150 camels to carry. In the two lists of goods coming to the Zhou court in 951, we find numbers not as large but still considerable, including more than 3000 pieces of sable skin in the first mission and 2100 *jin* of sal ammoniac in the second. The weight of these gifts needs to be considered in the context of the financial risk of procuring pack animals described in the previous section. Given the limited number of camels and horses they had under their command and the large amount of precious goods they transported, it is easy to imagine them using as much of the carrying capacity of pack animals for luxury items as they could.

Within this scheme, we can see why silk and other textiles were so central to the journeys of envoys. One *pi* of silk weighs about eleven *liang*, or just shy of five hundred grams.[140] The 1848 *pi* of silk given to the 878 mission from Dunhuang by the Tang emperor would have required about six camels to carry.[141] As one *pi* of silk regularly exchanged for around twenty-seven *shi* of grain in the Dunhuang market, this amount of silk would have been enough to purchase close to fifty thousand *shi* of grain, the transportation of which would have required 16,632 camels. While this math is theoretical, and frankly a bit absurd, it gives us a concrete sense of just *how light* silk was compared with its value. In fact, the relative value of silk was comparable to some of the most coveted treasures we encounter on the road. For instance, the same amount (in weight) of silver was only slightly more valuable than silk.[142]

Unlike virtually all other types of luxury items, which were specialties of certain regions (like jade, which was exclusively from Khotan), silk and other precious textiles were widely produced in all the major states in medieval Eastern Eurasia. Compound weave silk (*jin*) from Central Asia was particularly prized.[143] Among the lists of gifts recorded at the Tang and Song courts, compound weave silk from Persia and Kucha makes a regular appearance.[144] Cotton cloth was produced in large quantities in Turfan,[145] but Khotan also was famous for a particular kind of white cotton cloth.[146] These widely produced luxury textiles were also used in a much more diverse set of social settings than any other luxury items. Silk was made into sutra covers,[147] paintings, banners,[148] and clothes.[149] It was also used as currency, which assumed particular importance as bronze coin ceased to circulate in the region after the retreat of the Tang.[150] Therefore, I think the historian Peter Brown was not overly hyperbolic when he suggested that "silk and similar items were as central to the flow of power and prestige in eastern Eurasia as is the movement of enriched uranium between modern states."[151]

These luxury items traveled with diplomats on the road in a way that is not much different than food and texts. The travelers needed to load, move, and take proper care of them. But when they arrived at a stop and entered into interpersonal relations in the form of gift exchange, the lives of these items became much more complicated than that of a piece of bread that was consumed or a letter that was read. In chapter 6, I will further explore the complicated lives of luxury items as gifts.

## The Human-Thing Symbiosis on the Silk Road

Things and people are inseparable in contemporaneous Chinese records about envoys on the Silk Road. Official histories from the Tang or the Song court, such as the ones about the Uyghur envoys in *Cefu yuangui* discussed earlier, almost always mention the envoys along with the "tributes" they brought with them. Depictions of envoys in Chinese paintings also show them traveling with "tribute objects" that they offered to the Tang/Song court. In a well-known painting attributed to Yan Liben (c. 600–673), envoys carry elephants' tusks, strange stones, unidentified substances in pots of various sizes, and animals such as goats, horses, and birds (figure 3.4). These "tribute objects" are what defined the social identity of the people who carried them. Without these "things," neither the painter or the viewers would see these bizarrely clad travelers as envoys. Similarly, a Song dynasty painting entitled *Five Horses* shows not only the animals but also the people who delivered them to the Song court. In one case, a man with non-Chinese facial features, wearing a Central Asian gown and a pointed hat, stands holding the reins of a horse. The colophon describes the date of the arrival of the horse as well as its age and height; it tells us that this horse came from Khotan, and was given, at the Song court, the name of Stallion with a Phoenix Head.[152] The colophon, like the title of the painting, does not mention the man holding the reins of the horse. His presence seems to only echo the provenance of the horse: a Central Asian man leading the horse from Khotan. The man and the horse complete each other.

The record from *Cefu yuangui* mirrors Yan Liben's and Li Gonglin's paintings in that both see luxury gifts as the main, even the *only* companion of the incoming diplomats, and ignore all the other types of things that must have traveled with them. For observers at the destination and modern scholars who use their observations, the most salient human-thing relation was the one between the diplomatic traveler and the exotic gifts that he carried. But this view reflects only one dimension of a complex set of relations between things and human travelers on the road. As this chapter shows, humans traveled with much more than just luxury goods. Food, water, everyday clothes, pack animals, and texts of various functionalities also accompanied them. Different categories of things were often acquired at the same time before the journey: in a pre-trip contract, an envoy borrowed silk to fund his journey, but at the end of the contract, a note was added about the additional "road goods" that the envoy acquired, possibly from the lender, in the form of a jade waist belt, and a sheet of fine paper.[153] While on the road, these different categories of things were loaded on the same camels, or even put in the same "road bags."[154] Compared to records produced by the courts at the destinations of the travelers, the Dunhuang documents allow us to catch these travelers in action and see a more comprehensive picture of their symbiosis with a more diverse group of things.

My description above reveals the central tension in this symbiosis: the wish to carry more things and the limited carrying capacity of camels and

FIGURE 3.4 *Tribute Bearers*. Painting attributed to Yan Liben.

horses. The five types of things discussed here were all indispensable for a successful diplomatic trip. But the limits of carrying power meant that envoys had to make choices as to what to take to maximize the political, cultural, and material gains of the trip. Of course, traveling with one more camel would expand the carrying capacity. But there was a limit to how many camels a person could manage on a long-distance trip,[155] and hiring one more camel also significantly increased the financial risk of the journey. For instance, on his trip to the west, a monk sold his clothes so that he could buy two camels for the journey into the desert.[156] One might imagine that he had reached the limit of his ability to expand the carrying capacity of his journey.

With this dynamic in mind, it is easier to understand why deserts were such a potent deterrent to long-distance connection. It is not that people could not travel through deserts: the many examples of envoys moving between Dunhuang and Khotan testify to the traversability of the great desert that lay between these two kingdoms (see chapter 4). But in order to cross the desert, travelers

FIGURE 3.4 *Tribute Bearers (continued).*

had to carry greater quantities of food and water than did those traveling else-where, which reduced the percentage of profit/prestige-generating luxury goods that occupied the limited space of the camels' load. As a result, the things that came from the other side of a desert, in both directions, became meaningfully more valuable.

In this delicate balancing act, our envoys largely opted to be frugal in the daily necessities in order to maximize the number of important documents, luxury gifts, and rare animals that could join their journey. Therefore, at the beginning of their journey, most envoys carried only enough food and clothes for the first leg of the trip. Such shortage of daily necessities was a structural fea-ture of long-distance journeys. As the numerous accounts from the Dunhuang government show, envoys making stops in Dunhuang received ample replen-ishment of food, paper, clothes, and wine (see my discussion in chapters 5 and 6). The constant acquisition and replenishment of food and clothing, an antidote to this structural shortage, wove envoys in a series of overlapping networks of relations with their hosts on the road.

## Conclusion

This chapter has described the symbiosis of humans and things on the Silk Road. The things that traveled with their human companions included food, clothing, texts, animals, and luxury items. Each performed a different social function on the road: food and clothes were daily necessities that sustained the physical well-being of human travelers; texts gave their trips meaning; animals helped carry other things, but also provided companionship to human travelers; luxury items were most potent in negotiating the relations between diplomatic travelers and their hosts, and were often the very purpose of diplomatic journeys.

A diplomatic trip altered the fate of the things even more dramatically than it did the fate of an envoy. Foodstuff almost never lasted very long before being consumed by humans and animals; clothes grew old and tattered because of constant wear; horses and animals could be stolen or might run away, and, when desert was on the itinerary, death was not uncommon; texts were created and consulted during the trip and often donated or discarded after; luxury goods, of course, were particularly prone to the attention of bandits and enemies, and large amounts of goods could be taken away quickly. For these goods, a diplomatic trip might be the end of their life story.

For other goods, these trips could be transformational, a process nowhere clearer than in the category of luxury items. The exoticism that often defined these goods was *produced* by long-distance travel. A piece of *jin* silk manufactured in Kucha became "Kuchean *jin*" in Dunhuang; a watermelon from Turfan served as a rare gift when it traveled to Dunhuang; a war elephant in Central Asia became a dancing elephant in Kaifeng; a yak tail, when removed from the animal on the Tibetan Plateau and transported to the Chinese court, ascended to the imperial banner as a sign of royalty; a piece of jade from the Khotan River traveled over four thousand kilometers to adorn the headdress and clothing of the Song emperor. The transformation of the luxury items that traveled from the east to the west may have been less dramatic. As the majority of luxury items from North China—silverware, silk, clothes, and books— were products rather than natural resources, they were held in as high regard in Central and West Asia as in East Asia, albeit often in vastly different social contexts.

The discussion in chapters 2 and 3 is my answer to the question of *who* the travelers were on the Silk Road. The rich materials from Dunhuang have allowed me to paint a fuller picture of Silk Road travelers than we previously knew. The travelers I describe in this book include a diverse array of envoys who most typically voyaged in sizable diplomatic missions, but also the camels and horses they rode, the luxury goods they carried, the food they ate, the clothes they wore, and the texts they used. The different elements in these missions coexisted in constant tension: envoys argued and (occasionally) killed one another; potent things often set envoys in action; limited carrying capacity meant that rolls of silk had to compete with food and clothing for space on a camel's back. Therefore, a diplomatic mission was not only a complicated social space made up of diverse human travelers, it was also a unit of delicate human-thing symbiosis. With this complex profile in mind, let us see, in the next four chapters, how they actually fared on the road.

# Traveling

# 4

# Facing the Road

ONCE THE DIPLOMATIC mission was organized, the camels purchased, barbarian bread baked, and skeins of silk packed, the envoys were ready to begin their journey. But how did the journey actually materialize? How did the envoys travel along roads that they were not familiar with, deal with people of different cultural background and political affiliation, and communicate with speakers of unknown tongues? The Dunhuang materials provide a rich sourcebase to answer these questions about envoys' lives on the road, and this is the subject of the four chapters in part II. In this chapter, I first consider the road that our travelers faced.

What did the road of the "Silk Road" look like? Ferdinand von Richthofen visualized his new concept as one crooked yet continuous line that connected various key places of Eurasia such as Balkh (Baktra) and Dunhuang (Daxata) in a roughly east–west direction. The directionality of this road was determined by matching information from ancient Chinese travel accounts with the Greco-Roman cartographical tradition. Underlying this crude line was the dream of a German-engineered trans-Eurasian railroad (figure 4.1).[1] Subsequent scholars significantly revised Richthofen's picture of the road. By combining more historical information from well-documented travelers such as Xuanzang and Marco Polo with in-person examination of the landscape of Central Eurasia, the shape of the Silk Road grew from a single line to a network of interconnected branches.[2] The most nuanced treatment, such as the one included in the 2011 UNESCO project, further differentiates major routes from minor ones, on the basis of their frequency of use for premodern travelers.[3] The Silk Roads, in these visualizations, are like blood vessels, with arteries, arterioles, and capillaries channeling the travelers that animated the body that was the Eurasian continent.

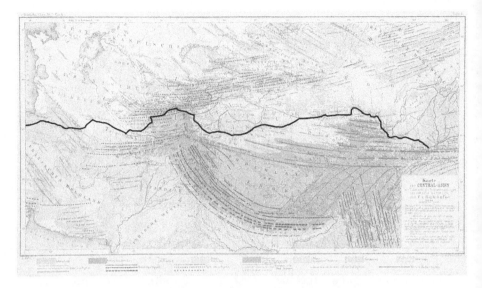

FIGURE 4.1 Richthofen's Silk Road.

On the other hand, some scholars have criticized the sense of certainty these cartographical visualizations convey. For example, Valerie Hansen argues that the "road" in Silk Road "was not an actual 'road' but a stretch of shifting, unmarked paths across massive expanses of deserts and mountains."[4] This view is useful in countering the unrealistic notion of the Silk Road being paved, supplied, and guarded like Roman imperial roads. If the Silk Road indeed was made up of mostly "shifting, unmarked paths," then the travelers upon it must have depended on their own spontaneous ingenuity on each of the trips they took, and the "Silk Road" would have looked different from one traveler to another, from one trip to another.

The Dunhuang documents provide a perspective qualitatively different from these pan-Eurasian (or sometimes Afro-Eurasian) visualizations of the Silk Road. They allow us to distance ourselves from an omniscient view, and see the road through the eyes of premodern travelers. The road that emerges from their lived experiences, as this chapter shows, is neither an all-encompassing network that connects China with Europe nor an uncharted territory navigable only through daily spontaneity. Instead, the Silk Road these travelers faced was a collection of regional routes of varying degrees traversability, conditioned by topographical features, the availability of water, and the reach of the state. Travelers navigated these routes by reading and reproducing geographical treatises, lists of place names, place-centered poems, and travelogues; they also relied on local guides and escorts for updated information about the roads.

By showing what the road looked like to long-distance travelers and how they navigated it, I argue that, while shifts in the geographical domains of states constantly reshaped the specific paths that travelers took and affected the conditions of the roads, the Silk Road was never, and could never be, "cut off" as a result of the rise or fall of states. Whether under large empires or during political fragmentation, with relatively comprehensive knowledge or severe informational lacunae, our enterprising travelers could always find a way.

## Understanding the Silk "Roads"

A driver living in a modern US city, wanting to reach another city, would be aware that they are facing not one single road but multiple different types of road. They will likely depart from their home on a city street, reach a state highway and/or an interstate, then enter the urban streets of their destination; if the destination is a small town, the driver might need to veer off the main streets and use country roads. Similarly, travelers on the Silk Road did not face a single, monotonous "road," but had to navigate a variety of natural landscapes and human establishments. Indeed, the diversity among the different sections of a single trip on the Silk Road must have been vastly greater than that experienced by a modern traveler behind the comfort of a wheel. The Dunhuang documents allow us to examine this variety of roads in a way that has not been done before in the existing scholarship. Let us begin by looking at the itinerary of a diplomatic trip.

This itinerary, now in the Kyōu Shooku collection in Osaka, Japan, lists the places a group of envoys from Dunhuang stayed at between the sixteenth day of the eighth month and the eighteenth day of the ninth month, in a certain year in the late ninth century (see table 4.1).[5] It is an incomplete list: only ten lines are found on this fragment, and the complete original text must have been more extensive. In the extant section, in a period of just over a month, the diplomats covered a distance of about a thousand *li* (540 kilometers). The itinerary describes in very terse language where the diplomats stopped and what their activities were at each stop. For instance, the first entry tells us that on the sixteenth day, they "arrived at the southern opening of the valley, and spent the night [there]." Not all of the twenty stops recorded in the itinerary are geographically identifiable. I am able to securely locate six of them.[6] Placing these on the map (map 4.1), we see that this was a trip from the "West

TABLE 4.1. Itinerary for a Ninth-Century Diplomatic Trip through Southern Mongolia

| Date | Name of Stop | Type of Stop | Activity |
|------|--------------|--------------|----------|
| 8.16 | Southern Opening of the Valley | 3 | Travel |
| 8.17 | ? | ? | ? |
| 8.18 | West Town of Subjugation | 2 | Travel |
| 8.19 | West Town (of Subjugation) | 2 | Rest |
| 8.20 | Fort of Four Twists | 2 | Travel |
| 8.21 | Wuhuai Fort | 2 | Travel |
| 8.22 | Wuhuai Fort | 2 | Rest |
| 8.23 | Garrison of Heavenly Virtue | 2 | Travel |
| 8.24 | Garrison of Heavenly Virtue | 2 | Playing polo game at reception |
| 8.25 | Garrison of Heavenly Virtue | 2 | Rest |
| 8.26 | Garrison of Heavenly Virtue | 2 | Rest |
| 8.27 | Garrison of Heavenly Virtue | 2 | Rest |
| 8.28 | Garrison of Heavenly Virtue | 2 | Rest |
| 8.29 | Garrison of Heavenly Virtue | 2 | Rest |
| 8.30 | Garrison of Heavenly Virtue | 2 | Rest |
| 9.1 | Garrison of Heavenly Virtue | 2 | Rest |
| 9.2 | Garrison of Heavenly Virtue | 2 | Rest |
| 9.3 | Wheat Pond | 3 | Travel |
| 9.4 | West River | 3 | Travel |
| 9.5 | Central Town of Subjugation | 2 | Travel |
| 9.6 | Divine Mountain Pass | 2 | Travel |
| 9.7 | Yunjia Pass | 2 | Travel |
| 9.8 | Yunjia Pass | 2 | Rest |
| 9.9 | Lasting Peace Post | 1 | Travel |
| 9.10 | Placating the People Post | 1 | Travel |
| 9.11 | Small River Post | 1 | Travel |
| 9.12 | Strengthening the Military Post | 1 | Travel |
| 9.13 | Lasting Benevolence Post | 1 | Travel |
| 9.14 | Garrison of Peaceful Border | 2 | Travel |
| 9.15 | Huyao Post | 1 | Travel |
| 9.16 | Pacifying the Barbarians Post | 1 | Travel |
| 9.17 | Heavenly Peace Post | 1 | Travel |
| 9.18 | Post at the Northern Entry to the Yanmen Pass | 1 | Travel |
| 9.19 | ? | ? | ? |

*Note*: the date 8.16 means the 16th day of the 8th month. Types of stop: 1, postal station; 2, other military/governmental establishment; 3, natural stop.

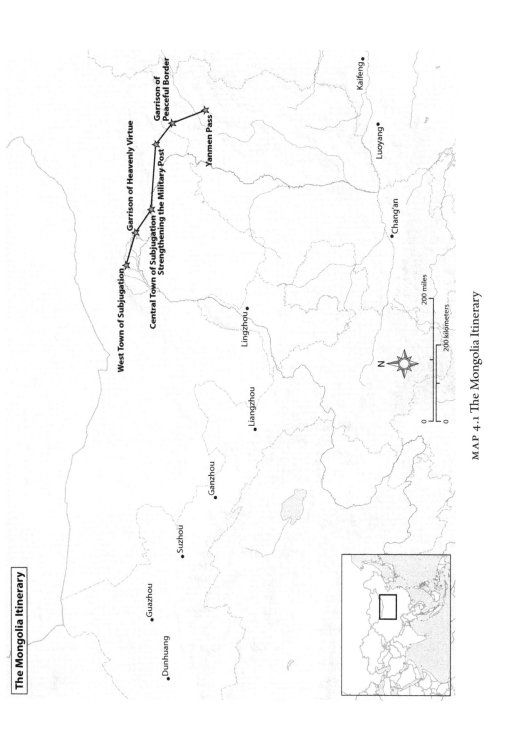

MAP 4.1 The Mongolia Itinerary

Town of Subjugation" (Xi Shouxiang Cheng 西受降城) to Yanmen Pass (Yan-men Guan 雁門關), which took the envoys through the southern part of what is now Inner Mongolia and into northern China, the "steppe route" section of the Silk Road.[7] I refer to this text as the "Mongolia Itinerary." From the shape of the route, we can guess that the envoys were traveling from Dunhuang to the Tang capitals, likely Luoyang but possibly Chang'an as well.

These twenty recorded stops includes towns (*cheng*), forts (*bao*), garrisons (*jun*), passes (*guan*), and, most commonly, postal stations (*yi*). In the first half of the itinerary (8.16 [the sixteenth day of the eighth month] to 9.7), the travelers mostly stayed in the towns, forts, garrisons, and passes, all of which were primarily military establishments of the Tang Empire. In the second half (9.9 to 9.18), as they moved closer to the Tang heartland, they stopped almost exclusively in postal stations, with the only exception being the Garrison of Peaceful Border (on 9.14). On three occasions (8.16, 9.3, and 9.4), the diplomats stayed at places not identified as either military establishments or postal stations; their names suggest that they were naturally formed locations suitable for overnight stays. The three types of stop—postal stations, other military/governmental establishments, and natural stops—determined the experience of travel for the diplomats and defined the contours of "the road" for them.

Postal stations were signature physical features of the empires in Eurasia. Large empires from the Mediterranean world to China all established their own postal systems.[8] The postal stations were generally evenly distributed between important administrative centers in order to facilitate travel. In the Tang Empire, for instance, postal stations were placed every thirty *li* (sixteen kilometers) on a government-maintained road.[9] The officially prescribed speed of travel in Tang China was seventy *li* per day on horseback, fifty *li* on foot or by donkey, and thirty *li* with a cart.[10] Therefore, one day's journey on foot would take the envoys conformably to the next postal station on a government road. A geographical treatise from the Dunhuang library cave (P. 2005) records the location and history of nineteen postal stations near Dunhuang. The Pure Spring Station, for instance, is located "40 *li* to the northeast of the city of Dunhuang, and 20 *li* to the Horizontal Valley Station. Following the postal-road, it is to the southwest of the Changle county of Guazhou."[11] The distance between the city of Dunhuang and Pure Spring Station broadly follows the prescriptions of the Tang government. In addition to the smaller postal stations on the road, major cities like Chang'an, Ganzhou, and Dunhuang functioned as the largest and most important postal stops.[12]

If such postal stations define the torsos of Eurasian empires, military establishments were their long arms. They were not designed for the comfort of
travelers, and their locations were not arranged primarily to facilitate the
timely renewal of supplies for travelers. For instance, the famous Jade Gate
Pass (Yumen Guan) was constructed at the order of Emperor Wudi of the Han
dynasty (156–87 BCE) as a western terminus of the chain of defense establishments in the Hexi region. When the eminent monk Xuanzang (602–64) began
his famous journey to India in 629, he first proceeded from the capital,
Chang'an, through the Hexi Corridor. Between Lanzhou and Liangzhou in
Hexi, he joined a group of people transporting horses for the government.
They likely used postal stations during this part of the trip. Yet, when Xuanzang ventured beyond Dunhuang to the area around the Jade Gate Pass, he
encountered a more precarious world without postal support. As a local con-
fidante told Xuanzang, "just beyond the [Hulu] river is the Jade Gate Pass,
which the westward road must pass through. It is the collar and the throat of
[the Tang's] western border. Beyond the pass, to the northwest, there are five
beacon fire towers, where military scouts are stationed. The towers are 100 *li*
apart, with no water nor grass in between."[13] This revealing conversation
shows that watch towers beyond the Jade Gate Pass were much more sparsely
distributed and not meant primarily to be a support system for travelers. Indeed, when Xuanzang had to approach them seeking water, he was first welcomed by a volley of arrows. Yet, after he convinced the scouts at the towers
of his good will and determination to travel further west, they treated him as
a guest, indicating that these military establishments did allow sanctioned
travelers a well-established place to stay and rest. By the ninth and tenth centuries, geographies found in the library cave tell us that the Jade Gate Pass was
located "160 *li* north of the county seat [of Dunhuang],"[14] and that the pass
measured 130 *bu* in perimeter (around 200 meters) and was 3 *zhang* (around
9 meters) tall.[15] Travelers at this time continued to stay at this pass, only without the vigorous military presence that once almost derailed the progress of
Xuanzang.

Natural stops, on the other hand, were places where little or no state-
sponsored constructions existed. The three stops listed in the Mongolia Itinerary are Southern Opening of the Valley (8.16), Wheat Pond (9.3) and West
River (9.4). Their names suggest that, when diplomats stayed in places without
governmental support, accessibility of water was the determining feature for
the making of a stop. Similarly, travelers leaving the Jade Gate Pass and heading
southeastward would have stayed at a "Pond of Foreign Merchants" after one

day's journey. According to the same geography from Dunhuang (P. 2005), "the water of this pond is salty and bitter, but the water from the nearby spring is drinkable. Foreign [*hu*] merchants traveling back and forth took the road of the Jade Pass. As a result, the pond is thus named."[16] The access to drinking water and its convenient location—50 *li* from the Jade Gate Pass and 110 *li* from the city of Dunhuang—together made this pond a must-stop for travelers. The three natural stops on the Mongolia Itinerary, although far less well known, were likely formed in the same way.

A fourth and final type of stop, in places with the harshest conditions, is not mentioned in this itinerary. The whole trip described in the Mongolia Itinerary, when not directly supported by governmental facilities, was at least operating in areas with sufficient supply of water and grass. But this was not the case everywhere on the Silk Road. Given the existence of actual roads, the popular image of Silk Road travelers, atop a string of camels, roaming through deserts, is largely a myth. It is nonetheless true that *parts* of the routes traversed by these travelers were indeed through terrain that ordinarily resisted travel. In certain regions under discussion in this book, particularly west of Dunhuang, travelers had to cross long stretches of desert. The desert to the northwest of Dunhuang, according to Xuanzang's biography, "stretches more than 800 *li* and was known since ancient times as the 'River of Sand.' There were no birds flying above and no animals running below. There was furthermore no water nor grass."[17] In these areas, animal or human bones often served as path markers.[18] One could assume that the stops indicated by these markers were likely much less geographically stable than the three previous types of stop.

The distinction among these kinds of stop may help explain why diplomats rested every three or four days in the first half of the itinerary (8.16–18 travel; 8.19 rest; 8.20–21 travel, 8.22 rest; 8.23 travel, 8.24–9.2 rest; 9.3–9.7 travel; 9.8 rest), but traveled continuously without stopping during the second half.[19] The four resting places were all military/governmental facilities. Evidently, these places, although not constructed solely (or even primarily) for the use of travelers, functioned as suitable resting places because of the abundance of governmental resources. Conversely, starting at 9.9, the diplomats entered the network of postal stations of the Tang, which provided reliable food and accommodation. These stations must have made the traveling experience considerably easier. As a result, the diplomats breezed through this area in eleven days without taking a single break.

The distinction between different types of stop was not absolute. With the shifting shape of the state, one type could easily morph into another. One of the best-known sources of water near Dunhuang was the Ershi Spring, about 130 *li* to the east. It was named after the Han dynasty general Li Guangli (?–89 BCE), who was known as General Ershi. He is famous for twice leading the Han army to Ferghana Valley, in one of the most daring military expeditions under the auspices of Emperor Wudi.[20] According to local lore in Dunhuang, when his army and horses, longing for water, passed Dunhuang on their way back from Central Asia, Li Guangli pierced a mountain with his sword and caused a stream of water to burst out, creating the Ershi Spring.[21] Its elevated placement in the mountain also earned this spring the alternative name Suspended Spring (Xuanquan).

The convenient location of this water source, three days' journey from Dunhuang according to a Dunhuang geography,[22] meant that the Suspended Spring has always been a place where travelers stopped. In the Han and Tang dynasties, when their territories firmly encompassed Dunhuang, this site was the location of a postal stop. Tens of thousands of documents written on wooden strips were discovered in the Han site of Suspended Spring Post (Xuanquan Zhi), attesting to the daily life of soldiers at this remote post of the empire.[23] Under the Tang, it was also used as a postal station (Xuanquan Yi), and, according to a geography found in Dunhuang, was 80 *li* from the station to its west and 40 *li* from the station to its east.[24] By the ninth and tenth centuries, after the retreat of the Tang Empire and the abandonment of its transportation infrastructure, Suspended Spring was no longer a postal station. But the Dunhuang government established a military garrison at the site (Xuanquan Zhen).[25] One document from 928 has the head official of the Suspended Spring Garrison reporting about the condition of "various beacon towers, roads, scouts, and the city."[26] The lord of Dunhuang once complained to the Uyghur khan about a group of Uyghurs who traveled to the Suspended Spring Garrison pretending to be envoys.[27] Another geographical text reveals that "the Ershi Shrine by the road has long been abandoned, but travelers still prayed for fortune in front of the stone camel and horse [near the shrine]."[28] We can gather from these sources that travelers continued to use this military establishment as a stop between Dunhuang and its eastern neighbors. Therefore, this location was originally a natural source of water, but became a postal station on the postal road (under the Han and the Tang) and a military establishment (in the ninth and tenth centuries), according to the type of state presence and its jurisdiction over the Ershi Spring. Throughout these changing times, travelers consistently stopped at the spring.[29]

What kinds of stops envoys passed through determined what the road looked like to them. Between postal stations, envoys would find the road well constructed and maintained, often with governmentally sponsored trees lining the roads.[30] For instance, in the eighth century, when envoys from a Central Asian country brought a lion to offer to the Tang court, it was at one point tied up to a "postal tree" on the way to Chang'an.[31] When envoys entered the Tang or Song heartland, as is the case in the second half of the Mongolia Itinerary, they made use of these postal roads. In Dunhuang in the ninth and tenth centuries, the retreat of the Tang presence meant that an extensive network of postal roads no longer existed. Yet there was clearly a well-maintained road that connected Dunhuang to its eastern neighbors. A letter from Cao Yuanzhong, the lord of Dunhuang, to the Uyghur khan speaks of diplomats traveling "on the main road [*dadao* 大道]."[32] A report of military affairs tells how bandits were traveling "on the main road to Guazhou [Guazhou *dadao* 瓜州大道]."[33] This "main road to Guazhou" was likely an extension the "Gua–Sha road," a section of well-maintained road between Guazhou and Dunhuang (Shazhou) under the rulership of the lord of Dunhuang.[34] Sometimes, a name was given to a longer stretch of road that joined several major towns. In the mid 920s, Cao Yijin launched a military campaign against the Uyghurs in Ganzhou in order to "reopen the old road of Hexi [Hexi *laodao* 河西老道]."[35] Because the goal of the campaign was to reconnect with North China, one might assume that this name describes the road the ran through the Hexi Corridor. In the eyes of travelers from Dunhuang, the road to the east, like the "old road of Hexi," was likely very well defined and maintained.

But not all roads were in such good condition. A geography of Turfan preserved in Dunhuang records eleven roads that led to Turfan from various directions.[36] One key piece of information contained in the geography is the condition of these roads. The best roads were those with abundant water and grass along the way that "people, horses, cows, and carts can pass." These roads were potentially even regularly examined and maintained. The three roads from Turfan running north through the mountain valleys to Tingzhou (Beshbalik; modern Jimsar) are described as roads of excellent condition. A bit less ideal were the roads on which cows could not travel, such as the ones leading west from Turfan to Chuyue and Agni (Kharashar), which are described as "traversable by carts and horses." Both of these roads are recorded as having abundant supplies of water and grass. The next group of roads, including the Tadi road and the Huagu (Flowery Valley) road, also abundant in water and grass, were only "traversable by humans and horses." One might assume that the terrain of these roads was difficult for carts or cows to pass. Worse yet, the Wugu road to Tingzhou, although also having grass and water, was "dangerous and precipitous with coarse rocks" that "only humans can pass, and horses travel-ing on the road are often harmed." But this road existed because it was little more than half the distance (400 compared with 730–740 *li*) of the other, easier roads to Tingzhou. So when speed was a priority, then travelers might consider this more difficult road. The diversity of the roads around Turfan shows that not all roads were well-maintained postal roads; shortcuts were often more precarious.

Finally, in the case of the road from Turfan to Dunhuang, travelers had few choices. The geography tells its readers that, on this long road of 1360 *li* (almost a thousand kilometers), "there are constantly running sands, and travelers often get lost. There are springs and wells, but [the water from them] is salty and bitter. There is no grass, and travelers have to carry water and load food. Walking over sand and rocks, going back and forth on the road is debilitat-ing."[37] The problem presented by this road was twofold: first, the terrain was so difficult that carts and cows would likely be unable to pass and human trav-elers often got lost; second, there were no good water or grass supplies, so travelers would have to prepare food and water to carry with them. This for-midable, barren road was ironically known as the Great Ocean Road (Dahai Dao 大海道), because the expansive sandy desert visually resembled a deadly ocean. As the main road connecting Turfan and Dunhuang, many travelers, including the envoys described in this book, must have traveled on it. The record about the Great Ocean Road echoes the account by Faxian of the road between Dunhuang and Khotan, where, in a "River of Sand," human remains were the only markers of the road one could find.[38] Whether heading north-west to Turfan or southwest to Khotan, travelers always had to endure long stretches of desert road once they left Dunhuang.

However, even the harshest of deserts did not completely deter travelers, and the supposed disorientation mentioned in the sources is likely exagger-ated. The fact that deserts were readily traversable is evident from the many cases of travelers in the Dunhuang documents. The monk-envoy Huide, for instance, went to Turfan, Khotan, and Ganzhou, all in the space of a single year.[39] His trips to Khotan and Turfan must have involved long stretches of desert or dry, sandy road, but such conditions did not prevent him from travel-ing.[40] Similarly, the envoy named Zhang Xiuzao who traveled to Turfan twice within three months and the Khotanese envoys who came to Dunhuang no fewer than seven times all had to use desert roads. It is easy to imagine that successful (and famous) travelers like Faxian had reasons to exaggerate the dangers of the road to make their deeds seem even more impressive. However, the regularity and predictability with which Dunhuang travelers navigated these deserts suggest that even in these desolate areas, roads were likely not constantly shifting, and that discernable paths must have been quite easy to identify.

Another reason to doubt the difficulty of traveling through the deserts is the travel speed recorded in the Dunhuang documents. The Mongolia Itinerary allows us to estimate the speed of the envoys' progress. From the West Town of Subjugation to the Garrison of Heavenly Virtue, in three days, the envoys covered 180 *li*; the 200 *li* between the Garrison of Heavenly Virtue and the Central Town of Subjugation also took three days; between Strengthening the Military Post and the Garrison of Peaceful Border, the envoys traveled 120 *li* in two days. Therefore, the average speed was about 60 to 66 *li*, or between thirty-two and thirty-five kilometers, a day.

One might assume that the speed of travel further to the west near Dunhuang, where a wide-ranging system of postal roads did not exist, would have been lower. But this does not seem to be the case. In a report to the Khotanese government, a Khotanese envoy recounted his journey between Dunhuang and Ganzhou: "I the humble servant went from Shazhou to Ganzhou on the twenty-eighth day of the month Skarhvāra [third winter month]. We came to Ganzhou on the fifteenth day of month Rrāhaja [fourth winter month]. And on the third day they conducted us to the presence of the khan."[41] The distance between Dunhuang and Ganzhou was 1800 *li* according to contemporary geographies, and is 609 kilometers on a modern road. The Khotanese envoy spent seventeen days, averaging 69 *li* (or 35.8 kilometers, if we estimate according to the length of the modern road) per day, at a slightly higher speed than the trip recorded in the Mongolia Itinerary. Such a pace shows that the road between Dunhuang and Ganzhou, part of the "Old Road of Hexi," was well maintained at the time and functioned as smoothly as a postal road in the Tang.

More surprising perhaps is how fast envoys were able to cross the desert regions to the west of Dunhuang. Suo Ziquan, an envoy on a mission to Khotan to bring gifts, for instance, left Dunhuang on the seventh day of the seventh month of 956 and arrived in Khotan on the twenty-second of the eighth month. As Khotan and Dunhuang are 1550 kilometers apart by modern road, Suo's forty-five-day journey would have proceeded at about 34.5 kilometers per day, almost exactly the same speed as the envoys recorded in the Mongolia Itinerary.[42] Similarly, *A Path to India*, an itinerary for traveling from western China to northern India, instructs its readers that it takes nine days to travel from Dunhuang to Yizhou.[43] The distance between these two places was measured in the Tang to be around seven hundred *li*.[44] The pace prescribed was therefore seventy-eight *li* per day (or about forty-six kilometers per day by modern roads), actually much faster than that recorded for the other, presumably better maintained, roads. Perhaps it was the need to conserve energy that compelled travelers to power through the deserts as swiftly as they could? In any case, there is little evidence to suggest, in spite of the ghosts and human remains that travelers like Faxian and Xuanzang so vividly described, that deserts posed any lethal threat to our travelers; for all we know, these deserts barely even slowed them down.

To conclude, documents from Dunhuang open up a window onto roads in medieval Eastern Eurasia. Diplomatic travelers experienced four types of places to stop: postal stations, military establishments, natural stops near water, and stops in deserts. The distribution of these four types of stop and the patchwork of roads that connected them were determined by both the physical landscape and the reach of states.

The physical landscape was by and large constant in historical times. The Hexi Corridor, for instance, was created by the Qilian Mountains in the south and the Beishan (literally, "northern mountain") mountains in the north. The reason Dunhuang was such a key location is because it sat at the western end of the Hexi Corridor. The harsh natural conditions to the north and, in particular, to the south of the Hexi Corridor meant that this long and narrow land bridge was the most commonly chosen path between China and Central Asia in historical times. Within this sharply defined landscape, travelers from prehistoric times onward searched for the most strategically located rivers, ponds, and springs, and strung a road together that maximized access to them without taking too much of a detour. By the ninth and tenth centuries, these water sources had acquired names and entered the geographical lexicon of the state as well as the folk knowledge of travelers. In this way, topographical features such as mountains and rivers shaped the broad contours of the "roads" on the Silk Road.

But physical landscape alone did not determine what the road looked like for our travelers. If we can imagine a surely nonexistent time without any state presence, then stops on the Silk Road would have comprised only ones with a water source (type 3) and those without (type 4). But as states small and large built postal stations and military garrisons next to favorable water sources and at key locations on naturally formed paths, they transformed many type 3 stops into type 1 or 2 stops. For travelers, these establishments formed the best places to rest and recuperate. The shift in the presence and the borders of certain states, however, did not fundamentally alter the shape of the road that connected these stops. The only time when the road was completely blocked was when warfare and social instability made travel along it too dangerous. In a message from the lord of Dunhuang to Khotanese envoys cited in a Khotanese report, the lord warned that "the [Ganzhou] country is in ruins. Therefore, the *ācāryas* [monks who traveled as envoys] will fall on a 'nonroad.'"[45] This intriguing expression, "nonroad" (*avadāya*), cannot be found, as far as I have seen, in texts in other languages and has to be treated as a Khotanese idiosyncrasy. What it means is nonetheless fairly clear: it is the *opposite* of a "road" that one can travel on. The political chaos of Ganzhou, the result of a succession dispute, meant that the road to the east of Dunhuang was perilous to the point of being untraversable. But other than these extreme cases, the changing shape of the state only affected how travelers used the road, and rarely cut the road off completely.

This understanding of the making of roads in medieval Central Eurasia allows me to reexamine a widely held belief about the history of the Silk Road. According to a recent synthesis:

> The development and prosperity of the Silk Road is guaranteed by military strength. Once stability and peace in the Western Territories [eastern Central Asia] was under control and sustained, the economic and cultural interactions of China with the Western Territories and Europe would take place smoothly. If effective control over the Western Territories was lost, the Silk Road would be broken up.[46]

Other scholars are less blunt, and less Sinocentric, but the idea that large, centralized empires like the Tang were crucial in maintaining open roads on the Silk Road is quite widespread. James Millward, for instance, suggests that "[the] eras of the most intense silk-road communications were those when not only the sedentary states of the Eurasian rim but also the nomadic confederations on the Eurasian steppe were relatively centralized."[47] For them, large, unified empires meant open roads and intense communications.

In chapter 2, I showed that in the ninth and tenth centuries, a period of imperial decline and political fragmentation, the number of transregional travelers was not minuscule, and perhaps did not even decrease from earlier periods of imperial unity. The discussion in this chapter has further explained how such sustained connection was possible by examining the roads travelers used. Although the presence of states, particularly large empires, did play a significant role in shaping how the road looked, the Silk Road was never "broken up" by the absence of empires, because it was never supported solely by them.

The retreat of large empires was often followed by, as was the case in Eastern Eurasia in the mid-ninth century onward, the creation of smaller regional and independent states in the places where the empire used to be. Their presence served a similar function to that once performed by the empires. For instance, the Suspended Spring site to the east of Dunhuang was a postal station at the height of the Tang Empire. The retreat of the Tang, instead of cutting the road off, resulted in the transition of Suspended Spring into a military establishment for the Dunhuang government. Throughout such changes, our envoys continued to journey on the well-trodden Gua–Sha road (between Dunhuang and Guazhou), and to stop and rest at Suspended Spring. Even when the state apparatus did disappear, as long as natural resources existed, what happened was simply that type 1 and 2 stops reverted to type 3 or, in case of extreme desertification, type 4 stops. Such absence of the state was rarely found, but the disappearance of the state of Kroraina (Loulan) might be an example.[48] In the ninth and tenth centuries, what had once been the prosperous kingdom of Kroraina, located between Dunhuang and Khotan, ceased to exist because of desertification.[49] This surely made life more difficult for travelers than it had been for their predecessors traveling in the same area in the third and fourth centuries. But as the many examples of travelers between Khotan and Dunhuang testify, the disappearance of the Kroraina kingdom did not prevent journeys through its old domain. Therefore, while shifts in the geographical territories of states constantly modified the specific conditions on a road, the Silk Road, as a living, breathing organism, was never cut off by the absence of large empires.

## Seeing Like an Envoy

Merely the existence of roads did not guarantee successful journeys. Envoys had to acquire knowledge of these roads. The transformation text (*bianwen*) devoted to the life of Zhang Yichao, founder of the independent state of Dunhuang in 848, includes an episode about a lost envoy named Chen Yuanhong, who was traveling from the Tang to the Turfan. As his mission approached Turfan, "at the southern slope of a snowy mountain," it was assaulted by a group of unknown Uyghurs; the insignia was taken and the diplomatic mission dispersed. Chen, fleeing the danger, "let his feet guide him" and inadvertently wandered southeastward into the domain of Dunhuang. When military officers in Dunhuang found him, he was "alone in the broad wilderness," clearly lost, and "floundering around all by himself." Fortunately, he was able to communicate with the officials patrolling the border of Dunhuang and to convince the officer that he "was not an evil person."[50] This story shows that to be separated from a diplomatic mission and deprived of geographical knowledge often led to the failure of the envoy to navigate the road. To succeed as transregional travelers, envoys had to possess knowledge about the roads they were taking. But how did they know, resting after a long day's journey, what lay ahead the next day? How did they *see* the Silk Road?

On many occasions, as envoys entered the jurisdiction of another state, they were provided with escorts and guides by that state, in what I call the "road protection" stage of the envoy/host relation.[51] In a letter from the governor of Lingzhou to the Uyghur khan of Ganzhou, the former explained in detail how both states made arrangements so that their respective escorts for a group of envoys from Guazhou, Dunhuang, and Ganzhou would transition seamlessly.[52] From this text we know that Later Tang personnel in different local governments worked in succession in escorting these envoys. Such road guides existed in Dunhuang as well. In an expenditure account from the Dunhuang government, four pieces of fine paper were offered to a certain Liu Xizhuochuo who was a road guide for the Canwei tribes to the south.[53] There is no comprehensive accounting of how many road guides and escorts the Dunhuang government provided for foreign envoys. But in a document from the fifth century, as mentioned in chapter 2, the Turfan government provided more than 1400 people as escorts for envoys from as far away as India and South China over a period of eleven months.[54] While it is possible that the Dunhuang government employed far fewer people in this capacity, their presence is evident. In fact, road guides could sometimes even be dangerous if they used their knowledge in the wrong way: Cao Yuanzhong, the lord of Dunhuang, complained to the Uyghur khan of Ganzhou about someone who had served as a road guide for one hundred Tatar bandits as they looted Guazhou.[55] In this instance, Cao was concerned precisely about the geographical knowledge that the road guides possessed. In most cases, however, guides and escorts quietly helped envoys proceed, as the letter of the governor of Lingzhou indicates. In these cases, envoys could simply rely on the knowledge of guides to navigate the road ahead.

But envoys often needed to travel without the guides from their host states. In these cases, they had to make active use of geographical information they possessed to orient themselves. Such information is found in abundance in the Dunhuang documents, including in copies of Tang geographies known as illustrated geographies (*tujing*)[56] and many later, shorter, and more portable local geographies.[57] Smaller administrative units such as counties also had their own geographies.[58] Certain journeys are further documented in travelogues that are preserved in Dunhuang, or in lists of place names organized sequentially. Such texts formed the reservoir of geographical knowledge available to long-distance travelers.

To show how these geographies could be useful for traveling envoys, let us look at one geographical text (P. 5034) that records six routes in a hazardous area, emanating from the Rock City (Shicheng) Garrison, a town between Khotan and Dunhuang founded in the early Tang by Sogdian immigrants.[59] The first two entries are about two roads, one northern and the other southern, between Rock City and Dunhuang:[60]

> The northern road: East of the [Rock City] garrison by 180 *li* is Tun City, where one takes the desert road at the "Western Pass" to Shazhou [Dunhuang]. The road is 1400 *li*. Altogether there are seven springs, but no water nor grass. The [Rock City] garrison is 1580 *li* from Shazhou.
>
> The southern road: From the [Rock City] garrison eastward to Shazhou [is] 1500 *li*. The road leads to Shazhou by way of the old Yang Pass. The road borders many precipitous places. There are eight springs [on this road], all possessing grassland. The road is treacherous and cannot be passed at night. In the two seasons of spring and fall, the snow is deep and the road not passable.

For someone planning a journey between the Rock City Garrison and Dunhuang, these entries allowed them to assess the condition of the roads that lay ahead. The northern road seems to have been open all year round, whereas the southern road, likely because of its proximity to the Southern Mountains hemming the Taklamakan Desert, was on more precipitous ground and open only during the warmer months. The lengths of the roads are similar—1580 and 1500 *li* respectively. Both have an array of springs, so that envoys should have access to a new water source every four or five days. Yet there is a crucial difference: while the southern road, fed by snow-melt water, had grassland near the springs, the northern road reportedly had none. Given this information, envoys then had to weigh their priorities. If they were traveling in large numbers with many animals and not pressed for time, it would be preferable to wait for the appropriate time and use the water-rich southern road; but if their trip was urgent, they would have to prepare enough fodder and take the northern road. In this way, the geographical manual helped travelers choose their road between the Rock City Garrison and Dunhuang, one of the most difficult stretches of the Silk Road.

The distinction between guided roads and roads that required self-navigation underlies a strange feature of the geographical writings found in Dunhuang. This feature is displayed in a manuscript discovered at Dunhuang entitled *A Path to India (Xitian lujing)*."[61] As the title indicates, it is a record of the road for the use of Buddhist pilgrims in China heading eventually to India. It begins, as many in this genre of writing do, with the capital of the Chinese regime at the time, the city of Kaifeng of the Song dynasty. The second stop in this guide is, however, nowhere near the capital, but at Lingzhou more than a thousand kilometers away. Only after Lingzhou does the text become a real road guide, as it starts listing the number of days a traveler would have to spend to reach the next stop, or the distance to the next stop. The distances between these stops also become drastically shorter. The text lists, after Lingzhou, four stops before it reaches Dunhuang (see map 4.2).

Similarly, A Tibetan manuscript from Dunhuang about a Chinese monk's route to India begins in this manner:

> Proceeding from Mount Wutai he arrived at the gold and turquoise halls of Hezhou; after that he arrived at the mountain of Dantig Shan; after that he arrived at the gold and turquoise halls of Tsongkha; after that he will arrive at the palace of Liangzhou; after that he will arrive at the castle of Ganzhou; after that he will arrive at Shazhou. After that he will certainly go to see the great teachers of Śrī Nālandā and the relics of Śākyamuni at the Vulture's Peak in India.[62]

If we put the places mentioned on a map, we have map 4.3. In both cases, the geographical narrative begins with the origin of the travelers (Kaifeng and Mount Wutai), but then jumps to the border of the Song state, Lingzhou and Hezhou. Only then does each text go into more detail about the stops these travelers made. I suggest that the reason for this peculiar way of recording geographical information is intimately connected to the way North China–based regimes like the Tang and the Song managed and escorted travelers within and beyond their domain. As the letter from the governor of Lingzhou in the Later Tang suggests, travelers were escorted throughout the domain of the Tang to the border. Therefore, it make sense that these travelers would not have needed to keep information about places *within* the Tang/Song borders.

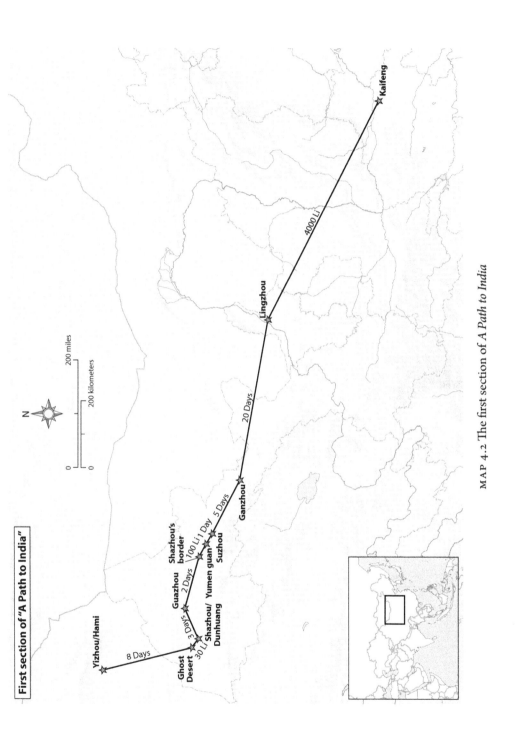

First section of "A Path to India"

Yizhou/Hami

8 Days

Ghost Desert

3 Days

30 Li Shazhou/ Dunhuang

Guazhou

2 Days

Shazhou's border

100 Li 1 Day

Yumen guan

Suzhou

5 Days

Ganzhou

20 Days

Lingzhou

4000 Li

Kaifeng

N

200 miles

200 kilometers

0

0

MAP 4.2 The first section of *A Path to India*

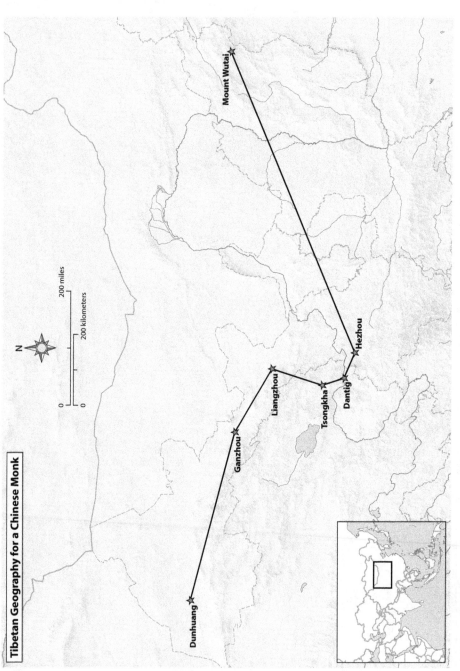

MAP 4.3 Route described in a Tibetan geography between Mount Wutai and Dunhuang

Both *A Path to India* and the account of the Tibetan geography were ostensibly made for Buddhist travelers. But many monks served as envoys at the same time, and it is possible that the monks using them had official duties too. After these texts were copied and transmitted, they could also easily have been *used* by envoys who were not monks. But more importantly, geographical texts definitely produced by envoys echo the feature revealed in these two texts. As I discussed in chapter 2, the Staël-Holstein manuscript contains two lists of geographical names, which helped orient the envoys that used this notebook. When I put these places on a map (map 2.1), it is clear that this record also stopped at Lingzhou on the Song border. We know that Khotan envoys regularly went to the Song court. So why did the geographical text they used cover only the route up to Lingzhou? I suggest that, like the users of the previous two texts, the envoys who used the Staël-Holstein manuscript did not record places within the Song borders because when they did go there, they would not have needed to find the way themselves.

Perhaps most intriguingly, this sequence of "capital + border town" in *A Path to India* is also found in a text produced much further west. *Ḥudūd al-'Ālam* ("Regions of the world") was a Persian geography composed in 982 CE by an anonymous author. It contains, among other things, a detailed description of the geography of the eastern border of the *Dār al-Islām* (regions under Muslim sovereignty). The section on China includes the following places: Khumdan (Chang'an), Kašan (?), Dunhuang (Sājū > Shazhou), Guazhou (Xājū), Kūγmar (?), Burj-i Sangīn ("Stone tower" < translation of Chinese Shibao Cheng), Suzhou (Sōkjū), Ganzhou (Xāmčū), Xālbak (?), Liangzhou (Kučān > Guzang), Baγšūr (< Tibetan 'Bug-chor), Khotan, and Kucha.[63] Not all of the places on this list are possible to identify, but if we place the identified ones on a map, a similar patter emerges (map 4.4). Other than the capital, Chang'an (Khumdan), the easternmost place named on this list is Liangzhou, using its older name of Guzang (Kučān). It could hardly be a mere coincidence that this unique way of recording places is found in both the Persian geography and the geographical texts used by envoys and monks in Dunhuang across texts in four languages. Underlying all of these texts is the use of road guides/escorts in long-distance travel. In fact, as I will discuss momentarily, envoys were transmitters of geographical knowledge, and it is conceivable that the editor of *Ḥudūd al-'Ālam* received information from envoys from the east, thus inheriting eastern idiosyncrasies.

By leaving out important places, these geographical texts reveal the way that travelers faced the road ahead. While they were under the protection and

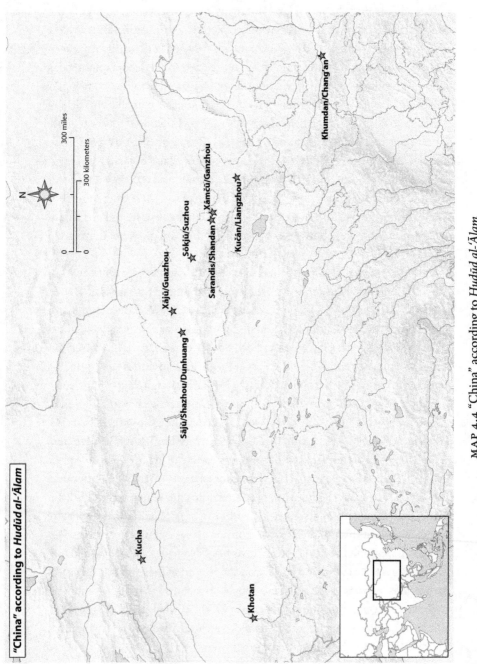

Kucha ☆

Khotan ☆

Sāǰū/Shazhou/Dunhuang ☆

Xāǰū/Guazhou ☆

Sōkǰū/Suzhou ☆

Sarandis/Shandan ☆ ☆ Xāmčū/Ganzhou

Kučān/Liangzhou ☆

Khumdan/Chang'an ☆

N

0                300 miles

0                300 kilometers

MAP 4.4 "China" according to *Hudūd al-ʿĀlam*

guidance of a state, they often did not need to actively seek out or use geographical texts. It was only when they traveled without such guidance that they would resort to the help of written geographies. Therefore, it is no surprise that border towns like Lingzhou, Hezhou, and Liangzhou acquired special status in the production of geographical knowledge for envoys and the states they dealt with. Lingzhou in particular is very well documented in this regard.[64] A fragmentary letter written in 850 by Dunhuang envoys to the Tang court is preserved in Dunhuang as repairing material for a Confucian text. Although about half of each line is missing, we can still gather enough information from what is left: seven envoys from Dunhuang reached Lingzhou, and with one missing for reasons unknown, six of them offered a map of Hexi to the Tang court.[65] This map of Hexi would have covered similar regions to those on the place list of Khotanese envoys and the section on China in *Hudūd al-'Ālam*. Because Lingzhou was on the Tang border and the first stop in Tang domain, the submission of the map occurred in Lingzhou. From this letter, we know that envoys not only used geographical texts but were also disseminators of such texts.

Lingzhou's special place is also made apparent by a letter (P. 2958) written by a "prince of Shuofang [Lingzhou]" named Hva (from Chinese *Han*?) Pa-kyau to the king of Khotan written in (or, more likely, translated into) Khotanese. In the letter, the lord of Lingzhou informs the king of Khotan that "the road to Ttāṃhtta has been disrupted."[66] Although it is difficult to know where this place Ttāṃhtta was, the fact that the information was conveyed to the king of Khotan by the lord of Lingzhou is significant, as the latter, situated in such a strategic location, seems to have a unique vantage point to know the condition of the roads in the area. Similarly, a Chinese monk named Guiwen who described the areas west of Lingzhou as a stretch of "ten thousand *li* of yellow sands" wrote his letter home from Lingzhou.[67] For many travelers, monks and envoys alike, Lingzhou at the Tang-Song border was a key place of the production and transmission of geographical knowledge.

It is no coincidence then that from Lingzhou we see one of the clearest examples of the production of geographical knowledge by envoys. The colophon of S. 367, a geography of Dunhuang (Shazhou) and Hami (Yizhou), reads:

> On the twenty-fifth day of the twelfth month of the first year of Guangqi era [February 2, 886], on the occasion of the arrival at our prefecture [Shazhou] of Master Si, the Pacifying Envoy from Lingzhou, Zhang Daqing copied this document from Envoy Si.[68]

When the diplomatic mission headed by Master Si from Lingzhou came to Dunhuang, a local official named Zhang Daqing took the opportunity to copy this geographical account from the envoys. The text Zhang copied contains extensive information not only on Dunhuang itself but also on Yizhou, a city northwest of Dunhuang. The beginning of the text is missing; the remaining portion contains eighty-six lines (not including double-lined notes). The first twenty-eight lines describe a few places under the jurisdiction of Dunhuang in the Tang administrative organization, including water sources such as the Suspended Spring (Xuanquan), the Sea of Longevity and Prosperity (Shouchang), several canals and valleys, and towns to the southwest of Dunhuang. The first listed town is the Rock City Garrison, the center of the records of roads discussed above. Then the other towns in the region between Dunhuang and Khotan, including Tun City, the New City, the Grape City, the Sapi City, Shanshan, the Old Tuncheng City, and the Puchang Sea, are all listed along with their distances from the Rock City Garrison. In this way, the first part of the geography Zhang copied offers a guide that is complimentary to the road guides discussed above.

The second part of the geography (lines twenty-nine to seventy-nine) turns north to the area called Yizhou (modern Hami), listing the names of counties, monasteries, military garrisons, and beacon towers—all standard information in a Tang geographical treatise (*tujing*). At the end of the text, several headings were copied, including Tingzhou (Jimsar) and Xizhou (Turfan), but no detailed information was included on these places. Evidently, this text was condensed from a longer text that contained geographical information on the entire region west of Dunhuang. The truncation may have already been present in the text brought to Dunhuang by the envoy from Lingzhou, or Zhang Daqing the copyist may have shortened the parts that he considered unimportant. In either case, it is evident that the intention of the maker of the text was to record information about the areas *immediately* to the southwest and northwest of Dunhuang. In this way, it offers a convenient roadmap to travelers heading in these two directions.

Master Si no doubt was an envoy from Lingzhou to Dunhuang. But nothing else is known about him. Zhang Daqing the copyist, on the other hand, is quite a well-known figure, and prolific copyist, among the Dunhuang documents. He copied a prophecy book in 860 when he was still a student,[69] and a transformation text on Maudgalyāyana (Mulian, a disciple of Buddha).[70] As an adult, he worked as a military advisor under the governor Zhang Huaishen.[71] More relevant to the topic under discussion, Zhang also appears in Khotanese documents. A letter from a Khotanese envoy named Thyai Paḍä-tsā tells us of an encounter he had in Ganzhou with an envoy from Lingzhou. This envoy from Lingzhou inquired about the kind of gifts Thyai Paḍä-tsā had for the Chinese emperor, then he informed Thyai Paḍä-tsā of a letter that had come from a certain Cā tteya khī (< Zhang Daqinng, with the typical loss of nasals in Khotanese) in Dunhuang.[72] This same name is also mentioned in a Khotanese painting.[73] Therefore, both the Chinese geography and the Khotanese envoy's report speak of a Zhang Daqing who interacted with envoys from Lingzhou. We are not sure if the Lingzhou envoys were the same person, but Zhang certainly played a central role in diplomatic affairs on behalf of the state of Dunhuang. He might have needed to copy the geography for his own reference, but it could very well have served as an easy guide for others on their trips to the west of Dunhuang.

Envoys also played a role in the transmission of geographical knowledge to the east. In the fifth month of 1083, a group of Khotanese envoys came to the Song court. Khotan was then under the rule of the Qarakhanids. After a meeting with the Song emperor Shenzong (r. 1067–85), the "Khotanese cheiftain" was ordered to "draw up a map of the distances of all Tatar states to the Han borders" and to give the map to a Song official who was planning a trip to the land of the Tatars.[74] Here, the Song emperor used the term *Han* to refer to his state. While the content of the map is not preserved, from its title we can surmise that it must have included information about key stops from the Song border to the land of the Tatars, and the distances between these stops. This map was produced by an envoy, and was explicitly meant to be used as a guide for a group of future envoys.

Beyond these information-rich geographical treatises and maps, other simpler sources could also assist envoys on their journeys. The envoys' notebook known as the Staël-Holstein manuscript, for instance, contains two lists of place names.[75] As I have explained, the first part is a list of the places one would have to pass going from Khotan to Lingzhou, and the second part is a list of cities near Turfan (see map 2.1). Many of the names on the list were originally Chinese, Tibetan, or Uyghur place-names; they were all transcribed into Khotanese script. The lists characterize places as "city" or "large city." The two sections do not intersect with each other. Therefore, for the Khotanese envoys from Central Asia, when they traveled towards Shuofang (Lingzhou), the border of China proper, they could just follow the places listed in List 1. If they planned to visit the areas around Turfan, they could follow List 2. Similarly, the records kept by Gao Juhui and Wang Yande, both of which were submitted to the courts in North China, also circulated among governmental officials before they were incorporated into the official histories. These records not only provide the names of major stops on the road but also give some information about the specific cultural and economic features of those places. The Mongolia Itinerary was potentially even more useful, because it was a record of the stops made on a daily basis. The fact that this itinerary made its way into the Dunhuang manuscript collection indicates that it was not only for the reference of the travelers on that particular journey but was either noted down during the trip and brought back and circulated in Dunhuang, or was copied from the original notes kept by the envoys. In either case, the itinerary must have had readers in Dunhuang beyond the original envoys, and could have served as a guide for them.

Moreover, envoys did not engage with the road they faced only in a utilitarian manner. The distance from home, the natural beauty of the landscape, and the uncertainty of life on the road all inspired, in those literarily inclined, poetic urges. The Korean monk Hyecho (704–87) wrote an account of his trip to India that tells us of an encounter between him and a Tang envoy to Tibet in the city of the king of Humi in northern Afghanistan. Hyecho was coming back from India to the Tang, while the envoy was traveling in the opposite direction, taking a Central Asian route to Tibet. Hyecho's poem captures the moment when "the honorable gentleman [the Tang envoy] abhors the distance to the foreign state to the west, while I lament the long road to the east."[76] The responding poem from the envoy has not survived. But there is no doubt that the Korean monk and the Chinese envoy had a conversation in northern Afghanistan, and poetry was their language.

Similarly, a unique set of poems written by an envoy is preserved in Dunhuang.[77] These poems were written by a late Tang envoy to Central Asia, who "traveled on official duty to Zhangye [Ganzhou]."[78] About half of the poems are devoted to places the official was visiting. A poem entitled "Jiuquan" (Fountain of Wine), for instance, highlights the cultural affinity of the Jiuquan area, also known as Suzhou, for the Tang.[79] Another poem, about the governor of Jiuquan, compares him to Zhang Qian (164–114 BCE) and Su Wu (140–60 BCE), famous Han dynasty figures in its entanglement with Central Asia.[80] In this sense, the poet was trying to make sense of the land he was traveling through in much the same way as Gao Juhui did in his travelogue: both invoked the deeds of Han dynasty travelers such as Zhang Qian to explain what they experienced. In other places, the poet saw more cultural hybridity: the poem on Dunhuang delineates its transition from a Tibetan province to a nominal Tang vassal state, while in the one on Ganzhou the poet eulogizes a "Han dynasty moon" while listening to barbarian tunes.[81] Further west, the poet found that the culture of Turfan "was different from that of China," and banquets he attended were accompanied by the performance of "barbarian lutes." Nonetheless, he expected to return from Turfan eventually: "Taking the grand thoroughfare to return to the Tang, the road will not take longer than three years!"[82] Collectively, these poems offered a mental map that oriented the poet and his readers in the culturally complicated world of Eastern Eurasia. In one of the last poems in this set, entitled "Iron Gate Pass," the poet wrote about the pass strategically located near Kharashar (Yanqi) on the road to Kucha:

> The east–west road outside the Iron Gate Pass,
> How many people from previous dynasties have traveled [this road]?
> The ruins of the guest houses still show their old traces,
> While the mountains and rivers are stacked up like fish scales.[83]

This poem might not have ranked among the finest Tang poems, and is certainly no rival of the poem by Cen Shen (715–70) on the same pass.[84] But it does convey the perceptions of a traveling envoy in the late ninth century. This pass, once part of the Tang military system, was no longer being maintained; the guest houses were abandoned and left in ruins. What did not change was the shape of the natural landscape, with mountains and rivers "stacked up like fish scales." In this way, the author was describing a place on the Silk Road that had transformed, according to my categorization above, from a type 2 to a type 3 stop. Such a change, as I argue in this chapter, did not prevent the author from traveling through the pass. Similar to the Mongolia Itinerary, this set of poems was copied and preserved in Dunhuang and made its way eventually into the library of the Sanjie Monastery. In addition to recording the experiences of this particular envoy, the poems were likely read and appreciated by later readers, and possibly also oriented later travelers on the Silk Road. The poet's lament at the Iron Gate Pass of "How many people from previous dynasties have traveled [this road]" would have been in the minds of the readers of the poem as they conducted their own journeys.

In these cases, in addition to traveling on the roads, envoys also *created* them. In writing poems like the ones about Dunhuang and Zhangye, compiling place lists such as the Mongolia Itinerary, and composing travelogues like Gao Juhui's and Wang Yande's, they organized information about different places into a meaningful sequence, thus producing a "road" that later readers of their texts could follow. Each successful journey thus generated knowledge that could inform a future journey. The envoys of the ninth and tenth centuries were operating in places long trodden by "people from previous dynasties," and many roads were already well established. The Wang Yande mission, on the return journey, was said to have "traveled on the same road that they came on."[85] Such regularity of the roads envoys took from Kaifeng to Turfan was the result of an accumulation of knowledge from the experiences of generations of travelers.

It is important to emphasize, however, that existing sources do not provide a complete picture of how envoys navigated the roads. Neither the Khotanese lists nor the Chinese travelogues nor the Mongolia Itinerary could have guided the precise movement of travelers as an omniscient modern GPS can. They simply allowed travelers, when they arrived at a stop, to check that they were *broadly* on the right track. For the spaces between these noted stops, not unlike how modern hikers follow a path in an unfamiliar forest, they would have relied on visual marks left by earlier travelers in the form of vaguely worn paths, accumulated animal bones, or man-made signs to recognize the road ahead on any given day. These experiences, however, are largely undocumented and thus invisible to us. Nonetheless, what is documented in the manuscripts from the Dunhuang library cave shows that medieval envoys had a large and diverse repertoire of sources available to them to make sense of the long roads that lay ahead.

## Conclusion

This chapter has shown that the Silk Road that envoys faced was a complex space. Close to the heartland of a major state, there were well-planned roads with staffed postal stations to attend to their needs; at the borders of these states, garrisons, passes, and other military outposts served as stops that connected the roads; beyond the domain of control of any established state, natural landmarks such as lakes, springs, and valleys functioned to orient the travelers on the road; finally, in long stretches of desert where such landmarks disappeared, travelers needed to rely on the water they brought themselves, the bones of animals and other deceased travelers for directions, and the protection of Bodhisattvas.[86]

In this diversity of roads also lies the Silk Road's resilience. Because it was not created by any one state, or maintained by any one government, the fall of a state or the shift of a governmental policy could not fundamentally change the shape of the Silk Road, much less cut it off entirely. Instead, it was created accumulatively by a mutually generative process of travel and knowledge construction and consumption, through the writing, copying, and reading of geographies, travelogues, place lists, and place-based poetry. Lacking a GPS system, medieval envoys made use of these tools, as well as the orally transmitted knowledge that is largely invisible to us, to navigate the complex roads in Central Eurasia. Neither entirely well-maintained thoroughfares nor utterly uncharted and unidentified paths, the Silk Road in the eyes of the envoys was complex and changing, but fundamentally knowable and therefore traversable.

# 5

# Praising the Host

IN THIS BOOK, I describe envoys as "travelers" on the Silk Road. They did indeed move through government-maintained postal stations, along naturally formed paths, and across long stretches of desert. But physical movement was only a part of their lives on the road. In the period recorded in the Mongolia Itinerary discussed in the previous chapter, the Dunhuang diplomats traveled two-thirds of the time, proceeding during the day and staying at a new stop each night. They rested four times during this period: the first break was in the West Town of Subjugation (8.19), the second at the Wuhuai Fort (8.22), and the fourth at the Yunjia Pass (9.8), all for a single day. The third break, in the Southern Inn of the city of the Garrison of Heavenly Virtue, was the longest and lasted for ten days. The diplomats arrived at this city on 8.23, and were invited to a polo game followed by a banquet.[1] This city is also the only place where the diplomats stayed in an inn (*guan*). For these diplomats, their brief or prolonged sojourns at different locations on the road constituted a crucial part of their traveling lives.

The distinction between the two types of day is worth noting because envoys engaged in different kinds of activities. On the traveling days, the goal was likely to make it safely to the next stop. But when staying at a city or a pass, they engaged their local hosts in activities such as polo games and banquets. This distinction can also exist within a traveling day, when diplomats were physically moving along the road, usually during the day, and stayed at some facility and interacted with the people there at night. Both sets of activities— the physical movement en route and the interactions with people where they stayed—belong to the category of "life on the Silk Road." In this chapter, I will examine how traveling diplomats interacted with their hosts.

The Mongolia Itinerary and most other travelogues tell us how diplomats "stayed overnight" (*su*) at different places.[2] What exactly does this mean? How did the process of arrival, accommodation, reception, and departure play out for these diplomats? To these questions, the laconic itinerary gives no direct answer. But many other Dunhuang documents were produced by envoys during their travels or in the process of diplomatic dealings, and they reveal the exact process of how traveling envoys dealt with their hosts. In the first section of this chapter, I surmise from these documents a "program" of successful envoy-host interaction that includes several standard sequential stages. In the second section, I assess some failed diplomatic trips by this program, and ask what went wrong in these cases. In the last section, I examine the social principles that governed such interactions: while it was the duty of the host to provide for the diplomatic travelers, the travelers were supposed to praise the generosity of the host. Diplomatic trips succeeded when such mutual obligations were observed, and faltered when one party failed to fulfill its responsibility.

## Successful Encounters

It was a transformative moment when traveling envoys met their host, either in a state that they were passing through or in the state of their destination. The envoys were no longer simply navigating the geographical landscape, but had to contend with new social realities. When crossing long stretches of desert, the envoys were likely no different than other types of travelers in how they conducted their lives on the road. It was when they met their hosts that the official nature of their trip gained salience. In a sense, only then did they really become *diplomatic* travelers.

When and where did the envoys first encounter their hosts? Obviously, each trip is unique, and no Dunhuang document preserves a complete picture of every step of an envoy-host interaction. Yet there does seem to be a general practice that was considered "appropriate" among travelers and hosts at the time. The most complete picture of an encounter comes from an unexpected place: a series of four consecutive reports made in the sixth month of 947 by the Office of Banquets and Hospitality in the Dunhuang government.[3] It lists all expenditure on food by the government, including food used in sacrificial rites and provisions for artisans, including carpenters, painters, sculptors, gold- and silversmiths, construction workers, cave makers, jade craftsmen, and quiver makers. A significant amount of the government's food also went to supplying foreign envoys. From the nineteenth to the twenty-fourth of the sixth month, for example, provisions were offered every day to a group of

TABLE 5.1. A Reception for Khotanese Envoys at Dunhuang

| Day | Reception | Provisions Offered by the Dunhuang Government |
|---|---|---|
| 6.19 | At Shouchang | Sixty rations of fine offering, [including] one barbarian flatbread [each]; one hundred barbarian flatbreads; four hundred oiled barbarian flatbreads; two *dou* of [?] flour; oil one *sheng* |
| 6.20 | To Khotanese prince | One hundred oiled barbarian flatbreads; two *dou* of [?] flour; oil one *sheng* |
| 6.21 | At Maquankou | Thirty rations of fine offering, [including] one barbarian flatbread [each]; twenty barbarian flatbreads; intestine noodles three *sheng* |
| 6.21 | Outside of the city | Twenty rations of fine offering, [including] one barbarian flatbread [each]; intestine noodle three *sheng*; ten rations of medium and inferior offering |
| 6.22 | To Khotanese prince | Fifteen rations of fine offering, [including] one barbarian flatbread [each] |
| 6.23 | At Great Court | Twenty-eight rations of fine offering, including two-thirds of a barbarian flatbread [each] |
| 6.24 | To Khotanese prince at Longxing Monastery | Fifteen rations of fine offering, [including] one barbarian flatbread [each]; eighty-five barbarian flatbreads |

incoming Khotanese envoys. Putting together all the relevant entries, a picture of this midsummer encounter emerges: the arrival of the Khotanese envoys resulted in three stages of envoy-host interaction: road protection, audience with the sovereign, and residency (see table 5.1).

The first meeting occurred in Shouchang, a town 120 *li* southwest of the city of Dunhuang according to contemporaneous geographies.[4] For Khotanese diplomats, Shouchang was a key stop on their way to Dunhuang: in the place list of the Staël-Holstein manuscript, Shouchang (Khotanese: Sucana) is the only place listed between Loulan and Dunhuang, and is described as a "city."[5] On the nineteenth day, the Dunhuang government delivered to Shouchang sixty "rations of fine offering," each including one barbarian flatbread. It also offered an extra hundred plain and four hundred oiled barbarian flatbreads.

The next day, a much smaller amount of food was given to a certain "crown prince" to be provided to the Khotanese envoys. From other sources we know that the term "crown prince" in the Dunhuang documents refers specifically to the prince of Khotan.[6] This prince might have been one of the many Khotanese dignitaries who had taken up a long-term, even semipermanent residency in Dunhuang.[7] His involvement in the reception of the Khotanese envoys complicates the idea of the "host": on this day, the Khotanese prince was not only a guest of the Dunhuang government, which was providing for him, but also served as liaison to his incoming compatriots, whom he escorted to the city of Dunhuang. The supply for the prince was much smaller than the supply for the first day, suggesting that the food given on the previous day was meant to be consumed on both days. Given that sixty rations of fine offering were provided that day, the number of envoys in this Khotanese mission should have been around thirty.

These first two days (the nineteenth and twentieth) mark the "road protection" stage of the envoys' interaction with their hosts, in which the Khotanese envoys were escorted by representatives of the Dunhuang government toward its capital. This stage continued the next day (6.21) when the diplomats and their entourage arrived at Maquankou ("Horse paddock mouth"), twenty-five *li* southwest of the city of Dunhuang. Maquankou fits the criteria for a natural halting place for travelers as it is at the mouth of a river.[8] Its proximity to the city and its location on the main road to the southwest meant that Maquankou was the juncture where departure and welcome ceremonies were often held. An envoy describes in a poem that "on my trip westward passing Maquan[kou], I look to the north to find the Yang Pass close. Turning back, I see the walls of the city [of Dunhuang], looming darkly among the trees."[9] In an official account of wine expenditure by the Dunhuang government, we find record of wine offered to departing envoys at Maquankou.[10] What the food expenditure account shows is that Maquankou was also where the welcoming ceremony was held for the Khotanese envoys. If it was a clear day when they arrived there, they could have, like the envoy-poet traveling in the other direction, had a first glimpse of the city of Dunhuang on the horizon.

Later on the same day, the Khotanese envoys arrived at the city. A banquet was held for them just outside of the city. This suburban location seems to be where many similar banquets were held.[11] An entry in an account of wine expenditure of the Dunhuang government tells us that one jar (*weng*) of wine was provided to the "Estate to the West of the City" in order to welcome the Khotanese envoys.[12] For other envoys, such receptions were held in the southern and eastern suburbs of the city.[13] The welcome ceremony just outside of the city concludes the "road protection" stage of the interaction between envoys and their host.

Then the envoys entered the city. After what must have been a restful night following a long trip, the Khotanese prince treated the newly arrived to yet another banquet on the twenty-second, this time in the comfort of the city. The main event of the diplomatic mission happened the following day, when the envoys met with the lord of Dunhuang at the "Great Court." This meeting, although perhaps brief, was a key moment for the Khotanese envoys. At this meeting, the envoys must have offered diplomatic letters to the host sovereign and presented gifts; the sovereign surely gave gifts in return, and perhaps even engaged in conversation with the envoys; these activities were customarily followed by yet another banquet. This major meeting with the lord of Dunhuang and the meetings and banquets associated with it mark the "audience with the sovereign" stage of the envoys' journey.

The end of the audience with the sovereign transitions to the beginning of what I term the "residency" stage of envoys' reception by their host. On the day after the Khotanese envoys' meeting with the lord of Dunhuang, the Khotanese prince again took responsibility for attending to the envoys, this time guiding them to Longxing Monastery, the main Buddhist monastery within the city of Dunhuang.[14] This trip might still have been semiofficial, as the exchanges among heads of the monastic communities in these states were as diplomatic as they were religious.[15] One might imagine that this trip to the Longxing Monastery would have been followed by further trips to other notable sites, including the Grottos of Unparalleled Height (Mogao ku) Buddhist complex, where the library cave is located. But this we cannot know for sure because the account was torn off and stops right after the entry for this day. As a result, it is also impossible to tell if the envoys were traveling to Dunhuang as their final destination, or just passing through Dunhuang on their way elsewhere. The answer to this question would have determined how long they stayed in Dunhuang.

Nevertheless, this account of food expenditure from the Dunhuang government reveals the three main stages of the reception of diplomatic travelers in Dunhuang: road protection, audience with the sovereign, and residency. To these one needs to add an earlier stage and a later stage to complete the "program" of guest/host interaction. The earlier stage, the first step of contact, can be termed "reconnaissance." In this report by the Office of Banquets and Hospitality, the interaction between the Dunhuang government and the Khotanese envoys began with the delivery of provisions to Shouchang. But for the

Dunhuang government to send food to the city of Shouchang, three day's journey away, it needed to have known about the incoming Khotanese envoys. Such news must have been conveyed by an even earlier, and likely much smaller-scale meeting between a messenger and representatives of the Dunhuang government. Additionally, after the envoys finished their residency stage in Dunhuang, they might have returned to Khotan, or continued further east. In either case, the Dunhuang government would have needed to provide road protection that mirrored the protection given to them when they entered the domain of Dunhuang. Only after Dunhuang escorts and guides left the Khotanese envoys at the end of this final road protection stage did this interaction between envoys and their hosts conclude successfully.

This five-stage "program" of envoy/host interaction is widely reflected in the Dunhuang documents and other contemporary sources. The existence of the stage of reconnaissance is revealed in another account about expenditure on wine by the Dunhuang government.[16] This account mentions a certain "Uyghur who came early to send the news,"[17] to whom the Dunhuang government provided half a *dou* of wine every two days. According to the account, this Uyghur traveler came to Dunhuang on the eighteenth day of the third month and left on the twentieth day of the eighth month, staying for a total of 150 days. The account does not specify what "news" he was sending, but another adjacent entry gives us a clear clue: from the twenty-fifth day of the third month to the twentieth day of the eighth month, the same day as the last supply of wine to the news-bearing Uyghur traveler, the Dunhuang government provided "daily wine" for diplomats from Ganzhou.[18] From the amount of wine offered we can deduce that this group consisted of twelve members. Comparing these two entries, it is evident that the "Uyghur who came early to send the news" came seven days before the main diplomatic mission from Ganzhou, stayed in Dunhuang with them for another 143 days, and all left together on the same day. In all likelihood, he was part of the Uyghur diplomatic mission, and traveled ahead to Dunhuang to convey the news of the imminent arrival of the mission. The seven-day notice would have allowed the Dunhuang government to send out escorts and guides, likely to the Suspended Spring Garrison,[19] 135 *li* and three day's journey to the east of the city, to welcome the incoming Uyghur envoys.

The existence of this stage of reconnaissance is also reflected in a letter from Khotanese envoys in Dunhuang back to the Khotanese court that describes these envoys' attempt to go to Ganzhou. Since Ganzhou was said to have been in a politically chaotic state following the death of a khan, the envoys pleaded with the lord of Dunhuang to "let us tentatively send one or two men to Gan-zhou and let them investigate what is said of good and bad, and we will go then."[20] These "one or two men" therefore functioned not only to connect the envoys to the next host (the government of Ganzhou) but also to test if the higher-ranked diplomats (described as "greater men" in this letter) could proceed safely. Similarly, the Jin envoy Gao Juhui, when talking about his journey from Kaifeng to Khotan, described his arrival at Dunhuang in this way: "Upon hearing of the imminent arrival of the Jin envoys [i.e., Gao's entourage], the governor Cao Yuanshen and others welcomed us in the suburb and inquired into the health of the Son of Heaven [of Later Jin]."[21] From this record, we know that the lord of Dunhuang learned of the "imminent arrival" of the envoys before preparing his suburban welcome. Such news must have been delivered by an earlier dispatch of reconnaissance from Gao's mission.

The next stage, road protection, the escorting of envoys within one's state, is a key step in a successful diplomatic journey. The geographical extent of the road protection from the oasis kingdom Dunhuang was rather limited, as Shouchang was only 120 *li* southwest of the city. For a larger state, like the Tang or the Song, the road protection extended to Lingzhou, which was 1250 *li* from the Tang capital of Chang'an.[22] Indeed, while state borders were shifting and porous in medieval Eurasia,[23] one might see the extent of such road protection as a good approximation of where the border of a state lay.

A letter from the governor of Lingzhou, likely written in 934 in the Later Tang dynasty, details how one group of envoys was relayed within and beyond the domain of the Later Tang and how the protection of the envoys transferred between different regional authorities.[24] This group of envoys heading west from the Later Tang capital of Luoyang was made up of envoys from Ganzhou, Dunhuang, and Guazhou, as well as "heavenly envoys" from the Later Tang. We meet them as they reach a place called Square Canal Garrison on the sixteenth day of the eighth month of 934. These envoys have been under the protection of the governors of Binzhou and Qingzhou, two local governments located about 550 and 680 kilometers to the northwest of Luoyang. The Square Canal Garrison was the final stop of their jurisdiction. After the arrival of the envoys there, the governors composed a letter to the governor of Lingzhou, some 200 kilometers away. This governor of Lingzhou, Zhang Xichong, received the letter on the twenty-first. From the letter, Zhang learned that the other governors intended to send the envoys away from the Square Canal Garrison on the fifth day of the ninth month and expected Zhang to receive them at a place called Mud Bridge the following morning. After receiving the letter on 8.21,

Zhang dispatched his own messenger the next day to deliver a positive response. On 9.3, then, Zhang sent his own men to Mud Bridge. They must have followed through on the plan and met with the envoys on 9.6, because on 9.9, they came back with the envoys to Lingzhou. Lingzhou was not the final destination, but only the beginning of the envoys' long trip further west. Having received the envoys, Governor Zhang then sent two messengers to the Uyghur khan of Ganzhou "asking for the khaghan to consider dispatching soldiers to welcome the envoys." The duty of the protection of envoys was further transferred westward, this time not to another prefecture but to another state. The constant communication through letter exchange and the use of soldier escorts allowed a successful transfer of the duty of road protection.

I present the dates and locations of this transaction in some detail because it is the most precise record of how the duty of road protection was organized between different states (Later Tang and the Ganzhou kingdom) and between regional powers of the same state (Lingzhou, Binzhou, and Qingzhou in the Later Tang). The practice revealed in the letter is as follows: After the arrival of envoys within one's own jurisdiction, the ruler of that particular place sends out a few messengers to the ruler of the next major stop on the envoys' intended route. Only after receiving a positive reply from the next ruler does the current one release the envoys. The regional governments within one state, such as the case of Binzhou/Qingzhou on the one hand and Lingzhou on the other, are often immediately adjacent, so that the envoys leaving the jurisdiction of the former in Square Canal Garrison on 9.5 would arrive in Mud Bridge on the morning of 9.6 under the jurisdiction of the latter. The transference of protective duties might not have been as smooth between states, and envoys might have needed to travel long stretches without clear state presence and protection, but as the action of the governor of Lingzhou toward the Uyghur khan shows, the principle of the transference of protective duties remained the same.

The road protection stage ended when envoys arrived at the capital city of the host state, where a banquet was often held in the suburbs of the city to welcome the incoming envoys. This banquet marked the transitional period, when envoys halted their physical movement and began the "audience with the sovereign" stage of the journey. In the case of the Khotanese envoys recorded in the food expenditure, they met the lord of Dunhuang at the Great Court in the city. But the audience with the sovereign could occur in many other places. When Gao Juhui arrived at Dunhuang, for instance, instead of following the standard protocol of meeting envoys in the city, Cao Yuanshen went out of his way and greeted them in the eastern suburb of Dunhuang. Usually the sovereign himself would not come out for this welcome ceremony, but would wait to meet with the envoys later in the city. Gao explains that such special treatment was because people in this region "were mostly Chinese" and therefore longed for an envoy from North China.[25]

The audience with the sovereign stage of the diplomatic trip played out expeditiously for this group of Khotanese envoys to Dunhuang recorded in the food expenditure. But for others, it was not always this easy. According to a Khotanese envoy report, a group of Khotanese envoys arrived at Ganzhou on the fifteenth day of a certain month, but only on the third day of the following month were they "conducted into the presence of the khan."[26] A prolonged delay before an audience with the sovereign was considered inappropriate. When Wang Yande, the envoy from the Song, arrived at Turfan in the fourth month of 982, he was unable to meet the khan for at least a month because the latter was escaping the summer heat in the northern part of the country.[27] The khan not only arranged to usher Wang and his entourage to his northern abode, but also sent a message that "I will pick a day to meet the envoys. Please do not be surprised by the long delay."[28]

In some cases, the audience with the sovereign happened more than once: the 878 Dunhuang mission to Chang'an offered its gifts to the Tang emperor, along with many other envoys and provincial officials, on New Year's Day. But its private meeting with the emperor happened much later, on the twenty-fifth day of the first month, at the Linde Hall of Daming Palace.[29] Often the audience also extended to meetings with high officials of the host state. The Khotanese envoys in Ganzhou, after meeting the khan, also met with officials with the title of *ügä* (counselor) and exchanged gifts with them;[30] the Dunhuang envoys in Chang'an in 878 similarly tried to deliver letters to "four prime ministers"—but only one accepted the letter.[31] During the meeting, gifts given by the envoys were often displayed,[32] and banquets and other amusements ensued. Wang Yande's meeting with the Turfan khan, for instance, was followed by "music and a banquet, where acrobatic performances were given," and then another more extravagant party in a boat on the following day.[33] This audience with the sovereign, with the exchange of gifts, the presentation of letters, and the conversation with the sovereign, was the central event of a diplomat's trip. Little wonder that, after meeting with the Uyghur khan and the ministers, the Khotanese envoys and their Uyghur hosts came to the understanding that the "official business was finished."[34]

Beyond the palace, the polo court was another venue for the official welcome ceremony of the host state. The longest stay in the Mongolia Itinerary happened between 8.24 and 9.3. In this entry, the itinerary notes that officials at the Tiande military garrison "played polo for and offered a banquet to" the Dunhuang diplomats.[35] Elsewhere, the itinerary recorded only that the diplomats "slept," "ate," and "rested" at a certain location on a certain day. Therefore, the polo game and the banquet must have been deemed two central and significant events in these diplomats' lives on the road to merit commenting.

The game of polo (Middle Persian *čawgān*) originated in Iran in the sixth century BCE. In the diplomatic cultures of Iran and the Roman world, polo playing allowed diplomats a chance to engage with their hosts. Matthew Canepa notes that in Iran, activities such as hunting, polo, chess, and backgammon "could demonstrate a sovereign's fitness to rule, something an astute envoy would be on the lookout for, and which the court would be eager to prove."[36] In Tang China, polo played a similar role in the imperial court, becoming an integral part of aristocratic leisure and diplomatic culture—even in the afterlife. In the corridor leading up to the main tomb chamber of Prince Li Xian (655–84), the son of Emperor Gaozong and Empress Wu, paintings of diplomats on the eastern wall face paintings of a polo game on the western wall.[37] Apparently, in the postmortem wanderings of this prince who died in his twenties, for which the tomb was meant to provide an arena, he was still entertaining diplomats and viewing polo games.[38] In the Song dynasty, the polo game became a part of diplomatic protocol that was codified in court rituals, and was used as a place to meet and entertain diplomats from the Jin dynasty.[39] Dunhuang diplomats' participation at a polo game confirms the long tradition of polo playing in Eurasian diplomatic communications.

But Dunhuang diplomats did not visit polo fields only in other parts of the world. There was a polo field in Dunhuang as well.[40] The envoy of the Tang emperor, for instance, delivered the edict to the lord of Dunhuang in a polo-field.[41] In a collection of letter models, an invitation to a polo game was copied immediately after a letter for "lowering the carrying pole," a phrase that indicates the arrival of travelers, who would lower their poles to put their luggage down.[42] This sequencing suggests that the meeting at the polo field generally followed the arrival of the guests. The polo field as a location for the deliverance of an imperial edict is codified in a ritual manual from Dunhuang, indicating a routinized practice.[43] The polo field was also where gifts of gold and silverware, as well as silk, brocade, and other precious textiles, were displayed, and served as a site for banquets. A government record of its flock of sheep tells us that the Bureau of Banquets in Dunhuang on one occasion used two brown sheep for a "polo-playing banquet."[44] Here, the polo field was functioning much like the palace, allowing the exchange of gifts and letters between the host and the visiting envoys. But compared with the more restrictive space of palaces, polo fields were capacious, open arenas that allowed the diplomatic ceremonies to involve more people. According to a panegyric poem for Zhang Huaishen, a reception for envoys from China at the polo field in Dunhuang caused "ten thousand people to acclaim in congratulation."[45] On this occasion, the polo field was transformed from the playground of the elite to a communal space where a diplomatic ceremony became a public spectacle.

After their meeting with the sovereign, envoys generally stayed in the city for a period of time. During this "residency" stage, envoys were free to engage in many endeavors, for the state and for themselves. The Khotanese envoys discussed above began their residency stage by visiting the Longxing Monastery on the day after their meeting with the lord of Dunhuang. In identical fashion, Wang Yande also visited the main Buddhist monastery of Turfan the day after his official meeting with the khan.[46] In these cases, the trip to the monastery could be considered a part of the welcome ceremony. But it could also be a leisurely one: Zhang Jinshan, the polyglot envoy from Khotan introduced in chapter 2, enjoyed the Buddhist sites and natural scenery of Dunhuang,[47] and the envoys recorded in the Staël-Holstein manuscript did the same.[48] We have particularly rich documentation of the residency of Khotanese elites in Dunhuang, who contributed, among other things, to the making of several caves among the Grottos of Unparalleled Height (Mogao ku) complex.[49] The residency of these envoys profoundly shaped the local culture in Dunhuang.

One feature of this residency stage of envoy-host interaction is that it could last for months, or even over a year. The Wang Yande embassy, for instance, stayed in Turfan for about a year and conducted various types of state and personal business, including a murderous plot against Kitan envoys who were also visiting Turfan.[50] One might argue that this sojourn was particularly prolonged because the trip between Turfan and Kaifeng was so time-consuming (taking about a year each way) that Wang and his government wanted to fully utilize the opportunity of his presence there to gather information and collect goods. But in another case, a Dunhuang envoy named Suo Ziquan stayed in Khotan for close to twenty-one months, despite the relatively short distance and close connections between the two states.[51] According to an account of wine expenditure in 964, the Dunhuang government provided wine for Turfan envoys for 91 days (1.24 to 4.25), one Khotanese envoy for 129 days (1.24 to 6.5) and another for 75 days (3.29 to 6.5), and Ganzhou envoys for 143 days (3.25 to 8.20).[52] Indeed, the Khotanese prince who was so profoundly involved in the reception of the Khotanese envoys was likely himself initially an envoy and decided to stay in Dunhuang for an extended period of time. We know of another Khotanese prince, named Congde, who came to Dunhuang in the eighth month of 964, lived there for around a year, traveled to Song as an envoy, and arrived at Kaifeng in the second moth of 966.[53] Such long residencies were a burden on the host states. For this reason, a Song edict stipulated that each diplomatic mission from Khotan to Kaifeng could not exceed fifty people, and they could not stay at the capital for more than one hundred days.[54] This injunction from the Song government attests to how widespread long residencies of envoys were in medieval Eastern Eurasia.

In all these examples of diplomatic residency, the envoys were fulfilling a function not unlike the permanent embassy in post-Westphalian European diplomacy. In modern practice, a diplomatic trip and a diplomatic residence are clearly distinguished. In the study of European diplomacy, the emergence of "resident diplomacy," where diplomats live in the target country long-term rather than just travel there temporarily, marked a major shift in the way diplomacy was conducted.[55] In the cases I have discussed above, however, these two functions were combined, and diplomatic travelers often took up long-term residency after their arrival at their destination. Such multimonth, sometimes even multiyear, residencies maintained a semipermanent diplomatic presence in the host state.

The final stage of the guest/host interaction was the road protection after the farewell ceremony for the departing envoys. Road protection for departing envoys followed a process that mirrors the first stage of road protection: a farewell banquet outside the city, and an escorted journey to a border town, all with provisions known as "road food."[56] Some of the departing ceremonies also involved large numbers of participants.[57] Only after the envoys left the domain of the state did the entire envoy-host interaction come to an end.

These five stages of a successful diplomatic encounter are summarized in table 5.2. This program was a widely accepted and observed diplomatic norm among states in medieval Eastern Eurasia. In his study of an earlier period, Jonathan Skaff observed a uniformity in diplomatic practices in the Tang and the Turkic Empires, which he believed to be a "product of military and diplomatic entanglements in Eurasia over the course of millennia."[58] Such entanglements persisted in the ninth and tenth centuries in Eastern Eurasia, and produced a

TABLE 5.2. A Program of Diplomatic Travelers' Interactions with Their Hosts

| Stage | Activities | Location |
|---|---|---|
| Reconnaissance | A small number of travelers arrive at the host state early to convey the news of the imminent arrival of the diplomatic mission | The border of the state |
| Road protection (incoming) | Provision of road guides, food, and protection for the envoys | From the border to the suburbs of the capital city |
| Audience with the sovereign | Meeting with the sovereign, banquets, gift and letter exchanges, gift display, meetings with ministers and officials | Capital city, but also polo field or suburbs |
| Residency | Visits to monasteries and famous sites, activities that accumulate merit | Capital city and the surrounding regions; sometimes also far-off regions within the state |
| Road protection (departing) | Provision of road guides, food, and protection for the envoys | From the suburbs of the capital to the border or the state |

general consensus of how diplomatic travelers ought to be received. In a letter written to an unspecified "foreign leader [*fanguan* 蕃官]," Lord Cao (it is unclear which one) of Dunhuang states:

> Now I am dispatching people to pay tribute to the court [in North China]. On the path they take, when they reach the region of your tribe, please follow the custom and offer manpower for security and assistance. Regarding the leader of my dispatch, make sure nothing is delayed or mishandled. Now I bestow on you slant-woven felt . . . and three yak tails, which you will receive when [the dispatch] arrives.[59]

The recipient of this letter was clearly not under the direct control of Cao, the lord of Dunhuang. It was thus necessary for Cao to make the plea that the "foreign leader" should "follow the custom" (*zhunli* 準例) in the treatment of the travelers. This "custom" must have comprised certain established procedures of diplomatic encounters, possibly not dissimilar to the five stages I describe above. In exchange for security and assistance, the unspecified foreign leader, who in other contexts of encounters on the road would have been considered a possible threat, received "slant-woven felt" and "three yak tails" as gifts. The assumption on the part of Cao that the foreign leader would understand and follow the "custom," something he did not even bother to elaborate on, indicates that a program of envoy-host interactions was self-explanatory and widely practiced, by Dunhuang and its (likely non-Chinese-speaking) neighbors alike.

## Failed Encounters

Like any program, this "appropriate" process of envoy-host encounters sometimes malfunctioned. Problems could occur at any of the stages outlined above. In a diplomatic letter to the Uyghur khan, the lord of Dunhuang Cao Yuanzhong complained about a group of eighteen bandits who, according to Cao, "were pretending to be envoys." These eighteen people, half on horseback and the other half on foot, took the "main road" all the way to the gate of the Suspended Spring Garrison, unannounced.[60] The Dunhuang army chased after them and captured the group, five of whom turned out to be young children. This unhappy encounter took place at Suspended Spring, where, like Shouchang to the southwest, the Dunhuang government began taking on the responsibility of escorting incoming envoys.[61] There is no corroborative account from the Uyghur side to confirm or refute Cao's version of the story. But it is not unreasonable to ask: Why would a group of bandits so blatantly and casually take the main road to the border of the state of Dunhuang? Why would they include five young children in their group? These actions taken by the eighteen Uyghurs strongly suggest that they might have initially started out as genuine envoys. Their mistake was the apparent lack of a messenger of reconnaissance. Indeed, Cao's complaint emphasizes that these pretend envoys marched "straight to the gate of the city [*zhizhi chengmen* 直至城門]," evidently startling the Dunhuang guards. Without reconnaissance, there was no way for the guards at Suspended Spring to know who was coming, and it was prudent to treat the unknown as the unfriendly. Hearing only Cao's side of the story, it is impossible for us to judge whether he was genuinely confused about the identities of these travelers or simply used this lack of reconnaissance from a group of envoys as a pretense to score a diplomatic win against the Uyghur khan. In either case, not having received a reconnaissance served as a reason for a potentially legitimate diplomatic mission to be condemned as a group of bandits.

In most cases, however, diplomatic journeys went awry at the "road protection" stage. In the same letter, Cao Yuanzhong complained about another incident in which Dunhuang envoys were traveling to Ganzhou to give gifts in return. This mission was ambushed in front of the Yonggui Garrison, still within the domain of Dunhuang, by a group of bandits, who killed one person and stole two or three horses.[62] Upon further investigation, the lord of Dunhuang found out that these bandits were Uyghurs who alleged that they were chasing after runaways. In this case, although Cao Yuanzhong blamed the Ganzhou khan for Uyghurs entering the domain of Dunhuang, it was clear that the government of Dunhuang itself had failed to provide adequate road protection for its envoys. In another letter, dated to 967, also from the lord of Dunhuang to the khan of Ganzhou, the lord asked the khan to investigate what had happened to a diplomatic mission from Dunhuang to the Song capital in the previous year.[63] According to the letter, this earlier mission had traveled safely from Ganzhou to "the border Liangzhou," but then was "thoroughly robbed, and the people [of the mission] were all scattered." By highlighting the location (at the border between Ganzhou and Liangzhou) of this robbery, the lord of Dunhuang insinuated that either the khan of Ganzhou or the ruler of Liangzhou had failed to perform his protective duty for the envoys.

More serious was the danger when supposed protectors not only ignored their duty but directly turned against the envoys. This was the case for a mission of more than seventy envoys to the Later Tang court in 934 led by a Dunhuang official Liang Xingde. This mission is fairly well known because of the records in two texts: Liang's portrait elegy (*miaozhen zan*) and a prayer text produced by Liang's sons after his death.[64] According to the elegy, the journey was initially successful, and the envoys were already on their way back from the Later Tang court, and "the appointments, endowments, clothing, and hats they were given were immeasurable."[65] With "immeasurable amounts of clothing and pearls" they arrived at Ganzhou. There, instead of being protected, they were imprisoned by the Uyghurs "like fish trapped in a net," and Liang Xingde was killed, along with many of his companions. In the prayer text, the sons of Liang Xingde offered a similar description: "[Our] father went to the prefectures of Qin and Liang [as an envoy]. On his way back [to Dunhuang], he encountered a catastrophe of the state [*guonan*, referring to the death of the Uyghur khan in Ganzhou]. [As a result], they lost not only their goods and fortune in Zhangye [Ganzhou] but also their lives in this foreign land."[66] This murderous act transpired partly because the Ganzhou government itself was unstable. The year before Liang was detained and killed in Ganzhou, Renyu Khan of Ganzhou had died and been succeeded by a new khan, Renmei.[67] Evidently, without a properly functioning government, not only was Ganzhou unable to perform the task of road protection for incoming envoys but certain factions of the government took the opportunity to actively harm envoys for material benefit.

It is for this reason that envoys often avoided traveling at times of political transition. In a letter from Khotanese envoys in Dunhuang to the king of Khotan, the envoys quoted a Dunhuang official as saying: "so the reverend ones [monks who were traveling as envoys to the east of Dunhuang] will go empty-handed! Who will lead them along the road? If there are no Uyghurs, who will lead them? With what will they go?"[68] The absence of Uyghurs who could guide the envoys on the road was, similar to the Liang Xingde case, a result of political chaos following the death of the Uyghur khan and the installation of a child as the new khan. For the letter writers, without proper road protection, envoys should not be expected to proceed, particularly when the political situation in the host state was known to be tumultuous.

Compared with the Liang Xingde murder case, another notable murder of an envoy in Dunhuang is shrouded in much greater mystery. The victim was named An Qianxiang, a Ganzhou official, likely of Sogdian descent. He appears in Chinese annals as the head of a mission from Ganzhou to the Later Tang in 924.[69] Then, two years later, he again traveled in a Ganzhou mission, which was accompanied by two other groups of envoys, from Dunhuang and Guazhou. This journey was as successful as the previous one. But, according to a letter written by the khan of Guazhou to the lord of Dunhuang the following year, "on the way back to the west," An Qianxiang was "murdered by Uyghurs on the road [*lushang bei Huihu shaque* 路上被回鶻煞却]."[70] The lord of Dunhuang initially suspected that An had really been killed by Zhang Baoshan and Liang Xingde (who, as mentioned above, was subsequently murdered himself on another mission), the head and deputy head of the Dunhuang subgroup in this composite diplomatic mission. But he later found out that an inexperienced young clerk named Zhang Yuanjin, who had become close with the Uyghur deputy head, was implicated in the matter. Exactly what role Zhang Yuanjin played in this murder is impossible to know, because the original letter about the matter was intentionally reticent. But it is clear that the joint Dunhuang-Guazhou-Ganzhou mission was attacked, potentially internally, when it was near or in the domain of Ganzhou. For a Ganzhou Uyghur official like An Qianxiang to be killed by "Uyghurs on the road" attests to the social complexity and the peril of these composite missions. One could not always count on even one's compatriots to be friendly.

In some cases, even though there was danger on the road, envoys were eventually able to overcome the difficulty and proceed on their journey. In a letter written to the king of Khotan, a Dunhuang envoy named Fuzhu stated that: "along the road, even though we encountered vile behavior and danger, bandits and killings, none of our group suffered any damage, and the gift [*xinwu*] to the great dynasty is also intact."[71] It is unclear what the nature of "bandits and killings" was. But the mission was able to fend off the threat and accomplish its goals. In this context, it is perhaps not unreasonable to read this line as a subtle accusation of the king of Khotan, who seems to have been derelict in his duty to guard the incoming envoys against danger on the road.

The most spectacular failures occurred when envoys encountered the wrong hosts. In 856, a major Tang diplomatic mission was dispatched to offer investiture to the Uyghur prince Pang Tegin (Pang Teqin) in Agni (Yanqi, Kharashar). This mission was important because it was the first attempt by the Tang government at establishing relations with the state newly founded by Uyghur migrants in that region after the fall of the Uyghur Empire.[72] It was led by the vice-minister of the Court of the Imperial Regalia (*Weiwei shaoqing*, rank 4a) named Wang Duanzhang, and two deputy heads, Li Xun and Li Ji. They were dispatched on December 12, 856, but when they reached the north of Yizhou (modern Hami) some two thousand kilometers away from Chang'an, they met a group of more than a thousand hostile Uyghur horsemen, who were not under the control of Pang Tegin. This encounter is recorded in a panegyric transformation text (*bianwen*) written for Zhang Yichao in Dunhuang, as well as on the tomb epitaph of Li Xun, the deputy of the mission.

Combining both records, we know that this group of "rebellious Uyghurs" threatened to murder the Tang envoys and to take possession of all their goods. The head of the mission, Wang Duanzhang, according to the clearly biased testimony in the epitaph of the deputy head Li Xun, intended to just offer the investiture to this group of Uyghurs instead. But when Wang held the imperial edict and started reading—a practice in line with the proper diplomatic procedure—the Uyghurs evidently were too impatient to wait until the end, and "attacked us and robbed us of the banners and insignia, chariots and horses, seals and gifts, clothes and luggage."[73] The Tang envoys were spared their lives; the three leaders all escaped and traveled back home, but one member of the mission became separated from the group and wandered to Dunhuang. The story of this member was recorded in the Dunhuang transformation text. From these records, we might deduce that, had the marauding Uyghurs decided to follow through with the investiture rituals, the Tang envoys might have gone along with the procedure and offered the title to this group. But the Uyghurs' unwillingness to even pretend to be a proper host spelled doom for the envoys.

As discussed in the previous chapter, envoys in medieval Eastern Eurasia traveled through postal stations, military establishments, natural locations with water sources, and deserts. Although the landscape that the envoys had to face was often hazardous, in the examples of failed diplomatic trips recorded in the Dunhuang documents, we rarely see deserts, mountains, or rivers appearing as the main culprits for their failure. In most cases, diplomatic journeys were foiled not by the difficult natural terrain—and difficult it no doubt was and remains—but by their hosts, either because of the dereliction of protective duties or through active hostility. These failed journeys point to the central importance of the envoy-host relation; to envoys on the Silk Road, people were often more dangerous than nature.

## Praising the Host: The Principle of the Guest-Host Relation

So far in this chapter, I have described a program of how hosts welcomed their diplomatic guests, and how diplomatic journeys broke down when proper practices were not followed. What I have not discussed is the reason that the hosts would agree to perform such duties in the first place. In all the encounters described above, the share of responsibility seems lopsided. The host provided protection, accommodation, and hospitality to the visiting envoys, whereas there is little record of material reciprocation in the other direction. Like any relationship, one would assume that both parties had to bear *some* responsibility for its maintenance. What did the envoys have to do for their hosts?

A natural guess would be the exchange of material goods. Indeed, as I will discuss in the next chapter, envoys offered gifts to their hosts, both at the destination state and to the hosting states along the road. But these gifts were primarily issued by the sovereign of the envoys' home state, and the hosts routinely reciprocated with return gifts to envoys and their sovereign. In the 878 journey of Dunhuang envoys to Chang'an, for instance, the diplomatic travelers did not contribute any gifts themselves, but merely delivered gifts from the lord of Dunhuang. In return, however, the Tang emperor gave gifts not only to the lord of Dunhuang but to all of the travelers. Thus, travelers' gifts were generally reciprocated and compensated by return gifts from their hosts;

so in and of themselves, these gifts served as little incentive for hosts to be generous.

While no source allows us to directly access the thinking of hosts, an assessment of the general mentality at the time might help us understand why they acted the way they did. In one of the collections of conversations and proverbs in Dunhuang, we find an axiom that gives instruction on the proper behavior of a host:

> When a bandit comes, he should be beaten;
> When a guest comes, he should be looked after.[74]

In no uncertain terms, this axiom informs its readers in Dunhuang that when a "guest" visits, he *should be* looked after. This rule of looking after a guest is here presented as a natural instinct. The text is a morality book that discusses the proper behavior of men and women in the context of marriage. It was widely circulated in Dunhuang, suggesting that this general sentiment toward guests was shared, or at the very least known, by many.

One reason for such a natural instinct is that the long-distance journeys taken by the guests were themselves seen as virtuous. In a Buddhist text popular in Dunhuang, a "good prince" traveled to the palace of the Nāga (dragon) king deep in the ocean in search of a Mani pearl that would cure all the woes in the world. After hearing a report about the prince at the gate of the palace, the Nāga king thought: "if not a virtuous and purely noble person, who would have traversed such a risky road?" The king then invited the prince into the palace, and asked, "Having deigned to travel from afar, what do you wish to acquire?" The prince responded that he wished to get the Mani pearl for the benefit of all sentient beings in Jambudvīpa. Hearing this request, the Nāga king stated: "If you agree to stay for seven days, I will be able to present you with my humble gift." The prince obliged, stayed for seven more days, and left with the pearl.

The process of the actual acquisition of the much-desired pearl seems almost anticlimactic after such a long and difficult journey, which involved, among other things, the departure and death of all five hundred of the prince's traveling companions. But it serves to illustrate a principle between guest and host: for a virtuous guest like the good prince, his long journey and his stay with his host were themselves his contributions to the Nāga king, who, as the host, reciprocated with the world-saving Mani pearl. This story was widely known among residents of Dunhuang and the surrounding regions because it is found in Buddhist sutras in Chinese,[75] Uyghur,[76] Sogdian,[77] and Tibetan,[78] all discovered in the library cave at Dunhuang. It was also depicted in mural paintings and in silk paintings from Dunhuang and was performed, according to the sutra-lecture manuscripts, for the public.[79] It would have been a familiar story to many of the travelers I discuss in this book, and the principle of the guest-host relation revealed in this story should not have been foreign to them.

It was this same spirit of hospitality that Marco Polo encountered in this region several centuries later. When he arrived at the city of Camul (Hami), Marco Polo recorded a local custom: "If a stranger passes through the region and comes to him to his house to lodge, [the host] is too much delighted at it, and receives him with great joy, and labors to do everything to please."[80] A more contemporary observer of Central Asian society also noted a similar sentiment. In the *Compendium of the Turkic Dialects*, Maḥmūd al-Kāshgarī made extensive remarks on the relation between a host and a guest. Under the entry for the word ōz (self), he quotes the following maxim:

> Put on fine garments for yourself;
> Make tasty food as a portion for others;
> Honor the guest,
> So that he spread your fame among the people.[81]

Much like the Dunhuang maxim, the attitude revealed by Marco Polo's story and the maxim recorded by Kāshgarī convey the same instinctual need on the part of hosts to treat their guests honorably and with care.[82]

If the thinking of hosts can be accessed only indirectly through popular maxims and stories, what the guests did to reciprocate the hospitality is better documented. A clue to this is present in the entry in Kāshgarī's dictionary cited above. After instructing hosts to treat guests with honor, the maxim clarifies that the reason for such treatment was so that the guest can "spread your fame among the people." Conversely, in the entry for uyra (going toward, intend), Kāshgarī quotes another maxim: "When the guest asks you for provisions and comes to you for it, give it to him; The guest will curse [you] if his reception is bad."[83] The reciprocal relation between a guest and a host is made abundantly clear by these sayings: if the host provides proper accommodation and provision, the guest responds by spreading the good name of the host; but if the host fails to provide such support, the guest responds by cursing the host, or spreading his bad name.

This idea is widely held not only in the Turkic-speaking world, as these maxims show; it is commonly found in many Dunhuang documents. In a letter from a Khotanese envoy to the Khotanese court, the envoy, who was in

Ganzhou at the time, explained that he wanted to go back to Dunhuang. But because of disorder in the Ganzhou government, it could not provide proper road protection. The message from the Ganzhou government was that "You must go if you can go safely, go. You can go. We cannot accept your good and bad name."[84] This phrase "good and bad name" (śirki viśū'na nāma) corresponds directly to the spirit of the Turkic maxims: a good host would acquire a "good name," while a derelict one a "bad name." The Ganzhou government was thus saying that it refused to take any responsibility for the fate of the Khotanese envoys. In another Khotanese letter, a monk who traveled to Dunhuang as an envoy described how he reproached the lord of Dunhuang as having done the envoys "great unpleasantness and dishonor." The lord of Dunhuang, according to this letter, responded by saying that "I made a bad name [viśū' nauma] here!"[85]

This same principle is also invoked in a Tibetan letter of introduction to a number of Tibetan monks for a Chinese Buddhist monk from a certain Ngog Luzhi Namka.[86] Namka claimed that "up to this point [in the monk's journey] both Chinese and Tibetans have [treated him] honorably . . . and conducted him stage by stage." He expected the same treatment from the recipients of the letter. But if the monk's progress were obstructed, Namka suggested, "the news will be carried away on the winds in the ten directions." The implication is, of course, that the potential reputation damage would be enough of a deterrent to any inappropriate behavior on the part of the host. The theme of the host's fame in this case also played a central part in the traveler-host relation.

The consequence of a "bad name" is evident from a Chinese letter about an ungrateful traveler. This letter was composed by the noble Lady Yin on behalf of herself and a certain lord (alang). One scholar has argued that this lady was the mother of Zhang Chengfeng, who was the ruler of Dunhuang from 894 to 910.[87] The letter is directed to a monk who traveled from somewhere west of Dunhuang to the east, and stayed at the residence of Lady Yin and her husband on his way. According to this letter, the monk was not just any "traveling monk," but the "teacher of the lord of the prefecture," an evidently official status. This important monk's journey should thus be considered semiofficial and not just religious. I quote the letter in full because it is a rare example of a message directed to a traveler.

Your disciple, [this] lady, has a small matter to report to the honorable one, and I hope you grant me your attention. Previously, when you were going to the east, your disciple expressed the deepest feelings of attachment [to you], and provided accommodation and service to the best of my abilities. Even with such hospitality [*yaole*, literally meaning "invitation and stopping (from going)"], you were not allowing [the possibility] of staying. Hence you went on ahead and departed from this confused person. Later, however, some officials told us in person that upon departure, the monk [the recipient of the letter] talked excessively about the inappropriateness of my lord [the lady's husband]. My lord soon heard about this and became very upset. This is because, when the monk was here, briefly [?] [we were] like older and younger brothers, like water and fish, and treated each other with respect without hearing about any unbecoming matters. Now for unknown reasons, [you] proclaim a bad name [for us]. When people around you hear about this, our fame will not be great. . . . We hope that the monk will return, and we will know your inner feelings. The disciple now longs for the honorable one to return to your monastery, which would fulfill my wish.[88]

This monk, it is said in the letter, enjoyed the accommodation and services provided by his hosts, and their relation appeared to have been intimate, like that between "older and younger brothers" and "water and fish." In spite of such intimacy, after the monk departed, he apparently slandered his hosts for some unknown reasons, giving them a "bad name" (*eming* 惡名). This slander prompted Lady Yin to compose this letter of inquiry, because "when people around you hear about this, our fame [literally, *mingjia* 名價, "the prize of our name"] will not be great." In this case, as in the Khotanese and Tibetan letters cited above, we see the "fame" or "good name" of the host being viewed as a crucial part of the relation between a guest and a host. If nothing else, a guest who enjoyed the accommodation of a host should proclaim the "good name" of the host. When this assumption was broken, it warranted an inquiry, at the very least. Therefore, underneath the extremely humble language of the letter lies a rather damning accusation. This accusation was made with the understanding that the monk most likely would return from the east and would have to pass Dunhuang and visit Lady Yin and her husband again. It is not difficult to see that if the monk could not give a reasonable explanation for what happened, he would not receive the same kind of accommodation on his return trip. The monk failed as a guest because he was seen as not fulfilling the reciprocal duty of spreading the good name of the host who had provided for him.

The celebration of the good name of the host also comes in the form of direct praise. Following is a model letter composed on the occasion of a traveler's departure:

*Gratitude for accommodation in the prefecture passed:*

A lowly certain someone and others, by the command of our own governor, passed your honorable land. Humbly we received double the normal amount of specially granted provisions and accommodations in the prefectures and garrisons within your jurisdiction along the road. This certain someone and others humbly feel unbearable gratitude and trepidation.[89]

In the note, the envoy is supposed to express gratitude (*gan'en* 感恩) because "humbly we received double the normal amount of specially granted provisions and accommodations." Therefore, this message serves as a "thank-you" note for hosts who have just provided provisions and protection in the road-protection stage of the interaction with envoys. Since the actual letters found at Dunhuang were commonly based on such model letters, the expression of gratitude through such a letter seems to have been a regular practice.

Therefore, travelers, including diplomatic travelers, repaid the proper accommodation and protection provided by their hosts through praising the hosts' generosity and spreading their "good name." The fact that this idea is found in Chinese, Turkic, Tibetan, and Khotanese sources shows that it was a widely held principle in medieval Eastern Eurasia, and a central dynamic for travelers on the Silk Road. Hosts, often the sovereigns of states, were interested in receiving a "good name" in exchange for the favorable treatment of travelers. Travelers, on the other hand, had a duty to spread the good name of their hosts. The fulfillment of this duty reaffirmed and reproduced the guest-host reciprocity for a future trip, but the dereliction of either party would risk, as in the case described in Lady Yin's letter, unsettling the guest/host amity. It was through this reciprocity of praise for hosts in exchange for protection and accommodation, rather than by commercial means, that diplomatic travelers organized their lives on the road.

## Conclusion

In this chapter, I have described how envoys interacted with their hosts on the road by dividing each envoy-host encounter into five stages: reconnaissance, incoming road protection, audience with the sovereign, residency, and outgoing road protection. The Dunhuang materials include rich documentation of each of these stages, demonstrating that they constituted a broadly observed "program" for diplomatic travelers in medieval Eastern Eurasia. The clarification of these stages allows me to identify exactly where and why the envoy-host relation could break down and a diplomatic journey fail. The success or failure of all envoy-host interactions, I argue, hinges on the reciprocal fulfilment of duties by both parties: while hosts provided accommodation and protection to envoys, envoys praised the generosity of their hosts and promised to spread their good name. The dynamic decidedly points to a noncommercial nature of envoys' interactions with their hosts on the Silk Road.

In the next chapter I further explore this noncommercial relationship by examining its central material manifestation: gifts. Almost every stage of the envoy-host interaction was accompanied by exchange of gifts large and small. Envoys came bearing gifts both luxurious and mundane; hosts reciprocated with gifts to the envoys and the sovereigns of their home states. These gifts were often displayed during the "audience with the sovereign" stage at palaces or polo fields, and the provisions given to the envoys by their hosts can be considered as gifts too. In a largely noncommercial world of relations, gifts served as the means by which envoys negotiated their relationship with their hosts, but also that with other people they met on the road. The central importance of gifts and gift exchange cannot be discussed as a subsidiary matter in this chapter, but deserves a fuller examination.

# 6

# Exchanging Gifts

## What Is a Gift?

The modern study of gifts and gift exchange began with Marcel Mauss's influential thesis.[1] Although he never gave a clear definition, his work argues for several fundamental features of a gift: it creates and recreates social relations; the donor of the gift assumes a higher social status than the receiver; and there is no "free" gift in the sense that even though recompense is not guaranteed, it is generally expected. The relation that a gift exchange creates is lucidly explained by Natalie Zemon Davis in her study of gift exchange in France:

> Every gift produces a return gift in a chain of events that accomplishes many things all at once: goods are exchanged and redistributed in societies that do not have distinct commercial markets; peace is maintained and sometimes solidarity and friendship; and status is confirmed or competed for, as in the potlatch among Indians of the Northwest coast of North America, where clan chiefs rival each other to see who can give away the most goods.[2]

Davis highlights three social functions of gifts: their economic function of redistribution, their political function of maintaining peace, and their social function of changing or confirming status. Diplomatic gifts in Dunhuang were used to accomplish all three of these goals. Even though Dunhuang and its neighboring states did have robust commercial markets, gifts remained distinct from commodities in that gifts tended to be luxury items, whereas commodities that were available in markets were mostly goods for daily use.[3] The sometimes jaw-dropping number of luxury goods exchanged as gifts, like the silk given by the Tang emperor in 878, invigorated the local economy of

TABLE 6.1. Words for "Gift" in the Dunhuang Manuscripts

| Language | | | | |
|---|---|---|---|---|
| Chinese | Tibetan | Khtoanese | Uyghur/Turkic | Sogdian |
| li 禮, gong 貢, xin 信, ci 賜 | bya-sga/bya-dga', skyes | skyaisa, mu'śda | beläk | p'l'k/pyr'k |

Dunhuang in ways that local transactions in cattle and grain could not. In diplomatic exchanges among states such as Dunhuang, Khotan, Turfan, and Ganzhou, gifts were also crucial to securing interstate peace. And the heads of states that were connected by envoys competed for higher status in their diplomatic networks through their gifts to one another. Gifts, with their diverse social functions, were as central to the lives of ninth- and tenth-century Eurasian envoys as they were in sixteenth-century France. In chapters 8 and 9, I will continue to explore the economic function of diplomatic gifts and their role in the kingly competition for status. In this chapter, I will restrict the discussion to the role they played in the lives of envoys.

The reference to gifts is prevalent in every type of Dunhuang document about envoys. In table 6.1, I list some of the most common terms for gifts in some of them main languages represented in the Dunhuang documents. These terms were not always used interchangeably. Some of them seem to point to specific aspects of gift exchange, while others denote general features. For instance, the Chinese term *li* signifies a generic gift without implying any difference in status between the giver and the receiver. The term *gong*, on the other hand, indicates an upward social movement of gifts, and is used almost exclusively for gifts to the emperor. Its downward counterpart, *ci*, has a broader semantic spectrum, denoting not only gifts from the emperor specifically but also from any person considered to be socially more prestigious than the receiver. Terms in other languages show similar distinctions. For instance, in Khotanese, the word *skyaisa* is used for both gifts that were attached to letters and gifts given out to establish diplomatic relations, while *mu'śda* seems to be more frequently used to mean gifts from someone of a higher social status. Interestingly, in both Sogdian and Khotanese, one of the common terms for "gift" is a loanword. In the Sogdian texts discovered in Dunhuang, the term for gift is *p'l'k* (or *pyr'k*), which derives from the Turkic *beläk*. The Khotanese term *skyaisa* derives from the Tibetan *skyes*. Such loanwords reflect the legacy of the Uyghur and Tibetan Empires and the inheritance of their ways of using gifts in the Sogdian and Khotanese communities.

The many terms for "gift" indicate a multiplicity of social scenarios in which gifts were exchanged. I use the term "gift" to describe all of these situations, because they are things that were, according to the Dunhuang documents where they appear, given without the immediate expectation of equal compensation. Many social events including marriages and funerals required the giving of gifts;[4] gifts to and from Buddhist institutions were equally prevalent.[5] In this chapter, however, I will discuss only gift exchanges that are relevant to the travel and transregional communications of envoys.

In many cases in medieval Eurasia, gifts were explicitly associated with travel. The Chinese term *gong*, for instance, often describes the gifts offered by a distant state of lower status, therefore incorporating the element of long-distance travel. In this regard, the Turkic terms are particularly well understood because of the existence of the eleventh-century *Compendium of the Turkic Dialects* (*Dīwān Lughāt at-Turk*) by Maḥmūd al-Kāshgarī. Kāshgarī's dictionary tells us that the term *ärtüt* means a gift "such as a horse, or the like, offered in the presence of emirs, or other; then every gift came to be called [with this term]."[6] This general term for "gift" is explicitly associated with diplomacy. Other terms for "gift" show a close connection to travel. For instance, *armāyan* means a gift "which a man returning from a successful journey brings for his relatives."[7] The term *beläk*, from which the Sogdian *p'l'k* derives, means a gift "which a traveler brings his relatives, or which is sent from one spot to another."[8] The way that *p'l'k* was used in a Sogdian text from Dunhuang, in which it describes a gift that was sent from one brother to another along with a letter, confirms its original meaning in Turkic.[9]

Another way in which gifts were inseparable from long-distance movement of people is through their association with letters.[10] It was a common practice at the time to attach gifts to a letter. When a certain Bäg Bars with the title of *tarqan* wrote to another Uyghur official, the sender complains: "I have heard that you are in Shazhou [Dunhuang]. . . . Because you have not come over here I got angry, and that's why I do not send letters or gifts."[11] According to the sender of the letter, the receiver should have visited him since he was, like the sender, also in Dunhuang. With the receiver failing to do so, he decided to refrain from sending letters or gifts. Similarly, in another Uyghur letter, the sender makes a request: "Now send all the news you have! I said, 'Yegän [meaning "nephew"] sends gifts and letters in all their fullness . . .' So I asked, but I did not find a gift or letter."[12] In these personal letters, the offering of gifts was inseparable from the exchange of letters, to the point that many discuss these two things as an indivisible unit. This close relation is seen in Chinese letters too: the common Chinese term *xin* 信, which can mean "message" or "messenger," is used in many Dunhuang letters to mean specifically the gifts that went along with letters.[13]

Because of the necessity of gifts in letter exchange, the offering of inadequate gifts is customarily, often self-effacingly, acknowledged in the writing of letters. A Sogdian letter written by someone named Tämär Quš to a Christian clergyman named George ends in this way: "I have sent [this letter] saying: Until [I,] his servant, may come [myself], may [my] letter not be empty. Having checked [it], [kindly] accept [my] little gift, [which is] in the hands of the head of the church, the priest Wanu čor. Don't be angry!"[14] In this letter, Tämär Quš describes his gifts as "little." Perhaps because he considers the gift inadequate, he begs at the end of the letter for the receiver to not become angry. Interestingly, the writer also indicates that, thanks to the small gift, his letter is not considered "empty."[15] For the same reason, in another letter, the writer gives the gift of "one *šay* [of] mulberries," but apologizes that "I have not sent you a finer gift."[16]

If an inadequate gift is something in need of excuses, even more so are letters without gifts. A Uyghur letter states: "As for me, I am at Sügču [Suzhou]. For this reason, I was not able to send you a gift. Do not be angry because there is no gift. In the next caravan I will send you the greatest gift."[17] In this case, a promise of a better gift in the future is meant to offset the current letter without a gift. Similarly, in a Tibetan letter, the writer confessed that after the death of his wife, he had married another woman who had carried debt with her. Because of this new debt and the fact that he had to take care of his children, he was unable to send any gifts. He hoped that the recipient would not be angry with him.[18] The close association between gifts and letters transcended cultural and linguistic boundaries, and was the standard practice in the world of medieval Dunhuang.

In many ways, therefore, gifts were inherently tied to the activity of long-distance travel, of both people and of letters. They permeated every aspect of envoys' lives on the road. Broadly speaking, we can distinguish two groups in the gifts with which Dunhuang envoys were most closely associated: the gifts that they transported for other people, and the gifts that they carried, gave, or received for themselves. The most important ones in the first group, because of the nature of envoys' travels, are the gifts between the sovereigns of the states that the envoys traveled to connect.[19]

## Gifts between Sovereigns

For a diplomatic mission, the most important type of gift is one from the mission's own sovereign to the sovereign of the destination state. These were the gifts that, in the case of the 878 mission to Chang'an, the Dunhuang envoys presented to the emperor on the New Year's Day celebration.[20] Almost every diplomatic mission traveled with such a list of gifts. In a letter a Khotanese envoy sent to the Khotanese court about his trip to the east, the envoy reported his activities upon arriving at Ganzhou (in Khotanese, Kamacū):

> We came to Ganzhou on the fifteenth day of month Rrāhaja. And on the third day they conducted us to the presence of the khan. And what I had as royal favor for the khan, that I presented according to the order. And the next day in the morning I gave the orders and gifts directed to the *ügä*s. And when they understood that the state business was finished, then the officer named Ttuḍīśä Saḍācī ttāttāhä: came to me.[21]

On the third day, upon arrival, the Khotanese envoy met with the khan of Ganzhou and offered the "royal favor," the gift from the Khotanese king. On the next day, he gave official letters and additional gifts to the *ügä*s, who were high officials in the Uyghur kingdom. The process described here is similar to that of the 878 mission in two ways. First, the presentation of gifts, more than anything else, seems to have been one of the main tasks of the envoy. Second, the gifts from the sovereign were intended not only for the other sovereign but also for his senior officials (prime ministers in the Tang case and *ügä*s in the Uyghur case). This kind of gift delivery by envoys was common practice at this time, constituting a crucial part of the "audience with the sovereign" stage of the envoy/host interaction.[22]

Just as gifts were attached to personal letters, these diplomatic gifts were often also considered attachments to official state letters. In a letter written by "seven princes," a group of Khotanese envoys, to the court of Dunhuang about their trip to China, they lamented their unfortunate situation: "All the animals our men had are lost. Our clothes are lost. . . . How [can] we then come to Shuofang [Lingzhou], since we have neither gift nor letter for the Chinese king?"[23] These envoys complained that they could not go further east, according to the original order of the Khotanese king, because they had lost everything they carried with them, and the consequent lack of gift and letter (*na . . . śkyesä u na pīḍakä*, "neither gift nor letter") prevented them from proceeding to Shuofang. For the Khotanese envoys, gifts and letters were appropriate only when offered in combination with each other.[24]

It turns out that the Khotanese envoys' concern was not unfounded. In the court records of the Song, we get to know a different group of Khotanese envoys who visited the Song court in the eleventh century:

> Office of Investigation of the Xihe circuit reported: "The kingdom of Khotan came and offered tribute without letter and petition from its king. According to the law [the tributes] should not be accepted. I have already ordered them to leave." The imperial edict ordered: "if they insist on offering the tribute, just allow it."[25]

In this case, already mentioned in chapter 3, the local Song official contended that the law prohibited the acceptance of tribute gifts without appropriate letters accompanying them. Diplomatic letters usually included a section describing the content and quantity of gifts attached, as well as the purpose of these gifts. Without the letters, the social significance of the gifts could not be properly understood. For this reason, the Song official refused to accept the Khotanese gifts because he could not make sense of them without a letter. Gifts and letters complemented each other in their roles not only in interpersonal communications but also in diplomatic ones. Neither could exist on its own.

There are many official letters from Dunhuang that include a list of gifts attached at the end. These lists give us an idea of the kinds of things that were used as gifts between sovereigns. At the end of a well-preserved royal edict from the king of Khotan to the lord of Dunhuang in 970, which reports on the recent victory of Khotan over the Qarakhanids to its west, we find the following list of gifts:

> First, one piece of medium jade of 42 *jin* [< Chinese 斤];
> And second, a piece of pure jade, 10 *jin*;
> and third, jade, 8.5 *jin*, which amounts to three pieces of jade
> 60 and a half *jin*.
> and one leather *baṃgāma*;
> and one hammer fitted with a handle made of horn;
> and one wagon and one drum.[26]

Several of the words in this list, as in many other lists of this nature in Chinese and Tibetan, have not been deciphered. The difficulty of knowing what they mean is itself informative: diplomatic gifts were usually lesser-known goods of exotic nature not common in daily usage; they often did not appear in standard glosses of the time, and subsequently have become obscure to us. Such obscurity potentially implies a high value placed on these goods. But even judging from the terms we do understand, including the three types of jade and the hammer, wagon, and drum, this list is already quite impressive, befitting the higher status of the Khotanese king than the lord of Dunhuang at the time of the letter.[27]

In 943, Cao Yijin, the king of Dunhuang, sent a letter to the ministers of the Uyghur kingdom in Ganzhou.[28] In the letter, "the older brother" Cao Yijin expressed his gratitude to "the younger brother" the khaghan for allowing the envoys from the Later Jin ("the heavenly envoy") to pass Ganzhou and reach Dunhuang. At the end of the letter, he attached a few "light tokens" (*qingxin* 輕信) for his gratitude, which included the following items:

1.  One piece of first-class carmine-surfaced jade, eight *jin*;
2.  White silk, five *pi*;
3.  Anxi [Kucha] cotton cloth [*xie*], two *pi*;
4.  Vertical-loom silk, eighteen *pi*;
5.  Government [produced] cloth, sixty *pi*.

To put these "light tokens" in context: items 2, 4, and 5 are common goods bought and sold in the markets of Dunhuang; together they would have been worth approximately 1335 *shi* of grain.[29] This amount of grain would have been enough to feed a couple (one adult man and one adult woman) for about 111 years.[30] But these are not the rarest or the most precious items on this list. The *xie*, a kind of cotton cloth from Kucha, was an exotic product not found in markets in Dunhuang, so there is no way to evaluate it precisely. For the same reason, it is difficult to determine the value of the highlight of the list, the "first-class carmine-surfaced jade" weighing eight *jin* (about five kilograms). There is almost no doubt that this piece of jade originated from the kingdom of Khotan, as Khotan was the only place where jade was produced in the region.[31] Given the fact that this is not a letter addressing an emergency or a serious crisis but just an expression of gratitude in a routinized practice, the amount offered in gifts is quite substantial. It is safe that say that the gifts on this list are by no means just "light tokens."

Yet these gifts from the Khotanese king and the lord of Dunhuang were light in a more literal sense of the word. While potentially worth more than all the rest of the gifts on the list combined, the piece of jade from the lord of Dunhuang was not particularly heavy, about five kilograms.[32] The gifts from the Khotanese king in 970, which mostly consisted of jade, weighed around

60.5 *jin*, or thirty-nine kilograms. One horse could have easily carried all the goods on both lists.[33] These gifts traveled a long distance with envoys, from Khotan to Dunhuang for the first list, and from Dunhuang to Ganzhou for the second; they had considerable value yet were fairly light in weight; several items on these lists were also clearly exotic goods. Therefore, these gifts are perfect examples of luxury goods transported on the Silk Road.

Gifts were sometimes so precious that their acquisition was itself the very reason for diplomatic traveling. For instance, in 969, a Khotanese envoy named Zhimoshan traveled to the Song court, and reported that in his own country of Khotan, there was a piece of jade that weighed 237 *jin* (154 kilograms). A single intact piece of jade that weighed this much was a rarity among this already precious category of stones. According to the Song record, "[the Khotanese] wanted to offer it [the jade], and begged [the Song court] to send an envoy to acquire it."[34] In this case, the sole reason for this round of diplomatic exchange was *news* about the acquisition of a large piece of jade. It is notable that the party that initiated the interaction was not the one receiving the gift (the Song court), but the one giving it (the Khotanese kingdom). For the Khotanese king, it was inappropriate to simply deliver this exceptionally large piece of jade to the Song court without notification, because of the expectation, shared between him and the Song emperor, of a counter-gift of potentially greater value from the latter (see my discussion later in this chapter). Therefore, the Khotanese king had to send an envoy to first inquire if the Song emperor was willing accept the newly discovered jade as a tributary gift. In this case, the Song emperor agreed to take the jade, and asked another Khotanese envoy, who came in a later mission offering asafetida, to return to Khotan and procure the jade for him.[35]

In other cases, envoys traveled specifically to demand gifts. In 1004, the governor of Dunhuang, Cao Zongshou, made a routine offering of jade and horses to the Song court, together with the following request for return gifts:

> Furthermore he [Cao Zongshou] said that monk Huizang entreated to be granted the master title, and that the Longxing and Lingtu temples were constructing statues [of Buddha] that [required] 100,000 pieces of gold leaf. It was his wish that these be granted. Furthermore, he also entreated that a bell maker as well as Chinese pearl connoisseurs should be sent to his province to teach the techniques.[36]

In addition to the request for titles, the lord of Dunhuang explicitly asked for gold for the construction of Buddhist statues, as well as for several artisans to be sent to Dunhuang. The Song emperor granted Huizang the master title and offered a certain amount of gold leaf, but refused the rest of the demand. Evidently, the requests of Cao Zongshou, in particular those for an exorbitant amount of gold leaf and artisans, were deemed inappropriately excessive.

As the exchange of gifts became a regular practice among states in the region, we see references to "return gifts" not only in Chinese sources but also in Tibetan. A letter from the king of Khotan to the lord of Dunhuang, written in Tibetan, mentions gifts that were "traded in return [*tshong lan du*]."[37] Two fairly complete documents record a "gift-recompensing envoy [*huili shi* 回禮使]" from Dunhuang to Khotan between 956 and 958. The first document was written by Suo Ziquan, the "gift-recompensing envoy" from Dunhuang, who delivered gifts to the king of Khotan and courtesans to the queen of Khotan.[38] As I explained in chapter 2, the gifts from the king of Khotan triggered multiple further rounds of envoys traveling thousands of kilometers over the course of two years, including Suo's mission to take counter-gifts and Fuzhu's mission to report the safe return of Suo. The exchange of gifts was the central theme of all of these trips. This shows that, similar to Natalie Davis's assertation that "every gift produces a return gift in a chain of events," important diplomatic gifts between sovereigns also produced a chain of further exchanges of envoys.

The fundamental role of gift exchange between sovereigns in the making of diplomatic relations can be seen in the very terms in which diplomatic relations were described. In a letter dated to 1026 written by the Kitan khan, Emperor Shengzong (r. 982–1031) of the Liao, to Maḥmūd (r. 971–1030), the ruler of the Ghaznavid dynasty in modern Afghanistan, the Kitan khan describes the subjugation of many of his surrounding states, who "constantly and without exception send their envoys, and their letters and presents follow upon one another." Here the close connection between letters and gifts and their relation to envoys are made as apparent as in the Dunhuang documents. The only king that did not send envoys, according to the Kitan khan, was the Ghaznavid ruler. Therefore, the Kitan khan dispatched a mission to establish contact with Maḥmūd. He claimed that the envoys were sent in order that "we may inform him [Maḥmūd] of how things stand with us, and communicate with him on what there is in the world, while establishing *the custom of mutual donations* [emphasis mine], in friendship with him."[39] For the Kitan khan, the exchange of diplomatic gifts through this "custom of mutual donations" was as important as the exchange of information ("what there is in the world") to this proposed diplomatic relation. Even though the proposal was ultimately rejected by Maḥmūd on the basis of the khan's non-Muslim status, the central importance of gift exchange in diplomatic traveling is nonetheless evident. Indeed, at the end of this same letter from the Kitan khan, in the same manner as many Dunhuang diplomatic letters, such as the one from the Khotanese king to the lord of Dunhuang (P. 5538), a list of gifts was attached that included silk clothing, sable martens, squirrels, musk, a bow and arrows, and a number of unidentified, potentially exotic and valuable, goods.[40]

Through my discussion of the exchange of gifts between sovereigns in the world of Dunhuang envoys, it is clear that such a "custom of mutual donations" characterized the diplomatic relations among these sovereigns as well. The donation of gifts likely facilitated the transmission of diplomatic information and the formation of interstate relations. But gifts were not just key components of a diplomatic mission. In many cases, the delivery and acquisition of gifts were themselves the primary goal of diplomacy.

But envoys were not merely transporting these gifts between sovereigns and other luminaries. They used gifts themselves in a much broader array of social settings. It is to the envoys' own use of gifts in their lives on the road that I now turn.

## Gifts for Envoys

The many ways in which envoys received gifts for their diplomatic missions can be seen in a fragmentary account of the grain expenditure of an unnamed Dunhuang monastery. In this account, there are four entries in which the accountant enumerates the amount of grain used to purchase wine for visiting envoys. This wine was intended to be provided for the funeral of a "heavenly envoy" from North China who had recently passed away in Dunhuang, a Buddhist teacher from Dunhuang who was about to depart for somewhere in the west, and Turfan and Khotanese envoys who were staying at the monastery.[41] These records, in a nutshell, capture the many dimensions of envoys' relations with gifts when they were on the road: not only were they given gifts prior to their departure (in the case of the Buddhist teacher), they were also consistently offered different kinds of gifts by their hosts when they were on the road (the Turfan and Khotanese envoys). In the case of the envoy from North China, wine was provided even for use in a posthumous ceremony. Such extensive use of gifts created and mediated the social relations envoys formed on their journeys.

Before departure, envoys usually received what is known as "road goods" (*songlu wu* 送路物). This practice was common in medieval Eastern Eurasia.

The diary of the famous Japanese monk Ennin (794–864), who visited the Tang capital of Chang'an in the mid-ninth century, mentions the road goods he received from a Censor Li just prior to his departure from Chang'an: "ten bolts of *shao-wu* damask, one piece of fragrant sandalwood, two sandalwood boxes with images, a bottle of incense, a five-pronged silver vajra [Buddhist ritual object], two felt hats, one scroll of the Diamond Sutra in silver characters, a pair of soft slippers, and two strings of coins."[42] In return, Ennin gave Li his robe and scarf. These return gifts did not match the material value of the road goods, but Censor Li's intention to "make offerings to them [the robe and scarf] for the rest of my life" indicates their tremendous symbolic importance to the recipient.

This practice of offering gifts to departing travelers is commonly found in the Dunhuang documents as well. The following is a letter model composed for the occasion of the departure of a traveler. In it, the traveler expresses gratitude for the gift of a horse:

> Letter [expressing] gratitude for a horse: Humbly I received the personal favor of this specially offered gift [of a horse]. Because of the long road ahead, it is hard to decline this gift; and the fleet-footed [horse] is just like Quanqi [a legendary horse]. Upon accepting this gift, I feel doubly profound gratitude. Thus, I have carefully constructed this note to express my gratitude. Humbly I hope you heed my words. Carefully petitioned.[43]

Unlike Ennin, the writer of the letter does not mention a counter-gift for the horse. The only response to the gift of the horse for the upcoming trip seems to have been the letter itself. Whether or not there were other measures of reciprocation is unknown.[44] What is transparent is that the horse was not bought or borrowed, as was the case with many horses envoys acquired prior to departure,[45] but offered as a gift without immediate material cost to the traveler. The fact that this narrative served as a model of letter writing suggests it was not a singular occurrence, but an accepted social practice in Dunhuang.

In other Dunhuang documents, we see many more examples of this type of road goods. They were similarly given to travelers, including envoys, without immediate request or expectation for compensation. Several of the references to this type of road goods appear in accounts of expenditure, especially those of the various monasteries in Dunhuang.[46] The Jingtu Monastery is particularly well documented in this regard. A certain military officer on a governmental trip received road goods in the form of one *pi* of vertical-loom cotton cloth and one *pi* of state-sanctioned cloth (*guanbu*) from the Jingtu

Monastery.[47] A significant amount of millet was used to purchase wine to be delivered as road goods for a General Gao's trip to the southern mountains.[48] Oil and millet were given to both governmental officials and monks for their trip to the east.[49] As well as monasteries, the Dunhuang government also provided road goods, including grain, flour, and wine to officials and artisans who traveled as envoys.[50] From a material perspective, in these cases, the road goods—food, oil, and wine—seem to have been mostly necessities travelers would use during their journeys.

Another type of road goods included things of a somewhat different nature. P. 3985 is a list of road goods that includes various types of cloth, including silk, given by as many as ten individuals or families.[51] The responsibility of the receiver is not specified. But the term "sending off on the road" (*songlu* 送路) implies that it was a list of gifts. In this case, the gifts were given not by a single monastery but by a collection of families. The collective nature of road goods can be seen in other contexts as well. In Dunhuang during this period, people sometimes organized themselves into mutual-help communities called *she* in order to shoulder risks collectively.[52] In a contract model for a *she* community, one finds the following responsibilities of the *she*-community members: "If traveling a long distance to the east or west as envoys, the departing members should be [properly] sent off, and the arriving ones should be [properly] received."[53] The offering of road goods should therefore be seen as a part of the proper sending-off ritual this contract model discusses. It is possible that P. 3985 is a list of people performing this type of ritual within a *she* community. The contents of this list suggest that it is not meant to provide for the basic needs of travelers, because the majority of the gifts are valuable textiles. One might speculate that they would serve travelers in other ways, perhaps as gifts or merchandise to be used on the trip in the future.[54]

These gifts given upon departure were not the only type of goods Dunhuang envoys received. When they arrived at a new place, they were often also greeted by their hosts with gifts. The following text from a letter model provides some insights into this second type of gift. According to this letter, a host is supposed to treat an envoy who has just arrived in this manner:

Offer to guests [who are] passing as they lower the carrying pole: *shi* silk [weft ribbed plain weave silk] one *pi*, damask one *pi*, and other listed goods. The aforementioned goods are cautiously ordered to be quickly sent, in order to account for the cost of the fodder for the next day. [I am] very ashamed of the small number [of gifts], they serve only to show my heartfelt feeling. Please do not take it as an offence, and grant me your acceptance [of the gifts].[55]

The term "lower the carrying pole" (*xiadan* 下擔) indicates, as I explained in chapter 5, the arrival of travelers, who would lower the poles they used to carry luggage with them on the road. In this sense, the term forms an interesting pair, along with "sending off on the road" (*songlu* 送路), which describes the occasion of travelers' departure. Underneath the extremely humble language on the part of the host, the basic matter dealt with in this letter is the following: the traveler who is simply passing through the region (*hengguo* 橫過)—as distinct from those whose destination was this region—is given two types of silk and other goods "to account for the cost of the fodder for the next day," thus serving their daily needs while on the road. Because the traveler is explicitly described as "passing through," one might assume that on the next day, they would have been on their way to the next stop. The reason for the host's gifts is said to be that "they serve only to show my heartfelt feeling." And the host will wait at the suburbs to see the guest off once they accept the gifts. There is no hint of the host demanding anything from the passing traveler.

In many other cases, envoys were not just "passing through" but staying at the place they had just reached, either as their destination or on the way to their destination. Upon arrival at the new place, they were provided with accommodation as well as various types of gifts. A few expenditure accounts produced by the Dunhuang government record these gifts to envoys in great detail. In accounts from the Office of Banquets, envoys from as far as China, India, and Persia, as well as the closer neighbors of Khotan, Ganzhou, Hami, and Turfan, were given certain rations of food.[56] Envoys from Ganzhou and Hami, in particular, enjoyed extensive provisions from the Dunhuang government, lasting for at least seventeen days. Similarly, the government also provided the envoys with wine. A group of thirty-five envoys from Turfan, for instance, received wine for at least thirty-two consecutive days.[57] In the same way, envoys from neighboring states such as Canwei and from North China also received cloth from the Dunhuang government, and envoys from Ganzhou, Suzhou, and North China, as well as few who were passing by, were given gifts of fine, coarse, and drawing paper for their use.[58] These gifts are similar in nature to many of the road goods envoys received prior to departure in that they are mostly goods for daily use. As I discussed in chapter 3, since envoys reserved their limited carrying capacity for more luxurious goods, their daily necessities were often met in the form of gifts from their hosts on the road.

Unlike the gifts exchanged between sovereigns, which tended to be high-value, luxury items, the gifts given to envoys were more diverse. There were high-value items such as silk, but more often, the gifts for envoys, both at departure and on arrival, comprised practical items such as horses, food, wine, paper, and clothes. These items were crucial in the daily lives of envoys on the road, both when they were staying with their hosts and when they were physically moving between cities and towns. They accounted for a significant portion of the "income" of envoys on a diplomatic mission.[59]

Another difference between these two types of gifts is that the exchange of gifts between sovereigns, despite discrepancies in the value of the gifts, seems to have been mutual in that both sovereigns were expected to send gifts in the "relation of mutual donation." For envoys, however, there is almost no record of them giving personal gifts *back* to the people who provided them with road goods before their departure, or to the hosts who offered them food, wine, and paper. The lack of return gifts is clear from their absence from the account books that recorded the gifts given to envoys. Because many of these account books from Dunhuang monasteries and the Dunhuang government were explicitly ones about *both* income and expenditure, one would assume that gifts from the envoys would have appeared in these accounts had there been any. The fact that none of these records exist implies that the road goods and provisions to envoys were generally unidirectionally offered and not immediately compensated. Such unidirectional gift giving indicates a structural imbalance in the relation between an envoy and a host: the former was constantly indebted to the latter.

## The Logic of Diplomatic Gifting

The discussion above shows that the exchange of gifts permeated many aspects of the lives of envoys on the road. They transported, delivered, and received gifts between sovereigns, offered gifts to other luminaries of the states they passed, and accepted gifts themselves from their home state as well as from the states they encountered on the road. The goods that served as gifts ranged from luxury items such as jade and silk to daily necessities like food and clothes to unique items such as elephants and watermelons. But why did gift givers decide to offer certain gifts? What did they expect to achieve? What was the relationship created and changed by a round of gift exchange? In this final section of the chapter, I explore these questions about the logic of gifting in the context of the envoys' lives on the road.

The most salient feature of all the gift exchanges described above is the inequality between the parties of exchange. For instance, during the 878 Dunhuang mission to Chang'an, in exchange for one piece of jade, one antelope horn, and a yak tail from Dunhuang, the Tang government offered 1848 *pi* of silk/cloth,[60] forty-two sets of clothes, and nineteen pieces silverware.[61] Such a drastic difference in material value between gifts exchanged might be unique, but the general principle of inequity displayed in this case is common. In fact, in letter after letter, writers describe their gifts as "small" and "light" while praising the gifts from the other party as "heavy." The inequity in gift exchange between sovereigns was openly acknowledged, even celebrated, by both parties of the exchange.

Where envoys received gifts, in particular from their hosts on the road, the inequity was even more pronounced because envoys usually did not respond with return gifts. When an envoy received food, wine, paper, and clothes, in addition to accommodation, from the Dunhuang government, for instance, it is unclear what he was doing in return. The unidirectional offering of gifts to envoys created a debt that had to be addressed. Instead of offering counter-gifts, the way envoys responded to these gifts was often a message of gratitude. In a model letter, a traveler expresses gratitude for the provisions given by the host:

> Because of certain matters of business, I arrived at your famous state. Due to my old yearning, I had the pleasure of glimpsing your face. Not having offered even a tiny bit [to you], my trepidation greatly increased. Honored by the invitation of the host, how dare I accept it? I wish to go to your mansion, and express my gratitude in person for the mountain-like favor. But after reconsideration I fear it might be bothersome. Therefore, I will wait for you to grant me a message. Cautiously I petition.[62]

The reference to "your famous state" suggests this letter model was meant to be used by someone visiting a foreign state, and the tone implies that the business involved was not personal. One can imagine a traveling envoy making use of this letter. The language of the letter is particularly humble because of the unequal relation between the traveler and the host. While the host provided a banquet for the traveler, the traveler was not able to offer "even a tiny bit" in return. This imbalance created great trepidation in the heart of the traveler, who profusely praised the host, and expressed the wish to further show gratitude in person. Thus the letter represents the traveler's attempt to address the host's "mountain-like favor" that they knew they had no hope of reciprocating.

This type of letter model is not rare among the Dunhuang documents. In another similar letter, the envoy explicitly expresses gratitude for the goods of "lowering the carrying pole"—the lamb and wine provided upon his arrival at the new place.

*Gratitude for lowering the carrying pole:*

> A lowly certain someone and others, by the command of our own governor, arrived at your honorable land. Before we had the honor of paying respect [to you], [you] have bestowed lamb and wine for [the occasion of] lowering the carrying pole. This certain someone and others feel unbearable gratitude and trepidation.[63]

This letter is clearly about an envoy, as it states that the writer was ordered to travel by the governor of his state. Like the previous letter, it also shows the envoy expressing "unbearable gratitude and trepidation" as a way of addressing the debt incurred by the goods given. Interestingly, a letter in actual use that was based on this letter model is also found among the Dunhuang documents. This real letter was written by a monk named Huiguang.[64] Huiguang's letter is essentially a verbatim copy of the letter model cited here, with the name "Huiguang and others" (*Huiguang deng* 惠廣等) replacing the "certain someone and others." Huiguang's case shows that the letter models were indeed used in the ways they were supposed to be, and the social practices seen in these letter models were accepted to the point of being formulaic. Huiguang's experience is the same as the one described above: not being able to (or not supposed to) directly give return gifts to reciprocate the provisions given by the host, he expressed his gratitude through a letter.

Such structural imbalance persisted even where an envoy did send gifts to his host. This case is found in the following letter, written by an envoy from the Song dynasty named Wang Ding to the lord of Dunhuang:

> Previously I acted out of order, and offered rough grass, only with the hope of receiving your honorable examination. How could I have hoped for the bestowment [meaning the gift given to him]? Now, because of the governor who widely opened the treasury, and specifically bestowed *qiong-yao* jade . . . Since I dare not refuse or decline, I can only hold it with trepidation.[65]

The language of this letter is embellished: the gift given to the host, the lord of Dunhuang, is described as "rough grass," whereas the return gift from the lord is compared to *qiong-yao* jade, a glimpse of which, according to Wang Ding, reminds one of the appearance of the autumn moon. But underneath the hyperbolic language, Wang Ding reveals the social principle for such gift exchange. According to him, his offer of "rough grass" was made "only with the hope of receiving your honorable examination." This statement suggests that at least rhetorically he did not initially expect counter-gifts. But had the governor not responded by opening the treasury and offering the gift of jade, Wang Ding would probably not have been satisfied. From the perspective of the lord of Dunhuang, gifts from Wang Ding had to be compensated with gifts greater in value, because of the higher social status of the lord. With his offering of counter-gifts, the lord of Dunhuang fulfilled his social duty, reaffirmed his superior status, and essentially "won" this gift competition. Yet the exchange did not end there. Wang Ding had to write a letter to show that he recognized the superiority of the lord's gifts and an unequal relation between him and the lord of Dunhuang. Only with this note of gratitude was the gift-exchange process complete, with the status of both parties reaffirmed and their relation strengthened. To terminate the process at any earlier point (for instance, if the lord had not responded with counter gifts, or if Wang Ding had not written the note) would result in a disruption of the equilibrium of the relation between the lord of Dunhuang and the Song envoy.

This imbalance between traveler and host created by the host's gift giving finds an astonishing expression in the case of another monk, who was traveling not as an envoy but as a pilgrim. In the third month of 924, a monk named Zhiyan from Fuzhou (鄜州, modern Shaanxi province) arrived in Dunhuang.[66] Like many before him, Zhiyan was on his pilgrimage to India for the procurement and transmission of Buddhist texts. After stating his purpose and wishing the well-being of the Chinese emperor, Governor Cao of Dunhuang, and the officials and commoners of Dunhuang, he went on to make a solemn vow:

> The day when Zhiyan returns, I vow to devote this vulgar body as an offering to the Great Sage Bodhisattva Mañjuśrī and burn this body, in order to repay the favor of protection on my way forth and back.[67]

Here, the monk Zhiyan recognized that he was unable to immediately return the favor offered by his host in Dunhuang. To address this debt, Zhiyan vowed to give the ultimate counter-gift: his own life. Self-immolation in medieval

China was inspired by the Lotus Sutra and other Jātaka stories about the sacrifices of bodhisattvas, and the purpose of self-immolation was to achieve *anuttarāsamyaksaṃbodhi* (complete and perfect enlightenment).[68] Yet in the case of Zhiyan, the goal of his proposed self-immolation was much more secular. His vow shows that the relation between him and his host was taken so seriously, and the debt thus incurred so severe, that he was willing to sacrifice his life to pay the debt to his host.

Therefore, unlike commercial exchanges, gift exchange in these cases was never about the transference of goods with (perceived) equal value. Scholars have long observed the unequal nature of gift exchange in diplomacy in medieval China. Jonathan Skaff, for instance, observes that "Tang gifts that exceeded the market value of tribute in livestock [from Turkic states] served as a hidden indemnity to guarantee a truce."[69] He sees the unequal gift exchange between the Tang its Turkic neighbors as the Tang giving in to military pressure. But as I have shown in the cases of Dunhuang envoys to the Tang, similar unequal gift exchange also occurred, when Dunhuang posed no military threat, thus needing no "hidden indemnity" from the Tang. Here, offering more gifts in an exchange was often a way to signify and consolidate one's superior status in a bilateral relation. This logic of gifting is revealed in a manuscript in Dunhuang on the various kinds of proper conduct a person should strive to follow:

> If one is blessed with the accommodation of another, till death does he remember the kindness; if one accepts salary and a place of honor, even the perishing of the body would not be sufficient in expressing the gratitude. . . . *One should much rather that others owe him, than he himself owe others.*[70]

The last sentence concisely sums up this logic of gifting. In gift exchanges in medieval Dunhuang, it was generally considered better to give without receiving in return than to receive without giving, because the latter solidified the perceived superior status of the giver of gifts. Such logic is also applicable in diplomatic gift exchanges, and explains why gift exchanges between sovereigns or between envoys and hosts were structurally unequal.

But no gifts were offered "for free." As the many letters cited above show, the imbalance created by unequal gift exchanges had to be addressed by the party receiving the more valuable gifts. One of the primary ways to address such debt was to praise the generosity of the gift giver. In a letter to the king of Khotan, he was addressed as "endowed with the experience of the great gift [*mistyi haurä*], from the four directions, in many lands, his great name had gone [*mestyi nāṃma tsva*]."[71] Because of his generosity in gift giving, this letter maintains, the Khotanese king's name traveled in all directions and lands. As in many other cases studied by anthropologists, giving more and superior gifts means that the giver achieves or solidifies higher social status.[72] This is why Marcel Mauss asserts that "the rich man who shows his wealth by spending recklessly is the man who wins prestige."[73] The kings of medieval Eastern Eurasia were similarly engaged in a process of competitive gifting so as to win prestige and influence. I demonstrated in chapter 5 that kings longed for the "good names" that they could acquire by performing their duties as hosts; this letter shows that gift giving was very much a part of the creation of a "good name." In this chapter about the material aspect of the relation between sovereigns of different status as well as that between envoys and their hosts, I have shown that the party of higher status often showered the one of lower status with more-valuable gifts, in order to reconfirm the imbalance of prestige and win in the competition of gifts.

## Conclusion

Diplomatic missions were laden with gifts. Before departure, envoys received "road goods" from friends, families, officials, monks, and other residents in their home state, and these gifts included both daily necessities and luxury items such as silk. When they departed, they carried with them the state gifts from the sovereign of their own state, typically consisting of high-value luxury items such as silk, jade, horses, slaves, and other types of exotica. While on the road, the envoys received gifts in the form of food, wine, clothes, paper, and horses from their host to support their stay and future trips. When they arrived at their final destination, they offered the state gifts to the head of the destination state and its high officials; in return, they received counter-gifts from the head of the state, partially intended to the sovereign of their home state and partially given to the envoys themselves. The busy engagement with gift exchange that we see in the 878 Dunhuang mission to Chang'an was typical for envoys of medieval Eastern Eurasia.

As Marshall Sahlins famously said: "If friends make gifts, gifts make friends."[74] Gifts were the medium through which relationships, be they between sovereigns or between envoys and their hosts, were formed. Unlike commercial exchanges, most of these gift exchanges were not "equal" in the material sense. The logic of gifting bends toward difference rather than equity. In this unbalanced relationship of gift exchange, the state of higher status reasserts its higher status, while the state of lower status receives material gains. In the 878 mission of Dunhuang envoys to Chang'an, for instance, the imbalance in the number of gifts exchanged reaffirmed the mutually recognized unequal relation between Dunhuang and the Tang. By spending wildly, like Mauss's "rich man," the Tang court acquired prestige and status vis-à-vis the state of Dunhuang. The governor of Lingzhou, a town on the western border of the Tang and on the road between Ganzhou and the Tang capital, once characterized the diplomatic relation between the Tang and the Uyghur kingdom of Ganzhou in this way: "The state [of the Tang] would acquire fame and luster, and the tribe [of the Uyghurs] would not be prevented from trading goods."[75] This phrase brilliantly captures the imbalance in diplomatic relations, and the primary goals of each party. Many such big and small imbalances, often results of gift exchanges, created the elevational differences like mountains and hills that kept the river of diplomatic travel constantly running on the Silk Road.

# 7

# Switching Languages

A JOKE CIRCULATED in the early 1110s at the Song court in Kaifeng. Wang Anzhong, a Hanlin academician, participated in the reception of a group of Khotanese (meaning Qarakhanid at this time) envoys. These envoys delivered a message from the king of Khotan to the Song emperor, which the court translators converted into Chinese. Wang found this translated message from the king of Khotan "abundantly funny," and shared it with other officials on duty. After Wang recited the message, "all [officials] present were greatly amused." Cai Tao, one of the participants in this banter, recorded the incident in his book of official anecdotes.[1] Chinese scholars and officials continued to find this message amusing, and included the episode in joke books centuries later.[2] According to the record of Cai Tao, the message from the Khotanese king read:

> The uncle Qarakhanid king [who rules] as the Tiaoguan [the meaning of this term, sometimes also written as Jiangguan, is unclear], lord of the five hundred kingdoms in the west, illuminated by the great brilliance of the sun that rises from the east, sends petition to the uncle great emperor [guanjia] [who rules] as the Tiaoguan lord of the four continents, illuminated by the great brilliance of the sun that rises from the east: about the jade that you asked for previously, I have devoted much effort; but it was difficult to find one of the size you asked. I have sent people to look for it. And if I do find one of the size you asked, I will send it along.[3]

Why was this message so funny to Wang Anzhong, Cai Tao, and their colleagues and continued to entertain generations of Chinese literati? I would venture that there are at least two main reasons. First, the audacity of the king of Khotan, a distant and insignificant Central Asian state, to rhetorically equate himself with the Song emperor naturally invited ridicule at the Song court. Second, and perhaps more important, is the tone that the message adopted: it addressed the

Song emperor as *guanjia*, which is a somewhat informal way of addressing the emperor and quite inappropriate for the king of Khotan to use.[4] Also, the content of the letter about the search for a piece of jade of the appropriate size is expressed in such a colloquial manner that it posed a drastic contrast in style to the tone of the titles of the two sovereigns. It is like a letter that addresses its recipient with Victorian formality and then narrates its content in the style of Twitter.

How did this funny letter come into being? Cai Tao, the first recorder of the letter, gives us an answer. At the meeting where Wang Anzhong related this letter, after the collective giggle, Cai remarked knowingly that "such a petition from the kingdom of Khotan has already been recorded in the Veritable Record of Emperor Shenzong [r. 1067–85]. That petition is similar to this one, only better in its literary style. I suspect it has been improved upon by the court historians."[5] After Cai's remark, which implies that the letter should have been funny only to those unaware of such established practice, his colleagues allegedly all fell into silence.

Cai's humorless pedantry aside, this story teaches us two lessons about the process of linguistic negotiation in diplomatic settings. First, the Khotanese envoys, who do not appear directly in the story, did not speak Chinese, but such lack of linguistic ability was no hinderance to effective, if rather crude, communication. Second, in diplomatic dealings, translation mattered not only between languages but also between different linguistic registers and styles of the same language.

As with many other matters, texts produced at the Song court address only the last stage of the complex processes of translation involved in a diplomatic journey, often with the foreign diplomat, as is in this case, silent. The Dunhuang documents, on the other hand, provide a richer and multilayered source base on the issue of translation and linguistic negotiation on the Silk Road. In this chapter, I will follow the steps of the envoys and examine the occasions where they needed to shift the language they used. What I have found is that, given the multicultural composition of most diplomatic missions, and with a few simple translingual tools, most monolingual or bilingual envoys could successfully navigate the dazzlingly complex linguistic landscape of medieval Eastern Eurasia. One did not need to be a polyglot to travel the Silk Road.

## The Search for a Lingua Franca

Eastern Eurasia in the ninth and tenth centuries was a world of many different languages. Prior to the mid-ninth century, three empires—the Tibetan Empire, the Uyghur Empire, and the Tang—dominated Eastern Eurasia.[6] The

administrative languages of these empires were Tibetan, Uyghur (a Turkic language) and possibly also Sogdian (a Middle Iranian language), and Classical
Chinese, respectively. Regional states like Khotan and Kucha used Khotanese
(another Middle Iranian language) and Tocharian (a unique eastern branch of
the Indo-European language family), while diaspora communities such as the
Sogdians also used their own language. With the decline and fall of the three
empires in the mid-ninth century, the linguistic landscape began to shift. Uyghur,
long the language of the steppe, migrated to smaller kingdoms such as Turfan and
Ganzhou as remnants of the old Uyghur khanate established regional states there.
The administrative language in the Dunhuang government, which claimed itself
a vassal of the Tang and other North China regimes, remained Classical Chinese
in the ninth and tenth centuries, as in the Tang, the Five Dynasties, and the Song.
The Kitan state of the Liao used both Chinese and Kitan. The kingdom of Khotan
continued using Khotanese as its administrative language. Other kingdoms and
tribes in the region, such as the Wenmo and the Mthong-khyab, may have been
remnants of the Tibetan empire and used Tibetan.

The distinctness seen in the administrative languages of various states—
Chinese in the Tang, the Song, and Dunhuang; Uyghur in Ganzhou and Turfan;
Khotanese in Khotan; and so on—masks a greater level of linguistic diversity
among the populace of any state. Such diversity is revealed by excavated documents in Khotan, Turfan, and Dunhuang. From archaeological discoveries in
Khotan, for instance, we know that, although Khotanese remained the administrative language, certain social and governmental documents were written
also in Chinese and Tibetan.[7] Because Dunhuang was under Tibetan rule for
more than half a century,[8] Tibetan was widely used in Dunhuang society. But
documents in the library cave also show the presence in Dunhuang of communities speaking Khotanese, Sogdian, and Uyghur.[9] Discoveries at various
sites in Turfan from the fourth to the fourteenth century represent as many as
twenty-two different languages and almost as many scripts that were used in
the Turfan government, private business transactions, Nestorian churches,
and Manichaean monasteries, among other social settings.[10] No comparable
archaeological discoveries exist for states further to the east, from Ganzhou to
the Tang, the Song, and the Liao, but there is no reason to underestimate the
linguistic diversity in these states.

Both the official administrative language and the languages spoken by regular residents were important to our travelers. As envoys, they were required to
deal with the apparatus of the states they encountered on the road, and thus
had to in some way communicate with state officials. But in their long journeys
from one state to the next, they unavoidably also entered a much broader

social world. As discussed in chapter 5, envoys had to both travel with escorts and guides and meet and consult with officials and sovereigns. How did they navigate such a diverse linguistic landscape?

Most existing research suggests that travelers on the Silk Road dealt with the issue of linguistic transition by using a lingua franca. James Millward, for instance, offers this synthesis about the Silk Road in medieval times (sixth to tenth centuries):

> By the middle of the first millennium, the most active silk-road integrators were speakers of Iranian languages; merchants under the Sasanids dominated sea trade not only around the Persian Gulf, but also in the Arabian Sea, along eastern Africa, coastal India and Sri Lanka, and as far as Malaysia and southern China. Persian merchants inhabited designated neighborhoods in Guangzhou (Canton)—then, as now, an export city. Sogdian merchants fanned out overland to Armenia, throughout Central Asia, across north China, and even as far as Manchuria and Korea. Thanks to the prominence of these groups, Persian would become the lingua franca of silk-road commerce and communication, especially along more southward-lying routes, and would remain so even after the Arab conquests of Persia and Central Asia.[11]

A quibble with this characterization is that Sogdian and Persian were, though both Iranian languages, never mutually intelligible. Thus, it does not make sense to say that Persian was the lingua franca in a world connected by Sogdian traders. But Millward's effort to look for a common tongue in which travelers supposedly communicated is representative of how scholars think about linguistic negotiations on the Silk Road. A plethora of languages, including Chinese, Sogdian, Tibetan, and even Cuman, have been identified by scholars as the lingua franca of the Silk Road at different times and places.[12]

For the region and time period covered by this book, two languages have been proposed as the lingua franca. Étienne de la Vaissière argues for Sogdian:

> A little while afterward [after the end of Tibetan rule in Central Asia], the over-representation of persons of Sogdian origin in ambassadorial circles is certain. About 874/879, a mission was sent to China, and while the two titular ambassadors indeed bore Chinese names, we find four Sogdians among the managerial officers. At Khotan as at Turfan we also find traces of ambassadors from Sogdian families or using Sogdian as a lingua franca.[13]

In a footnote, La Vaissière makes clear that the mission to China that he refers to is the 878 mission of Dunhuang envoys to Chang'an that I will discuss in detail in chapter 8, and that the example cited for "Sogdian as a lingua franca" in Khotan is the case of Zhang Jinshan, the Sino-Khotanese envoy who signed his name in Sogdian letters. But the problem with the argument for Sogdian as the lingua franca in ninth- and tenth-century Dunhuang is that in neither of these cases can we be sure that anyone actually *spoke* Sogdian. The four envoys who bore Sogdian surnames in the 878 mission may have been descendants of Sogdian immigrants, but it is by no means clear that they were still using Sogdian at this time. In fact, all evidence seems to point to these people of Sogdian descent being thoroughly integrated into Dunhuang society by this time.[14] Similarly, there is also no evidence that the envoy Zhang Jinshan had any actual capability to use Sogdian beyond a simple signature.

A more plausible case is made for Tibetan. The Tibetan-language materials preserved in Dunhuang, including secular documents, were initially assumed to have been produced when Dunhuang was under the Tibetan rule. In 1981, however, the Hungarian Tibetologist Uray Géza published a study of a group Tibetan letters that he argued should be dated to the Guiyijun period after the end of the Tibetan rule in Dunhuang.[15] This suggestion has been further substantiated by both Uray and Takeuchi Tsuguhito.[16] The evidence they have presented is indisputable, and the view that Tibetan was the lingua franca in Dunhuang and the surrounding regions is now widely accepted.[17] In particular, these Tibetan letters are relevant to my purpose here because many of them are diplomatic letters between states such as Dunhuang, Ganzhou, and Khotan. In another article, Takeuchi calls Tibetan in this period (ninth to tenth centuries) "an international *lingua franca.*"[18] Does this mean that the travelers I discuss in this book, regardless of their cultural backgrounds, all (or mostly) had knowledge of Tibetan? Was knowing Tibetan (or being multilingual in general) a prerequisite for working as an envoy?

To answer these questions, I will examine the activities of envoys on the road, focusing on times when they needed to switch the language they used. This examination begins with an assessment, to the extent that our evidence allows, of the languages our envoys spoke.

## Were Envoys Multilingual?

Among the envoys that I have introduced in earlier chapters, some were clearly bilingual or multilingual: Zhang Jinshan wrote in both Khotanese and Chinese.[19] Hun Ziying was said to have been able to speak a "barbarian language" in addition to Chinese.[20] Zhang Yichao, the founder of the independent polity of Dunhuang, might also have been able to read and write Tibetan.[21] A story recorded in the *Songshi* tells of an enterprising border official named Zheng Wenbao (953–1013), who traveled across Song's northeastern border twelve times into Lingwu in order to learn the language of the region, likely Tangut.[22] But other than these individual cases, there is little evidence that many, much less most, of the travelers I describe in this book were true polyglots in the way that An Lushan or Marco Polo might have been.[23] The extensive participation of the Dunhuang population in diplomatic travel, discussed in chapter 2, also indicates that there was likely not a multilingual requirement for traveling as an envoy. Indeed, the language of the elegy of Hun Ziying, which praised Hun's exceptional ability as an interpreter,[24] seems to suggest that most envoys were not fluently multilingual as he was.

Indeed, there is an interesting record about the *lack* of linguistic ability. In a letter back to the Khotanese court, a Khotanese envoy described the condition of the envoys in Dunhuang. Some of them were in economic trouble; others had even been imprisoned.[25] But at the very end of the letter, the writer includes a line that reads: "Hvai Lā-ttai, the Chinese, knows Chinese fully, but he does not know Khotanese."[26] The identity of this Hvai Lā-ttai is unclear. But judging from the context, he likely was part of the diplomatic mission that included Ana Saṃgaa, the writer of the letter. His lack of Khotanese language skills thus would have stood out, and become a topic worth commenting upon. This short comment shows that, while one might assume that everyone in a diplomatic mission from the Khotanese government would have been able to speak Khotanese, it was not necessarily the case. But Hvai could have functioned in this mission because there must have been other members who knew both Chinese and Khotanese. Like the members of the mission with Chinese names recorded in the Staël-Holstein manuscript, Hvai must have also performed tasks that made him valuable to the mission, despite his lack of linguistic competence.

As the extensive diplomatic network described in previous chapters shows, such limited linguistic abilities did not prevent envoys from functioning properly as intermediaries between states that used different languages. To understand how they did it, it is necessary to first identity the *subject* of the linguistic negotiations. As I showed in chapter 2, under normal conditions, diplomatic travelers banded into groups on their journeys. These diplomatic missions ranged from a dozen to over a hundred members. We do not often have information about the constituents of the missions, but whenever we do, it almost invariably shows the members of the mission as coming from different cultural backgrounds. The mission from Khotan to Dunhuang recorded in the

Staël-Holstein manuscript, for instance, consisted of people with Chinese, Khotanese, and Tibetan names.[27] A 1004 mission from Ganzhou to the Song court was headed by a monk, an envoy with a Chinese name, and an envoy with a non-Chinese, likely transcribed Uyghur name.[28] In these cases, the diplomatic mission as a whole might be bilingual or trilingual, even if most of its members were monolingual. In some other diplomatic missions, certain people were designated as interpreters. For instance, a 1012 mission dispatched by the Song government to Ganzhou was headed by a certain Yang Zhijin and an interpreter (presumably between Chinese and Uyghur) named Guo Min.[29] After the arrival of the Yang mission in Ganzhou, the road back to the Song border was blocked by a warlord in Liangzhou. The Ganzhou khan, knowing the danger, refused to let the head envoy return to the Song and sent back only Guo Min the interpreter. Guo was able to convey the message of the khan to the Song, no doubt thanks to his linguistic ability.[30] In a diplomatic mission like this, it was not necessary for every individual to be multilingual to fully participate, as long as there were multilingual members included.

A particularly well-documented case of a diplomatic mission that was likely multilingual was led by the Khotanese envoy Liu Zaisheng. According to the *New History of the Five Dynasties*, the Khotanese king "dispatched *dudu* Liu Zaisheng to offer one thousand *jin* of jade, as well as a jade seal, demon-suppressing *vajra*, and other things."[31] Liu led this group from Khotan, arrived at Kaifeng in early 943, and left a few months later.[32] Fortunately for us, Liu also left many traces in the Dunhuang documents. He signed his name, at the end of a Sanskrit dharani, in Chinese as "Sikong Liu Zaisheng, the tribute-bearing envoy of the Great Jeweled kingdom of Khotan."[33] In a shortened Khotanese version of the Lotus Sutra, Liu is twice mentioned as the donor.[34] In this way, Liu was similar to Zhang Jinshan in that both were envoys from the Khotanese kingdom bearing a Chinese name.

The most revealing document about Liu Zaisheng for our purpose here, however, is written in Tibetan.[35] This document (figure 7.1) was written on the back of a Tibetan multiplication formula. Its beginning reads: "On the sixteenth day of the first month of the fall of the pig year, at the time of departure of the Khotanese envoy Liu Sikong and Zho gam and others, the envoys are promised to be dispatched to Khotan without danger." Then the note lists nine names of additional envoys. The first one had the Turkish title of *ügä*, the second through the fifth all had the Sino-Turkish title of *dudu* (*totog*, meaning "general"), while the remaining four had no title. The title given to Liu makes it likely that this envoy was indeed the same person as Liu

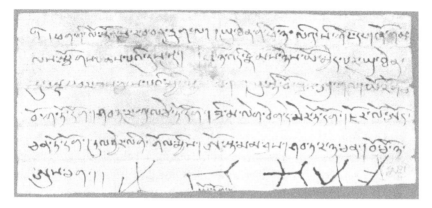

FIGURE 7.1 A Tibetan note (travel permit?) from Liu Zaisheng's diplomatic mission.
*Credit*: Bibliothèque nationale de France.

Zaisheng, who had the title *sikong* in his Chinese signature.[36] The note is dated to a pig year, likely 951.[37] Therefore, it was written for another mission that Liu undertook after the journey to China in 943. The specific language used—"the envoys are promised to be dispatched to Khotan without danger [pho nya 'di rnams nyes o myed par yu-then du brdzang par khas blangs pa]"— suggests that this note functioned as a kind of travel permit. Given that there were Tibetan tribes living south of Dunhuang and between Dunhuang and Khotan, this might be a note from the lord of Dunhuang to the Tibetan-speaking peoples on the way to Khotan. As I mentioned in chapter 5, in a Chinese letter, the lord of Dunhuang asked a "foreign leader" to "follow the custom and offer manpower for security and assistance" to his envoys to make sure "nothing is delayed or mishandled."[38] This note might have accompanied such a message. Indeed, the fact that the note has been folded (see figure 7.1 for the fold lines) much like a letter suggests that it likely traveled with the envoys; the broken writing, or signs, on the lower edge may have been part of a certification mechanism in which the other half of the document was preserved somewhere else.[39] For now it is difficult to reconstruct the meaning of the names transcribed in Tibetan. But it is nonetheless evident that this small diplomatic mission, like the one recorded on the Staël-Holstein manuscript, was multicultural, with Chinese, Khotanese, Tibetan, and likely Uyghur members. We do not know how many of these members were multilingual, but, collectively, they were capable of communicating in all the major languages spoken in the region.

Another reason that most envoys did not need to be multilingual is that they were probably not allowed to speak in any official capacity for most of their time on the road. P. 4044 preserves a rare text that was an instruction from the lord of Dunhuang (in this case, likely Zhang Chengfeng) to envoys traveling to Ganzhou:

> When you serve as an envoy to Ganzhou, you need to cultivate friendship and harmony. When passing through forts, garrisons, prefectures, and cities, in each you should maintain their rituals and rules. Follow the verbal instruction of only the head of the mission, and do not wildly discuss rights and wrongs. Along the road on the way back, you should follow this same rule, and restrict yourself to performing your own duty. If you are stubborn in the east and unruly in the west, and engage in unfounded and wild conversations, the head of the mission will take note of your name, and you will be severely punished when you come back to [our] prefecture.[40]

Indeed, communicating liberally with officials of other states was considered inappropriate and, sometimes, criminal. In a murder case discussed in chapter 5, An Qianxiang, an envoy from Ganzhou, was killed by Uyghurs while traveling back from China with Uyghur envoys. In this murder, a young clerk named Zhang Yuanjin had become "close friends with the deputy head of the Uyghur mission, and discussed the situation [with the Uyghur envoy] and was made aware of the incident." In a letter written by the lord of Guazhou, a neighbor of Dunhuang and Ganzhou, Zhang's action was explained as his "not having any experience of difficult travel and therefore [being] unfamiliar with the rituals [li] of the state."[41] These rituals that the young clerk failed to follow are likely similar to the instructions the lord of Dunhuang gave to his envoys to Ganzhou: one was not supposed to privately communicate with officials of other states without the authorization of the head envoy. In a similar spirit, a much later Song edict stipulates that the escorts dispatched to accompany foreign envoys should be "over sixty years old, illiterate, with proper conduct and no criminal records."[42] Illiteracy, like prescribed silence, helped ensure ritual propriety in diplomatic matters. Under this custom, monolingual travelers would not only fit right in, they might even be more desirable for certain roles than their multilingual counterparts.

Thus, while many, perhaps most, envoys might very well have been monolingual, a typical diplomatic mission was in all likelihood bilingual or multilingual because of the multicultural makeup of its personnel. These diplomatic missions, when on the road, marshalled the abilities of their members and relied on help from the host state to engage in linguistic negotiations, both in written and in oral form. The next two sections explore these two forms respectively.

## Written Mediation

One of the major tasks of a diplomatic mission was the transmission of information, for which purpose envoys carried both official and private letters. The most important written texts are, as I discussed in chapter 3, the edicts and state letters that envoys delivered from their own state to the sovereign and officials of the destination state. What language would a letter be written in between two states with different administrative languages? What was the role of envoys in this translingual activity? From both Tang-Song sources and Dunhuang materials, we know that states large and small at the time all had translators to deal with letters in foreign languages. In the Tang, for instance, the Central Secretariat (Zhongshu Sheng) employed ten translators.[43] The Song had the Office for the Exchange of State Letters (Zhuguan Wanglai Guoxin Suo), where twenty translators were on staff.[44]

Because in Dunhuang there was no descriptive summary of the bureaucratic system like the *Tang liudian* (for the Tang) or the *Song huiyao* (for the Song), the situation in Dunhuang is not explicitly recorded. But from the activities of the Dunhuang government, we can observe the presence of similar translators. In a wine-expenditure account from the Dunhuang government, we find references to clerks (*kongmu*) in charge of "the writing of Xizhou" (Xizhou *wenzi*), Ganzhou, and Khotan. These clerks were in charge of translating between Chinese and Uyghur as well as Khotanese. The specific places we find them in the account are also informative. On the sixteenth day of the sixth month, the account shows, one *weng* (= 6 *dou*) of wine was offered to welcome "envoys of Ganzhuo." The next day, one *jiao* (= 0.25 *weng*, or 1.5 *dou*) of wine was offered to a clerk "in charge of the writing of Ganzhou."[45] The incoming Ganzhou envoys must have brought with them Uyghur letters that the clerk had to process. The relatively meagre offering to the clerk indicates that the amount of text processed must have been quite limited.

In contrast, another series of records about Khotanese envoys reveals a greater amount of translation work involved. According to the account, the Dunhuang government provided wine for a certain Gelu from Khotan from 1.24 to 6.5, for 129 days, and a "Minister Luo" from Khotan from 3.19 to 6.5, for 75 days. These two groups of Khotanese envoys must have left Dunhuang together on the fifth day of the sixth month. Indeed, two days earlier, the

Khotanese prince, the representative of the Khotanese government in Dunhuang, held what must have amounted to a farewell banquet for these Khotanese envoys, with delicacies such as "fermented sheepskin wine."[46] Following these records, we find that from 5.28 to 6.5, the day that the Khotanese envoys left, a "clerk in charge of Khotanese writing" was given wine by the government for seven days. The timing of these offerings leaves little doubt that the clerk was tasked with processing Khotanese documents prior to the departure of the Khotanese envoys.[47] The fact that it took seven days attests to the amount of text that must have been handled before the departure of the Khotanese envoys. The account also includes a clerk in charge of "Xizhou [Turfan] writing," which seems to suggest that the Uyghur kingdom in Turfan had different writing practices than those of Ganzhou. In any case, this account shows not only that the Dunhuang government employed specialists to process texts in Khotanese and Uyghur, but also that these specialists were busiest at the arrival and departure of envoys from those states.

What kinds of texts were processed by these translators? Chinese court sources point to the central importance of non-Chinese official letters and edicts, but none of the letters were preserved or even transcribed. In some rare cases, like the letter from the king of Khotan cited at the beginning of the chapter, translations of these letters are extant.[48] The Dunhuang library cave, on the other hand, contains many official letters exchanged between heads of states (including Dunhuang, Ganzhou, Turfan, Khotan, and the Song) and delivered by envoys.[49] A thorough examination of all these letters from the different states is not possible here, because of both the number of letters and the multitude of bilateral relations involved. Here, I shall isolate one set of such relations and examine the letters sent out in one direction, in order to cut through possible confusion. The case I pick is the communications from the king of Khotan to the lord of Dunhuang, a particularly well-documented bilateral relation between two states with different administrative languages.

In what language did the Khotanese king write to the lord of Dunhuang? To answer this question, we first need to distinguish two types of letters. The first type includes letters that carry official seals, which are written in a way that is much more enlarged and spaced out than everyday letters. This intentionally wasteful way of writing exhibits the material richness of the court that issued the letters.[50] Letters with these formal features can be considered "original" edicts. Five such edicts from the king of Khotan to the lord of Dunhuang are preserved. The second type of letter lacks the seal and the conspicuousness of the official edict, and these should therefore usually be considered drafts. The life trajectories

FIGURE 7.2 The end of a Khotanese royal edict (Pelliot
chinois 5538). A smaller character *chi* (勅) can be seen to
the upper left of the large *chi*.
*Credit*: Bibliothèque nationale de France.

of these letters are instructive in our understanding of the process of transmission and translation of non-Chinese letters to the state of Dunhuang.

The five edicts in the first group are Pelliot chinois 5538, Pelliot tibétain 44, Pelliot chinois 4091, Pelliot chinois 2826, and 羽 686. P. 5538 is the edict from the king of Khotan Viśa' Śūra to the lord of Dunhuang Cao Yuanzhong where the king boasts about the acquisition of the elephant mentioned in chapter 3. The best-known feature of this letter, the Chinese letter *chi* (meaning "imperial edict") that occupied an entire piece of paper, conveys the higher, even imperial, status of the king of Khotan over the lord of Dunhuang (figure 7.2). After the edict had served its diplomatic function, it remained in Dunhuang, possibly

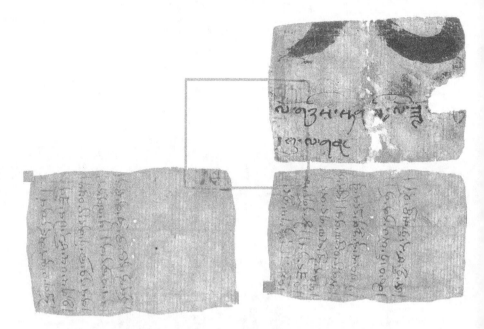

FIGURE 7.3 Reconstruction of a royal edict from Khotan written in Tibetan. The square indicates a reconstruction by Takeuchi Tsuguhito of the shape of the official seal.
*Credit*: Bibliothèque nationale de France. Photo author's own.

with the Khotanese residents there, and a practice draft of an envoy report as well as a Sanskrit-Khotanese bilingual phrasebook were later copied onto the back of the edict.[51] Eventually, this piece of paper was donated to a monastery in Dunhuang, likely intended to be used for restoring Buddhist texts because of its high-quality paper.

Pelliot tibétain 44 is a small codex in Tibetan about Padmasambhava, the Buddhist mystic who allegedly introduced Tantric Buddhism to Tibet.[52] But its cover used to be the lower part of an edict, with the lower edge of the outsized character *chi* (edict) still extant (on the upper right fragment in figure 7.3). Two additional folios from this codex also belonged to the same edict, and their original relation to the cover can be reconstructed because traces of a seal (the outline of which is drawn in figure 7.3) are still visible on all three fragments.[53] The papers used for the other parts of this codex, however, are unrelated. Therefore, parts of this edict were reused to make the Tibetan Buddhist codex, evidently also because the high-quality paper on which the royal edict was written.

FIGURE 7.4 A fragment of a Khotanese royal edict
(Pelliot chinois 4091), with parts having been cut away.
*Credit*: Bibliothèque nationale de France.

In the case of P. 4091 (figure 7.4), another Khotanese royal letter, we can
see the process of reuse after donation with much greater precision. It is a
fragmentary piece that resembles P. 5538 in its formal features. Only the left
half of the document is still extant, while the right half was unevenly cut off
and not preserved. When backlit (figure 7.5), however, it becomes immediately clear that the uneven cut was not randomly made. Rather, the missing
paper was likely cut off to make paper flowers.[54] When we compare the shape
of P. 4091 and actual paper flowers (figure 7.6) preserved in the Dunhuang
library cave, we can see that the lower right corner was cut off to make petals,
while the square shape cut out above became the background.[55] The connection

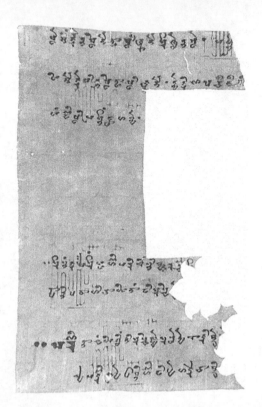

FIGURE 7.5 P. 4091 backlit. It seems likely to me that the missing parts were removed to make paper flowers (see figure 7.6). The missing square in the middle of the right-hand side was cut to make the support, and the lower parts were turned into petals.

*Credit*: Bibliothèque nationale de France.

FIGURE 7.6 A paper flower from Dunhuang.
*Credit*: The British Library.

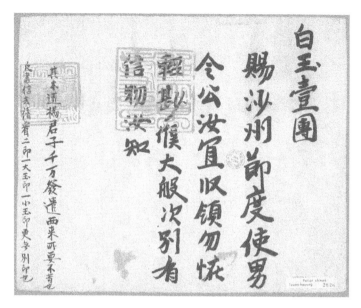

FIGURE 7.7 A message from the king of Khotan to the lord of Dunhuang.
*Credit*: Bibliothèque nationale de France.

between this Khotanese edict and paper flowers is further corroborated by a Dunhuang document that talks about a Khotanese princess donating "government-crafted flowers and trees," "new flowers and trees," and "cloth trees."[56] The language of this document, which uses the word *zao* (造; "to craft, to produce"), makes clear that the flowers and trees were not natural flora but likely made of other materials such as paper and cloth. One can imagine a scenario in which this Khotanese edict, after it was no longer current, was cut up to make paper flowers to be used in a Buddhist ritual setting. The leftover part of the edict was then donated to a Buddhist monastery, perhaps because it was still sizeable enough to be used in other ways.

P. 2826 is a short message in Chinese about the delivery of a piece of white jade sent by the Khotanese king to the lord of Dunhuang as a gift (figure 7.7). At the end of the letter, in a small hand, the king made a request for a carpenter and noted which seals Khotanese official letters used. The back of this letter is unused, suggesting that it entered the library of the Sanjie Monastery as paper to be preserved for future use. The king's note about the seals reads: "Whenever a letter arrives, please check two seals: one large jade seal and one small jade seal. There are no other seals."[57] Indeed, on the letter, we can clearly see

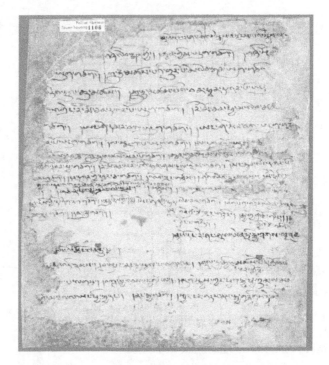

FIGURE 7.8 A draft letter from the king of Khotan to the lord of Dunhuang in Tibetan.
*Credit*: Bibliothèque nationale de France.

that two seals, one large and one small, have been applied. Therefore, the note also served as a way of authenticating future letters from the king.

羽 686, now preserved in Kyōu Shooku in Osaka, Japan, is another short note, similarly to P. 2826 about the delivery of gifts. The gifts sent included lumps of jade, jade horse gears, three horses, and 16.5 *jin* of steel. As with P. 2826, two seals, one large (twice) and one small, have been applied to the letter. The larger seal, which reads "Newly cast seal made upon imperial order [*shuzhao xinzhu zhiyin* 書詔新鑄之印]," is the same as that seen on P. 5538. The care with which the seals were used in these five edicts suggests that they should be considered original letters from the king of Khotan.[58]

The sole letter in the second group that I can find from the king of Khotan to Dunhuang looks quite different. This letter (Pelliot tibétain 1106; figure 7.8), in Tibetan, is also about the delivery of gifts and contains a large number of undeciphered names of goods.[59] The first line of the letter reads "To *teŋri* Shangshu, the younger brother, the return gifts of the gifts dispatched [earlier]." In contrast to the imperial edicts, this letter is written densely, and no seal has been applied (the round seal visible on the letter is modern).

Collectively, what do these letters tell us about how the kings of Khotan communicated with the kings of Dunhuang? From this small sample, it seems that we can draw a few preliminary conclusions. The main diplomatic message, which was often lengthy and contained complicated discussion of political and military matters, was written and sent in Khotanese. P. 5538, which runs to eighty-one lines, fits this description. P. 4091, although only partially preserved, is of the same nature as P. 5538. The most curious case is Pelliot tibétain 44, which formally resembles these two Khotanese letters, but is written in Tibetan. As Takeuchi has perceptively noticed, the dating formula in this letter does not fit the typical Tibetan way of dating.[60] Thus it might have been a translation (or, to use Takeuchi's term, "calque") from Khotanese. The two edicts in Chinese, on the other hand, are both short lists of gifts. Since the Khotanese kings were likely multilingual,[61] it is not out of the question that they produced messages such as P. 2826 themselves. Finally, Pelliot tibétain 1106 is similarly a list of gifts, but written in Tibetan. Because it lacks the formal features of an imperial edict, it might have been a translation, most likely from Khotanese, produced either in Khotan or in Dunhuang.

These edicts and gift lists do not constitute the entirety of the Khotanese government's communications with the lord of Dunhuang. Another important category of materials was produced by envoys from Khotan and delivered to the lord of Dunhuang. As envoys first arrived at Dunhuang, they would have delivered, during the "audience with the sovereign" stage of the envoy-host interaction, letters from the Khotanese king such as the ones discussed above. But as the envoys entered into the "residency" stage, they also continued to produce documents and convey messages to both the sovereign of their own state and their host.[62] Even though there are many (around twenty) Khotanese letters written by Khotanese envoys in Dunhuang,[63] they were all meant for the king of Khotan or the government of Khotan. The letters written by Khotanese envoys to the lord of Dunhuang include the Tibetan messages found in the Staël-Holstein manuscript and the Chinese letter from Reverend Long.[64] The Tibetan message was a request to the lord of Dunhuang for the envoys to go back to Khotan, whereas the Chinese letter was a direct plea for clothing. Therefore, when Khotanese envoys had to communicate with the lord of Dunhuang while they were under his jurisdiction, they sometimes wrote in Tibetan (for longer messages) and sometimes in Chinese (for shorter requests). The distinction here is similar to that of the official edicts: when only a brief message was needed, the Khotanese produced the letter in Chinese, presumably for the convenience of the lord of Dunhuang. But when they needed to send a longer message to Dunhuang, they usually did not use Chinese, but wrote in (or translated into) Tibetan instead.

Here, I have examined one kind of diplomatic relationship (between Khotan and Dunhuang), and focused on one direction (from Khotan to Dunhuang) of communication. As I have described in previous chapters, in medieval Eastern Eurasia there was a complex network of diplomatic relations involving many states with many different administrative languages. Examining these interactions in full would require its own monograph. This brief consideration of the topic, however, does hint at a general practice. Longer edicts were composed in the administrative language of the sender (Khotanese); shorter notes were composed in the administrative language of the receiver (Chinese). It is important to point out, however, that both types of letter, because of their formal features of calligraphy and seals, were likely produced in Khotan and by the office of the king of Khotan. Tibetan then served as an intermediary language. The translation of edicts and gift lists into Tibetan would conceivably have facilitated understanding of the messages by their receivers in Dunhuang, given the widespread Tibetan literacy there.[65] Judging from the formal features of these two Tibetan letters, one might assume that the edict was translated by the Khotanese government (therefore preserving the royal "*chi*" and the seals), while the gift list was translated either by the envoys themselves or by the Dunhuang government. The same pattern of writing shorter messages in the language of the receiver (Chinese) and longer messages in the intermediate language (Tibetan) seems to exist in the letters composed by envoys, too. In these cases, envoys were not just delivering messages; they had to have the linguistic ability to compose messages themselves.

This scenario of translingual practice between two states will need to be tested further with other materials produced by the various states, each with its own set of languages. But one result of this complex web of translation processes is clear from our sources: the proliferation of loanwords in official documents. In particular, words were borrowed from Chinese, Tibetan, and Uyghur, the administrative languages of the three empires of previous centuries, when established practices of governance and diplomacy had exerted a significant impact on how things were talked about in regional languages such as Khotanese and Sogdian. In the diplomatic setting, for the word "gift," we see a Sogdian loanword from Uyghur and a Khotanese loanword from Tibetan, as discussed in the previous chapter. In Khotanese, many ninth- and tenth-century official titles were borrowed from Chinese, to the extent that they seem to have been considered even more prestigious than local Khotanese official titles.[66] Sogdian similarly has loanwords such as the title *dudu* from Chinese.[67] In a Sogdian letter from a Ganzhou official to a Christian churchman, the official informs the churchman of recent diplomatic developments in Ganzhou, particularly the achievement of a peace treaty. The letter contains two key loanwords, *tnk* (< Ch. *Ding* 定), meaning "to conclude [an agreement]," and *cwn ywzy* (< Ch. *Chuan yuzhi* \*傳御旨), meaning "the bearer of an edict."[68] These loanwords show how deeply Uyghur (and also Sogdian) diplomatic practices were impacted by those of the Tang dynasty.

The most surprising loanword, however, is one that was borrowed *into* Chinese. In a Chinese letter written by the lord of Guazhou to the lord of Dunhuang about the Uyghur envoy An Qianxiang's murder, discussed in some detail in chapter 5, he referred to the young Dunhuang envoy as the *chaoding* (朝定) of a Uyghur envoy.[69] As Yang Baoyu and Wu Liyu pointed out, this term, meaning "friend," was borrowed from Kitan. According to one Song source, the Liao emperor Abaoji, upon learning of the death of the Later Tang emperor Li Cunxu, cried out, "My *chaoding* is dead!"[70] In a note that follows this line, the author indicates that "what the barbarians mean by *chaoding*, in Chinese we call 'friend.'" Both references appear in diplomatic, transregional settings, denoting the relation between the Kitan emperor and the Late Tang emperor in one case, and that between a Dunhuang envoy and a Uyghur envoy in another. It is thus possible that this term, still unidentified in the original Kitan, might have meant a "friend" in the diplomatic sense. But regardless of whether we can confirm this nuance in its meaning, the fact that the Kitan word appeared in a Dunhuang document attests to the profound connection between Kitan and the Hexi region in the diplomatic realm.

The information revealed in edicts and letters allows one to assess the linguistic ability needed to be an effective envoy. First, envoys did not need to be multilingual themselves to be effective deliverers of these multilingual state letters. Some of the letters were produced by multilingual sovereigns themselves. Others, to the extent that they were translated, were translated either at the court of the home state or upon arrival at the destination state. At both locations, this translation was carried out by linguistic experts, such as the "clerk in charge of the Ganzhou [Uyghur] language." The visual features of these letters, the large character *chi*, for instance, make their status apparent to readers, including the envoys who delivered them, regardless of whether the reader understood the language. Indeed, even the illiterate could not have missed the significance of these letters.

On the other hand, envoys also had written communications with their various host states. On these occasions, they really needed to have a level of mastery of the administrative language of the host state, or at least a mutually recognized intermediate language. But even then, it was the linguistic ability of the *entire diplomatic mission* rather than of any individual envoy that mattered. As long as there were members of the mission who were capable of producing documents in the language needed, communication would not be hindered. Thus, most envoys likely did not need to be literate in multiple languages.

The letters I have discussed in this section were either delivered or composed by envoys. But such written messages constituted only a part of the translingual activities. At various points in their lives on the road, they also needed to communicate orally. The next section turns to this more elusive aspect of how envoys navigated the linguistic complexities of the Silk Road.

## Oral Mediation

Oral communications were often intimately intertwined with written ones. We can begin to understand their relation from a letter, written in Chinese in 931, by the lord of Dunhuang Cao Yijin to Shunhua Khan of Ganzhou.[71] After a standard greeting, Cao explained that the letter was composed to express his gratitude for the khan's assistance with the passage of the heavenly envoys of the Later Tang in the previous year.[72] This main message included a retrospective account of a few recent diplomatic encounters between the two states, and was followed, as was customary, by a list of the gifts that accompanied the letter. As such, Cao's message is a typical diplomatic letter between two sovereigns.[73]

Uniquely, however, this written letter refers to three occasions of oral communication. These are the relevant passages from the letter:

> Last year, the older brother, the great king [meaning Cao Yijin himself] visited Ganzhou personally and discussed matters of state that were of lasting consequence with the younger brother, the Son of Heaven [meaning the Uyghur khan] in person.

> In the fifth month of last year, the heavenly envoys and Shazhou [Dunhuang] envoys arrived at Ganzhou safely. The younger brother the Son of Heaven dispatched General Dinglüci to Shazhou to report this private message. Careless people [the general?] had a few words [with me?].

> I have additional messages that will be delivered in detail orally by General Jia.

The first occasion was when Cao had visited Shunhua the previous year in person and discussed matters of state, including the maintenance of the open road between Dunhuang and Ganzhou. This rare case of an in-person meeting of two heads of state reveals that they were able to communicate directly with each other, either because one or both of them were bilingual, or because they used an interpreter. The context of the second occasion is unclear: the Ganzhou envoy visited Dunhuang to report the arrival of envoys from the Later Tang and the returning envoys of Dunhuang. But the letter does not specify exactly who the "careless person" was, even though Cao implies that the words of this person were unsavory. Nonetheless, they did not seem to have negatively affected the relation between the two states. It is possible that Cao was here simply acknowledging that he had received the verbal message from the khan without specifying what the message was. In contrast, the third occasion of oral communication is plainly laid out in the letter: General Jia, likely the head envoy to Ganzhou tasked with the deliverance of the official letter, would also convey personal messages to the khan orally. In this case, again, Jia and the khan may have been bilingual, or he could have been speaking through an interpreter. In fact, in an expenditure account, we know of a "General Jia" who went on a diplomatic mission to the east in the same year. The title in these two names, "general" (*dutou*), suggests that they may be the same person. If this is the case, then he seems to have been a frequent diplomatic traveler routinely tasked with journeys to Ganzhou.[74] Even though the exact oral messages in all three cases are unspecified in the letter, the references to these meetings show that official letters were never meant to communicate the entirety of the message sent by a sovereign: verbal messages were vital parts of the communication as well.

If the delivery of official letters required little linguistic ability from envoys, the oral aspect of the task was a different matter. As discussed in chapter 5, "reconnaissance," "road protection," and "audience with the sovereign" were all important steps in the "program" of envoys' interactions with their hosts. In each of these steps, envoys had to deal with real human beings from the host state, who likely spoke a different language. The messenger at the reconnaissance stage must have been able to communicate precisely when and where the main mission would be expected to arrive; the envoys at the road protection stage had to inform their escorts of their daily needs; the head envoy, as the one who led the mission, at the audience with the sovereign had to manage to converse with the king or lord in front of him. How did diplomatic travelers like General Jia accomplish these goals?

One possibility is that the diplomatic mission included people who had mastered the language of the host state. The Song interpreter Guo Min and the Dunhuang interpreter Hun Ziying discussed above were able to excel at their jobs precisely because of their linguistic abilities. The elegy of Hun Ziying, in claiming that "His tongue is refined and his lips are sweet," highlights his capability in oral interpretation.

Another possibility is that the host state would have staff at hand to assist the envoys. From Song dynasty sources, for instance, we know that interpreters were part of the entourage that welcomed incoming envoys, and the Song government arranged for the interpreters to "copy letters, listen, and be attentive to the conversations" at the postal station.[75] Because of their intermediate role in diplomatic matters, these official interpreters sometimes amassed considerable influence. A story from around the mid-eleventh century reveals one Song official's view on interstate interpreters.[76] A group of Khotanese envoys were said to have been behaving badly in Qinzhou at the Song border, "damaging goods at postal stations." The governor of the region, after learning about the unruly behavior, observed that "envoys do not misbehave of their own accord; it usually is the interpreters who taught them [to act as such]." This observation, he noted, was based on his earlier experience managing Kitan envoys. Therefore, instead of directly admonishing the Khotanese envoys, he offered stern warnings to the interpreters: "for those entering my domain, if there is even a minor unlawful act, I will behead you." As a result, during the entire interaction between the Khotanese envoys and the governor, "none [of the Khotanese envoys] would dare even speak loudly." In this case, the power of the interpreters, who were likely provided by the Song government, was painfully recognized by their contemporaries.

But in cases where such official interpreters were lacking on both sides, the problem of an unknown spoken language could still be partially resolved by using phrasebooks, which helped the speaker of one language mimic the sound of certain words and phrases in other languages. The fact that such phrasebooks are still widely used by modern travelers attests to their lasting appeal. A number of such bilingual phrasebooks are preserved in Dunhuang, including Sino-Tibetan,[77] Sino-Khotanese,[78] Sanskrit-Khotanese, and Turco-Khotanese.[79] Existing research on these phrasebooks has focused on the linguistic information they contain.[80] But more can be said about their social underpinnings. Of interest to my purpose is that fact that many of these phrasebooks were intimately connected to the activities of envoys, even though some of them are primarily Buddhist in nature. A Sino-Khotanese phrasebook, for example, was written on the same manuscript as a few Kho-tanese letters by monks who traveled as Khotanese envoys.[81] One of these letters mentions that "when we came here to Shazhou [Dunhuang], the *ling-gong* [the lord of Dunhuang] deigned look very kindly upon the royal favor [gift] here."[82] Another phrasebook was copied on the back of P. 5538, the Khotanese royal edict discussed above that was delivered from Khotan to Dunhuang by envoys. Thus it is virtually certain that envoys had access to, or perhaps even produced, these phrasebooks.

How would the phrasebooks be used? In the following lists, I have di-vided the topics discussed in P. 5538, the most extensive of such bilingual lists, into categories and give English translations of the sentences and words included:[83]

On Traveling:
I shall see China and afterwards return.
Stay a little while, one or two months.
I shall not stay.
I shall go at once.

On Provisions:
Do you have equipment for the road or not?
I do not like equipment for the road.
A horse or two and I shall go.
Have you any books or not?
I have some.

On Other Activities on the Road:
Did you fare well?
I am very content in my mind.
I will go to bed.
Eat food.

Categorized Word Lists:
*People:* "woman," "pupil," "attendant"
*Adjectives:* "old," "long," "short"
*Colors:* "black," "white," "yellow," "red," "green," "blue"

These phrases and words would have allowed envoys to have brief communi-cations within predictable parameters of social interaction. They would have been able to, when encountering an official from the host state, identify who they were and where they came from. The Sino-Khotanese phrasebooks, for instance, allow travelers to ask "Where is he going?" and say "I am going to the court" in both Chinese and Khotanese.[84] When under the guardianship of escorts and guides, envoys would have been able to ask for food and drink and describe their own needs. For these purposes, they could use phrases such as "Bring water!" "Bring the salt!" or "Do you wish for anything?"[85] Finally, like any modern language learner can attest to, one of the first phrases to learn in a new language is "I don't speak language *X*." In the Sino-Khotanese phrasebook, we also find the question "Do you know Chinese?"[86] These phrasebooks would have been invaluable tools for envoys encountering hosts who did not speak their language.

One of the best-documented occasions of oral communication is at the "audience with the sovereign stage" of envoy/host interaction. Typically, the sovereign of the host state had an official meeting with the envoys, where they engaged in oral communication. The kind of information that the envoys needed to convey was often quite simple. The *Songshi* records two conversations between a Song emperor and a Khotanese envoy at an imperial audience. In the first conversation, Emperor Zhenzong (968–1022) asked the Khotanese envoy "how long he [had] traveled on the road, and how many *li* away [his home state] was from here."[87] In the second conversation, Emperor Shenzong (1048–85) asked the envoy: "How long has he be away from his kingdom? What states did he pass by? And were there any bandits on the road?"[88] To both sets of questions the Khotanese envoys were able to give satisfactory answers. It is possible that these envoys were conversational in Chinese; they may also have relied on the help of Song official interpreters. On one occasion, for instance, when an Arabic envoy arrived at the Song court in 995, it was explicitly recorded that, at the Chongzheng Palace during an audience with Emperor Taizong (936–97), the interpreter communicated orally on the envoy's behalf.[89]

Yet another possibility is that the envoys learned just enough to convey the information regularly asked at such meetings. It is notable that the questions of the Song emperors touch on the same issues covered in the Sanskrit-Khotanese phrasebook, which includes phrases such as:

Whence have you come? I have come from Khotan.
When did you come from India? Two years ago.
Where did you stay in Khotan? I stayed in a monastery.
Did you duly see the king or not? I duly saw him.

They summon you to the palace.
I made a report to the court.[90]

The references to the palace and the court point to the phrasebook's usefulness for monks and envoys alike. Indeed, certain basic phrases are so common in these bilingual phrasebooks that one can imagine that envoys, regardless of their daily linguistic ability, could have learned them in multiple languages. For instance, in three such phrasebooks, we find questions about a traveler's destination:

> *Sino-Khotanese:* Where does he deign to go? (S. 5212)
> *Sanskrit-Khotanese:* Where are you going? (P. 5538)
> *Tibeto-Chinese:* Where [are you] going? (S. 2726)

Access to these phrasebooks, therefore, would theoretically have allowed the envoys to say this phrase in four different languages: Chinese, Khotanese, Tibetan, and Sanskrit.

To conclude, oral communications were perhaps as important as written messages in diplomatic dealings. Transmitted sources certainly include many examples of brilliant interpreters active in diplomatic negotiations.[91] But what the Dunhuang materials show is that, even for those lacking such linguistic prowess, there was assistance available in the form of learning manuals that helped them conduct basic conversations and get through the task at hand. Just as in the case of written communications, even monolingual envoys could have a role to play.

## Conclusion

Unlike popular accounts of the history of the Silk Road, which often see travelers on it as broadly multilingual, I have tried to discuss with some precision two issues in this chapter. First: Were travelers on the Silk Road, in this case envoys traveling in Eastern Eurasia between Khotan and Kaifeng, really multilingual? Second: At what specific places in their journeys would linguistic abilities, in both written and oral forms, be required?

The Dunhuang materials provide many direct and indirect pieces of evidence to answer these questions. My examination shows that while there were indeed envoys who excelled at writing and speaking many languages, they were likely the exceptions. Many, if not most, of the diplomatic travelers were likely monolingual or at best bilingual. But heads of state, when they assembled their diplomatic missions, intentionally selected multicultural (and thus likely also multilingual) members. These members, many of whom were no doubt monolingual, could nonetheless form a multilingual diplomatic mission.

Such diplomatic missions were tasked with delivering state letters in different languages, a substantial number of which are preserved in the Dunhuang library cave. The existence of translation offices in virtually all the states on the Silk Road meant that traveling envoys themselves were not necessarily the ones who produced these multilingual letters. It was only when they were in residency at the host state and needed to communicate through letters in a foreign language that their linguistic ability would be put to use. Similarly, multilingual skills were certainly useful in communicating orally with guides, escorts, and sovereigns. But with the help of interpreters and bilingual phrasebooks, even monolingual envoys could, and did, successfully conduct these translingual communications.

Finally, the argument for Tibetan as a lingua franca makes sense in a very restricted area, in letters exchanged between Ganzhou, Dunhuang, and Khotan—all states that were, until the mid-ninth century, under the rule of the Tibetan Empire. It is possible, as Takeuchi has suggested, that a widespread capability in Tibetan among the people in the region played a role in why Tibetan continued to be an international language after the fall of the Tibetan Empire.[92] I suspect that as Tibetan was no longer the administrative language of any major state in the region, its political neutrality might also have been appealing. In any case, the role of Tibetan was certainly not as profound as that of the original lingua franca in the late antique to medieval Mediterranean, or the role of French in early modern European diplomacy. The linguistic complexity that travelers faced, and historians continue to face, in medieval Eurasia is not easily solved by a single lingua franca.

———

So far in this book, I have presented a *descriptive* account of diplomatic travelers between China and Central Asia, including who they were and what they did while traveling. In long poem by a Qarakhanid official named Yūsuf Khāṣṣ Ḥājib (ca. 1019–90), we are fortunate to find a *prescriptive* account of what an envoy ought to be. Yūsuf, originally from Balāsāghūn, composed *Kutadgu Bilig* (*Wisdom of Royal Glory*) in the tradition of the "mirror for princes" genre popular in medieval Eurasia. This poem, presented to the khan in Kashgar in 1069 or 1070, imagines an ideal state in which the king engages in conversations with a vizier, a sage, and an ascetic about the best ways to govern.[93] In one of these conversations, the king (named "Rising Sun") asks the sage (named "Highly Praised") "what sort of man is required to serve as envoy, so the prince may depend on him and send him off to traverse the land?" To this question, the sage gives a long answer:

> The envoy ought to be choicest of mankind, wise, intelligent, and courageous. . . . So the envoy must be intelligent, steady, and wise, and a good interpreter of words. Words are his business: he has to know them inside and out; then matters arranged by him will succeed.[94]

Here, the sage lays out the general characteristics of an ideal envoy and emphasizes the significance of "words" to his profession. Then, the sage offers some details about more specific qualities of a good envoy:

> He should be loyal, content in eye and heart, reliable, sincere, and upright. . . . As for the greedy-eyed man: he has no self control and so is unfit for the office of envoy. . . . He should be modest, quiet mannered, and discreet, but also worldly-wise. . . . As a mark of ready wit, he should know how to draw up all sorts of documents, how to read and write, and how to listen. . . . He should be not only well-read and well-spoken, but also well versed in poetry and himself able to compose. He ought further to have some knowledge of astrology and medicine, and the interpretation of dreams, also arithmetic, geometry, trigonometry, and cadastre. Then he should be able to play backgammon and chess, well enough to make his rivals howl. He should excel in polo and in archery, also in fowling and in hunting. . . . Finally, he must know all tongues when he opens his mouth to speak, and know all scripts when he takes pen in hand. . . . The man sent as envoy must be very virtuous, excelling his adversaries in every kind of negotiation. . . . [W]hatever sorts of men he converses with, he must be able to understand what they say and to keep their deliberations confidential. When the envoy is master of all these virtues, his prince's name grows great in the land. . . . He should be able to grasp what people say quickly and be ready with the proper answer. So he must not drink wine but rather must keep in control of himself. . . . He must have a good mind and a skilled tongue. Then he will retain in his memory what others have said, and through his own speech he will be effective and his affairs will succeed. . . . He should be handsome of appearance, neat and trim, and of good stature. And he should be valiant and high-minded—these two qualities are the

measure of a man's worth. Finally, he should be soft-spoken and honey-tongued, for the great and the small alike soften at sweet words. The envoy's job consists in so much speech: if his words are right, he will reach his goal.[95]

After listing these fine qualities, the sage concludes that "should His Majesty find a man such as this, then he may give him the title of envoy and send him on any mission, whether to distant strangers or nearby neighbors."

I quote extensively from this conversation because of Yūsuf Khāṣṣ Ḥājib's proximity to the world I describe in this book. Yūsuf was born only a few years after the closure of the Dunhuang library cave, and he lived just across the Taklamakan Desert from Dunhuang. The qualities of an ideal envoy in Yūsuf's imagination mirror the actions of envoys described in the preceding chapters, who delivered and wrote official letters, engaged in oral communication with other sovereigns, composed poems, participated in diplomatic games such as polo, and tried to spread the good name of the sovereign. Certain envoys like Zhang Jinshan, the Sino-Khotanese polyglot, possessed the kind of knowledge about medicine that Yūsuf praised, while others such as Zhang Yuanjin, the young and inexperienced envoy implicated in the murder of An Qianxiang, failed as an envoy because he lacked the desired personal qualities of being "modest, quiet-mannered, and discreet." No similar account about what an envoy ought to be is found in Dunhuang or transmitted sources in Chinese, and what the Dunhuang documents show is that real diplomacy was more forgiving—even those who fell far short of such standards engaged in, and often excelled in, their journeys as envoys. Nonetheless, it seems clear from the similarity of diplomatic actions involved that both the stories of envoys presented in this book and the account from Yūsuf reflect the shared values and common realities of a connected world of medieval Eurasian diplomacy. The experience of envoys found in the Dunhuang documents finds echoes in the much broader Eurasian world.

# PART III

# The King's Road

# 8

# The Economics of Diplomacy

PARTS I AND II of this book have offered a portrayal of diplomatic travelers and examined their lives on the road. Collectively, these travelers created a dense network of state-sponsored connections on the Silk Road. But this is not the whole story. What motivated these travelers to undertake arduous and often dangerous journeys? Why did states sponsor such expensive ventures? Who funded these trips? And, after the travelers came back, what changed because of their journeys? In part III, I tackle these questions of motivation and impact in three realms: economy, kingship, and international relations. These three chapters reconstruct the world that propelled the envoys on their journeys and was simultaneously shaped by them.

In this chapter, I demonstrate the economic incentives and impacts of diplomatic journeys in Dunhuang by digging into economic and social documents—most notably, the large number of contracts found in the Dunhuang library cave. The economic decisions of residents of medieval Dunhuang reflected in these documents reveal to us an unfamiliar, sometimes even surprising world profoundly shaped by diplomacy on the Silk Road. We will meet people who self-funded their diplomatic journeys by selling their houses, who lost all they owned because of a failed trip, and who accrued a life-altering amount of wealth after a successful one. This chapter, I hope, will help explain their decisions and actions, and assess the economic impact they had. To enter this unique and still largely unexamined economic world, let us begin with a different kind of document: a popular lyrical poem (*quizi ci*):

Opening [the road to] Khotan—
There will be cotton and silk filling every household.
Live dragons and jade bowls will be brought to the view of the
   commoners.

The *shangshu* [lord of Dunhuang] oversees the Bureau of Guests,
And warfare has ceased at the four borders.
May our lord live for a thousand years,
And let Ganzhou splinter on its own![1]

The poem describes the relation between Dunhuang and its two most important neighbors: Khotan and Ganzhou. The poet suggests that as long as the road to Khotan is open, the lord of Dunhuang need not worry about the chaos in Ganzhou to the east. The reference to the "Bureau of Guests [*dianke*]," the branch of the Dunhuang government in charge of the accommodation of foreign envoys, makes clear that the poem is discussing the opening of the road for diplomatic travelers.[2] The first few lines of the poem direct our attention to the economic impact of these diplomatic connections: the opening of the road to Khotan not only promises peace between the two states, it also brings prosperity in the form of "cotton and silk" and "live dragons [I am unsure what this means] and jade bowls." The poet makes an apparent distinction between two groups of luxury goods: while the live dragons and jade bowls will be offered by the Khotanese "to the view of the commoners," the cotton and silk will "fill every household." The first group of luxury goods would become the possessions of the king of Dunhuang and would be accessible to commoners only through a kingly display, while the second group, of cotton and silk, would enter every household, including, one might presume, those of the commoners in Dunhuang.

This view that diplomatic connections financially benefited common people in Dunhuang is corroborated by the song of New Year exorcism that opens the introduction of this book. This song, readers might recall, depicts an ideal world where "ten thousand commoners sing songs with full bellies like drums" and where the envoys from the east and the west offered tributes in luxury goods to Dunhuang. As a result, "all within the border [of Dunhuang] chant the song of happiness."[3] The lyrical poem and the song seem to share the view that diplomacy brought riches (and happiness) to the people of Dunhuang.

Did diplomatic connections really have a such significant, even structural impact on the economy of Dunhuang? This chapter answers this question by conducting a four-part examination. Each part describes an economic phenomenon in Dunhuang society. These four phenomena are:

1. Dunhuang envoys acquired tremendous numbers of return gifts and exchanged goods on their diplomatic trips.

2. The primary income of the average household in Dunhuang came from agriculture.
3. Residents in Dunhuang took great financial risks to travel as envoys.
4. Envoys shared their profits and risks among a wide spectrum of Dunhuang society.

I argue that these four phenomena were historically connected: the significant rate of financial return of trips as envoys, in the context of the agrarian society of Dunhuang where economic opportunities were limited, meant that diplomacy provided an obvious and outsized economic opportunity for Dunhuang residents, and many took great risks in pursuing the profits of diplomacy. Such risks and fortunes were transferred to and distributed among residents of Dunhuang who did not personally travel as envoys, thus shaping the economy of the entire society. Once we "follow the money," the reason people of Dunhuang were so eager to engage in such long and dangerous journeys as envoys becomes apparent. Diplomacy not only connected Dunhuang politically with other neighboring states, its promise of material gains also animated the Dunhuang economy in a way that few other forces were capable of doing.

## The Profits of Diplomacy

In previous chapters, I have mentioned several times the mission from Dunhuang in 878 to the Tang court and the different types of gift exchange that happened in this mission. Here I return to this valuable account to show the economic nature of the gift exchange. What made this mission worthy of further investigation is that not only the types of gifts but the *exact amounts*, from both sides, are recorded.[4] As a reminder, on this trip, in addition to the letter of petition, the envoys of Dunhuang delivered three gifts: one piece of jade, one antelope horn, and one yak tail. In return, the Tang court offered return gifts to the lord and other officials in Dunhuang, as well as to the envoys themselves. For the sake of clarity, I display these items in table 8.1. Put together, these return gifts amount to 1848 *pi* (around 22,176 meters) of silk, forty-two sets of cotton clothing, and nineteen articles of silver, a tremendous quantity, clearly exceeding the gifts from Dunhuang in value.[5] This disparity illustrates, as I showed in chapter 6, the unequal nature of gift exchange. More relevant for the purpose of the current chapter, however, is the fact that the return gifts were not lumped together as a whole, but distinguished as two categories.

TABLE 8.1. Return Gifts from the Tang Court in 878

| Recipient | Gift |
| --- | --- |
| **Gifts to Officials in Dunhuang** | |
| Lord of Dunhuang | As an answering token, 70 *pi* of silk; as an asking token, 50 *pi* of silk, one set of clothing, one silver box, one silver bowl, one imperial edict |
| Administrative manager (*panguan*) | 25 *pi* of silk, one set of clothing, one silver bowl |
| Chief general (*duyaya*) | 25 *pi* of silk, one set of clothing, one silver bowl |
| Each of the five officials in group 1 | 15 *pi* of silk, one set of clothing |
| Each of the five officials in group 2 | 10 *pi* of silk, one set of clothing |
| Each of the eight officials in group 3 | 7 *pi* of silk |
| **Gifts to Envoys** | |
| All twenty-nine members of the diplomatic mission, the "price of camel and horse" | 43.84 *pi* of silk |
| Each of the three generals | 15 *pi* of silk, one silver bowl, one set of cooked cotton clothing, one set of brocade cotton clothing |
| Each of the thirteen lieutenants | 10 *pi* of silk, one silver wine cup, one set of brocade cotton clothing |
| Each of the thirteen traveling assistants | 5 *pi* of silk, one set of cotton clothing |

The first category of gifts targeted luminaries in the Dunhuang government who had not traveled to Chang'an themselves. Even though it had officially been the lord of Dunhuang, Zhang Huaishen, who gave the gifts to the Tang court, the return gifts were not reserved for him alone. He did get his fair share, but so did his senior officials, the administrative manager (*panguan*) and chief general (*duyaya*), and another eighteen officials in the Dunhuang government. The eighteen officials were divided into three groups, presumably on the basis of rank. These gifts all went to the top echelons of the Dunhuang government, people who had remained in Dunhuang. The wide reach of the gifts allowed the Tang emperor to form a personal and economic relation not only with the lord of Dunhuang but also with his most important officials.

The second category of return gifts comprised those given to the twenty-nine people who had actually traveled to Chang'an on behalf of the lord of

Dunhuang. This part of the gift list is further divided into two groups. The first group is "the price of camel and horse," a term used to indicate the expenses that travelers incurred in their long journey. In this category, each of the twenty-nine members, regardless of rank, was given the same amount: 43.84 pi (43 pi and 3.36 *zhang*) of silk. As I have mentioned, thirteen of the twenty-nine envoys traveled to Chang'an, while the other sixteen stayed in Lingzhou. The group that went to Chang'an therefore traveled about 1200 kilometers further than those who stayed in Lingzhou. Yet the compensation for travel costs made no such distinction, indicating that during the trip between Lingzhou and Chang'an, these thirteen envoys were already accommodated by the Tang government, in the road protection stage of the envoy-host interaction, thus requiring no further compensation.[6] The second group, on the other hand, is differentiated by rank among three generals (*yaya*), the leaders of the mission, thirteen lieutenants (*junjiang*), and thirteen other "traveling assistants" (*changxing*). Combined, the gifts for envoys amounted to 1511.36 pi of silk, dwarfing the first category of gifts for the lord of Dunhuang and his officials (351 pi), and indicating that in this particular diplomatic dealing, the vast majority of the return gifts went to the ones who had transported the diplomatic gifts (the envoys) and not to those who nominally gave them (the lord of Dunhuang).

The Tang emperor rejected the request of the lord of Dunhuang for the title of governor (*jiedu shi*) that was conveyed by the envoys in 878. But he showered the envoys with gifts far exceeding the amount of their own gifts, exhibiting in the process his prestige and magnanimity. By participating in this process of unbalanced gift exchange, the ruler of Dunhuang also reaffirmed his connection with the Tang. But perhaps more importantly, he and the officials of his government collected significant economic compensation. The envoys, in addition to gaining personal status and prestige, also obtained gifts that more than made up for the cost of the journey. Although this mission did not achieve its political goal, for its members, it was nonetheless an economic success.

This document, rare as it is, is not the only testament to gifts from the Tang to Dunhuang. A structurally similar document records the gift exchanges of another mission from Dunhuang to the Tang. The information is not complete, as only the lower half of the document is preserved.[7] Yet judging from the remaining fragment, it is clear that this document is concerned with similar things, such as the granting of "the price of camel and horse," as well as gifts that included fifteen pi of silk and a silver cup for each traveling envoy.[8] The similarity in the language of gift giving and in the types of gifts offered to Dunhuang envoys indicates a regular practice: envoys to the Tang court often acquired not only ample compensation for travel costs but also additional gifts to show the magnanimity of the emperor. Such a practice is confirmed by records in non-Chinese sources. For instance, in the mission recorded in the Staël-Holstein manuscript, the Khotanese envoys not only exchanged gifts between the Khotanese king and the lord of Dunhuang but also received gifts from the lord for their work as envoys.[9]

The gifts that traveled from Dunhuang to the Tang in the 878 mission (one piece of jade, one antelope horn, and one yak tail) made up an unusually meagre list. On many other occasions, envoys from Dunhuang and other kingdoms in the region went to the court in North China bringing gifts of much greater value. For instance, in 964, a group of forty-seven Uyghur envoys reached the Song court bearing "100 chunks of jade, one cow tail, 60 white yak tails, 110 sable skins, 535 jade beads, 125 jade fragments, 110 jade *diexie* belts, 65 horses, and 19 camels."[10] In 965, a combined embassy from Dunhuang, Guazhou, and the Ganzhou Uyghur kingdom sent a large collection of gifts to the Song court, including "1000 horses, 500 camels, 500 pieces of jade, 500 *jin* of amber, 40 *jin* of sal ammoniac, 8 pieces of coral, and 1000 *pi* of felt, as well as a jade belt and jade saddle."[11] The return gifts from the Song court on these occasions are not recorded. But given the practice of unequal gifting, by which the Song customarily offered more value in return, the exchange of goods accomplished in these missions must have been considerable.

The imbalance between gifts from Dunhuang and return gifts from Chang'an seen in the 878 trip is echoed in other documents about diplomatic gift exchange. S. 8444 is a record from the Imperial Treasury of Chang'an, an institution in charge of the management of the emperor's personal life, including the production and supply of his clothing and other imperial trappings.[12] It details the exchange of gifts between the Ganzhou Uyghur khan, his relatives, and his officials on one side and the Tang government on the other. The gifts given by specific Uyghur personnel are listed first, and the return gifts from the Tang that served as requital for that particular item follow on the next line. This document, too, is incomplete. A few intact entries to illustrate the nature of the document are shown in table 8.2. Scholars have compared this list with lists of officially sanctioned prices of things in the Tang market, and found that the Tang return gifts clearly exceeded the market price of the Uyghur gifts.[13] But the margin is much smaller than in the case of the 878 mission from

TABLE 8.2. Gifts Exchanged between the Uyghur Khan of Ganzhou and the Tang Emperor

| Gift from the Uyghur Khan | Return Gift from the Tang Emperor |
|---|---|
| One *pi* of Persian brocade | Two *pi* of fine brocade |
| One chariot assemblage and ten arrows | Five *pi* of silk and three *pi* of fine brocade |
| One chunk of ivory | Twenty *pi* of silk |
| Thirty pairs of antelope horns | Twenty-five *pi* of "grand silk" |

Dunhuang. Because this list only targeted the Uyghur luminaries in Ganzhou, one might suspect, on the basis of the two documents discussed above, that they constituted only the equivalent of the "Gifts to Officials" of the return gifts in the case of the 878 mission. A separate list of return gifts that included travel costs and add-on gifts would have been offered to envoys who came to the Tang court.

This type of gift exchange existed in all diplomatic dealings between states in the Eurasian world. But aside from the documentation from Dunhuang, only in a few other cases, such as the exchange between the Song and the Champa kingdom in what is now Vietnam, are the return gifts from the Chinese side recorded as well.[14] While the state with the lower diplomatic status often initiated the visit and the gift exchange, the return gifts from the state with higher status satisfied the economic needs of the initiating state. Furthermore, the Dunhuang documents tell us that the traveling envoys themselves received substantial economic compensation for their diplomatic trips. In a dispute over yet another politically failed trip to China, a Dunhuang envoy lamented that "for twenty years, how many lowly minions came here but could not achieve official appointment!"[15] But these "lowly minions" were not traveling thousands of kilometers out of a pure sense of duty to the Dunhuang government. Instead, even those with the lowest status in the 878 mission—those the Tang government refused to allow into the Tang domain—acquired 48.84 *pi* of silk (43.84 *pi* for travel expenses and 5 *pi* of additional gifts) and one set of cotton clothing.

Apart from highly profitable gift exchange, envoys also engaged in straightforward commerce. In 923, a commoner named Zhang Xiuzao rented camels for his trip as an envoy to Turfan from two different residents of Dunhuang, both bearing the title of "general" (*yaya*). The two transactions happened only three months apart: the first in the fourth month, the second in the seventh month.[16] The second contract lays out the conditions of repayment clearly: the rent is to be paid within three days of Zhang's return from Turfan. If the camel was stolen by bandits, one was to refer to the "grand precedent."[17] If the camel died of illness, the rental price was to be converted to the sale price of the camel and paid. If the camel ran away, it was to be the fault of Zhang Xiuzao and not the owner of the camel, and Zhang was to pay back the price of the camel, not just the rental price. On these two occasions, Zhang Xiuzao paid sixteen and ten *pi* of state-sanctioned cloth (*guanbu*) to creditors as rent for the camel. The outbound trip from Dunhuang to Turfan takes around ten days at full speed. But considering that his trip was a diplomatic one, Zhang would presumably have had to perform certain governmental duties while he was in Turfan. Therefore, to estimate the time spent on this trip as something around one month would be conservative. If Zhang did spend just one month on the first trip, he waited only two more months to go to Turfan again.

Zhang invested a significant amount of capital into borrowing camels to travel. If the camels were to go missing on the road, he would have needed to pay even more to make up the loss. There is no record of what Zhang did in Turfan, but it seems reasonable to suppose that it was something profitable enough to justify the rental expense. And documents in Dunhuang do show envoys from other states engaging in trade. The monks of Dunhuang, for instance, purchased farming tools from envoys from Ganzhou,[18] and clothes from envoys from Turfan.[19] In a contract an envoy made to borrow silk prior to his trip, the lender explicitly says that the silk borrowed "can be speculated at will," as long as the loaned silk is repaid with interest after the diplomatic trip.[20] In these cases, envoys took advantage of the opportunity of long-distance travel and conducted commercial transactions. It is possible that travelers like Zhang Xiuzao also engaged in similar endeavors. The profit he made from them, along with the potentially greater number of gifts that he would have received from his hosts in Turfan, must have been enough to convince him to borrow camels and travel to Turfan as an envoy twice in quick succession.

But how much were the gifts from the Tang emperor, or Zhang Xiuzao's investment in camels, worth to the regular residents of Dunhuang? Did what the envoys could gain on these trips serve as a real incentive for commoners and officials in Dunhuang to pursue such trips? Did the influx of gifts have any impact on the economy of Dunhuang as a whole? To answer these questions, we need to examine the economic lives of ordinary people in Dunhuang.

## The Economy of Dunhuang

Dunhuang was an oasis state situated in an extremely dry environment. Its agrarian production was supported by an extensive irrigation system extending from the city of Dunhuang into rural areas.[21] Landownership there was transitioning from the state to private households in the ninth and tenth centuries.[22] Much of the language used in documents between the state and households still adhered to the old terminology, with the households "requesting" (*qing*) and "accepting" (*shou*) land from the state.[23] But in practice, private households could and did own, sell, and buy land.

The presence of private land ownership meant that inequality of landed property among Dunhuang households was quite stark. At one end of the spectrum, many households owned more than one hundred *mu* (one *mu* is 520 square meters, or a little more than an eighth of an acre)[24] of land, with some reaching more than five hundred *mu* (roughly sixty-four acres).[25] At the other end, the household of Linghu Anding and his brother, for instance, owned only fifteen *mu* (less than two acres). In a petition by Linghu to the Dunhuang government asking for more land, he described the fifteen *mu* of land he and his brother owned as "extremely meagre and narrow."[26] For this reason, they wanted the government to grant them the land of Yin Shiwu, the female head of a household that owned land next to theirs. Yin Shiwu's household, which also owned fifteen *mu* of land, was clearly doing even worse, as it was not able to pay taxes on the land it owned. Both households thus stood at the poorer end of the wealth spectrum of Dunhuang households—but they were by no means the poorest. There were also people without any land, who had to resort to cultivating land rented from other households.[27] It is likely, because of her inability to pay taxes, that Yin Shiwu was destined to slide into this category, had the Linghu brothers been successful in taking her land away. Liu Jinbao points out in his study of the economy of Dunhuang that "on average, a commoner household in Dunhuang had about five members, and owned 30–40 *mu* of land."[28] For this average family with thirty to forty *mu* of land, the economic precarity experienced by the Linghu and Yin families was not at all unimaginable.

To understand the broad contours of economic life for a Dunhuang household, I will examine a particularly well-documented household, that of Suo Qingnu. Дх. 2954 contains a report of landholding filed in 952 by the Suo household. It lists six members: Suo Qingnu, his wife, and four sons, and forty-eight *mu* of land dispersed in seven different locations, including six pieces of farmland and a half-*mu* of garden.[29] In this way, Suo's family was a bit better off than the average Dunhuang household. As the average produce from one *mu* of land was about one *shi* (sixty liters) of grain,[30] the annual production of Suo Qingnu's land would have been close to fifty *shi*.[31] This amount of produce provides a useful benchmark for understanding the economic lives of commoners in Dunhuang.

It was on these pieces of land that the Suo family paid taxes. The taxation system of Dunhuang at this time was based almost exclusively on landholding; no tax was levied on commerce or individuals.[32] The land tax included at least four types of materials collected by the government on the basis of acreage: grain, cloth, grass, and firewood. These categories combined would amount to slightly less than 10 percent of average produce, a fairly lenient rate.[33] The family of Suo Qingnu would have been required to pay a total tax of around five *shi* of grain.

In comparison, food consumed an even larger share of the Suo family's income. According to Huang Zhengjian's study of the Dunhuang documents, an adult male at this time would consume about 2.2 *sheng* of grain (1.32 liters) per day, which amounts to about 800 *sheng*, or 8 *shi* (480 liters), per year, whereas an adult female would consume 1.4 *sheng* of grain ($=$ 500 *sheng* or 5 *shi* per year), and nonadult males and females each just below 1 *sheng* of grain per day ($=$ 350 *sheng* or 3.5 *shi* per year).[34] Thus Suo Qingnu's six-member household would have consumed (assuming the four sons were nonadults) 27 *shi* as food out of the 50 *shi* of grain produced by the land they owned. After the roughly 10 percent tax (5 *shi*) and food consumption, the Suo household would have had a surplus of 18 *shi* that they could spend on other non-food-related items such as clothing or reinvest in agricultural work for future years. The numbers are approximations, based on a combination of separate sources. Nonetheless, they give us some idea of the scale, or rather the scarcity, of resources available to a somewhat better-than-average Dunhuang household.

What did it mean for a family to have a surplus of eighteen *shi* of grain per year? Direct comparison to the value of other things is not very straightforward, because Dunhuang in this period was not strictly speaking a "money economy." Coins, which had been common in the area in the seventh and eighth centuries, by the ninth century had gradually exited circulation.[35] Instead, silk, other types of cloth, and grain served as generally accepted media of exchange.[36] In the various sale and loan contracts preserved in Dunhuang, silk, cloth, and grain were exchanged for land, labor, livestock ranging from donkeys to cows, agricultural tools such as iron plows, and daily items including bamboo tea containers.[37] By comparing the items involved in the contracts, we can get a general sense of the value of things in the Dunhuang economy.

In our modern world, housing is one of the major expenditures of any household; and so it was in Dunhuang, too. In 897, Zhang Yiquan sold his house along with its yard for 50 *shi* of grain. His house measured 1.35 × 2.25 *zhang*, which equals 27.34 square meters (4.05 × 6.75 meters), and his yard measured 0.4 × 1.13 *zhang*, which equals 4.07 square meters (1.2 × 3.39 meters).[38] In another case in 936, Yang Hulüpu sold his smaller house (14.18 square meters) and yard (6.3 square meters) for 33.7 *shi* of grain.[39] In this second sale, the contract specified that the price paid also included that of the pillars and beams of the house. In the first case, the rate is 1.59 *shi* per square meter, whereas in the second case it is 1.65 *shi* per square meter. The prices represented by these two deals four decades apart in time are remarkably similar, and give us a general sense of how expensive houses were for Dunhuang residents.

Next let us look at the cost of labor. In a certain *dingsi* year (897 or 957), a commoner bought one five-year-old cow for agricultural work from a fellow commoner, and paid one *pi* of raw silk, which was valued at around twenty-seven *shi* of grain.[40] In 932, another commoner loaned an eight-year-old cow to work for him for one year at the rate of one *shi* of grain per month.[41] One can imagine that both men were likely managing land much greater in size than that of the Suo family to merit such significant investment. Unsurprisingly, those who employed human labor were also among the better-off in Dunhuang. Across different transactions, the pay rate for an adult male worker in Dunhuang contracts was actually remarkably stable over the ninth and tenth centuries: twenty-four *shi* of grain per year, or two *shi* per month.[42] There are cases where the rate is slightly lower, sometimes because the male laborer could not work for a whole year.[43] This average yearly pay (twenty-four *shi*) for an adult male was three times the amount of food he would consume (eight *shi*) in the same period. With an annual surplus of merely eighteen *shi*, the Suo family would certainly struggle if they wanted to hire an additional worker.

In contrast, the price of a slave differed wildly from one case to another. Even though slave ownership was not sanctioned by the state, rich households undoubtedly kept slaves, often at the expense of poorer households. In 916, a certain Awu, the widow of Wang Zaiying, sold her seven-year-old son for 30 *shi* of grain.[44] In 991, a man named Han Yuanding sold his twenty-eight-year-old daughter for five *pi* of silk (three *pi* raw silk, two *pi* processed silk), amounting to 135 *shi* of grain.[45] In 943, three brothers formed a pact and sold one of them into bondage for 23 *shi* of grain.[46] The price of slaves varied depending on the age and gender of the slave and the circumstances of the purchase. The three brothers in the pact stated that "their family was destitute and deeply in debt"— it is easy to imagine that they were hardly in a place to get a better deal.

With this broad understanding of the value of things in Dunhuang, we can place the regular household income and the financial gains from diplomatic travel into the context of the Dunhuang economy. In table 8.3, three examples of profits are considered: the annual surplus (income minus food and tax) from agriculture in an average Dunhuang household, represented by the household of Suo Ziquan (eighteen *shi*); the amount of counter-gifts from the Tang emperor for a low-level envoy on the 878 trip (48.84 *pi* of silk); and the amount Zhang Xiuzao put down to rent a camel to travel as an envoy to Turfan (16 *pi* of state-sanctioned cloth). The grain, silk, and cloth used in these cases also represent the three types of goods most often used as currency in commercial dealings in Dunhuang. Because the conversion rates between these three types of goods are well known, we can have a sense of their relative values. For convenience's sake, I have converted the value of silk and cloth to that of grain. These three amounts are then compared to quantities representing four types of local commercial dealing in Dunhuang. Like the three types of profits, I have also converted these to their equivalent amount of grain. Table 8.3 then directly compares the two sets of quantities, showing, for example, how many houses like the one Zhang Yiquan sold could be purchased with the profits from a year of agricultural work for an average Dunhuang household. The table thus shows where value resided in the Dunhuang economy.

As discussed above, the envoy of the lowest status in the diplomatic mission of 878 obtained 48.84 *pi* of silk, which translates to about 1319 *shi* of grain. This amount would be equivalent to the total income produced in 26 years of farming by Suo Qingnu's household on an average-sized property (50 *mu*), or enough to pay the tax of Suo's family for 260 years. It would also be enough to buy twenty-six houses like the one sold by Zhang Yiquan in 897. If this envoy were to use what he gained in this trip to rent a laborer (whose pay would be 24 *shi* a year), he could have his employee working for him for 55 years. If he converted this amount into food to feed himself, it would sustain him for 165 years. Had he decided to purchase a slave like the daughter of Han Yuanding, he could buy almost ten slaves. And, as noted above, Han's daughter was among the pricier slaves. If he chose to buy someone at the price of Awu's son, the returning envoy could theoretically own, with the gifts

TABLE 8.3. Locations of Value in Dunhuang's Economy

| Profit | Value | Value in Grain | Zhang Yiquan's House (= 50 shi of grain) | A Hired Laborer per Year (= 24 shi of grain) | Food for Adult Man per Year (= 8 shi of grain) | Han Yuanding's Daughter (= 135 shi of grain) |
|---|---|---|---|---|---|---|
| Annual produce on Suo Qingnu's land | 18 shi | 18 shi | 0.36 houses | 0.75 years | 2.25 years | 0.13 |
| For an envoy on the 878 mission | 48.84 pi of silk | 1319 shi | 26 houses | 55 years | 165 years | 9.7 |
| Zhang Xiuzao's camel rental (first trip) | 16 pi of state-sanctioned cloth | 64 shi | 1.28 houses | 2.67 years | 8 years | 0.46 |

he acquired, forty-four slaves. The value in gifts that the envoy received from the Tang emperor in his trip to Chang'an would have made him *very* rich back home in Dunhuang.

The shorter trip Zhang Xiuzao took to Turfan was likely not nearly as profitable. Even though there is no record of how much profit Zhang acquired in his trip, the amount that he spent in borrowing a camel might be indicative of the scale of costs involved in this shorter diplomatic trip. To borrow a camel, Zhang spent the equivalent of more than one house, two and half years' wages for a male laborer, enough food to feed an adult male for eight years, or half the price of an adult female slave like Han Yuanding's daughter. As a comparison, the rent one would have paid for a camel to the Chinese capital was around 135 to 162 *shi* of grain, about three times the amount Zhang invested.[47] Clearly, the farther the diplomatic trip, the larger the investment and the profit. But even for a relatively short trip, like the one Zhang Xiuzao took, the investment in a camel would have been the equivalent of three and half years of income from agriculture for an average family like Suo Qingnu's. The economic profit (and investment) of diplomacy, over both long and short distances, far exceeded the income one could hope for from agriculture.

If this hypothetical math exercise seems ridiculous, that is precisely my intention. I am not suggesting that the earnings from a trip would be devoted entirely to, say, feeding a person for 165 years. But these comparisons give us a sense of the economic significance of diplomacy. The value of the things that envoys handled before, during, and after their trips was so dramatically—indeed absurdly—greater than the value of things in the daily lives of Dunhuang residents that they almost belong to separate spheres of value.[48] In addition to the potential to increase one's social and bureaucratic status, which I discussed in chapter 2, participation in diplomacy also brought envoys the kind of wealth otherwise unimaginable in an agrarian society like Dunhuang. There is little wonder, then, that people would risk so much to try to become envoys.

## The Financial Risks of Being an envoy

Indeed, there were great risks involved in being an envoy. If the diplomatic mission were thwarted, one could be detained and enslaved.[49] The risk of bandits was always present, even for well-equipped envoys from North China.[50] Some high-profile envoys were murdered, either by bandits (in the case of An Qianxiang) or by fellow envoys (in the case of Liang Xingde).[51] In his preface to a dharani sutra, Zhang Qiu, a famous member of the literati of Dunhuang, tells a story of how he narrowly escaped mortal peril on the road. Zhang was tasked with transporting grain to Liangzhou after it was newly conquered by Dunhuang. While in Liangzhou, he met a group of envoys from China who were also heading towards Dunhuang. Initially they planned to travel with Zhang, but were dissuaded because they saw him as a bookish official unlikely to be of use when confronted with bandits. Therefore Zhang Qiu's mission, more than one hundred strong, headed back without the envoys and safely reached the Jade Gate Pass. The envoys from China, however, fell into the hands of Tibetan bandits. The head envoy was killed and the rest suffered "immeasurable harm." To highlight his proximity to danger, Zhang reveals that the night the envoys from China were attacked, they were staying at the exact same spot where Zhang's men had been the day before, so soon after that "the lingering ember of the previous fire was not entirely extinguished."[52] In addition to demonstrating the stability of the routes between Dunhuang and Liangzhou discussed in chapter 5, this detail also shows that danger was constantly present in the life of a long-distance traveler. Deaths of envoys were such a common occurrence that the Dunhuang government routinely provided help with their funerals.[53] Physical harm from long-distance travel, which often lasted months or even years, through difficult terrain, was one of the greatest risks envoys faced.

Beyond physical danger, diplomatic trips often exposed envoys to financial risk as well. In 941, Jia Yanchang borrowed one *pi* of silk and one *pi* of white camel brocade from Xinshan, the abbot of Longxing Monastery, for his trip as an envoy to Turfan.[54] It was stipulated in the contract that the interest would be two *pi* of vertical-loom cotton cloth. The contract describes two situations that would result in different financial outcomes for Jia: if "the mission is not secure on the road," the guarantor, Jia Yanchang's brother Jia Yanyou, would be responsible for paying back the original amount of the silk, without the interest; but if the mission was completed safely, Jia Yanchang was to pay the interest on the day of return, and the original amount within a month. These stipulations are broadly similar to those in contracts made by other envoys.[55] By taking out these loans, Jia put himself and his brother at considerable financial risk. The amount Jia borrowed, one *pi* of silk (= twenty-seven *shi* of grain) and one *pi* of white camel brocade (= eighty-eight *shi* of grain), would be enough to buy Zhang Yiquan's house twice (fifty *shi* of grain), with some change. Had Jia Yanchang indeed failed to come back, an exorbitant debt would have fallen on his brother.

In a more reckless case, a commoner named Li Wenwen sold his house to another commoner named Song Wenzi in 950 to fund his trip to the Chinese capital, which was Luoyang at the time.[56] In exchange, he was able to acquire at least eight *shi* of grain,[57] and an eight-year-old yellow male camel. The journey, according to this contract, was a task given by the Dunhuang government: Li talks about how he was "traveling to the capital upon an order." Thus, this contract is a clear example that the Dunhuang government did not provide enough funding for its diplomatic travelers. Those involved had to fund themselves by putting down what was to them a life-changing amount of investment so that they could travel as envoys. A house might not have accounted for as great a portion of one's income in medieval Dunhuang as it does for most twenty-first century urbanites, and Li might have had more than one house. But it is equally possible that Li was in fact cash-strapped and that the house represented a last bit of financial cushion, on which he was ready to make a gamble. In either case, selling a house to buy food and a camel for a diplomatic journey had to be a major event in the economic life of Li Wenwen. This decision, as much as any discussed in this chapter, demonstrates the unique and central role of diplomacy in Dunhuang's economy.

Regarding Jia and Li, we do not know if their journeys were successful, so we can only guess if they benefitted or suffered financially as a result. In another case, however, we can closely observe what a failed diplomatic mission could mean financially. In the twelfth month of 959, a commoner named Cao Baosheng sent a petition to the lord of Dunhuang about a distressing piece of news he had received recently. His brother Cao Baoding, he had learned, had died on the road as an envoy to Kaifeng. The brother's body was in Ganzhou at the time, and Cao Baosheng asked to be allowed to go to Ganzhou to collect it. In the petition, Cao Baosheng stated that in the year prior to the trip, his brother had "borrowed saddles, horses, and goods from various people for the road." He further lamented that "I am sad to see that [my brother] could not return from his trip to the capital; the debt thus owed is broad and profound, and there is no way I can repay this debt."[58] It is possible that, as Jia Yanyou had for his brother Jia Yanchang, Cao Baosheng also served as cosignatory of the loan contracts made by his brother prior to this trip. Now that the traveler would not return safely with the expected profit, he had to shoulder the costs of this risky venture, which could easily bankrupt a commoner's household.

Such financial risk was not found only among Dunhuang envoys. A report to the king of Khotan describes a daring case of risk-taking by someone intending to become an envoy for the kingdom of Khotan:

> There were those servants [of yours] here who made a petition to the royal court, saying, "We shall go to the China land [and] do service." [Among them] there was Lā Sīkau from Saga, who was a monk. He renounced monkhood and with his [two?] lay brothers received everything from [their] parents and sold [it]. He made a petition, saying, "I shall go to the China land."[59]

This case is instructive in a number of ways. The former monk had to ask permission to become an envoy to China on behalf of the king of Khotan. In order to fund his trip, he and his two brothers sold everything they had inherited from their parents. This brotherly alliance from Khotan resembles the relation of the Jia and Cao brothers discussed above. As with those other brothers, the financial risk was worth it to the envoy-to-be because of the potentially great profit from a trip to China. And, like envoys from Dunhuang, this envoy from Khotan looked at the diplomatic trip as a way of increasing his economic standing. Given that the economic basis in the oasis towns around Dunhuang, including Khotan, Ganzhou, and Turfan, was broadly similar to that of Dunhuang, it is likely that diplomacy served just as great an economic stimulus in these states.

What the Khotanese case and that of Cao Baosheng also show is the involvement of one's family in the perilous endeavors of diplomacy. Family members shared the risk by contributing goods and serving as guarantors for the person who actually traveled as an envoy. Presumably, they would share the fortune if the trip proved successful. Both the risks of and the fortunes to be made by serving as an envoy, particularly to a place as far away as North China from Khotan, were so great that the fate of an entire family hinged on the outcome of the mission. But this sharing of the risks and fortunes of diplomacy was not limited to the envoy's immediate family members. As I will show in the next section, a much broader segment of Dunhuang society also took part.

## Sharing the Risks and Fortunes of Diplomacy

In 941, Luo Xianxin borrowed one *pi* of raw silk before his trip as an envoy to the capital of the Later Jin (936–47) in Kaifeng.[60] According to the contract written on that occasion, he was to pay the creditor two *pi* of raw silk upon his return. If he failed to return, his brother Luo Hengheng, the commissioner of soldiers and horses, would inherit the debt. This transaction was guaranteed by a witness surnamed He with the same official title as Luo Hengheng. It is notable that the envoy, his brother, and the witness all bore Sogdian surnames. Because of the length of Luo's trip, about 2300 kilometers from Dunhuang to Kaifeng, the interest on the loan was 100 percent, much higher than in the contracts made for shorter diplomatic trips. The entire transaction seems to have been purely commercial, with the brother serving as guarantor in much the same way as in the cases discussed earlier.

What makes this contract peculiar is that at the end a note was added, apparently by the same hand, stating that one jade belt and one piece of fine silk were to be given to the envoy as "road goods" (figure 8.1). Some argue that the same creditor gave these gifts.[61] The juxtaposition of the commercial activity of lending and the noncommercial offering of gifts indicates that they should not always be treated separately. In this case, both the borrowed silk and the road goods were offered to Luo, albeit in different forms, by nontraveling residents of Dunhuang; both constitute parts of the resources Luo Xianxin collected in preparation for the trip. The creditor and Luo's brother certainly would bear the brunt of the risk that Luo might not return safely, but the witness of the contract and the unnamed giver of the road goods also shared the financial risk of Luo Xianxin's trip.

In Luo's case, it is impossible to know where the gifts, or road goods, came from. But in many other cases, we see a broad spectrum of social groups in Dunhuang all offering road goods to envoys. In this way, these gift givers all took a financial risk in diplomatic traveling. For a trip to the Song capital in 996, a list of "those who made contributions to the offerings to the Son of Heaven [the Song emperor]" is preserved in the Dunhuang cave.[62] This list,

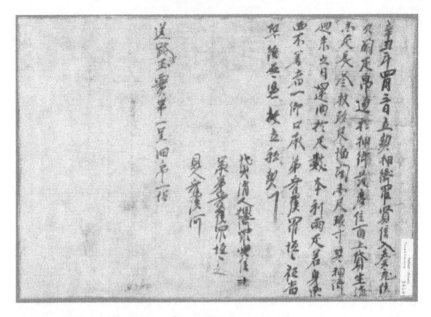

FIGURE 8.1 Envoy Luo Xianxin's contract.
*Credit*: Bibliothèque nationale de France.

which details the type and amount of each silk contribution, reads like a *Who's Who* of Dunhuang dignitaries. Starting with Monastic General Zhang, sixty-four officials of different stature and specialization each contributed to the goods offered to the Son of Heaven. The vast majority of the people in this list are not given their full names, only their surnames and titles, such as An *zhenshi* (Garrison Commissioner An). These abbreviated names indicate that the compiler of the document was likely familiar with the people who made contributions. With the two exceptions of the great secretary (*da shangshu*) and Commander Suo (Suo *zhihui*), each of whom put up two *pi*, all the listed contributors, despite differing official ranks, made equal contributions of one *pi* of silk. One might assume that the profit generated by the return gifts from the Song would have been distributed equally among these people as well. The people mentioned in this list also appear as a group in other documents, including two lists of wedding banquet guests and another list for an unknown purpose.[63] In particular, the guest list for the wedding banquet of lady Yin in 994 included 631 people (about 2 percent of the population of Dunhuang),[64] ranging from Khotanese princes and queens to Dunhuang officials and their families. The fact that the list of wedding guests and the list of diplomatic gift givers overlap to such an extent suggests that these people formed the ruling class of Dunhuang society. The members of this ruling class might not all travel as envoys, but they fully participated in diplomatic gift exchange on the Silk Road by pitching in their share of silk to the mission to the Song capital in 996. The contributions of these wealthy individuals must have played a central role in the envoys' ability to fund their trips.

Such pooling of resources occurred not only at the very top of the social hierarchy in Dunhuang. Another list of road goods includes goods of much lower value.[65] Like the list discussed above, this list does not usually give full names. Instead, the contributors are primarily family units, such as the Zhang family or the Yin family. The ones that are not families are often artisans of various kinds, such as carpenters, which are the only cases in which the full name of the contributor is given. The omission indicates, yet again, a closely knit network of people in which a reference to just a "Zhang family" could point to a specific family. One might speculate that this network could have existed in the context of the same village or neighborhood (known as a "ward") in the city, where one or more members were about to begin a long-distance journey, prompting the collection of contributions. Unlike the previous list, which primarily consisted of silk, the goods contributed in this list are both more varied in kind and modest in value. They include both silk and plainer types of cloth like state-sanctioned cloth, felt carpet, six pieces of jade, and one *pi* of cotton cloth from Kucha. Thus, these goods were not all necessities for travel in the forms of food, clothing, or means of transportation. They were goods to be exchanged, rather than consumed, by the travelers either as gifts or as commodities on the road. In this way, each family that contributed to the travelers had a stake in these potential future exchanges, and the profits gained by the travelers would presumably also be shared among the contributors. The meticulousness of the list, in which not only the types of cloth but also the exact width and length of each piece are recorded, speaks to the businesslike nature of this enterprise.

Other lists, such as an undated list of goods to be delivered to Turfan,[66] are more differentiated: this one includes not only silk and other kinds of cloth but also arrows, lacquered plates, and lacquered cups. Unlike the first list of contributions from the ruling class, in which most contributors gave one *pi* of silk, there is a clear hierarchy in this text in terms of the amount contributed: an unnamed contributor called a "big man [*dajia*]" offered twenty *pi* of silk, whereas all other contributors gave one or two *pi*. This list is only partially preserved, so it is difficult to gauge the number of people involved. But it shows the pooling of significant resources occurred not only for trips to places like the Song capital Kaifeng but also for shorter trips such as this one to Turfan.

Residents of Dunhuang sometimes organized into mutual-help groups called "societies" (*she*) to deal with the large expenses in life such as funerals and weddings.[67] Among the Dunhuang documents, there are a substantial number of texts that were originally used by these *she* societies. In one of these texts, we find a stipulation of the rules of the Society for Long-Distance Travel (Yuanxing She 遠行社):

> The *Society for Long-Distance Travel* stipulates that close relatives, brothers, sisters, men and women (or daughters and sons) of the *society* should each contribute one *pi* of cloth on the occasion of return from long-distance travel or death [during the trip]. For those who travel more than 1000 *li*, on the day of departure for a trip for governmental matters, [each member of the society] should deliver one urn of wine; upon return, [each] should arrange for two urns of wine at the welcoming banquet. Trips for private purposes do not fall within the parameters [of this stipulation].[68]

The presence of a mutual-help group specifically relating to officially sanctioned long-distance travel indicates both the frequency of such journeys and the exorbitant cost that they could accrue. According to this stipulation, members of the society were responsible for providing goods to those who returned successfully and for those who died on the road. They were also tasked with holding banquets for the departing and arriving travelers who were society members. It is particularly telling that this document explicitly excludes private trips (*sixing* 私行) from the coverage. These residents of Dunhuang were willing to share the costs of long-distance trips, as long as the travelers were sent by the state as envoys.

One might assume that, when the envoys successfully returned, they would have to share whatever profit they acquired with those who initially helped fund the trips. Unfortunately I have found no direct evidence about the return gifts for these road goods. But there are several significant cases where gifts, after their initial exchange, were redistributed to the broader society of Dunhuang. In a document produced by Cao Yijin, the lord of Dunhuang, when he made a massive offering for a bodhimaṇḍala in 933, we find various types of gifting activities in a single event.[69] In this case, Cao Yijin contributed gifts to a Buddhist monastery at Dunhuang. The list of gifts included funding for a sutra-turning ritual that lasted seventeen days, communal meals for 1750 people, the initiation of seventeen monks and nuns, and fine clothes and silk.

At this time Dunhuang had a population of between thirty and forty thousand.[70] This banquet therefore involved about 4–6 percent of the state's entire population, a public event on a scale rarely seen in any other context in medieval Dunhuang.

Among the gifts that Cao gave to the monastery on this public occasion, one finds a "purple brocade jacket with coiled dragon." Next to this line a note was added indicating that it was "in exchange from the Khotanese prime minister."[71] Thus, this jacket was a gift from a Khotanese official to the lord of Dunhuang. Cao Yijin regifted this extremely extravagant item with imperial symbols to the monastery, perhaps because he did not feel he was entitled to such a garment with imperial images.[72] That this jacket was the first mentioned in the list of gifts highlights its value and significance. The jacket is followed in the list by other luxury items, such as "one jacket made of red palace-style brocade, one short-sleeved shirt made of purple silk, one pair of trousers made of white silk with single-wreath-shaped patterns," and other kinds of cloth. These luxurious gifts to the monastery should be understood in the context of the gifts monasteries regularly provided to envoys, discussed in chapter 6. Cao Yijin's offerings served as a spectacular compensation to the monastery.

These gifts were not, however, meant only for monasteries. As the text states, the goal of this event was to wish for fortune and prosperity for both the emperor in China and the lord of Dunhuang. In particular, peace on the road was one of the more specific goals of these prayers: "May the envoys to the Eastern Court soon sight the Heavenly Countenance; may the envoys from Khotan come and go without interference." Thus the gifts transported on the Silk Road from places like Khotan were not only redistributed into the local economic life of Dunhuang, they also contributed to a collective prayer for peace on the road that would enable further transportation of similar goods. At the end of the text, Cao Yijin expresses the wish that the merit accumulated from this event would be further transferred to the general public. In this way, an exotic gift from a prime minister of Khotan not only became the actual possession of a monastery but also had symbolic significance for a much greater number of the Dunhuang public, many of whom were present at this ceremony. Like the luxury goods mentioned in the poem cited at the beginning of this chapter, Cao's gifts here were also "brought to the view of the commoners."

Redistribution of gifts did not occur only in the case of gifts between sovereigns and senior officials. There is evidence that gifts acquired by envoys too were shared when they came back to their home state. In a letter to an official in Dunhuang, the letter writer, an unnamed official in Suzhou just to the east of Dunhuang, discussed an array of official matters.[73] The first three are about an order to bring families of stationed troops to Liaoquan station within ten days to calm morale, a request to have painted screens and two sculptors sent to him along with another person, and the delayed shipment of previous requested goods from the commissioner of horses and soldiers. These matters show the close connection between these two places within the domain of the kingdom of Dunhuang. After laying out these three matters, the letter goes on to say that Wang Jingyi, an official serving as the head envoy of a mission to North China, has arrived in Suzhou. The letter writer explained that "previously, because of the large number of officials in various cities and garrisons, you have not [yet] received the gifts of benevolence [from the Chinese emperor]." He assured the official in Dunhuang that "this [lack of gifts] was not because I procured them for myself, please be aware." What this crucial sentence shows is that many "officials in various cities and garrisons" in Dunhuang *expected* to receive a certain share of the gifts of the Chinese emperor from the returning Dunhuang envoys.

Upon the arrival of the envoy Wang Jingyi, the letter writer received a new batch of gifts, and immediately dispatched someone to deliver these gifts, including one set of clothing and one silver bowl, to the previous letter recipient. It is surely not a coincidence that these items are the exact same kinds of gifts from the Tang emperor recorded in the documents discussed above for the 878 mission. In fact, in both cases, the gifts were said to have been wrapped up and sealed in a bag, with the seals being marked "intact" (*quan* 全).[74] Evidently, the gifts acquired by officials traveling as envoys did not belong only to them. A much larger group of officials in Dunhuang, like the recipient of this letter, also had claims and expectations of a share. The apologetic attitude of the letter writer about the earlier absence of gifts also shows that the practice of acquiring and redistributing gifts from China among officials was so routinized that the occasional temporary lapse demanded explanation. In this way, the profits of diplomacy were shared by a much larger spectrum of Dunhuang society than those who directly participated as envoys.

As a result of the acquisition and redistribution of goods through diplomacy, luxury items in the form of silk and other textiles found their way into households of Dunhuang. In an account of the property of an unnamed household in 991, we find a dazzling array of silk items.[75] The list begins with some pieces with fantastical names: seven *pi* of "yellow deer fetus," and three *pi* of "red translucent seashell." The only way for us to know that they were silk or at least some kind of textile is the counting word *pi*. The list continues, with dragon (patterned) yellow damask, yellow imperial (*yu* 御) damask, and white imperial damask. The "imperial" appellation and patterns of these pieces of textile show that they were associated with the Chinese emperor and could conceivably have been diplomatic gifts from the emperor. After these items, the list then includes other precious textiles, such as red patterned silk, silver brocade, yellow-black floral-patterned silk, and three *pi* of "sand in clear sky." Only at the very end of the list, likely indicating the lowest end of the value spectrum, do we find regular white, yellow, purple, or blue silk, both raw and processed, the kind of silk usually exchanged in the contracts discussed above. While we do not know which household this particular list belonged to, it is clear that it owned things the value of which far exceeded anything the local agrarian economy of Dunhuang could produce. Many of these luxurious textiles, particularly those associated with the Chinese emperor, may have come into this household through the network of envoys. Here we see that diplomacy could reshape what was economically possible for a household in Dunhuang.

Finally, I want to approach the issue of scale. The stories of economic decisions are informative in showing the role of diplomacy in the individual lives of diplomatic travelers. But to what extent did these journeys affect the economy of Dunhuang *as a whole*? Were these just exceptional cases that did not have any structural impact on Dunhuang's economy, and thus mattered little to most people in Dunhuang? These questions are similar to the one I raised in chapter 2 about the number of people who traveled as envoys in Dunhuang, and they are similarly difficult to answer. Nevertheless, some of the examples I have presented above, although each having its specific social and economic context, seem to indicate the broad impact of diplomacy on Dunhuang's economy. The significant number of people involved in the wedding and Buddhist banquets, where they were exposed to the riches imported through diplomatic connections, suggests that a great many of the residents in Dunhuang must have been aware of diplomacy as a means of gaining wealth. The large number of people who traveled as state envoys, as I explained in chapter 2, also means that the economic successes and failures of diplomats did not affect only a small group of people.

In addition, there is one number that might be statistically meaningful. Eric Trombert, a pioneer in the study of the economic history of Dunhuang, noticed that in Dunhuang contracts from the tenth century, travel was "the only reason that was explicitly given in the contracts."[76] Of the forty-seven contracts he studied for this period, nineteen quoted journeys to places like Turfan, Khotan, Ganzhou, and Kaifeng/Chang'an as the reason for the economic transactions recorded. As Trombert pointed out, the other twenty-eight contracts generally did not explicitly state the purpose for the contract, offering instead the vague reason of "lacking wealth in the household." For all we know, they could have been used for travelers as well. Among the nineteen that specifically cite travel, only one was made for a commercial trip. The purpose of the trip was, according to the contract, "to buy and sell things in the Southern Mountains [Nanshan maimai 南山買賣]."[77] The other eighteen contracts— I have analyzed several of them in some detail in this chapter—were each created by someone who went on an official journey to a foreign state on behalf of the Dunhuang government.

I ask readers to pause and consider just how strange this number is. To put it differently, in Dunhuang in the tenth century, among the forty-seven loan contracts collected by Trombert, about 40 percent were made by people borrowing things for diplomatic journeys. This very specific activity—acquiring the goods necessary for one's diplomatic journey—accounts for a tiny fraction of the economic activity in any modern state where readers may live. Yet in tenth-century Dunhuang, it assumed a highly visible presence in the local economy. It is, of course, important to acknowledge the inherent bias of the documentation we have. But the accidental nature of the Dunhuang archive (see chapter 1) would suggest that the group of forty-seven contracts is at least *to some extent* a random sample of economic activity in Dunhuang. This high representation of contracts for diplomats should thus not be dismissed as a mere coincidence. Indeed, if anywhere near this percentage of all the contractual activity in Dunhuang's economy involved diplomacy, then we are looking at an economy that was to a significant extent defined by the activities of diplomatic travelers. If diplomacy is a specialized bureaucratic endeavor in most modern states, to many residents of medieval Dunhuang it was a way of life, and a means of livelihood.

## Conclusion

In this chapter, I have argued that diplomacy was central to the economy of Dunhuang. Envoys who traveled on diplomatic missions exchanged luxury items and acquired expensive gifts; often they also contributed significant investment locally in purchasing or borrowing materials to prepare for the trip. When placed in the context of the agrarian economy of Dunhuang, it becomes clear that long-distance travel as an envoy, with its tremendous amount of investment and profit, was a uniquely lucrative endeavor for people in Dunhuang. The profits of diplomacy lured Dunhuang residents into serving as envoys, often taking great personal and financial risks.

Such risks were mitigated by the fact that people from a wide spectrum of Dunhuang society participated in the costs and benefits of long-distance travel, often without serving as envoys themselves. These people included creditors and debtors in loans relating to envoys' trips, family members of envoys who guaranteed them in these loans, sworn brothers and sisters of the Society for Long-Distance Travel, officials who collectively contributed gifts to the Chinese emperor, and people who pooled materials as sending-off gifts. They formed a complex local network that supported the people who actually went on the road, shouldered the risks of long-distance diplomatic travel, and shared the profits. In this way, the economics of diplomacy not only affected the sovereigns who gave and received gifts and the envoys who traveled, but also shaped many other aspects of the economy in Dunhuang.

At the beginning of this chapter, I quoted a lyrical poem composed in Dunhuang that states that, through the opening of a diplomatic connection with Khotan, "there will be cotton and silk filling every household." This poem's claim of a close connection between the smooth functioning of diplomacy and the economic well-being of Dunhuang residents, after my discussion in this chapter, becomes easy to understand. Read in the context of the many cases of economic decisions made by residents of Dunhuang discussed above, these lines appear not to be merely a poetic fantasy but reflect the central, and previously unexplored, role of diplomacy in the economy of Dunhuang.

# 9

# The Kingly Exchange

THE ECONOMY of Dunhuang society at large was shaped, as I showed in chapter 8, by diplomatic connections on the Silk Road. Envoys, many of whom were commoners in Dunhuang, were incentivized to participate in diplomacy because of the potential material gains. But how about the social group at the very top: the kings, the royal families, and their close associates? These kings consistently dispatched envoys to other states, exchanged gifts with other kings, and offered foreign envoys accommodation and protection: all indications that they were willing, even eager participants in the diplomatic network on the Silk Road. Why were kings so invested in creating and sustaining this network? What did they stand to gain? Did the diplomatic network change the behavior of these kings? This chapter is my attempt to understand the actions of kings connected by the "King's Road."

To answer these questions, I first discuss the material gains kings made through this diplomatic network. I show that luxury goods that were exchanged as diplomatic gifts often went into the kings' private coffers rather than the state treasury, giving them a strong personal incentive to create and maintain the diplomatic network. The luxury gifts, once acquired, were used as corporal decoration or augmentation for the kings, distinguishing them from their more ordinary subjects. And the rigorous sharing of diplomatic gifts among kings of Eastern Eurasia resulted in a curious phenomenon: in images produced thousands of kilometers apart, kings and queens often were depicted as dressing in comparable ways, donning similar luxury goods that were exchanged on the Silk Road. For all these kings, the exhibition of luxury was a key ingredient in their display of power.

But the kings acquired more than luxury goods in the diplomatic network. Through the use of official state letters and ad hoc oral communications with envoys, kings kept abreast of changes in the world—the death of another king, the movement of rebels, the outcome of a war. This network of political information allowed kings to frequently reassess their relative political and military strength vis-à-vis their neighbors and adjust their policy priorities and political rhetoric. The news regarding the fall of the Tang, for instance, brought about novel political experiments in Dunhuang, where the king claimed to be the "Son of Heaven," and in Khotan, where the king assumed the tile of "king of kings of China."

Therefore, the diplomatic network channeled exotic luxuries and political news, and enabled association with fellow kings, all indispensable in the kings' self-fashioning and legitimation. The kings' interests aligned well with those of the envoys in creating and sustaining the diplomatic network on the Silk Road.

## The King's Coffer

According to a story recorded by Cai Tao, a court insider in the early Southern Song, whenever Emperor Huizong (r. 1100–1126), the penultimate emperor of the Northern Song, left the palace, his eunuchs always carried two pieces of weaponry.[1] The first was a stick made of pure iron that Emperor Taizu (927–76), the founder of the Song dynasty, used "when he was obscure"—meaning before he became emperor. Emperor Taizu's grip was so strong that the imprint of his fingers was said to be still visible in Emperor Huizong's time, more than 150 years later. The lesson of this iron stick seems clear: by holding it, Emperor Huizong invoked the military prowess of his imperial ancestor, an important aspect of Song worship of its founders.[2]

The other item points to a different dimension of kingship in the Song. It was a "jade fist" made of "real Khotanese jade, much bigger than the human fist, attached to a string made of red *jin*-silk." The exact use of this fist is not recorded. Might Emperor Huizong have actually used it to strike at an insubordinate official? It is impossible to know. But there seems little doubt that the fist, just like the iron stick, symbolized imperial power, only in a different way. If the significance of the iron stick derived from Emperor Taizu's ancestral grip, the fist was fitting for imperial use because it was made of a rather sizable piece of "real Khotanese jade," a rarity from thousands of kilometers away in Khotan, the main source of jade in all of Eastern Eurasia at the time.[3] Emperor Huizong's use of this jade fist directs our attention to the close relation between luxurious and exotic things and the expression of kingly power.[4]

Luxuries were not always exotic imports: the red silk string that was attached to the jade fist was likely of Song domestic origin. But often, it was the long-distance journeys, particularly those across boundaries between states, that turned things from ordinary to luxurious (see chapter 3). In this chapter, I shall explore the relation between luxury and power by tracing how kings acquired luxury items and analyzing the ways in which they used them. The central significance of foreign goods in the representation of kingship was a forceful motive for kings to create and maintain a diplomatic network with their neighbors.

Let us first turn back to the 878 journey of Dunhuang envoys to Chang'an, a diplomatic mission characterized by an extremely unequal exchange of gifts, which I discussed in some detail in chapter 8. Why would the Tang emperor shower the envoys with silk, clothing, and silverware, when all he received was a yak tail, an antelope horn, and a piece of jade? The dynamics of gift exchange offers part of the explanation: by giving significantly more than the lord of Dunhuang, the Tang emperor reasserted his superior status in their relation. A reputation as a gift giver was considered worth pursuing, and was often incorporated into celebrations of kingly power in premodern Eurasia.[5]

Acquiring a reputation as a magnanimous gift giver, however, is not the whole story. If we follow the gifts from the Dunhuang envoys after they were offered, another more materialistic dimension emerges, which further explains the behavior of the Tang emperor. Although the whereabouts of these three gifts are not specifically recorded, from Tang regulations we can make an educated guess that they most likely ended up in the Qionglin (Forest of Jade) Treasury, located in the Daming Palace.[6] The Tang Empire had a complex treasury system to store the income of the state from different channels.[7] Relevant to our purpose here is the presence of two distinct treasuries: the national treasury, the "Left Treasury," and the emperor's personal treasury, the "Inner Treasury" (neiku). A mid-Tang critic of the emperors' private greed cited an earlier rationale for this distinction, of which he disapproved: "Taxation should be given to the administration for the use of the state; gifts and tributes should belong to the Son of Heaven for the personal banquets and offerings of the emperor."[8] This critic suggested that the emperor abolish his personal Inner Treasury, whose existence as a destination for state revenues he saw as damaging the finances of the state. But, judging from other sources, such personal treasuries only expanded in the late Tang.[9] The most likely destination for the three gifts in 878 was thus the personal treasury of the Tang emperor.

On the other hand, the supplies for foreign envoys and gifts to them were not exclusively, or even primarily, from the emperor's personal treasury. An edict from 758 explicitly states that the supplies for "foreign guests" should come from the national, rather than the emperor's private, treasury.[10] The silk and textiles, which accounted for the bulk of the return gifts from the Tang emperor, very likely also came from the national treasury of the Tang government. Indeed, raw silk was one of the main items of taxation in the Tang, and the national treasury had ample supply of raw silk.[11] It is possible that some other items that the Tang emperor gave out as gifts might have come from his personal treasury, especially when these gifts were goods that were not part of the Tang taxation regime. The silverware, for instance, may have been gifts from other states that ended up in his private treasury.[12] This practice of regifting may have been behind the piece of jade, likely from Khotan, that was offered to the Tang emperor by the Dunhuang mission in 878. Nonetheless, because a significant part of the gifts from the Tang emperor came from the state treasury, while all gifts from other kings went to his personal treasury, it is more than likely that the Tang emperor was never the poorer personally, even though he gave more gifts than he received.

At the other end of the exchange of 878, the king of Dunhuang also made significant personal gains. I described how much the envoys personally acquired as gifts during this trip (chapter 8), and how potentially life changing these gifts could have been for commoners in Dunhuang. The gains of regular envoys (ranging from 48 to 58 *pi* of silk, in addition to silver bowls and clothing), however, pale in comparison to the gifts intended for the lord of Dunhuang, which included 120 *pi* of silk, a set of clothing, a silver box, a silver bowl, and an imperial edict. As the kings of Dunhuang regularly sent envoys to their neighbors, such return gifts must have been a routine stream of income for them.

While there is no direct record of these gifts going to the personal treasury of the kings of Dunhuang, the structural distinction between a governmental treasury and an "inner" treasury existed here too. The governmental treasury, known as the Treasury of Military Expenditure (Junzi Ku 軍資庫),[13] stored taxation from subjects of the Dunhuang government. Its expenditure included significant outlays for the accommodation of foreign envoys. The majority of the paper, wine, clothes, and food given to these envoys came from the governmental treasury, not the personal, inner treasury of the lord of Dunhuang.[14] But similar to the case of the Tang, some goods and gifts to envoys must have come from the inner treasury. For instance, a petition from the manager of the inner treasury states that "three cotton jackets and a Sogdian [*hu*] bed" were dispensed for the use of a large group of Tatar visitors.[15] The king therefore used some of his personal wealth to help foreign travelers in need. Nonetheless, these occasions were exceptions, and the governmental treasury generally handled the daily expenses of visiting envoys.[16] Therefore, the kings of Dunhuang enjoyed the same kind of structural benefit as the Tang emperor in diplomatic gift exchanges.

The sovereigns' invested personal interest in diplomatic gifts can be seen in the ways they treated these gifts. During the reign of Emperor Dezong (r. 779–805) of the Tang, the emperor dispatched a eunuch to Khotan to seek jade. The search was successful, and the eunuch acquired a substantial number of decorative jade items. Instead of delivering these precious pieces to the emperor, however, the eneuch fabricated a story that the treasures had been robbed by Uyghurs on the way back. This brazen attempt at embezzlement was eventually uncovered and the eunuch was exiled to, and soon died in, a province in the deep south.[17] Relevant here is the fact that the task of procuring Khotanese jade was given to a eunuch rather than a regular official. This decision shows the personal nature of these endeavors, because eunuchs were part of the personal entourage of the emperor and not answerable to the regular bureaucracy.

In another case, Emperor Xuanzong, the great-grandfather of Dezong, proclaimed in an edict that "I the emperor cherish only grains and value only the virtuous people. I neither accrue useless expenses nor value things from afar. Therefore, brocade, silk, pearls, and jade are burned in the imperial courtyard, and giant clams and agate stones are offered to the vassal states."[18] The brocade, silk, pearls, and jade must have included those that entered the Tang court through diplomacy. The two emperors' attitudes toward luxury goods were diametrically opposed: one actively sought them out, while the other argued against their value. What unites them is that both considered these luxury things their *personal* possessions, free for them to obtain and to destroy. Since the sovereigns were in personal control of diplomatic dealings and the flow of gifts, it is easy to imagine that they would make sure they did not come away with a deficit.

Preston Torbert, in his study of the Qing imperial court, observes that "the exchange of tributary gifts, while functioning as a vehicle for the conduct of international relations, also contributed to the emperor's personal fortune."[19] Commenting more broadly, Christopher Bayly notes that:

> This common ideology also inflected the logic behind royal consumption over much of Asia and beyond, bringing large quantities of graded goods

and products into treasuries each tagged and docketed with the name of the ruler, chief and region from which it came and the auspiciousness of the day on which it was received.[20]

These cases show that the practice of retaining diplomatic gifts for the personal use of emperors and kings was not unique to medieval Eastern Eurasia.

As a result of this general practice, the kings of Dunhuang became personally wealthy. While no accounting of their wealth exists, we know that they routinely donated luxury silks to the local monasteries.[21] Within seven months between 933 and 934, for instance, Cao Yijin made at least four rounds of donations to the Buddhist communities in Dunhuang, which included two banquets that hosted 1500 and 1600 people respectively, as well as precious textiles and ready-made clothes.[22] In another, possibly related, record that dates to 936, the central financial bureau of the Buddhist community in Dunhuang lists its possessions.[23] The largest part of these possessions came from auctions held upon the death of members of the community or its devout followers, and donations made by those followers. In this list, all of the various goods were valued in plain hemp cloth, one of the currencies at the time.[24] Within three years (934–36), the Buddhist community had newly acquired goods valued at 58,502 *chi* (about 17,550 meters) of hemp cloth, of which Cao Yijin and his family had contributed 28,520 *chi*, or about 49 percent. Since 1 *chi* of hemp cloth was valued at about one *dou* of grain, these donations by the royal family of Dunhuang would have amounted to close to three thousand *shi* of grain, enough (if we remember the math in chapter 8) to purchase sixty houses. It is likely that the other kings discussed in this book, those of Khotan, Turfan, and Ganzhou, would have been similarly wealthy.

## Adorning the Kings

What did the kings do with their wealth, a significant portion of which must have been acquired through diplomatic gift exchange? Much of it likely would have been donated to Buddhist institutions for the accumulation of merit, as the Cao kings did. But religious donations are not the full picture. Let us return once again to the three gifts given to the Tang emperor by the lord of Dunhuang in 878: an antelope horn, a yak tail, and a piece of jade. None of these three items was local to Dunhuang: jade was at this time exclusively produced by the kingdom of Khotan to the west,[25] the yak tail originated from the Tibetan Plateau to the south, and the antelope horn would have hailed from places even farther west, likely Western Asia or Africa—one earlier appearance of antelope as a gift at the Tang court came from Byzantine envoys.[26] When these objects already foreign to Dunhuang were delivered to the Tang court, their exotic appeal became even more pronounced. After their arrival at the Tang court, the jade might be made into various royal accessories for the emperor,[27] the yak tail likely ended up embellishing the banners of the royal procession,[28] and the antelope horn, when ground and mixed with honey, served to alleviate fever in elite bodies.[29] In all three cases, the gifts were used in a *corporal* way: they were closely connected to the body of the sovereign.

This proximity to the kingly person characterized luxury goods transmitted on the Silk Road. A diverse array of goods, including horses, glassware, and different kinds of medicine and aromatics, traveled as diplomatic gifts and served the needs of the kings and elites of Eastern Eurasia. For instance, the majority of the gifts offered by the two Uyghur diplomatic missions in 951 (see chapter 3) were readily consumable by the kings, and did not enter the revenue stream of the state. In 1030, a combined diplomatic mission from Kucha and Dunhuang offered to the Song court the following gifts:

> From Kucha: jade belts, pearls, jade axe, [jade?] shield, pistil-patterned cotton cloth, gilded iron armor, frankincense, sal ammoniac, horses, single-humped camels [dromedaries], big-tailed sheep.

> From Dunhuang: jade, jade plates, black jade, jade bridle, pearl, frankincense, sal ammoniac, "tears of the wutong tree," fibroferrite [*huangfan* 黄矾], pistil-patterned cotton cloth, whitish-brown horses.[30]

These gifts came from a vast geographical span of the Eurasian continent: frankincense was most likely from Arabia or East Africa,[31] dromedaries almost certainly traveled from the Arabian Peninsula, and the various jade objects were, as always, from Khotan. The presence of these goods implies an extensive network of material exchange further to the west of Kucha and Dunhuang that is not always directly visible in our sources. But there were also more local gifts on both lists: pistil-patterned cotton cloth (*huarui bu* 花蕊布) came from Kucha itself,[32] whereas the "tears of the wutong tree" and fibroferrite were both local products of Dunhuang and nearby Guazhou, which was under the rule of the lord of Dunhuang.[33] Therefore, envoys from Kucha and Dunhuang offered gifts to the Song court that were either local products or regifted goods from farther west.

What unites this diverse group of items is their connection to the body of the sovereign at the Song court. The medicine, culinary rarities, and aromatics helped sustain and enhance sovereigns' bodies, while the cloth physically adorned them. These goods were sometimes bestowed on the elites by kings and were used similarly. In 1063, for instance, a group of Khotanese envoys came to the Song court and offered, among other things, pistil-patterned cotton cloth, the same exotica that the kings of Kucha and Dunhuang delivered in 1030. Emperor Renzong (1010–63), upon receiving the cotton cloth, regifted it to "officials from the prime ministers down," as a royal favor. According to Ouyang Xiu, who was one of the highest-ranked officials at the Song court at the time (*canzhi zhengshi* rank 2a) and a recipient of the cloth, it was "sturdy and white as solidified fat; when used against the wind, [it keeps] you warm in a way no less effective than cloth made of camel hair."[34] By wearing this precious piece of clothing, Ouyang Xiu showed off his status as one among an exclusive group of Song elites who had access to these objects of kingly grandeur.

Other items on the gift lists, such as the jade objects and armor, would have been prominently displayed in an imperial procession. For the Tang and the Song emperors, prescriptive instructions about how they should dress survive in the "chariot and clothing" chapters of standard dynastic histories. From these chapters we know that for the most sacred rituals, the emperor rode a "jade chariot" that had its tips decorated with pieces of jade.[35] The unprocessed pieces of jade on these two lists might have been used for the chariot of the emperor, like the jade bridle and the horses that pulled their chariots. The jade plates were used to inscribe imperial edicts;[36] jade belts and pearls were worn by emperors and other elites;[37] jade axes and gilded iron armor were displayed by imperial guards at royal processions.[38] In their suburban sacrifices, Tang emperors not only rode jade chariots, but also offered silk and jade to Heaven.[39] Such exotic goods acquired through diplomacy were central to the expression and legitimation of Tang-Song kingship.

Indeed, an early thirteenth-century official remarked about the Song court that "the ritual objects of our dynasty, the adornments and transportation of the emperor, were mostly made of Khotanese jade."[40] The imperial seal, a central ritual object of Song imperial power, was made of jade.[41] The extensive use of Khotanese jade in state rituals necessitated a steady stream of Khotanese envoys to maintain the supply chain, which is amply attested in both transmitted sources and Dunhuang documents. As Rong Xinjiang and Zhu Lishuang point out, because of the need for Khotanese jade was so great, the Song court could not always wait for the next diplomatic mission from Khotan to arrive of its own accord.[42] In 977, for instance, the Song court sent an envoy to Ganzhou and Dunhuang to offer gifts in order to "acquire famous horses and beautiful jade for use in chariots and ritual objects."[43] The initiator of this action and benefactor of these goods was the Song emperor. It is also telling that, like the case of Emperor Dezong of the Tang discussed earlier, the person sent on this mission was also a eunuch, the personal servant of the emperor, rather than a regular official of the Song government.

The use of jade in imperial adornment was not restricted to the Song but was shared by the Kitan state of the Liao. In 1018, a young Kitan princess, who was a grand-daughter of Emperor Jingzong (r. 969–82) and born in 1001, died. She was buried with her husband, a Kitan nobleman. Their joint tomb, discovered in 1985, is one of the only tombs of members of the Liao imperial family that has been found largely undisturbed. The burial goods included many jade pieces, from bird- and fish-shaped pendants to jade belts, along with other visually stunning decorative objects in gold, silver, amber, and agate.[44] Many of these goods are known to have been gifts to Kitan from the west.[45] More specifically, in 1006, according to the *History of the Liao*, "from Shazhou [Dunhuang], the king of Dunhuang Cao Zongshou sent envoys to offer horses from the Tajik and fine jade; [the Kitan emperor] bestowed matching clothes [*duiyi*] and silver objects."[46] Like the Song court, the Kitan court was also an active participant in the Eurasian diplomatic network through which jade and other precious stones moved.

If jade was the most conspicuous kind of goods that traveled from Central Asia to the Song and the Kitan courts, the most prominent category of gifts that went in the other direction was precious textiles, either in the form of ready-made clothes or in rolls or even pieces of cloth. As Zhao Feng and Wang Le show in their survey of references to silk in the Dunhuang documents, virtually every part of the standard dress of the time could be made of silk.[47] Among the more familiar items, such as jackets and shawls, one finds a mysteriously named "warmer" (*nuanzi* 暖子), which Zhao considers to be a kind of luxury bathrobe. Emperor Wenzong of the Tang, when examining the imperial treasury, was said to have found two such warmers decorated with golden birds, which had belonged to Emperor Xuanzong and his consort Yang.[48] In a donation record from Dunhuang, we see that Cao Yijin donated two warmers (one in red compound weave silk from the palace, the other in purple compound weave silk) to a monastery in Dunhuang.[49] The kingly quality of these silk warmers was highlighted both by the reference to their origin (*gong* 宫, "palace") and their special color.[50] They might have been acquired directly from the Tang/Song court or made locally in imitation of those from North China. The fact that Tang emperors and the lords of Dunhuang possessed similar bathrobes made of *jin*, or compound weave silk, points to one consequence of

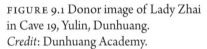

FIGURE 9.1 Donor image of Lady Zhai in Cave 19, Yulin, Dunhuang. *Credit*: Dunhuang Academy.

FIGURE 9.2 Donor image of Cao Yuanzhong in Cave 19, Yulin, Dunhuang. *Credit*: Dunhuang Academy.

the intense exchange of gifts intended to decorate the body of the sovereign—namely, the creation of a shared culture of kingly dress.

Thanks to the preservation of royal images, we can probe this question of kingly decoration a bit further. The best-documented royal images are from the courts of the Northern Song (owing to the preservation of court paintings) and of Dunhuang (the mural paintings of donor images in the Dunhuang caves). To demonstrate the impact of the exchange of luxury goods on the self-representation of kings of Eastern Eurasia, I will briefly examine the images of two royal couples: Cao Yuanzhong (?–974), the king of Dunhuang, and his queen, Lady Zhai, and Emperor Renzong (1010–63) of the Song and Empress Cao (1016–79). The images I selected are those of Lady Zhai (figure 9.1) and Cao Yuanzhong (figure 9.2) preserved in Cave 19 in the Yulin Cave Complex near Dunhuang,[51] and those of Empress Cao (figure 9.3) and Emperor

FIGURE 9.3 Portrait of Empress Cao of the Song (with attendants).
*Credit*: National Palace Museum, Taipei

Renzong (figure 9.4) preserved through the imperial collection of the Qing dynasty and now in the Palace Museum in Taipei.[52]

The portrait of Song emperor Renzong (figure 9.4), like other existing portraits of Song emperors, shows a subdued figure dressed rather modestly in the style of an official. One of the only places where status is indicated is the emperor's crimson belt decorated with a large piece of white jade, known as the "jade-decorated red waist belt" (*yuzhuang hong shudai* 玉裝紅束帶).[53] Given the centrality of Khotanese jade in the Song court discussed above, it is difficult to imagine that the jade on the emperor's belt would have come from anywhere else. Indeed, jade belts were one of the staple gifts from Khotan

FIGURE 9.4 Portrait Emperor Renzong of the Song.
*Credit*: National Palace Museum, Taipei

to the Song court.[54] So it is not impossible that the entire belt, rather than just the piece of jade, was imported from Khotan. In like manner, Cao Yuanzhong, the lord of Dunhuang, is also wearing a jade-decorated belt in the mural painting in Yulin Cave 19 (figure 9.2). His robe and hat also resemble those of the Song emperor. The robe was originally painted red but has turned brown owing to oxidation. Even to untrained eyes, such similarity is hard to miss.

FIGURE 9.5 Details of the portraits of Empress Cao (figure 9.3) and Lady Zhai (figure 9.1), showing the headdresses.
*Credit*: Dunhuang Academy and National Palace Museum, Taipei.

On the other hand, the images of Lady Zhai and Empress Cao diverge significantly. The dragons prominently displayed on the borders of Empress Cao's robe (see figure 9.3) are more visually captivating than the simple floral patterns on Lady Zhai's robe (see figure 9.1). Their headdresses are also different: Empress Cao's headdress is decorated with a flying dragon, whereas Lady Zhai's is shaped like a phoenix (figure 9.5).[55] Nonetheless, both royal ladies are lavishly adorned with precious jewelry such as pearls and jade, and wear intricately woven shawls and robes, certainly made of luxury textiles like silk. Particularly alike are the facial decorations, known as *huadian*, where pearls and jade pieces were attached to the women's cheeks and foreheads. The necklaces, too, are both made of precious jewels. If the images of these two royal ladies differ in details, they are both transparent displays of the tremendous wealth and luxury available to the royal families, something shown in a more restrained manner in the images of their male counterparts.

The similarity in how the royals were depicted was not simply a result of the kings of Dunhuang learning to dress like the emperors of the Tang or the Song. In fact, the diverse origins of the royal dress can be seen in the very same image (figure 9.2) in Yulin Cave 19. Here, just behind Cao Yuanzhong stands a boy identified as his son Cao Yanlu, the future king of Dunhuang. Cao Yanlu is dressed quite differently from his father (figure 9.6). In fact, if we compare his dress with that of male royal donors in images discovered in Turfan (figure 9.7),[56] it is apparent that whoever drew the Dunhuang prince was consciously modeling his dress on that of male Uyghur royal figures. The thin belts of both Cao Yanlu and the Uyghur donors, with intricate hanging blade and other pendants, contrast with the wider belts of Cao Yuanzhong and Emperor Renzong. The floral pattern of Cao Yanlu's robe is very similar to those of the Turfan donors, especially the middle one of the three. The men in both images are holding flowers, albeit of different kinds. The headdresses of the Uyghur donors are much more intricate than that of Cao Yanlu, but both differ drastically from those of Cao Yuanzhong and Emperor Renzong.[57] When we place the portraits of Cao Yuanzhong and Cao Yanlu in the context of other royal images, it is clear that the royals of Dunhuang shared very similar dress with their neighbors both to the east and to the west.

A most spectacular example of this sharing of royal attire, and the prominence of luxury items, is the image of the king of Kho-

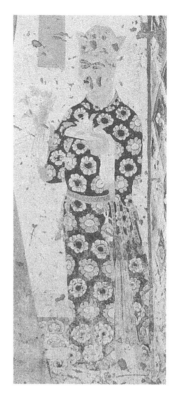

FIGURE 9.6 Detail of the donor image of Cao Yuanzhong (figure 9.2) showing his son Cao Yanlu.
*Credit*: Dunhuang Academy.

tan found in Dunhuang Cave 98. The corridors of the cave are decorated with life-sized portraits of generations of lords of Dunhuang, dressed in largely the same way as Cao Yuanzhong in figure 9.2. On the eastern wall of the main chamber, however, one finds an image of a king of Khotan that stands 2.92 meters high (figure 9.8), the largest donor image not only in this cave but among all the Dunhuang mural paintings. Scholars generally agree that this is an image is of the king Viśa' Saṃbhava/Li Shengtian.[58] In this image, Viśa' Saṃbhava has the typical trappings of Chinese emperor. His image resembles the canonical depictions of Chinese emperors found in, for instance, the work of Yan Liben (閻立本; 601–73). Figures 9.8 and 9.9 juxtapose the image of Viśa' Saṃbhava with that of Sima Yan (司馬炎; 236–90), Emperor Wudi of

FIGURE 9.7 Image of royal donors from Turfan in Bezkilik Cave 20.

the Jin Dynasty, from Yan's celebrated *Portraits of Generations of Emperors* (*Lidai diwang tu* 歷代帝王圖).[59] The Khotanese king's headdress (*mian* 冕), used exclusively by Chinese emperors, has the bejeweled *liu* (旒) strings dangling on both the front and back (figure 9.8); the number of strings (twelve) shows that this was a headdress appropriate to the most solemn of occasions. Similarly, the robe (*yi* 衣) and lower garment (*shang* 裳) bear the auspicious symbols (*zhang* 章) of Chinese emperors as seen in Emperor Wudi's portrait (figure 9.9). For tenth-century viewers of the cave, what was depicted in this image was unambiguously a Chinese emperor. Unlike Emperor Wudi, however, the Khotanese king's image in Cave 98 is lavishly decorated with jade: both the top of the headdress and the twelve *liu* strings are

大朝大寶于闐國大聖大明天子

FIGURE 9.8 A king of Khotan, believed to be Viśa' Saṃbhava, in Dunhuang Cave 98.
*Credit*: Dunhuang Academy.

晋武帝司馬炎

FIGURE 9.9 Emperor Wudi of the Jin dynasty,
according to Yan Liben's *Lidai diwang tu*.

dotted with turquoise-colored jade pieces. He is even wearing jade rings on both hands. In this case, the luxury was not exotic, because jade was the most important product of Khotan. Instead, it became a trademark visual feature that, along with the inscription next to the emperor, allowed viewers to unmistakably identify the larger-than-life figure as the Khotanese king.

These royal images differ in painting medium and social context. Despite these differences, even my very cursory survey shows, I hope, that the rulers shared many features in the types of clothes and headdresses they donned and the belts they wore. One key commonality of all these images is the prominent place of luxury goods in the corporeal adornment of the kings. Whether subdued (in the cases of Cao Yuanzhong and Emperor Renzong), transparent (Empress Cao and Lady Zhai), or pronounced (Viśa' Saṃbhava), luxury goods such as jade from Khotan, silk from North China, and pearls from the

FIGURE 9.10 Detail from the portrait of the
Khotanese king in Dunhuang Cave 98.
*Credit*: Dunhuang Academy.

coasts of the Indian Ocean or the Persian Gulf are included in each of the
images. From the textual evidence presented earlier, we know that royal adornment involved also brocade from Central Asia and yak tails from Tibet. Many,
if not most, of these goods were accessed through the diplomatic network
I describe in this book. Therefore, the royals of Eastern Eurasia were incentivized to send envoys on difficult journeys because they could acquire gifts that
not only enriched their coffers, but also, the most conspicuous examples being
jade and silk, were central to the ways the kings chose to be seen.

A detail of the image of the Khotanese king in Cave 98 merits a closer look.
Like Cao Yuanzhong in Yulin Cave 19, the king of Khotan is also depicted as
carrying a lavishly decorated sword on his belt. If we look more closely (figure 9.10), we can see that the pommel of the sword was made in the shape of
a fist, which is holding a red string (now turned brown from centuries of oxidation). Is this what the jade fist of the Song emperor introduced earlier would
have looked like? There are some apparent differences between the two fists:
in the Khotanese king's image, the fist as the pommel of a sword was smaller
than the king's hand, whereas the Song emperor's fist was said to be much
bigger than a normal hand; and it is unclear what the pommel and the string
were made of in the mind of the painter in Dunhuang. Nonetheless, the connection in both cases between Khotan, jade, and a fist as part of a kingly image
is hard to ignore. To both the Song emperor and the Khotanese king, luxury
materials were made into artificial fists as symbols of their kingly power.

## An Information Network

The kings and elites of Eastern Eurasia desired more than just material gains and the display of exotica in their daily lives. They also craved information about distant places. Such information was conveyed to the kings through oral communication and written messages. In 1009, when a group of Khotanese envoys arrived at Kaifeng, Emperor Zhenzong (r. 997–1022) of the Song asked them about how long they had been traveling and the conditions on the road.[60] In 1083, emperor Shenzong (r. 1067–85) asked Khotanese envoys at his court similar questions.[61] The records composed by envoys such as Gao Juhui and Wang Yande apprised the Later Jin and Song emperors of the kingdoms the envoys had encountered on the road. The Song ambassadors to the Liao similarly learned about the land and customs of the northern state, which in turn shaped how the Song viewed itself.[62] From these records, we know that the emperors in North China were most interested in the local products and political status of other kings, as well as the length of the journey and conditions on the road.

Dunhuang materials show that these smaller kingdoms in the west, such as Dunhuang and Khotan, were no less well-informed. Unlike with Song emperors, whose documentation was mediated by later historical compilations, we have access to some of the original (or close copies of) diplomatic letters the kings of Dunhuang used. They allow an unparalleled look at the inner workings of this information network. For instance, an envoy's report from 884 reveals the kind of information that interested the lord of Dunhuang. This letter was delivered by a messenger to the officials in charge of the military garrison in Suzhou on Dunhuang's eastern border.[63] The text mainly deals with the whereabouts of four different missions to the Tang court that the lord of Dunhuang had dispatched.[64] The most dramatic piece of news, however, was inserted into the letter between information about two of these Dunhuang missions (figure 9.11). The inserted part states that "the brigand Huang Chao was killed by Shang Rang along with Huang Chao's brother in Xichuang; and the emperor returned and entered Chang'an on the seventh day of the tenth month." The death of Huang Chao, the rebel who had almost toppled the Tang dynasty, was one of the most discussed issues in Tang historiography.[65] Different sources offer accounts with different details of the manner of his death. But most agree that Huang Chao was hunted and beheaded by a Tang general called Lin Yin. The information contained in the diplomatic letter is therefore an outlier. In fact, the strikethrough at the bottom of line 5 from the right (in

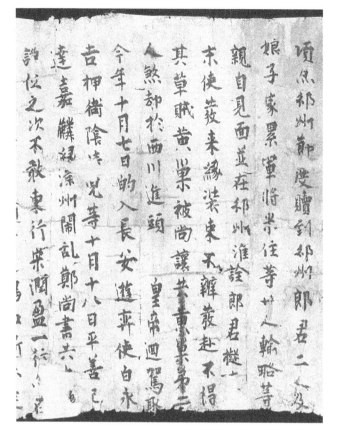

FIGURE 9.11 News about the death of Huang Chao.
*Credit*: The British Library.

figure 9.11) removed the phrase "along with Huang Chao's brother [*gong Huang Chao di* 共黃巢弟]," thus betraying the uncertainty of the composer and/or copyist of the letter about what really occurred in a surely fluid and chaotic situation. Nonetheless, the letter did convey two key pieces of information—the death of Huang Chao and the return of the Tang emperor to Chang'an—in a timely and accurate manner to the lord of Dunhuang.

This letter revealing a prompt flow of political news is by no means exceptional. The four diplomatic missions from Dunhuang, were they successful in returning home, must have carried news about further developments in the stimulating political drama. Indeed, a copy of the amnesty decree by the Tang emperor after his return to Chang'an in the following year is also preserved in the Dunhuang library cave, and might have been passed on to Dunhuang by one of these diplomatic missions.[66] The specific route of transmission by which this document ended up in the library cave is unrecoverable. But the Dunhuang government was undoubtedly keeping a close eye on the political shifts in the Tang capital Chang'an at the delicate moment following the death of Huang Chao and the restoration of the Tang emperor.

In one other case, we can trace with greater precision the particular way in which political information from North China was conveyed to Dunhuang. Our knowledge here is based on a single document produced during the Later Jin dynasty, likely in its capital Kaifeng. This document, S. 4473, is a three-meter-long scroll with writing on both sides. On the first side (figure 9.12) there are five texts, including:

1. "Eulogy for the Emperor of the Great Jin [Shi Jingtang, 892–942]"
2. "Letter from the Emperor of the Great Jin to the Emperor of the Northern Dynasty [Emperor Taizong, Yelü Deguang (902–74), of the Kitan Liao state]"
3. "Petition to Give a Posthumous Title to the Deceased Emperor"
4. "Seven Petitions to Decline Reappointment by the Jixian Minister after the Death of His Mother"
5. "Eulogy for the Deceased Mother"

All were copied tightly on this side of the scroll, by the same hand. On the other side (figure 9.13), there are three letters written by midlevel officials of the Later Jin state.[67]

Scholars have pointed out that the texts on the first side are all works of Li Song (?–948) of the Later Jin dynasty.[68] Li, a descendant of the Tang royal family, served the Later Tang and the Later Jin. By the time of the death of Shi Jingtang, Li Song had ascended to the illustrious office of prime minister.[69] In 941, according to texts 4 and 5 on side one, the author, a "prime minister" surnamed Li wrote six petitions to ask for temporary relief of official duty to mourn his mother, who had recently passed away. In the biography of Li Song in the *Old History of the Five Dynasties*, we see that he did indeed write to the emperor repeatedly to decline the order to reenter officialdom after his mother's death.[70] Given that there were two prime ministers at the time (the other being Sang Weihan), there is no doubt that the author of texts 4 and 5, the "prime minister Li," was in fact Li Song. As Li was known for his literary talent and tasked with drafting critical state documents and diplomatic letters, it is very probable that the other three texts—all official documents produced after the death of the Jin emperor Shi Jingtang—also came from Li's hand.

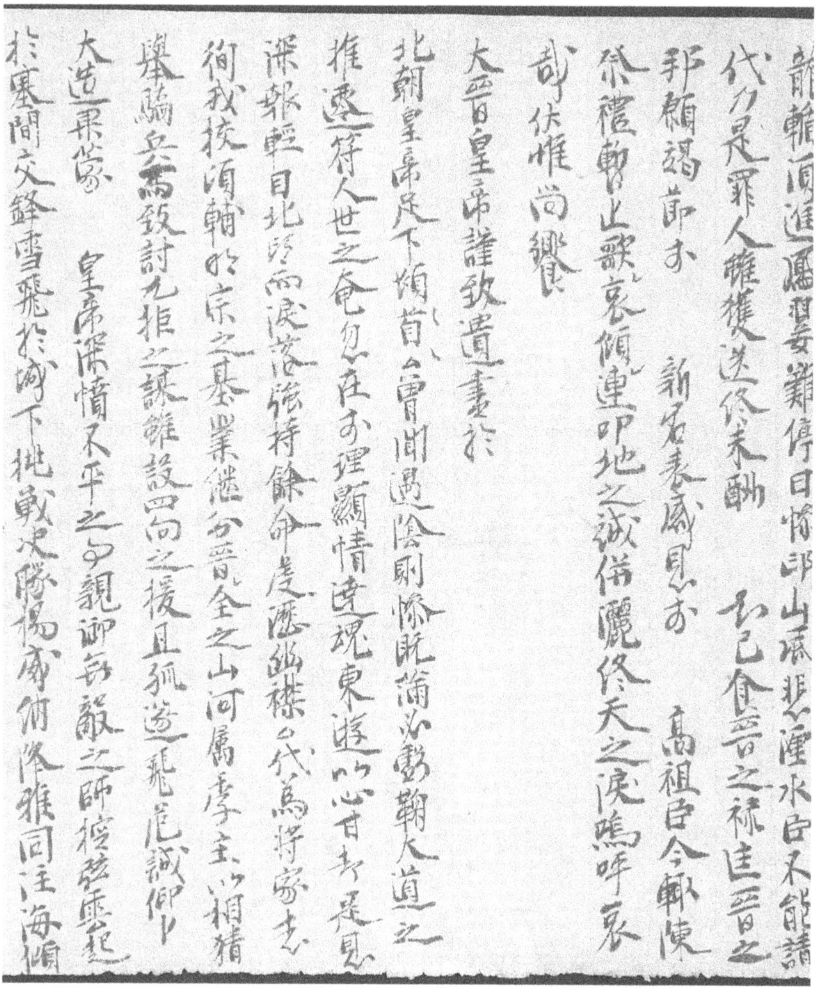

FIGURE 9.12 Beginning of the copy of the Jin emperor's letter to the Kitan emperor (text 2).
*Credit*: The British Library.

But how did this collection of a Jin prime minister's writing make its way to Dunhuang? Existing scholarship does not address this issue directly. I believe the clue lies on the other side of the same document. The historical importance of the texts on side one, particularly those dealing with the death of Shi Jingtang, has convinced scholars to treat it as the "recto" side and side two as the "verso."[71] But from both the content of the texts on the other side of this document and the physical features of the document as a whole, it is clear to

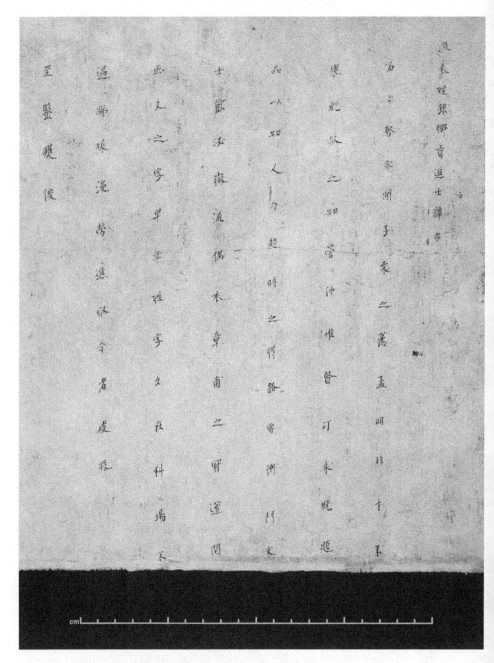

FIGURE 9.13 Beginning of Tan's petition (letter 3).
*Credit*: The British Library.

FIGURE 9.14 End of letter 1 (right) and end of letter 2 and beginning of letter 3 (left) on the recto side of S. 4473. The texts were written in different hands, and spaced widely following the practice of official writing. The given names of the letter writers are in smaller size to show humility.
*Credit*: The British Library.

me that the texts on side two were in fact written first. The first document on side two is a short, routine message of greeting from a general to a high official. The other two texts are both self-recommendation letters. One is written by a county head to the deputy minister of personnel (*libu shilang*) to ask for a new official appointment closer to the writer's hometown; the other is from a "provincial tribute" (*xianggong jinshi*) to his grand uncle for official recommendation. Thus, all three were letters drafted by officials of lower status to ones of higher status, perhaps even to the same person. These three texts were written in different hands (see figure 9.14) and strictly in accordance with the formal requirements of official documents at the time, with widely spaced characters and lines, and adherence to the proper arrangement and sizing of characters. The letter writers' names in the first two letters were written in smaller characters to show humility. Therefore, unlike the texts on side one, all of which are copies made by the same hand, the three letters on side two are likely originals. These letters were written on eight sheets of paper, each *within* units of sheets—letter one on sheet one, letter two on sheets two to four, and letter three on sheets five to eight (see the left-hand image in figure 9.14 for the connection line between sheets four and five)—whereas on the other side, texts were copied *across* connection lines between different sheets.[72] All these details show that the three texts on side two were written first, and these were then pasted together to form a longer scroll, the back of which was then used to copy the texts on side one, by a single person, possibly in one sitting.[73]

Understanding the making of this scroll helps us see the social context of the transmission of political information. All three letters on side two, or the recto side, are requests to unnamed high officials for help in the bureaucratic advancement of the letter writer, and at least one of them (letter two) was written by a county head in Hebei, around 150 kilometers from the coast of the Bohai Bay and 1500 kilometers from Dunhuang. It is virtually impossible that these recommendation letters would have been composed in Dunhuang. The far more likely scenario is that they were written and delivered to high officials in Kaifeng, the Later Jin capital.

After their delivery, the letters ran their course of usefulness, and became waste paper. They were then pasted together, in a form of recycling and reuse not unlike that we have seen locally in Dunhuang (see chapter 1), and formed a long scroll on which five texts by Li Song were copied. It is hard to know who in Kaifeng made these copies. It may have been someone in Li Song's household—indeed, the recommendation letters might have been originally addressed to Li. Or, they could have been copied by some other official keen on keeping up with the news of the day, and were subsequently acquired by representatives of the Dunhuang government. It is also possible that Dunhuang envoys requested that these copies be made, or even made the copies themselves from Li's writing circulating in the capital. In any case, the making of the long scroll shows that Dunhuang envoys actively sought political information in Kaifeng, organized the information in a single scroll, and brought it back to Dunhuang.

Through this scroll, the king of Dunhuang was made aware of not only what had happened in the Jin state, but also how it happened. The newly aggressive rhetoric the new emperor of the Later Jin adopted toward the Kitan emperor was a crucial factor, which changed the attitude of the Kitan and triggered a Kitan invasion.[74] This political rhetoric was immediately conveyed to the king of Dunhuang. In addition, the king also learned about the internal policies of the new emperor and changes in personnel at the highest echelons of the Jin bureaucracy. All this information was useful in the policy decisions of the king of Dunhuang. The fact that Dunhuang envoys had copies of diplomatic exchanges occurring between *other states* (the Later Jin and the Kitan) attests to the depth of this information network on the Silk Road.

The kings of Dunhuang were paying attention not only to the happenings in the east. P. 5538 is a letter from the king of Khotan Viśa' Śūra to the king of Dunhuang Cao Yuanzhong. The letter reports the recent military victories of Khotan against the Qarakhanids and includes a lengthy, and to us quite obscure, description of the movement of soldiers—information of obvious military and strategical significance. At the end of the letter, the Khotanese king recommends continued communication between the two sovereigns:

> If We deign to be successful in making [Our] brother the great king satisfied, if the couriers go, you will make a report in letters in detail for us about how it is in your mind, whether your heart harbors worry or whether it is appropriate that no mercy [meaning gift] comes here or whether you harbor satisfaction with the taking of the land.[75]

The Khotanese king explains that his military needs prevent him from sending more gifts—although the end of the letter does include a handsome number of gifts, featuring primarily jade—for which the Khotanese king asks for understanding. He wishes that this lack of proper gifts should not prevent the king of Dunhuang from continuing to deliver information, including "a report in letters in detail for us about how it is in your mind."

Similar wishes to maintain open information channels are seen in letters exchanged among other kings. In a letter dated to 931 from Cao Yijin to the Ganzhou khan Shunhua, Cao explains that "previously, all the matters of the world in the west [*xitou suoyou shijie shiyi* 西頭所有世界事宜] have been passed on [to you] repeatedly whenever there is a diplomatic mission. I suppose that it [the information] has reached you."[76] Here, it is notable that, as the western neighbor of Ganzhou, the king of Dunhuang Cao Yijin was responsible for conveying not only information about his own state, but also occurrences in the wider world to the west of Dunhuang.

In addition to carrying messages between kings, traveling envoys also constantly wrote back to their king about the political situation on the road. For instance, several well-preserved and lengthy letters written to the Khotanese king by Khotanese envoys in Dunhuang and further to the east are preserved. The envoys talk about conditions on the road, interactions with their hosts, and the political situations in the places they traveled to. The death of the

Uyghur khan in Ganzhou caused political chaos in his state and was meticulously reported on by the Khotanese envoy.[77] This information was useful for the king of Khotan in adjusting his broader foreign policy and making the specific decision of whether or not to send envoys to the east.

In this way, through the exchange of letters with other kings, reports by envoys, the copying of official documents from other states, and direct conversations with envoys from other states (see chapter 7), kings from Khotan to Kaifeng shared up-to-date news with one another. The news about the death of Huang Chao and the Khotanese king's defeat of the Qarakhanids, for instance, flowed swiftly on the Silk Road, likely making its way into every court in the region in a few months. The mutual exchange of gifts and personnel supported this network of political information.

Why was this kind of political information important? While we need not deny that the kings could have simply been curious about the outside world, it is easy to imagine that such knowledge also constituted a particular kind of exotica that, like jade and silk, further distinguished kings from others. Indeed, imperial edicts, physical carriers of political information, were placed on the leading horse while on the road and stored in specially designated houses after they were delivered.[78] This kind of treatment would elevated the edicts to the status of the rarest of luxury goods.

The use of information as a status marker is conceivable, but not well discussed in our sources. Better documented are the political implications of this information network in the decision-making of kings on the Silk Road. In the next section, I turn to a few cases of extraordinary political projects among kings of Dunhuang and Khotan, and demonstrate that their policy decisions were made with the help of the influx of both political information and luxury goods on the Silk Road.

## Kingly Claims

As the kings of Dunhuang and its neighbors kept a close eye on the political shifts in North China, they could not have missed the biggest news story of the time: the fall of the Tang dynasty. Even though the Tang ruling house had been in decline for decades, its official fall in 907 was no less consequential and caused immediate changes of state policy in a number of independent states that sprung up in the aftermath of the Tang collapse.[79] Zhang Chengfeng, the lord of Dunhuang at the time, swiftly dispatched a group of envoys to the newly founded Liang state after the fall of the Tang. Whatever Zhang learned from his envoys about the Liang—this information is not preserved—apparently did not impress him.[80] Therefore, shortly after the return of the envoys, around 909, Zhang founded a new state named "the Golden Mountain Kingdom of the Western Han" and declared himself "Son of Heaven" and "the White-Clothed Emperor of the Western Han."[81]

The elements of metal/gold and whiteness in the names of the kingdom and the emperor are clear indications of the relation between Zhang's new regime and the Tang Empire. According to the five-element theory, the element befitting a ruler changes in a patterned cycle.[82] The element of metal/gold succeeds that of earth, and in parallel the color white succeeds yellow. Because earth and yellow had been the element and color of the Tang, the element of metal/gold and color white were used in the political terminology of the new empire in Dunhuang to signify that Zhang Chengfeng had the objective of not merely breaking away from the regimes in North China but of succeeding the Tang and achieving the status of emperor.

The contours of Zhang's political ambition can be seen in the lines of a celebratory poem composed by a Dunhuang official after the sighting of a white sparrow. White sparrows had appeared as a political omen on several other occasions, such as the founding of the Tang, the creation of the local Western Liang dynasty (400–421) in Dunhuang, and the establishment of the Former Shu (907–25) dynasty, another state claiming to be a Tang successor in the tenth century.[83] Therefore, the convenient appearance of one in Dunhuang at this time served the political goals of Zhang Chengfeng. This goal is spelt out in the poem itself:

> His Highness the Son of Heaven of Golden Mountain Kingdom, from above he received the mysterious emblem and obtained the book [of mandate] of Heaven and Earth; from below he accorded the wish of the people, and facing south he became the lord. He will follow as the restoration of the Five Liangs, and occupy the great places of the eight prefectures.[84]

Unlike his ancestors, who had tied the rationale of their state to the recognition of the Tang court, Zhang Chengfeng traced an alternative history that he could "restore." What he found were the five kingdoms, all bearing the state name Liang—the Former Liang (320–76), Later Liang (386–403), Southern Liang (397–414), Western Liang (400–421), and Northern Liang (397–439)—that ruled parts of the Hexi region in the fourth and fifth centuries. Such political regionalism was found in other post-Tang states, particularly in South China, such as the Former Shu and the Southern Han.[85]

Zhang's experiment was not successful. His ambition to reconquer "the great places of the eight prefectures," which equates more or less to the entire Hexi region, was unrealistic because only two prefectures were under his control at the time. His military campaign against Ganzhou was quickly thwarted, and the counterstrike from Ganzhou, which reached the city of Dunhuang, forced him to give up his "imperial" ambitions. In circumstances still unclear to us, in 914 Cao Yijin replaced Zhang and established the Cao family rule of Dunhuang that lasted until 1036. This watershed moment in the political history of Dunhuang came as a direct result of the wild ambitions of Zhang Chengfeng triggered by the news of the fall of the Tang.

The political news about the fall of the Tang also reached further west and reshaped ideas of kingship in Khotan. When Gao Juhui (see his journey, discussed in chapter 1) arrived in Khotan about three decades after the official fall of the Tang, he met with a king who acted like a Chinese emperor:

> [The Khotanese king Li] Shengtian's clothes and hats were like those of the Zhongguo [the Central Country]. His palaces all faced east, and [one of them] was called Jince Dian [Golden Ordained Palace]. There was a mansion called Qifeng Lou [Mansion of Seven Phoenixes].... There were fifty monks dressed in purple in attendance at the king's abode. The year was the twenty-ninth year of the Tongqing reign.

Viśa' Saṃbhava (Ch. Li Shengtian) is the first post-Tibetan Khotanese king we know. He enjoyed a long reign from 912 to 966. Among our limited textual sources, we find that his royal titles included "lion king" and "king of kings."[86] The lion image was connected to the king in the Indian tradition (Skt. *Rājasiṃha*),[87] while the grand title of "king of kings," a Near Eastern way of addressing a supreme ruler, implies a status similar to that of an emperor. His claim to be a descendant of the Tang imperial house may have been related to his use of this grand title. Such possibilities were further substantiated in the titles of Viśa' Saṃbhava's son, the next Khotanese king, Viśa' Śūra:

> In the happy time of the reign of Tianzun, sheep year, Ttumjārā month, seventeenth day, dwelling in the palace, ruling in the Law, the bodhisattva Viśa' Śūra, king of kings of China.[88]

This is an unambiguous example presenting the king of Khotan as the "king of kings of China [*caiga rāṃdānä rrādi*]."[89] This title creatively fuses the Indo-Iranian elements of the traditional Khotanese kingship ideology ("king of kings") with a new claim of being a descendant of the Tang ruling house ("of

China"). This novel title can be understood in the context of the portrait of the Khotanese king as a Chinese emperor mentioned above (figure 9.8). The adoption of this title also affected how the Khotanese kings used their official documents and seals. At the end of Khotanese edict P. 5538 we find a large Chinese character *chi*, meaning "edict" (see figure 7.2) written in imitation of the edicts of Tang-Song emperors (compare the *chi* in figure 7.2 to that in figure 1.1). Further substantiation of this new claim can be found in a Chinese letter written by the Khotanese king to the lord of Dunhuang discussed earlier (figure 7.7). Here, a Chinese seal, the smaller one of the two seals, reads "Seal commissioned by the Han Son of Heaven of great Khotan [大于闐漢天子製印]."[90] The Chinese title *tianzi* (Son of Heaven) can be seen as an equivalent of the Khotanese "king of kings," both denoting a supreme political figure of (claimed) translocal power.[91] These paintings, documents, and seals together show that the new claim of being a "king of kings of China" was visible in many aspects of governmental functions in Khotan.[92]

Although the exact timing of this broad claim of "Chineseness" cannot be established as firmly as the king of Dunhuang's claim to be the "emperor," there is no doubt that it happened after, and as a response to, the fall of the Tang. In fact, along with the new title, the Khotanese government also adopted several key official titles from the government in North China. At least one, *shumi* (chancellor, transcribed in Khtoanese as *chū-bīra*),[93] became prominent only in the tenth century after the fall of the Tang.[94] The Khotanese king was intimately aware of the political and institutional changes of Khotan's neighbors, particularly the states in North China. Underlying the new claims of the Khotanese kings was thus an information network that conveyed the institutional knowledge of Chinese kingship to Khotan.

While the fall of the Tang emboldened the king of Dunhuang to elevate his status, the news of the military victory of Khotan had the opposite effect. As mentioned earlier, in the late 960s, the king of Khotan Viśa' Śūra scored a decisive victory over the Qarakhanids and conveyed the information to the king of Dunhuang Cao Yuanzhong in a royal edict (P. 5538). Fortunately, a letter from Cao to Viśa' Śūra, which is very likely a response to the news of the Khotanese victory, is preserved in the form of a copy. Here, faced with the Khotanese military ascendency, Cao Yuanzhong assumed an exceptionally subservient tone. The letter begins: "Humbly I have received the specifically issued edict from the emperor, together with gifts. I cannot bear the extremity of my gratitude."[95] By addressing Viśa' Śūra as the "emperor" (*huangdi*) and calling his letter an edict, Cao acknowledges his subordinate status vis-à-vis the Khotanese king. Cao continues to say that he has learned about the military victory of Viśa' Śūra over the Qarakhanids, and compares the Khotanese king to Emperor Gaozu of the Han dynasty. After this victory, Cao claims toward the end of the letter that "not only do the Qarakhanids [Dashi of the Black Clothes] fear the Emperor, [everyone] up to the Tang kingdom is in awe of your power, too." Notable is the reference to the "Tang kingdom" (Tangguo 唐國). As the Tang dynasty had fallen decades ago by this time, the term is not a specific reference to the Tang but should be taken to mean generally the state in North China. By designating this state (the Song, that is) as a "kingdom" (guo) but the king of Khotan as an emperor (huangdi), Cao Yuanzhong clearly indicates that, for him, the center of the political world at this moment is not Kaifeng, but Khotan.

The way the king of Dunhuang saw himself in this world can be further observed in a more concrete setting, in one of the largest caves of the Dunhuang Mogao cave complex. Constructed in 924 by the king of Dunhuang Cao Yijin, Cave 98 was known as "the cave of the great king [dawang ku 大王窟]" and is described by a modern scholar as "political propaganda on an unprecedented scale."[96] It is consisted of a large rectangular main chamber (15.2 × 12.8 meters) and a wide corridor 6.8 meters long.[97] Now designated as a "special cave" (teku 特窟) by the Dunhuang Academy, it is not always open to visitors. But if you have the good fortune of visiting when it is open, you can take a walk through it much as Dunhuang residents in the tenth century would, and witness the world of power in medieval Dunhuang.

As you enter the corridor, you will see the larger-than-life portrait of Cao Yijin, the king of Dunhuang who commissioned the cave, on the southern wall, wearing a crimson outfit similar to that worn by Cao Yuanzhong analyzed above (figure 9.2). Following Cao Yijin are slightly smaller portraits of his sons Cao Yuande and Cao Yuanshen. On the other side of the corridor you can find portraits of previous rulers of Dunhuang (Zhang Yichao, Zhang Huaishen, Suo Xun). The walk through the corridor thus introduces the viewer to generations of Dunhuang's sovereigns. Upon entering the main chamber, your eyes will likely be caught by the massive transformation paintings (jingbian hua 經變畫) representing various different Buddhist sutras on all four walls. But before long, you will also notice the long lines of more than two hundred human figures, all Dunhuang elites who served as donors, underneath the transformation paintings. Of those, the most prominent are painted on the eastern wall, on both sides of the corridor. On the south side, the procession is led by the Khotanese king Viśa' Saṃbhava (Li Shengtian) and his queen Lady Cao, dressed as Chinese emperor and empress. On the north side, the opposite procession is headed by wives of Cao Yijin, the first of whom is Lady Li the Heavenly Princess, daughter of the Uyghur khan of Ganzhou.[98]

These luminaries appear in the cave for good reason. The Uyghur princess Lady Li, along with Lady Suo painted just behind her, are the wives of Cao Yijin. Likely a daughter of Cao Yijin and the Uyghur princess, Lady Cao married the king of Khotan Viśa' Saṃbhava.[99] The three ruling families of Dunhuang, Khotan, and Ganzhou were thus linked with two marriages, and all were represented in Cave 98 constructed by Cao Yijin. For any visitors to this cave, medieval or modern, the power dynamic among the three ruling families does not reveal any clear hierarchy. The portrait of Cao Yijin might have greeted visitors first, but the portraits of Viśa' Saṃbhava and the Uyghur princess are larger and visually more ornate. Rather than honoring the unique status of the king of Dunhuang, the portraits of the cave should be seen as a celebration of Dunhuang's successful diplomatic connection with two of its most important neighbors.[100]

What makes this cave a uniquely productive site to study the self-representation of the Dunhuang king, however, goes beyond these elaborate portraits. We are fortunate to have the prayer text that Cao Yijin used when the roof of the cave was completed in 920. Here I quote a few key sentences from this prayer:

> The emperor of the Great Liang will reside in Penglai [the island of immortals] in perpetuity. . . . Our governor of Hexi, the minister [meaning the lord of Dunhuang] . . . opened the House of Phoenix in the east, and becomes the belly and heart of the emperor; he quenched the smoke of the Rong [a derogatory term for non-Han peoples] in the west, and rules Shazhou [Dunhuang] forever after. The Heavenly Princess Baolang [Lady Li, the Uyghur princess] will always possess the virtue of pine trees; the appearance of the noble lady [Cao's Chinese wife] will forever boast the beauty of the harp. . . . The four directions are safe, and envoys will not be trapped and prevented from proceeding; to the north and the south military actions all cease, and travelers on horseback come back and forth without delay. . . . Therefore, the three borders all pronounce peace, and the passes do not have the worry of beacon fires; guests from the four borders all gather and there is marvel at the treasures from the road.[101]

Not appearing at all in the cave itself, the emperor of the Later Liang took pride of place in the prayer. The connection to Ganzhou is conveyed by the inclusion of the Uyghur wife and the elevation of her over the Chinese wives of the Dunhuang king in both the cave and the prayer. But the king and the queen of Khotan are nowhere to be found.

In addition, the prayer also reveals a view on the relation between diplomacy and the celebration of the king of Dunhuang. The writer wishes both for an open road, on which the traveling envoys will not be hindered from going to foreign lands, and peace at the borders to allow foreign envoys to visit Dunhuang. Why was this network so important to the king of Dunhuang? The last line of the prayer gives a clue: when the road is open and the envoys continue to visit, the writer suggests, "there is marvel at the treasures from the road." The parallelism of Chinese poetic construction means that the writer considered the treasures from the road to be of comparable importance to the topic of the previous sentence, peace on the borders.

These three cases—the "emperor of Dunhuang," "king of kings of China," and Cave 98—illustrate two features of kingly claims on the Silk Road. First, the kings of Dunhuang and Khotan demonstrated political flexibility in their manners of self-fashioning. When they sensed the growth of their own power and the decline of an important neighbor, they did not hesitate to elevate themselves to the status of "Son of Heaven" and "king of kings" in dealings with that neighbor. On the other hand, when they encountered a stronger rival state, or perceived their own state as being in decline, they were also quick to adopt the status of vassal, often elevating another neighbor king to the status of "emperor." In doing so, they made full use of the linguistic resources available, and claimed such elevated status in more than one language. The cultural affiliations that scholars often assign to them—the *Han Chinese* state of Dunhuang, the *Khotanese* state of Khotan—did not prevent them from making transcultural claims of kingship. The Khotanese king claimed to be "king of kings of China" and "Han Son of Heaven," while the son of the Dunhuang king dressed like a Uyghur elite.[102]

From the traditional Chinese sources like the official annals of the Tang and the Song dynasties, states like Dunhuang, Khotan, and Turfan were border polities participating in the tributary system centered in Chang'an and Kaifeng. But when we examine the relations among these states revealed in the Dunhuang documents, the picture changes dramatically. From this perspective, it becomes clear that the rhetoric of the tributary system masked a more fluid power structure among kings of Eastern Eurasia. In the letter from the king of Dunhuang to the king of Khotan cited above, a Chinese-speaking state (Dunhuang) offered tribute to a non-Chinese-speaking state (Khotan), and resigned itself to the status of a vassal. Here, the assumptions of the tributary system were turned on their head. Such a lack of intellectual coherence was a strength that allowed kings on the Silk Road to constantly adjust the way they related to their neighbors.

A second feature of Silk Road kingship revealed in these cases is that the policy decisions of self-aggrandization or degradation were embedded in the flow of luxury goods and information on the Silk Road. The flow of information allowed the kings to constantly reassess their military power and political capital vis-à-vis their neighbors, and adjust policies accordingly. The flow of luxury goods, on the other hand, gave the kings the resources necessary to make such claims. To become a "king of kings of China," for instance, the Khotanese king needed to have an open channel for importing clothes and decorations from North China to dress like a Chinese emperor. The accumulation of and adornment with luxury gifts, both in real life and in pictorial depictions, were key aspects of the kingly claim to status and grandeur. Gifts and news transmitted through the diplomatic network were thus both crucial to the kings on the Silk Road.

## Conclusion

This chapter has shown how intensive material and informational exchanges shaped the kings of Eastern Eurasia from 850 to 1000. There were many kings in Eastern Eurasia during this period. Telling the full story of the kings of even a single state would require an entire monograph. Rather than being comprehensive, therefore, this chapter has captured a few particularly well-documented and revealing moments in the lives of kings through their edicts, letters, portraits, and chronicles in order to examine how they viewed and used the diplomatic network that I have described in the previous chapters of this book.

The kings of Eastern Eurasia were interested in the maintenance of the diplomatic network for a number of reasons. Because of the fiscal structure of their courts, the kings usually stood to personally benefit from the gifts exchanged with other kings; they also desired information that only envoys from distant lands could bring. The legitimacy of their rule was bolstered by an association with other kings, whether such association existed among equals or between two parties of distinctly different status. In Dunhuang, this foreign presence is reflected in the depiction of foreign rulers in the Buddhist caves. All these factors contributed to the eagerness of kings of Eastern Eurasia to send envoys to other states.

Foreign people, goods, and news were used by the kings to distinguish themselves, visually and rhetorically, from the commoners under their rule. Speaking of globalization before the nineteenth century, historian Christopher Bayly reminds us that "whereas modern complexity demands the uniformity of Levis and trainers, the archaic simplicity of everyday life demanded that great men prized difference in goods, learned servants, women and animals and sought to capture their qualities."[103] The Silk Road created a kind of social elite of great men and women who sought such status differentiation by exchanging gifts and information with other members of the elite. In the process, kings became more and more distant from the subjects they ruled, but more like one another, not only socially but also in their actual appearance. These kings, with their silks and jade, were the international elites of medieval Eastern Eurasia.

Therefore, I agree with Peter Brown's assessment of the Silk Road that "elements of an 'archaic globalization' were brought to the fore by constant diplomacy and warfare, and not by the invisible hand of the market," and that "from one end of Eurasia to the other, the game of the day was the game of the competing glory of the kings."[104] In order to participate in this "game of . . . competing glory" that brought distant goods and political information, kings needed to stay on good terms with their neighbors, particularly the ones through whose domains their envoys needed to travel. The safety of the roads that the envoys took thus became a central concern of the state. In the next and final chapter, we will witness what the kings and commoners of Dunhuang did to try to keep the road open.

# 10

# The Politics of the Road

IN THE PREVIOUS chapters, we have witnessed how a wide spectrum of Dunhuang society—from commoners to kings—made material and symbolic gains through maintaining a diplomatic network that connected Dunhuang to its neighbors. In this final chapter, I turn to the "road" that sustained this diplomatic network. An awareness of roads shared with other states and the wish for peace on these roads, I will suggest, were consistent features in political expression in Dunhuang and its neighboring states, and became the basis on which international relations were constructed.

I approach the politics of Dunhuang at this time by analyzing three realms of state activity: war, diplomacy, and Buddhist and popular rituals. These three realms are accessible through a wide range of Dunhuang manuscripts. Biographical accounts of generals, panegyric poems for rulers, and documents produced by governments contain information about the rationale and the process of military campaigns.[1] Diplomatic letters and envoys' reports form the basis for understanding diplomatic rhetoric and practice between Dunhuang and other states.[2] Prayer texts (*fayuan wen* 發願文) and lyrical poems performed on ritualistic occasions also reveal features of political ideology.[3] Collectively, they offer a multiperspective view of the political culture of Dunhuang and, to some extent, the region around it. On each of these fronts, the wish to maintain peace on the road was a central concern.

## Fighting for the Road

In Eastern Eurasia, the period between 850 and 1000 was characterized by imperial collapse and political fragmentation. Yet, as I explained in chapter 1, we should not equate political fragmentation with sheer chaos. In fact, after an initial period of instability in the late ninth century, when political hostage taking featured prominently in regional diplomacy,[4] the states in the Hexi region reached a kind of power equilibrium early in the tenth century, partly through an extensive and complex network of diplomatic marriages among Dunhuang, Khotan, and Ganzhou. The regional peace thus established not only sustained the longevity of the ruling houses in these states but also made long-distance travel for our envoys possible.

In spite of this regional peace, warfare did break out sometimes. From the records in the Dunhuang documents, we know of two major wars in the tenth century, both between Dunhuang and Ganzhou. In this section, I will first discuss what we know about these two wars and show that central to both wars was the wish to keep open the main road that ran through the Hexi region. Then I will discuss another smaller-scale military conflict, between Dunhuang and the Southern Mountain tribes to its south, which reveals a similar underlying rationale for conflict. The need to maintain peace on the road featured prominently in these decisions to go to war.

The first major conflict was a direct result of the fall of the Tang. On the first of June 907, Zhu Wen (852–912), the most powerful warlord in North China and de facto ruler of the ailing Tang Empire, ended months of performative reluctance and ascended the throne as the new emperor of the Liang. The news of the official end of the Tang must have been relayed quickly to Dunhuang, and led to Zhang Chengfeng's decision to found his own independent state, the "Golden Mountain Kingdom of Western Han [Xihan Jinshan Guo 西漢金山國]," and to claim to be an "emperor."[5]

In creating his new state, as I explained in chapter 9, Zhang looked back in history and found a precedent for regional rule in the Five Liang dynasties.[6] A panegyric poem for the founding of the new state expresses Zhang's ambition to "follow in a restoration of the Five Liangs, and occupy the great places of the eight prefectures."[7] Another panegyric poem spells out this ambition with more specificity: its author, a "great prime minister [da zaixiang]" surnamed Zhang, proposed that the new emperor "destroy Ganzhou and occupy the land of the Five Liangs."[8] Thus the campaign against the Uyghur state of Ganzhou served Zhang's ambition of rising as a regional power after the fall of the Tang. In order to achieve this objective of reconquering the domain of these earlier Liang states, which included the region ruled by Ganzhou, Zhang Chengfeng opted to ally with the remnants of Tibetan forces, the long-term enemy of the Tang and the Uyghur khanate, in order to attack the Uyghurs in Ganzhou. This campaign, however, proved disastrous. In 911, only two years after Zhang created the new regime, he found the city of Dunhuang surrounded by the counterattacking Uyghur army.[9]

We know a great deal about the war because of an extraordinary letter allegedly written by "ten thousand commoners in Dunhuang" to the Uyghur khan as the Uyghur army were laying siege to the city.[10] The vision these commoners had of the place of Dunhuang in the region was drastically different from that of Zhang Chengfeng. Instead of wanting to attack and conquer Ganzhou and establish a regional state in the image of the Liang states, the commoners argued that Dunhuang and Ganzhou should return to the amicable relation that they had maintained in previous decades, when both states nominally acknowledged the suzerainty of the Tang. The letter describes this recent past in the following terms:

> In the second year of Dazhong era [848], our governor Taibao [Zhang Yichao], arising from a first-rank family in Dunhuang, expelled the Tibetans and restored the land again. . . . His sons and grandsons thereafter have guarded the western gate [of the empire] until now. In the meantime, the Heavenly Khaghan dwelled in Zhangye [Ganzhou] and [we both] served the same family [the Tang] without a second thought. *The eastern road was open and the heavenly envoys were never blocked.*[11] (Emphasis added)

Such favorable conditions were disrupted by Zhang Chengfeng's war, one consequence of which was that "all the prefectures and garrisons on the road [between Ganzhou and Khotan] were successively destroyed." Therefore, unlike the earlier condition of an "open" road, Zhang's war with the Uyghurs wrecked the "eastern road" and the transregional connection it enabled. The ten thousand commoners were so furious about Zhang's decision to go to war that they referred to him, still the ruler of their state, with clear contempt: on Zhang's decision to collaborate with the Tibetan tribes, the commoners claimed that "the Son of Heaven [Zhang Chengfeng] acted anxiously on his impulse, and the commoners all disagreed with that."[12] While the details of what followed this letter are murky, we know that eventually the vision of the ten thousand commoners prevailed. The Uyghur army retreated, a Dunhuang-Ganzhou agreement was reached, and after a year or two, Zhang himself was deposed. This war was fought as a result of political instability caused by the fall of the Tang and the unrealistic and opportunistic aspirations of Zhang Chengfeng. But the commoners cited the fact that Zhang's ambition had become an obstacle to the road as one of their major reasons for opposing his war. In this case, whether the "eastern road" was open or not was a major consideration in the decision to seek peace or to go to war.

If the role of the "road" was indirectly revealed in Zhang Chengfeng's war in the voice of his dissenters, the second war I discuss was explicitly fought to keep the road open. This campaign occurred between 924 and 926. Information about it is preserved in biographical texts (in particular the "portrait elegies," 邈真讚), lyrical poems, and official documents. Rong Xinjiang has patched together these diverse texts and recovered a rough outline of the campaign:[13] Somewhere between late 924 and early 925, the government of Dunhuang under Cao Yijin initiated a campaign against Ganzhou. In early 925, partly because of the internal succession crisis of the Uyghurs and partly because of a great fire that ravaged the city of Ganzhou, the army of Dunhuang prevailed. Just over a year later, however, Ganzhou regrouped and launched a counterattack, reaching the Jade Gate, the eastern border of Dunhuang. The fighting this time was equally fierce, with "blood filling the field" at the Jade Gate.[14] In a follow-up battle in the city of Suzhou, a notable general and multilingual envoy of Dunhuang named Hun Ziying died in combat.[15] Eventually, however, the Dunhuang army prevailed again, forcing Ganzhou not only to retreat but to recognize Dunhuang's superior place in their bilateral relation. Because of the connected nature of these battles (924–25 in Ganzhou, 926 at the Jade Gate, 926 in Suzhou), they were considered different stages of the same campaign.

The 924–26 campaign is significant for the local history of Dunhuang because it was the first major battle fought by the state of Dunhuang after the transition of power from the Zhang family to the Cao family in 914. As it turned out, it was also the last. After this campaign, until its conquest by the Tangut Xia state in 1036, Dunhuang maintained largely peaceful relations with its neighbors for another century. Why did the government of Dunhuang feel the need to wage such a campaign just fifteen years after its humiliating defeat at the hands of the Ganzhou Uyghurs? And, more importantly, why was the diplomatic order established after this campaign capable of maintaining relative regional stability for over a century? The answer to both questions, I argue, lies in the role of the shared road in the political culture of Dunhuang and other states in the region.

The most complete account of the reasons for and consequences of this campaign is found in a lyrical poem titled "Erlang-wei," a type of popular song regularly performed in Dunhuang during the exorcist ritual on New Year's Day like the one I opened the book with.[16] These songs often recounted history and discussed current events. The public setting of their performance meant that they conveyed messages that could be heard by a wide spectrum of Dunhuang society.[17] The subject of this particular song is "matters of the recent past [*jindai shifei* 近代是非]." The most crucial matter of the recent past, as the song made clear, was the 924–26 campaign. The song begins with the condition of the region just prior to the campaign:

> Hexi is the old land of the Han family
> As a blockade in the middle lived the Xianyun [meaning the Uyghurs]
> For several years, the road to the east was obstructed,
> [making people in Dunhuang feel] like a fish in a small pond.[18]

These lines make it clear that just before the campaign, the Uyghurs were blocking the connection between Dunhuang and North China. This obstruction was particularly egregious in the minds of people in Dunhuang, because the Hexi region (the area roughly between Liangzhou and Dunhuang, see map i.1) had long been considered a land of the "Han."[19] Because of the Ganzhou blockage, people in Dunhuang felt like "a fish in a small pond." This situation had to be addressed, and fortunately, as the song continues, there was just the right person to do it:

> Now we encounter the fortuitous transformation of the brilliant king
> to reopen the road and boulevard of He-Long [Hexi and Longyou],
> The Taibao [a title of the king of Dunhuang] thus initiated rage with
>     his divine might,
> subsequently counting military armor for soldiers.[20]

The term "He-Long" refers to two geographical names—Hexi (west of the [Yellow] River) and Longyou (right [east] of the Long Mountains)—that both refer to the area of the Gansu Corridor. Therefore, the road that Cao Yijin (the "Taibao") reopened was the main road that connected Dunhuang with Ganzhou and other oasis towns all the way to the border of the North China regimes in Lingzhou. With this intention, the Dunhuang army marched toward the city of Ganzhou. How the actual battle played out is not described in detail: one line, "there was nowhere for the Uyghurs to hide," sufficed for the writer to show the outcome of the fighting. What mattered to the lyricist more was the broader consequences of this military success, which the song spells out in some detail:

> Thereafter, one worries not about the Eastern Road,
> as [one lives] in the age of [the sage emperors] Shun and Yao.

Envoys from the inner land [North China] newly descend upon [our]
   western garrison,
and the Son of Heaven congratulates our righteous army.
To the west all the way till Khotan,
all offer tributes such as jade and glass.[21]

The military triumph puts the minds of people in Dunhuang at ease: they
no longer need to worry about the uncertain conditions on the "eastern road,"
a central concern of the "ten thousand commoners" just fifteen years earlier.
The reestablished connection with the court in North China signified a sagely
age like those of the mythic Shun and Yao emperors. In this new era, Dunhuang
restored its place on the reopened road as a key stop that connected North
China in the east to Khotan in the west. And the newly reopened road to Khotan promised tributes of jade and glass. The message of this song is essentially
identical to those of two other two songs I have cited (in the introduction and
in chapter 8), which both celebrate the open road and the influx of luxury from
afar. Dunhuang after this campaign was no longer confined like "a fish in a small
pond." It had access to an ocean of wealth and connections.

The central importance of the road seen in this song is corroborated in
other governmental sources produced during this campaign. In a petition sent
to the king of Dunhuang in 925, Liu Shaoyan, who had been stationed in Liangzhou to the east of Ganzhou by the Zhang family rulers, reminisced about
a time when "the road of Hexi was peaceful" under the Zhang family.[22] The
peace on the road allowed him and many others originally from Dunhuang to
be garrisoned in the city of Liangzhou to the *east* of Ganzhou. Even after the
rise of Ganzhou, because the road was still largely unobstructed, Liu and his
comrades maintained control of Liangzhou as a kind of Dunhuang enclave.
Yet in the few years before the campaign, Liu went on to say, "the Uyghurs in
Ganzhou possessed fierce soldiers and strong horses, and would not allow the
envoys of Liangzhou to visit Shazhou [Dunhuang]." Here the petition shows
the other side of the Uyghur blockage: not only were envoys of Dunhuang
prevented from going to the east, envoys from places east of Ganzhou, such as
Liangzhou, were also not allowed to go to westward to visit Dunhuang. The
blockage turned into sheer chaos when the Uyghurs in Ganzhou fell into internecine fights that escalated with the military involvement of a group of
Tibetans and their raiding of Liangzhou.[23] Only after Cao Yijin's campaign that
"reopened the old road of Hexi" was order restored.[24] The ultimate goal of
Liu's petition was to implore Cao to send provisions to Liangzhou, an act

made possible by the successful campaign that had secured the road. But by laying out the historical background for his petition, Liu reveals the rationale and consequence of the 924–26 campaign from the perspective of one of its beneficiaries. For both Liu and the anonymous lyricist cited above, the blocked road was the reason for war.

In these two accounts, the campaign's success seems to have been achieved fairly easily. Biographical sketches found in the portrait elegies, however, reveal that the war was hard-won. The portrait elegies of Yin Shanxiong and Hun Ziying describe prolonged and at times bloody battles.[25] Dunhuang suffered setbacks at different points in the three-year period, but, eventually, all the sources agree that the army of Dunhuang—described in the portrait elegy of Zhang Mingji as "the great troops opening the road [*dajun kailu* 大軍開路]"— was successful.[26] These texts of different genres—poems, portrait elegies, official petition—each have their objectives and emphasize different aspects of the campaign. But they all agree that the campaign was triggered by the blocking of the road, and that with military success the road was reopened. This war, the only major campaign against a neighboring state (that we know of) in more than a century of Cao-family rule of Dunhuang proves again the central importance of an unobstructed road in Dunhuang politics.

Compared with these two campaigns between Dunhuang and Ganzhou, the third conflict I shall discuss, the one against an elusive tribal organization called Southern Mountain (Nanshan 南山), is much harder to describe in detail.[27] Several of the portrait elegies of the generals mentioned above make references to a campaign against Southern Mountain.[28] Yet without any corroboration from official documents, the specific dates of the Southern Mountain campaign cannot be securely established. For all we know, there may have been multiple operations against this group. But existing sources do offer some clues to the rationale for the campaign (or campaigns). The portrait elegy of Zhang Mingji, for instance, tells us that "when Southern Mountain stole the road, our lord was first to volunteer. On the battlefield he swept the front and exited from the end."[29] The unusual term "*toulu*" (偷路) is translated literally here as "stealing the road." In isolation this term might not have had a clear meaning. But activities of people from the Southern Mountain recorded in other documents may help us understand it. The Southern Mountain people are often called a "tribe" (*buluo* 部落) and discussed in the context of their looting of horses and envoys.[30] People who felt that it was hard to make a living in Dunhuang sometimes fled to the Southern Mountain tribes,[31] and members of the Southern Mountain tribes raided herds of sheep kept by the Dunhuang government.[32] In two cases, they even detained and robbed envoys sent by Dunhuang.[33] For these reasons, unlike Ganzhou and Khotan, which were sometimes considered adversarial but always treated as proper states, people from Southern Mountain are most commonly referred to in the Dunhuang documents as "bandits" (zei 賊). From the portrait elegy of Zhang Mingji we know that he was involved in a successful campaign against the Southern Mountain tribes sometime just before 924. Yet, as there are many examples of disruptions of travelers by the Southern Mountain tribes, it is likely that this would not have been Dunhuang's only campaign against them.

The Southern Mountain tribes were located to Dunhuang's southwest. Whereas the goal of the war with Ganzhou was to secure the road to the east, the war with the Southern Mountain tribes, who were known as predators on the road, was to secure the road to the west. The outcome of the campaign against the Southern Mountain tribes was that the connection between Dunhuang and its western neighbors, in particular Khotan, was preserved—the "stolen" road was, in this sense, recovered. The policy objective of the Dunhuang government was to keep *both* the eastern and the western roads open, a goal that it was willing to achieve through force. It is notable that, at least from Dunhuang's perspective, these tenth-century wars were fought not over territory but over routes of connection—after its victories, the Dunhuang government did not attempt to occupy Ganzhou or the Southern Mountain tribes.

Nonetheless, when placed in the broader political history of Dunhuang and the region, these military actions were the exceptions, extreme measures taken rarely and cautiously. In most cases, an open road was achieved through diplomatic means.

## Negotiating for the Road

Unlike the warfare that we hear of only indirectly in the sources, much more first-hand testimony exists for diplomatic dealings, through diplomatic letters preserved in the Dunhuang collection. A comprehensive account of the many twists and turns of diplomatic relations between Dunhuang and its neighbors has been offered elsewhere.[34] Here I will focus on a few incidents when the relation between Dunhuang and Ganzhou, its most important eastern neighbor, was tested. By analyzing the ways these incidents were resolved without resorting to warfare, I highlight the role of a shared road in creating a pragmatic approach to diplomacy.

The first incident is the murder of Liang Xingde, an envoy of Dunhuang, in 934.[35] As discussed in chapter 5, Liang led a mission of more than seventy envoys to the Chinese court, but was trapped and ultimately killed in Ganzhou on his way back.[36] The year before Liang's murder, Renyu Khan of Ganzhou passed away and was succeeded by a new khan, Renmei. The year after Liang's death, Cao Yijin, the architect of the new Dunhuang-Ganzhou relationship, also died. With the passing of the two heads of state, the Dunhuang-Ganzhou relation was bound to experience a period of readjustment—and Liang Xingde's murder further complicated the matter.

In order to mitigate the negative impact of the Liang incident and ensure the smooth passage of envoys from North China, Cao Yuande, who had recently succeeded Cao Yijin, sent an extraordinarily subservient letter to the Uyghur ministers of Ganzhou. Because this well-preserved, and relatively brief, message touches on many of the themes I discuss in this section, here I translate it in full:

> Ministers: Please consider that [our] two places are not of different states, and that by the road we become one family [*tulu yijia* 途路一家]. On the day when the envoys arrive, if you allow them to come to the west [to Dunhuang], it would be a great favor [*enxing* 恩幸]. Indeed, since the road to the court (of North China) passes Ganzhou, do our two places have only this one occasion of envoys passing? Or do we expect such passage in the future as well? As for the dispatch of heavenly envoys, I wish you would allow their passage to the west. [If that occurs,] people hearing it from near and far, [would they] not consider this name of "pain and heat?" That would be fortunate! Now I am sending Buddhist monk-manager Qingfu, the general Wang Tongxin, and their companions to connect our happiness and express my goodwill. For each of the ministers I have attached ten *pi* of white flower-braided wool, one *pi* of white silk, as a token of the memories of my father the great king. When they [the envoys] arrive, please check and collect [the gifts]. Since the ministers have established with the great king [Cao Yijin] the relationship between a son and a father, now that the great king has passed away, such feeling of "pain and heat" cannot be abandoned. Please wisely consult and report to the khan, [who is] the Son of Heaven, so that he agrees with all of the affairs of the world. [If he does,] it would be thanks to the maneuvering of the ministers. Not exhausting my intent, I humbly petition.[37]

This letter touches on a number of the issues that I have discussed in this book, including the employment of a monk as an envoy (head envoy, in this case) and the offering of a significant amount of diplomatic gifts. But the main objective of the letter needs further explanation. At the start of the letter, Cao Yuande reminds the ministers of the established relation between Dunhuang and Ganzhou: "[our] two places are not of different states, and . . . by the road we become one family [*sheji wu'er, tulu yijia* 社稷無二, 途路一家]." This expression is significant in that it combines the two essential elements of this regional diplomacy—road and family—into a single argument: for Cao Yuande, the fact that Dunhuang and Ganzhou were on the same road turned them into "one family."

After stating this general diplomatic principle, Cao Yuande then delves into the practical matter the letter was trying to accomplish, the passage of envoys from the Later Tang court: "if you allow them to come to the west [to Dunhuang], it would be a great favor." To bolster the request for a favor, he points out the obvious: "do our two places have only this one occasion of envoys passing?" The implication is that to return the favor, he will allow their envoys to pass through areas under his rule. Then he invokes a strange expression of "pain and heat [*tongre* 痛热]" that is not attested in transmitted sources and appears only in the Dunhuang materials. As this term appears again later in the letter, it is clear that it refers to the close relationship between Dunhuang and Ganzhou. Cao Yuande argues that the "feeling of pain and heat cannot be abandoned" at such a delicate time, when his father, the founder of Cao family rule at Dunhuang, had just passed away. Perhaps because of this sentiment, but certainly in line with the general diplomatic practice of the time, fine gifts of silk and wool were given to the ministers. Invoking precedent, sending envoys, and offering gifts, the diplomatic relation with Ganzhou was thus reestablished. For Cao Yuande, it was not worth it to risk undermining this relation to revenge the death of an envoy, so he chose not to bring up the matter in this letter.

In this way, Cao Yuande seems to be following the precedent established by his father, Cao Yijin, after the death of another envoy. About ten years earlier, a Ganzhou envoy named An Qianxiang—his surname An implies Sogdian origin—had been killed by fellow Uyghurs on his way back from the Chinese court (see my discussion in chapter 5).[38] This otherwise internal Uyghur matter implicated people from Dunhuang, because the envoys Zhang Baoshan and Liang Xingde (the same one who would later be killed himself) were traveling with An Qianxiang on their way back. In a letter that recounts these complicated events, the lord of Guazhou, a town between Dunhuang and Ganzhou that was occasionally independent but usually under the rule of Dunhuang, gives advice to Cao Yijin on how to avoid escalation: "It is not worth it to break the road of ten thousand years for this minor infraction. The dead man is gone and cannot be revived, but the communication between the brothers [i.e., Ganzhou and Dunhuang] should not break for a thousand years."[39] Hyperbole aside, the sentiment conveyed in this letter is in line with that found in the case of Liang Xingde: compared with the maintenance of the road, the death of envoys, even important ones such as Liang and An, was only a "minor infraction" (*xiaoxia* 小瑕) that should not sever the brotherly relation of these states on the same road.

Such forgiveness of perceived wrongs also appeared in other cases of diplomatic dealings. The text of a negotiation over a covenant is preserved in P. 2786, the letter by the Khotanese envoy Ana Saṃgaa. The Khotanese envoys not only managed the relation between Khotan and Ganzhou but also acted as intermediaries between Ganzhou and Dunhuang. In his letter, Ana Saṃgaa reports the following incident, which occurred on the road between Ganzhou and Dunhuang:[40]

> Then, in Cvāvaja [first] month, on the thirteenth day, five envoys, Tcyauvä Aṃmäga and others, left. In their hands, the *linggong* [lord of Dunhuang] sent a letter to Ganzhou, as follows: "As for the old hostility, I no longer seek it nor ask [about it], if indeed a good time should please [both of us]. Those who are our men, to all [of them] fame and peace. You are not controlling even one of them. You will also open the road to China [*caigą-kṣīrāṣṭä padä*]."[41]

According to this letter, five Khotanese envoys had departed Dunhuang with a letter from the lord of Dunhuang to Ganzhou. The unnamed lord proposes to look beyond old hostility and reestablish relations with Ganzhou. In exchange for his forgetting the old hostility, the Uyghur khan in Ganzhou should, according to the lord of Dunhuang, control the enemies and open "the road to China." The result would be that "our men" would obtain "fame and peace." The wording of the letter suggests that the enemies in question are those who stood in the way of opening the road to China. This report corroborates the observations made above in my discussion of the Chinese letters written by lord of Dunhuang to Ganzhou. In both letters, the primary goal of peaceful diplomatic relations is the maintenance of a road suitable for travel. It was through this cycle of constant making and remaking of treaties that peace on the road in this region was sustained.

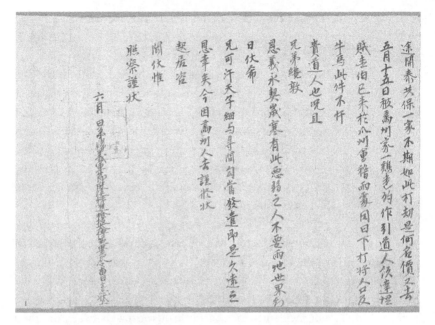

FIGURE 10.1 The end of Cao Yuanzhong's letter to the Uyghur khan of Ganzhou.
*Credit*: Bibliothèque nationale de France.

Another factor disrupting the relation between Dunhuang and Ganzhou was banditry. P. 2155 verso (figure 10.1) is an original letter, elegantly copied and impressed with an official seal, from Cao Yuanzhong to the Uyghur khan written sometime between 956 and 963.[42] In this letter, he complains about three disturbances on the road. In the first incident, "bandits" had robbed an embassy taking return gifts to the Uyghurs. They had killed one person and stolen two or three horses. Upon further investigation, it became apparent that the bandits were runaway Uyghurs from Ganzhou. The second incident occurred seven days after the first one. According to Cao Yuanzhong, eighteen "bandits," half on horse and half on foot, were pretending to be envoys and marching on the main road to the town of Xuanquan. Similarly in this case, the perpetrators were Uyghurs who claimed that they were chasing after runaways. In the third incident, a certain Yiji Xizhou from Suzhou had worked as a road guide for one hundred Tatar bandits who attacked Guazhou and Kuaiji on the same day and carried off people as well as cattle.

The juxtaposition of the first two cases, which I discussed in chapter 5, and the third in one letter is intriguing, as the last incident in fact had nothing to do with the Uyghur khan. Cao Yuanzhong himself said as much when he noted "this [the third] incident is not the fault of people from your honored province [meaning Ganzhou]." Yet by putting them together in the same letter, Cao implied to his recipient that these incidents were of the same nature: these travelers had behaved in inappropriate ways. After laying out the infringements, Cao inquired of the Uyghur khan: since previous cases of possible runaways had only been discussed through letters, why were recent cases being pursued in such a violent manner? "Now that the road is open and prosperous, and we maintain [it] as one family [*daotu kaitai, gongbao yijia* 道途開泰, 共保一家]," Cao asks, why would the Uyghurs commit such acts of banditry?[43]

What was the answer of the Uyghur khan? It is hard to know for sure, because if there was any letter in response, it is not preserved. However, in another letter sent by Cao Yuanzhong a few years later in 967, we get a sense of how these kinds of incidents were generally dealt with.[44] Cao begins by indicating that previously there had been cases of banditry, about which petitions had already been sent. He then quotes a response letter from the Uyghur khan, which states that "I have dispatched Prime Minister Biruq to go to Suzhou to renew an oath: from now on, if there are bandits within our tribe, they will be eliminated on the spot." To reciprocate, Cao Yuanzhong makes a promise of his own. As he explains, the state of Turfan was in political chaos at the time, and many "unsavory people" from Turfan were traveling east and unlawfully going to Ganzhou. Cao would issue an order that was to be posted and publicized in various small towns along the way: "From now on, if there is anyone who is traveling to Ganzhou illicitly, officials of the respective place should deal with him on the spot." Having made this promise, Cao then makes another request: "in the previous year, when our envoys to the court [in North China] reached the realm of Liangzhou, they were all robbed and the whole mission was destroyed. Your honorable land shares a border with Liangzhou. I hope you can . . . go to Liangzhou to inquire after the case."

The text is cut off at this point, and what happens afterward is unknown. But the extant section already illustrates the interconnectedness of these towns on the road between Turfan and Liangzhou. While Ganzhou guarantees the elimination of bandits and negotiates with Liangzhou on behalf of Dunhuang, Dunhuang makes sure that bandits from Turfan do not reach Ganzhou. This interstate dynamic clearly demonstrates the fact that these four places shared a single road, the road that connected North China with Central Asia.

The importance of the road in diplomatic dealings in the region is also seen in a Tibetan letter and the treaty it quotes. Pelliot tibétain 1189r is a letter written to the governor Cao of Dunhuang (who bore the title *ha se tser to* < Ch. *Hexi jiedu* 河西節度) by the governor of Suzhou (Tibetan *Sug cu*). In this case, four groups—Dunhuang, Tatar (Da tar), Zhongyun (Ju ngul), and Ganzhou Uyghur (Hor)—swore an oath. Each party performed a whipping ritual on this occasion. The letter preserves a precious piece of the actual treaty itself:

> At Yar-sha-cab, from today onward, we will not show the horse heads nor make any noise. Whoever goes secretly or runs and loads horse gear, if one commits robbery and rape in the direction of [meaning toward] Shazhou [Dunhuang], if the son does it, may the father die; if the younger brother does, may the older brother die.[45]

The initial treaty was agreed upon in the Dayun temple (*de'i yun zi 'i gtsugs lag khang*) in Suzhou. It was Empress Wu who, in the late seventh century, ordered the construction of a Dayun temple in both capitals (Chang'an and Luoyang) and in every prefecture, in order to store the Buddhist text *Dayun jing* (大雲經).[46] By the tenth century, these Dayun temples in Hexi had become some of the largest Buddhist institutions regionally. Grand, yet somewhat apolitical, a Dayun temple was a suitable place for such a ceremony. More specifically, the ceremony was performed in front of Vaiśravaṇa, the guardian of the north and one of the four *lokapālas*—"world protectors," or Heavenly Kings. The ability of Vaiśravaṇa to guard the peace of the area was well known and will be explored further in the next section. While the exact meaning of phrases such as "show the horse heads" in the treaty awaits further investigation,[47] the general sense expressed is fairly clear: any secret use of horses was not allowed, because these riders were committing robbery and rape "in the direction of Dunhuang [*sha cu phyogs*]." Therefore, in this monastery, Vaiśravaṇa was witnessing and guaranteeing a treaty that guarded against illicit activities on the road to Dunhuang.

This brotherhood on the road between Ganzhou and Dunhuang was widely understood, as revealed by a collection of letter models.[48] These models, scholars have discovered, were based on the actual letters sent by the governor of Lingzhou in the early tenth century.[49] Letter number 17 in this collection, the longest and most studied, is a petition sent by the governor of Lingzhou to the Uyghur khan of Ganzhou, both to persuade Ganzhou to pay tribute to the North China court and to convince it to allow Dunhuang to do so as well. After relating the historical analogy of the relation between the Xiongnu and the Han, the Lingzhou governor argues that the Uyghurs should follow suit and send envoys to the Chinese court. Then the letter turns to the matter of

Dunhuang. The governor of Lingzhou claims that the lord of Dunhuang and the Uyghur khan of Ganzhou "share the same predilection and follow the same principles. Even though the road [between the two] were longer than a thousand *li*, are the gratitude and amity [shared by the two] unlike those of one family?"[50]

The letter continues to say that between Dunhuang and Ganzhou, "the bond is like that between the kingdoms of Lu and Wei [*qingdun* Lu Wei 情敦魯衛]." During the spring and autumn period, the kingdom of Lu was the fief of the Duke of Zhou and the kingdom of Wei that of his brother Kangshu (康叔). According to Confucius, "the policies of Lu and Wei were those of the brothers [魯衛之政, 兄弟也]."[51] After such a characterization of the Dunhuang-Ganzhou relation, the letter sails on to ask that "from now on, when they [Dunhuang envoys] travel through [your state], please remove any animosity." Finally, as a parting warning, the governor of Lingzhou says, "if your honorable prefecture [Ganzhou] decides to hold them [Dunhuang envoys], our humble state [Lingzhou] will have to do the same [to your envoys]." Ganzhou was located to the east of Dunhuang in the same way that Lingzhou was to the east of Ganzhou (see map i.1). The governor of Lingzhou makes clear that denying passage to Dunhuang envoys would trigger a chain reaction that would eventually harm Ganzhou as well. In this way, the road that ran through the Hexi Corridor connected these three states, and many others, and prevented any one from monopolizing control over the route. Agreement on this shared control became the basis of diplomacy and coexistence.

While the disruptive incidents between Dunhuang and Ganzhou described above are different in nature, the language used to mitigate tension and reestablish trust is consistent. When dealing with the detention and death of Liang Xingde and the blocking of envoys from China by the Uyghurs, Cao Yuande claimed "[our] two places are not of different states, and . . . by the road we become one family."[52] When inquiring about incidents of Uyghur bandits on the road, Cao Yuanzhong described the relation between Dunhuang and Ganzhou in these terms: "The road is open and prosperous, and we maintain [it] as one family."[53] When trying to persuade the Ganzhou khan to ensure a smooth passage for envoys of Dunhuang to the east, the governor of Lingzhou asked rhetorically: "Even though the road [between the two] were longer than one thousand *li*, are the gratitude and amity [shared by the two] unlike those of one family?"[54] The idea that the road made these states a family was an understanding shared broadly—or proclaimed as something that ought to be shared—by the participants in diplomatic dealings. By repeatedly resorting to the binding power of the road, the states on the Hexi road between North China and Central Asia were able to avoid escalating isolated incidents into large-scale warfare during much of the tenth century.

Having explained the role of the road in the political rhetoric of war and diplomacy, in the next section I expand my purview to different occasions of Buddhist or secular rituals, and argue that this understanding of the central importance of the road for the state and the people of Dunhuang was not only the diplomatic consensus among Dunhuang and its neighbors but also became a crucial part of the hopes and fears of a wide spectrum of people in Dunhuang society.

## Praying for the Road

In 947, on the fifteenth day of the seventh month, the ghost festival, Cao Yuanzhong ordered a series of Buddhist images to be printed.[55] About a dozen of these single-sheet prints found their way into the library cave collection.[56] The ghost festival was a time of renewal, and as Stephen Teiser points out: "coming at the junction of the full moon, the new season, the fall harvest, the peak of monastic asceticism, the rebirth of ancestors, and the assembly of the local community, the ghost festival was celebrated on a broad scale by all classes of people throughout medieval Chinese society."[57] The ghost festival in Dunhuang shared this communal character, which was further accentuated by Cao's use of printing. From the multiple copies of each print preserved in the library cave collection, we know that Cao Yuanzhong must have distributed them quite extensively. Deploying the new technology of mass reproduction and propaganda at a festival celebrated by "all classes of people," Cao clearly wanted the message on the prints to reach as many as possible in Dunhuang society. What was the message?

As can be seen in figures 10.2 and 10.3, the prints are of a composite nature. The upper portion is a line drawing of a Buddhist deity, the lower portion the prayer text by Cao Yuanzhong. For the prints of Vaiśravaṇa (figure 10.2), the lord of the north among the Four Heavenly Kings, Cao's colophon is relatively brief: he wished that by producing the prints for Vaiśravaṇa "the state will be secure and the populace content; the government will constantly prosper; the road will be peaceful; and all under heaven happy and joyous."[58] Along with a general concern about the well-being of the populace and the fortunes of the state, Cao Yuanzhong included the importance of peace on the road in

FIGURE 10.2 Print commissioned by Cao Yuanzhong:
Vaiśravaṇa.
*Credit*: Bibliothèque nationale de France.

his prayer. This concern about the road is more explicitly spelled out in the
prints for Avalokiteśvara (figure 10.3), the bodhisattva of compassion, where
Cao prays that "the city god will be peaceful and content, the entire prefecture
will be healthy and tranquil. The road of the east and west will be open, and
the enemies of the south and the north will be subservient."[59]

Here, Cao Yuanzhong identifies the political allies as from the east and the
west of Dunhuang, including, one might assume, Ganzhou, Khotan, and Turfan. Political enemies of Dunhuang, on the other hand, resided to its north

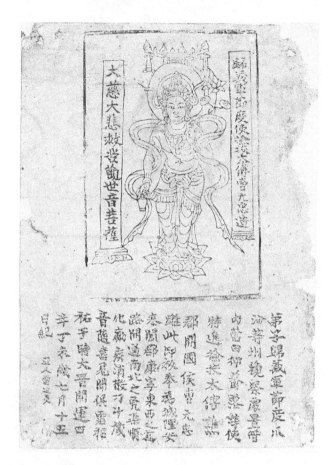

FIGURE 10.3 Print commissioned by Cao Yuanzhong:
Avalokiteśvara.
*Credit*: Bibliothèque nationale de France.

and south in the mountainous regions: the Southern Mountain tribes, as
I have shown above, were among the main disruptors of travel on the road. In
this sense, these two wishes were linked not only rhetorically but also substan-
tively: only when the enemies of the north and the south were subservient
could the road that ran from the east to the west continue to be open and
peaceful. The security of an open road was as important in the prayer as the
city god and the welfare of the state in general.[60]

That Cao Yuanzhong should pray for peace on the road in the prints graced
by Avalokiteśvara and Vaiśravaṇa is not a coincidence. The belief that these

two deities could protect travelers and maintain the safety of the road was widely shared by people in Dunhuang at the time. A model prayer implores:

> May Avalokiteśvara lead the way, so that there is no danger for ten thousand *li*; may the Four Heavenly Kings stand guard in pairs of two; may the people and horses be safe and arrive at the heavenly court promptly; may they dance contentedly in front of the palace with their wishes fulfilled; may the back and forth of the envoys on the four roads not be blocked by passes and mountains.[61]

In this case, both Avalokiteśvara and the Four Heavenly Kings (of which Vaiśravaṇa is one) are explicitly invoked as guardians for diplomatic travelers. In another prayer, also written by an envoy, Vaiśravaṇa in particular was summoned as a guardian deity:

> Now for an undertaking of the king I embark on a long journey. The road will be treacherous and long, and the passes and mountains that hinder the road will be precipitous. To pray that I arrive safely, I uphold the Three Worthies. Respectfully offering precious treasures, I hope they ensure my ease and security. I wish that the heavenly general Vajra would lead the way, and that wherever I go [the road] would be open; and that the king Vaiśravaṇa would secretly support me so that the back and forth will be safe and smooth.[62]

For this traveler about to embark on a long journey for "an undertaking of the king [*wangshi* 王事]," Vaiśravaṇa and other Buddhist deities were supposed to ensure that he enjoy a safe and leisurely trip. On this point, the reader might also recall the treaty reached at the Dayun temple in front of Vaiśravaṇa discussed in the previous section. Cao Yuanzhong's invocation of Avalokiteśvara and Vaiśravaṇa in his prayers for peace on the road would have been recognizable by a wide spectrum of people in Dunhuang.

Cao Yuanzhong was not alone in his view about the centrality of the road for the well-being of Dunhuang state. Back in 933, when Cao Yijin held a banquet for 1500 commoners and seventeen monks and nuns, and made donations for the transfer of merits, he prayed that "the envoys to the Eastern Court will promptly witness the Heavenly visage of the emperor; the envoys to Khotan will come and go without hindrance."[63] In this case, Cao Yijin was not only wishing for safety on the road in general but referring specifically to the road between North China and Khotan. Closely mirroring Cao Yijin's wish, in a record of the virtue accrued through commissioning Buddhist paintings, an unnamed prime minister of Khotan prayed that "the old and the young on this journey enjoy peace without danger along the road; [traveling for] the communications of the two countries, may they reach safely and quickly their homeland."[64] In a text composed for a Buddhist banquet she hosted, the Heavenly Princess, who was the Uyghur wife of Cao Yijin, prayed for safety on the road at least three times, hoping that "the road will be open and peaceful, and the five grains will be abundant," "[the people on] the four roads will all bow their heads, and the eight directions will exhibit their admiration," and "the eastern and western roads will be safe so that envoys will not be hindered by the passes and mountains."[65] Evidently, the elite class in Dunhuang, both domestic and foreign, all embraced the paramount significance of safety on the road for the fortunes of the state of Dunhuang and its neighbors.

Even the construction of the Mogao caves, the place where the collection of Dunhuang manuscripts was discovered, was often linked with diplomacy and the hope for peace on the road. In 935, after the death of their father Liang Xingde discussed in the previous section, Liang Yuanqing and Liang Daolin finished constructing what is now known as Cave 36, which Liang Xingde had initiated. According to the *Record on the Merit [from Constructing] the Mogao Caves*, the two brothers built a pagoda at their estate, completed the sculptures and statues in the cave, and erected a stela with a portrait elegy of Liang Xingde.[66] At the end of this record, the brothers prayed that "the state be peaceful and the people be content, the prefect live for one thousand years; the four roads be tranquil so as to guarantee the prosperity and fortune [of Dunhuang]." Like Cao Yuanzhong, the Liang brothers also prayed for peace on the road, and the fact that the cave originally featured the image of Vaiśravana is thus not accidental.[67] This prayer is especially poignant given that the Liangs' father not only was originally responsible for the construction of the cave but had just been killed on the road on his way back from North China. In this case, the prayer for peace on the road reveals personal pain.

The ideology of the state and the elite expressed in these prints and prayers was echoed more broadly among other prayer texts by other social groups in Dunhuang. In some of these prayer texts, the language follow that used by Cao Yuanzhong closely. In 985, Yuan Yuansheng, Zhang Fuding, and Li Changzhi hired a scribe to write the first chapter of the *Pratyutpanna-bhadrakalpa-sahasra-buddhanāma-sūtra* (Ch. Xianjie qianfoming jing 賢劫千佛名經), to be donated to a monk named Shunzi (figure 10.4).[68] Yuan and Li were identified as "fortunate women [xingpo 幸婆]," and Zhang a "fortunate man [xingzhe 幸者]." In the colophon to this text, they expressed an array of different wishes: "the state will be peaceful and the people will be content; the government will constantly prosper; the four roads will be tranquil and open, and the eight directions will all succumb."[69] This list is also almost a verbatim repetition of the prayer in the printed Vaiśravaṇa text of 947 (see figure 10.2), suggesting the effectiveness of Cao Yuanzhong's message.[70] Other prayers, such as P. 2733 in which the writers wished that "the city god will be peaceful and content and there will be no danger on the road,"[71] also remind one of the language Cao used on the Avalokiteśvara prints. These similarities indicate that the general belief, and sometimes even the specific language, of the lords of Dunhuang had penetrated the minds of the populace. The prints and their mass circulation seem to have connected the ideology of the state with the wishes of the commoners.

Finally, in the colophons to a copy of the Mahāsaṃnipāta Sūtra, the writer wished "that the king's road [*wanglu* 王路] continue to be open

FIGURE 10.4 A colophon to Xianjie qianfoming jing. The text here resembles the message contained in Cao Yuanzhong's print shown in figure 10.2.
*Credit*: The British Library.

and the enemies and bandits disappear; that the plague does not rise and the wind and rain remain timely; that all the suffering sentient beings be promptly liberated."[72] The reference to the "king's road" is a clear indication that the road in the mind of the colophon writer was used primarily for interstate connections maintained by the heads of states. The central role of this "king's road" in the well-being of Dunhuang—both the state and the people—is made apparent in this text.

These prayers show that the kings, officials, and commoners in Dunhuang were all keenly aware of the fact that they lived on a road that they shared with Dunhuang's neighbors, and that the continued peace on and connections through the road had become major concerns in their lives. The profound reach of such concern is also discernable from a children's song composed at the time of Cao Yijin's military victory over Ganzhou. The song begins with a general description of people's lives in Dunhuang: "[People] of the six prefectures [under Dunhuang's rule] all declare that they live in the time of the King Yao [an ancient sage king]." Then the song turns to a more specific celebration of Cao Yijin's accomplishment in forming new relations with Dunhuang's neighbors:

> Foreigners in four directions all come and kneel down;
> Offering camels and sending horses without interruption.
> The khaghan of Ganzhou personally dispatched envoys;
> And expressed the wish to be the son of the *Aye* ["father," meaning
>     Cao Yijin].
> The road to the Han at this day has no obstacles;
> The journeys back and forth cause no concern.[73]

In this song, Cao's status as the king is connected to the submission of "foreigners in four directions." The invocation of the foreigners (*fan*, sometimes also with clear negative connotations that should be translated as "barbarian") is a common trope in premodern Chinese thinking about its international relations.[74] The singer acclaims the reestablishment of Dunhuang's amity with Ganzhou, because it not only produced a new interstate (or, rather, intersovereign) dynamic that was favorable to the Cao ruler, but also ensured that the "road to the Han" (*hanlu*)—the "old road of Hexi" that connected Dunhuang to North China—remain unobstructed. So far, the rhetoric of this song resembles that of several other songs discussed earlier in the book. Like the other lyricists, who rejoiced in the influx of luxury goods and the opening of the road, the singer here also mentions camels and horses that were offered to Dunhuang because of a reopened road. What is different, however, is the alleged identity of the singer, which is revealed immediately after the lines about the "road to the Han":

> Please do not blame the babblings of small boys and girls;
> This children's song came from our little son.
> Wishing that Alang [meaning Cao Yijin] live for tens of thousands of
>     years;
> And the Lady [the wife of Cao Yijin] and others be sturdy without
>     falling.
> The father was rushed over to bear witness;
> And the mother also served to guarantee.[75]

The last stanzas reveal the genesis of the song. The parents testify that these well-wishes for the king and the lady were not their concoctions, but came from "our little son." To this claim, the father and mother both served as witnesses, in a manner that reminds one of the contracts found in Dunhuang. As Chen Sanping has pointed out, in premodern China, "of all folk songs, children's ballads or rhymes occupied a particularly important place: they were often regarded as 'vox Dei,' or oracles from heaven."[76] Therefore, this song, which notably centered on the continued connections of the road, was seen by the parents as an auspicious sign for the future prosperity of Dunhuang under Cao Yijin.

Finally, the last two lines further involve the parents (and presumably the boy) in the world of the Silk Road. After laying out the natural—indeed, the supernatural—genesis of this song, the parents ask to be compensated for their effort in presenting these auspicious lines to the lord of Dunhuang:

> We pray that you bestow one *pi* of compound weave silk [*jin*] on us;
> So that we can make a set of daily clothing.

Not land, nor official titles. The parents ask for the very thing that defines the connections that their boy's song celebrates: silk. It is hardly coincidental that the goods they seek are the most popular item shared and exchanged in this diplomatic network they celebrate. Had their request been granted, this family would have to be counted among those enriched by connections on the Silk Road, mirroring the view of the poem "Opening [the road to] Khotan," which wishes for "cotton and silk filling every household."[77]

There is no way to know if such a boy ever existed; the parents could have made up the song and invented their testimonies. It is also entirely possible that this whole episode was fabricated by an imaginative official in the Dunhuang government in an effort to craft the appearance of political support among commoners in Dunhuang. But any such concoction, whether by the parents or some unnamed official, would need to conform with the sentiment of Dunhuang society at the time to be credible to Cao Yijin and to those among whom the song was circulating. Therefore, the idea expressed by the song should be taken seriously. The boy who supposedly uttered these lines was as much a participant in the world of the Silk Road as the kings that were eulogized in them.

People in Dunhuang prayed for the prosperity of the state, the health of the people, and the moderation of the weather, like people in other parts of the world. Uniquely, however, they also prayed for continued peace and free passage on the road that connected Dunhuang to its eastern and western neighbors. No such emphasis on the road is found, for instance, in the prayers contained in a group of more than 1600 dedicatory Buddhist inscriptions from North China in the fifth and sixth centuries.[78] An unobstructed road was thought to bring both peace and prosperity to people in Dunhuang in a way that no other social institution could. Thus, the wish to keep the road open did not only dictate major political decisions in war and diplomacy, from lords to officials, monks to commoners, reaching all the way to the alleged words of a young boy, this wish also saturated every social stratum of Dunhuang society and appears to have become a political and social consensus.

## Conclusion

In the previous two chapters, I showed that the influx of luxury goods, primarily through diplomatic exchange carried out by envoys, was central to the economy and the kingship of Dunhuang. This chapter completes my demonstration of the centrality of the road in the lives of people in Dunhuang. When we read the song performed on New Year's Day (discussed in the introduction), the one about the opening of the road to Khotan (chapter 8), and the young boy's song, it seems clear to me that people in Dunhuang did not just understand the importance of the road and luxury goods, they also considered them closely intertwined, because keeping the road open, they believed, would naturally result in a flow of luxury goods that promised to benefit a wide range of people in Dunhuang. In these songs, as in the economic decisions of envoys and political decisions of kings, I argue that we see a phenomenon intriguingly close to the standard understanding of the "Silk Road"—a network of transregional routes used to carry and exchange luxury goods.

The people of medieval Dunhuang certainly would not have used or heard the term "Silk Road," and I remain skeptical of applying this term to Dunhuang in an undifferentiated manner. During the Tang or Tibetan rule, as well as under Zhang family rule, many of the characteristics discussed in this chapter are not detectable in the sources.[79] But, with the discussion in the last three chapters in mind, I argue that the term "Silk Road" would not have been meaningless to the kings or the commoners of Dunhuang. Perhaps unwittingly, the term created by Ferdinand von Richthofen was anticipated nearly a thousand years earlier in the popular songs of tenth-century Dunhuang. While Richthofen's inspiration was the accounts of classical authors of the luxurious silk products and the lure of the East, the concerns of the residents in Dunhuang were much more immediate. They hoped that an open road would not only maintain peace with their neighboring states but also bring in goods and economic opportunities difficult to acquire in Dunhuang. It is in the lives of these kings, travelers, and commoners that the meaning of the term "Silk Road" finds its fullest expression.

# Conclusion

THIS BOOK attempts to reconstruct the world of diplomatic travelers on the Silk Road based primarily on the Dunhuang documents. I have described who these travelers were (part I); how they traveled (part II); and the economic, political, and social impacts of the network they created (part III). To conclude my reconstruction, I remind readers of the song quoted at the opening of the book:

> The ten thousand commoners sing songs with full bellies like drums,
> [living in] a time like that under [the sage kings] Shun and Yao.
> Do not worry about the eastern road being blocked.
> In the spring, the heavenly envoys will arrive,
> and they will contribute large *jin*-silks with coiled dragons,
> and different kinds of damask, gauze, plain silk, colored silk.
>
> . . . . . . . . . . . . . . . . . . . . . . . . . . . . . . . . . . . . . . . . . . . . . . . . . . . . . . . . . . .
>
> To the west all the way until Khotan
> the road is smoother than those covered in cotton cloth.
> [The Khotanese] will offer precious artifacts and white jade,
> as well as a thousand rolls of cotton, damask, and miscellaneous fabrics.
> All within the border [of Dunhuang] chant the song of happiness
> and enjoy a long life like Ancestor Peng![1]

To this Dunhuang lyricist, luxury goods like silk and jade were expected to enter Dunhuang with diplomatic travelers to enrich the "ten thousand commoners" and bring about an ideal world of prosperity and longevity. In the preceding pages, I have sought to show that the vision of this song was deeply rooted in the social realities of medieval Dunhuang and Eastern Eurasia. In effect, the song was describing the same network of long-distance connections, albeit much more concisely, as I have reconstructed in this book—the network that I call the "King's Road."

I do not choose the overused term "network" lightly.[2] A few sporadic cases of travelers do not make a network of long-distance connections. Like most societies we have any knowledge about in the world prior to 1000, Dunhuang and its neighbors in this book have not left us statistical records such as census data or GDP breakdowns. But certain documents do allow one to assess the number of diplomatic travelers, the frequency of their journeys, and the proportion of their impact on Dunhuang's economy and society. Throughout the book, wherever possible, I have sought to ask the question of *scale*. When we see, for example, an envoy from Khotan going to Dunhuang for his seventh trip; a Dunhuang monk serving on diplomatic trips to Khotan, Ganzhou, and Turfan all in the same year; the king of Dunhuang simultaneously managing four missions to the Tang; and 40 percent of contracts found in Dunhuang implicating traveling envoys I suggest that the use of the term "network" is warranted.

I call this network the "King's Road" because the kings of Eastern Eurasia performed central roles in its creation and maintenance. They longed for goods from afar for corporal use—consumption and decoration of themselves, the royal family, and the elite—they also deemed it essential to be well-informed about the political news of their neighbors, and made political decisions on the basis of such information. In order to sustain the network of luxury goods and political information, these kings constructed postal stations, hired interpreters, and supplied accommodation to foreign envoys; they also sent out envoys, almost unfailingly bearing gifts, to visit other kings in foreign lands. They provided much of the infrastructure, and part of the motivation, of the network described in this book.

But the kings are not the only, perhaps not even the most crucial, characters in this story. The daily operation of the King's Road was made possible by diplomatic travelers. They collected gifts and daily necessities before their journeys, trudged through the formidable Central Eurasian terrain, dealt with hosts and bandits on the road, and, if they were lucky, delivered messages and gifts on behalf of their kings. In addition to serving kings, however, these envoys also visited Buddhist sites, conducted personal business dealings, and formed (sometimes illicit) friendships with envoys of other states. Occasionally, we even find honest and unflattering views about their kings from these envoys. They regularly praised the foreign kings they encountered on the road in order to receive adequate accommodation and guidance; but, sometimes, they also acted irreverently toward their hosts, lost their way on the road, or murdered (or were murdered by) their companions. Their experiences, views, motivations, and interests did not always align with those of the kings. Both groups were indispensable in the making of the King's Road. Thus it makes just as much sense to call this network the "Envoy's Road."

This road, as a collective noun, refers to the routes that connected states in Eastern Eurasia from Khotan to Kaifeng. According to the Dunhuang documents, this road was not uniform and could not be easily defined: it could be a guarded and guided postal road, a well-marked natural road, or a shifting path in the desert. It was also not simply a physical presence: the road became a central concern of kings, envoys, and commoners in places like Dunhuang, and entered policy making and the personal prayers of people in Dunhuang. The importance of the road reveals itself in its interactions with the travelers, as we have witnessed how travelers used geographical texts, location-based poetry, and human guides to help them navigate and tame the road. In this book, I have sought to portray the road not just as something that envoys trod but as a character with its own idiosyncrasies and history.

The King's Road had a visible impact on the societies on its route, the best documented of which is Dunhuang itself. Beyond the kings and envoys, many other people in Dunhuang society were involved in the maintenance of the King's Road. They contributed goods to departing envoys, provided services as local guides to incoming envoys, offered spiritual support through their prayers for all travelers, and shared the personal and financial risks of diplomatic travel. The King's Road in turn also changed their economic lives and broadened their political and cultural horizons. It is true that the network did not always function smoothly. The people of Dunhuang certainly did not simply "sing songs with bellies completely filled," nor did the road realistically "fill every household with silk and brocade," as some Dunhuang poets envisioned. But the lives of many, if not most, in Dunhuang were nonetheless profoundly shaped by the road that connected Dunhuang with its neighbors. The world of the King's Road did not end where the travelers stopped; we see rippling effects of this network in the societies that it connected, reaching deep into the everyday lives of commoners. Such impacts, produced by the combined force of luxury goods ("silk") and the land-based means of transportation and travel ("road"), mean that the "Silk Road" is an accurate term to describe this diplomatic network. To put it simply, to residents of medieval Dunhuang, there *was* a Silk Road. Thus, I use the term "King's Road" not to replace "Silk Road" but to underscore its diplomatic dimension.

This book is concerned primarily with a world centered on Dunhuang between 850 and 1000. How should we assess the broader significance of the experiences of envoys and kings that have unfolded in the preceding pages? To conclude, I place the stories I have told in the *King's Road* within the scholarly discussion of the Silk Road, medieval China, and Eastern Eurasia, and consider the contributions and limits of this book.

## Toward a Traveler-Centered Definition of the "Silk Road"

At its core, this book is a social history of long-distance travel. Unlike much existing scholarship on the Silk Road, which uses primarily the archives of empire, from Chinese annals to Roman histories,[3] I take the perspective of the creators of these connections: the transregional diplomatic travelers who left their traces in the Dunhuang library cave. By following the footsteps of these diplomatic travelers, we can observe what it was really like to travel on the Silk Road: Travelers sometimes cruised to their destinations, but, as often, they were delayed, obstructed, and even ambushed. They traveled on postal roads and through deserts, participated in polo games and joined banquets with kings. They wrote reports and delivered letters and gifts; they praised their hosts but also complained to and argued with them. It was a messy world of difficult and exhilarating life on the road.

In the process of reconstructing these stories, we have encountered many colorful figures: the erudite polyglot Zhang Jinshan, the skilled interpreter turned war hero Hun Ziying, the desperate house-selling envoy Li Wenwen, the female attendant to the Khotanese princess and astute organizer of long-distance exchange Youding, the confused and lost envoy Chen Yuanhong, the inexperienced juvenile attaché Zhang Yuanjin, and the murdered head envoy Liang Xingde. These diplomatic travelers included high-level governmental officials and impoverished commoners, even slaves. Their stories contribute to a central observation of the book: in medieval Dunhuang and its surrounding states on the Silk Road, diplomacy was not the prerogative of a small, tight-knit group of highly trained bureaucrats, as in most modern states, but a way of life open to a wide spectrum of people in society.

Along with these envoys, we have also met other marvelous travelers, such as dancing elephants, jade fists, and a magic cauldron. Equally important, however, were the mundane things that time has rendered invisible in our sources, such as the food, water, and clothing that sustained human travelers. Pack animals such as horses and camels also feature prominently in our stories, not only as a means to carry other things, but also as an economic investment that shaped the human travelers' relation with broader society. Finally, we have also seen skeins of silk and other luxury cloth traveling hundreds or thousands of kilometers from camels' backs to the bodies of kings and, occasionally, the households of regular people.

A type of diplomatic traveler central to this book is the manuscript. Some of the manuscripts I discuss in this book, such as the envoys' notebook (the Staël-Holstein manuscript; chapter 2) and the collection of political information from the Later Jin (chapter 9), were likely compiled by envoys; others, like the edicts of the Khotanese king (chapter 7), were brought to Dunhuang by envoys. I have also introduced contracts and personal letters created by envoys at different stages of their lives. While most of the envoys and things that once traveled on the Silk Road have long since perished and disappeared, these documents, some of which must have accompanied envoys on the Silk Road, are still with us. In this book, I treat these documents not only as carriers of text but as objects with long and exciting lives of their own.[4]

Envoys, luxury goods, animals, and manuscripts were all diplomatic travelers, and none traveled by themselves. It is not in any one type of traveler but the *relationships* among them—the human-thing symbiosis—that we find the defining characteristic of the travelers I describe in this book. This symbiosis can be summarized in this way: The largely riverless landscape of Central Eurasia meant that the most powerful means of transportation was domesticated Bactrian camels. To make full use of their capacity, the envoys-to-be invested heavily, even recklessly, to acquire camels; but the high prices of raising and caring for camels meant that even the richest travelers could have only so many, which limited the quantity of goods they could bring on their trips. With this calculation in mind, these travelers opted to bring mostly high-value, low-weight luxury goods at the expense of food and water; as a result, our travelers acquired much of the food they needed from their hosts on the road, thus obligating them to enter into guest-host relations in the societies they passed through. This chain of relations, which governed life on the road, is clear only when we consider human and nonhuman travelers together.

Clarifying the relations among these components of a diplomatic journey helps us determine where the medieval travelers fit in a longer history of transregional travel in Eurasia. How do our travelers differ from other long-distance travelers in Eurasian history? While a detailed discussion of this topic is impossible here, I can point to broad differences between the travelers

I discuss in this book and three other types of traveler who are often also described as participants of the Silk Road.

1. Before the domestication of camels in the third millennium BCE and their widespread use as pack animals, the bulk and weight of goods Bronze Age travelers could haul over long distances must have been even less (and tended to be more luxurious) for the trips to make sense, and the distance this earlier human-thing symbiotic unit could cover must also have been drastically shorter than that of the travelers I describe.[5]

2. Maritime travelers had vastly greater carrying capacity, which allowed them to transport not only lightweight luxury goods but also porcelain,[6] grain,[7] wine, and other household items. Maritime travelers could also carry all the food and clothes they would require for the whole journey, thus eliminating the constant need to ask for provisions that faced overland travelers. The goods maritime travelers loaded on their boats, due to the sheer number and relatively lower value (again, compared to the overland route), also could reach a much broader spectrum of the society that they sailed to.

3. Modern Eurasian travelers on railways and in automobiles move much faster. The isolated environment of the train and the car also largely shields human travelers from having to form the kind of reciprocal relations our envoys needed to make with their hosts on the road.[8] Trains and cars can also carry an almost infinitely greater amount of goods per operating person than was possible for medieval travelers, but their heavier reliance on infrastructure also means that travelers are more beholden to the state.

These three types of traveler—on foot, on boats, and on trains—are similar to the travelers I discuss in this book (we can call them travelers "on camels") in that they all cover long distances and exchange goods. But because of the different human-thing symbioses involved in each type, the social, economic, and cultural impacts of these four types of traveler must have been—and this is my hypothesis—significantly distinct from one another. Because of this distinction, I propose that, instead of calling all four types "Silk Road" travelers, we reserve this term for the land-based travelers who made use of pack animals in their long-distance journeys. The temporal scope of these travelers would be from the domestication and extensive use of pack animals such as camels and horses until the widespread use of railroads. To put it another way,

I define the "Silk Road" as a *premodern network of land routes in Eurasia where people primarily used pack animals to transport high-value, low-weight things.*

This definition covers a broader chronological range than the original (and implicit) definition of the Silk Road by Richthofen, who dated this phenomenon to the Han-Roman period. I believe that restricting the "Silk Road" to only this period exaggerates the uniqueness of the Han-Roman world—there are few discernible qualitative differences between how the Silk Road functioned in the first century than, say, in the tenth century—and thus diminishes the value of this concept.

On the other hand, the common scholarly and popular use of the term "Silk Road," which often lumps together prehistoric transmission of languages and agriculture, maritime exchange in the premodern era, and even modern transportation of goods on trans-Eurasian train tracks, is also unhelpful because it is too broad.[9] While there is nothing wrong per se with this more general approach, such omnipresence of the term "Silk Road" deprives it of any chronological and spatial specificity, thus similarly rendering it less helpful in understanding historical change. As a result, the "Silk Road" becomes simply a vague and exoticizing way of talking about cultural and material exchange. I hope my traveler-centered definition of the Silk Road, which takes a middle path between Richthofen and many modern historians, retains an internal coherence that makes this idea the most useful.

## The Nature and the Chronology of the Silk Road

This book's focus on diplomatic travelers and the "King's Road" is the result of the preponderance of evidence about the two in the Dunhuang archive. Our sources describe the travelers as "envoys" and the goods they exchanged as "gifts."[10] The activities of these envoys almost always included delivering official letters, meeting with kings, and the exchange of gifts. The infrastructure of the road was maintained by the different governments of Eastern Eurasia, which offered accommodation and replenishment of provisions for these travelers. The goods that these travelers exchanged and transported, as we see in Dunhuang, occasionally entered the everyday markets, but more often they were stored in the treasuries of kings and the elite. Travelers without insignia showing their official status were often prevented from participating in diplomacy. It is hardly a coincidence that the guidelines of the mutual-help group in Dunhuang, the Society for Long Distance Travel, explicitly stated that "trips for private purposes do not fall within the parameters [of this stipulation]."[11]

Aside from the private business that travelers sometimes engaged in when they were on the road, there is very little that can be described as strictly "commercial" in the stories of envoys and kings told in this book.

The portrait of the diplomatic dimension of the Silk Road in this book reminds us that diplomatic travelers are never invisible in the transmitted sources and caches of excavated documents on the Silk Road. It was Zhang Qian, the envoy who led a mission to Central Asia in the second century BCE, who is often (but wrongly) credited as "opening the Silk Road."[12] Aḥmad ibn Faḍlān, the renowned medieval traveler whose account of the Vikings has fascinated readers since medieval times, traveled to northern Europe from Baghdad as an envoy.[13] Other renowned travelers not primarily known as envoys in fact also played diplomatic roles at certain points of their trips. Xuanzang, the famous Chinese monk who visited India, was able to move with ease between Turfan and western Central Asia because he carried the insignia of an envoy from the king of Turfan.[14] Marco Polo was primarily a merchant on his trip from Venice to the Mongol court and used the commercial network established by his father and uncle. But on his way back, in particular during the trip between the Mongol courts in North China and Iran, his primary role was that of an envoy.[15] From archaeological sources, one of the largest known groups of travelers on the Silk Road ever recorded was a diplomatic mission from Khotan to Han China that included 1074 members.[16] The record about envoy-escorts in fifth-century Turfan, as I have mentioned several times, involved about 15 percent of the adult male population of the kingdom.[17] As a result, many of the best-known areas of cultural exchange in the premodern era were facilitated by envoys.[18] The importance of envoys also manifested itself in visual forms: For instance, in Afrasiyab near the ancient city of Samarkand, an extravagant "Ambassadors' Hall" was constructed in the seventh century, with paintings of kings and luminaries from the Roman, Turkic, and Chinese worlds.[19] The hands and eyes of the kings and their envoys were often central, and rarely absent, in the stories of long-distance connection in premodern Eurasia.

The transregional connections in our modern world since the sixteenth century are indeed animated primarily by a capitalist commerce network.[20] But should we see premodern Eurasia as connected primarily by commerce, only of a smaller amount and more limited scale? Or should we follow the suggestion of Peter Brown and see the medieval connections as motivated primarily by "the game of the competing glory of the kings"?[21] On these questions, I think the jury is still out. For three reasons, the fact that the overwhelming majority of long-distance travelers in the Dunhuang documents were diplomatic should *not* lead to the simplistic conclusion that the Silk Road was primarily a diplomatic network.

First, the Dunhuang archive, although somewhat randomly assembled, is likely biased toward recording more about official travelers and less about private traders. Therefore, the absence of commercial travelers in the Dunhuang archive is not entirely unexpected.

Second, the period covered in this book is one of extreme political fragmentation, when many independent kings were vying for power and prestige through diplomacy. But this extreme political fragmentation was by no means the norm in Eurasian history. In the era of large land-based empires, such as the Tang and the Mongol Empire, the dynamics of long-distance connection may have been different.

Third, and most important, there is indisputable evidence of the commercial dimension of the Silk Road. The fourth-century Sogdian Ancient Letters, from a Great Wall ruin site near Dunhuang, attest to an early yet extensive network of Sogdian traders.[22] In Turfan documents from the fifth to the eighth centuries, we also see "trading foreigners" (*xinghu* or *xingsheng hu*) participating in various aspects of Turfan's social life.[23] Even in the Dunhuang materials, there are still cases where we see traders engaging in long-distance journeys.[24] The relative importance of one type of traveler compared with another in any given society—and indeed the complex relation and mixture of these "types" of travelers—needs to be studied on a case-by-case basis, and the situation in Dunhuang in the ninth and tenth centuries should not be seen as generalizable.

Nevertheless, I do hope that the stories from the Dunhuang materials can help put the widespread and commonly accepted assumption of the commercial nature of the Silk Road into question.[25] Scholars have long been a bit too ready to interpret ambiguous evidence as traces of commerce on the Silk Road.[26] As a result, the presence of commerce in our sources is often assumed and exaggerated rather than demonstrated. By highlighting the diplomatic nature of *some* connections on the Silk Road, I hope this book will remind readers and scholars to be more cautious when encountering an object or a person that has traveled far in premodern Eurasia. Instead of immediately connecting them to merchants and commerce, one should be open to interpreting them in other possible social contexts, such as diplomacy.[27]

One example of this overeagerness to see commerce where little evidence exists is the argument about merchants "pretending" to be envoys. Owen

Lattimore once observed, regarding "the celebrated Silk Route trade," that "oasis rulers carried on trade in a disguised form, by sending embassies with gifts to the Chinese Court."[28] This claim of merchants "pretending" to be envoys is sometimes still repeated and requires a bit of clarification.[29] While there are perhaps rare cases of intentional deception,[30] most diplomatic travelers should not be regarded simply as merchants in disguise. As I have shown in this book, envoys were dispatched by kings; they needed official insignia, royal edicts, gifts, and information to be admitted as such; while traveling on roads sanctioned and maintained by a network of states, they enjoyed material support from these states. These features of diplomatic travelers are not found in the lives of private merchants, such as the ones who appear in the Sogdian Ancient Letters in the early fourth century.[31] The distinction between envoys and merchants, and the different ways governments on the Silk Road treated them, is also visible from other oasis towns, like Turfan.[32] I would suggest that the more meaningful distinction lies, not between "real" envoys and merchants who sometimes (supposedly) pretended to be envoys,[33] but between exchanges (through gifts or trade) conducted by envoys that states sanctioned and organized within an explicitly diplomatic network, on the one hand, and private trade by merchants in which states did not directly participate but might have condoned, on the other.

Another aspect of the history of the Silk Road that I wanted to address in this book is its chronology. Most scholars who attempt such a chronology have linked the fate of the Silk Road with that of the empires—to put it simply, they suggest that the Silk Road rose and fell with the empires that supposedly sustained it. The global historian Philip Curtin, for instance, highlights three periods—the Han-Parthian-Roman period, the Tang-Abbasid period, and the Mongol Empire—that featured "relatively open trade across Asia" as the heydays of cross-cultural trade in the premodern world.[34] Jerry Bentley goes one step further and divides world history into six periods following the rise and fall of the Silk Road, which according to him reflect the ebb and flow of support from unified empires.[35] Curtin's and Bentley's hypothesis would maintain that the five centuries between the heyday of the Tang and the Mongol Empire (750–1250) are an era of decline in the history of the Silk Road in Eastern Eurasia.

This hypothesis is based on the assumption that large empires, through their various unifying measures and protective apparatus, reduced the dangers and costs of traveling on the road, thus making them facilitators of cross-cultural exchange and connections.[36] But stricter and more centralized control also meant that empires could *prevent* people from traveling. Take Xuanzang and the early Tang Empire as an example: as he was making his way from Chang'an to India, Xuanzang first traveled through the Hexi Corridor under the rule of the Tang, where he was threatened, harassed, stopped, even temporarily imprisoned, because he was not authorized to travel. Then he crossed the Great Ocean Desert, entered Turfan, and, after an extended sojourn there, journeyed further west into the eastern half of Central Asia, which was made up of many independent kingdoms.[37] In this second leg of the journey, Xuanzang met with courteous treatment and received gifts and assistance, because of both his Buddhist learning and the help of the king of Turfan. How should we understand the role of the Tang Empire in Xuanzang's journey? It was certainly not a facilitatory one. The pro-connection or anti-connection impulses of an empire should both be considered in order to have a more accurate assessment of that empire's role in activities on the Silk Road.

Just as unified empires did not always promote transregional connections, political fragmentation likewise did not always weaken these ties. What this book has shown is that at least *one type* of activity on the Silk Road—diplomatic travel—was not in decline in the era of political fragmentation. Instead, we witness an unexplored dynamic where increased political fragmentation produced a large number of relatively small states vying for status and seeking to strengthen their diplomatic connections, which may even have further incentivized diplomatic travel. After the fall of the Tang, Tibetan, and Uyghur empires, and the dissolution of the Sogdian merchant network that spanned much of Eastern Eurasia, the Silk Road did not simply dwindle into stagnation. The kings and envoys from regional states in the postimperial age were fully capable of remaking a network of long-distance connections to serve their own needs.[38] Therefore, both empires and smaller regional states had competing and complex interests regarding long-distance connections. The existing chronology of the Silk Road as rhyming only with the "rise and fall" of large transregional empires, at the current state of our research, seems suspicious and scantly supported by empirical evidence. The history of the Silk Road might very well have its own, autonomous rhythm that is yet to be fully understood.

## Eastern Eurasian Diplomacy

This book is not, as I explained in the introduction, about well-trodden areas in the field of the history of international relations, such as military strategy and decision-making in court. But the process of dissecting the lives and motivations of diplomatic travelers and their sovereigns naturally leads me to important issues in this field. Because the existing scholarship largely centers on Eastern Eurasia's great imperial powers, the ways in which Dunhuang, a former province of both the Tang and the Tibetan empires, dealt with its neighbors has much to teach us about the world of diplomacy in Eastern Eurasia between 850 and 1000. With its lack of a widely recognized imperial center, this world differed from those of both the High Tang and the Song-Liao after the Chanyuan Covenant in 1005, and is not yet well understood.

Through examining the actions of Dunhuang kings and envoys, whose relation toward regimes in North China (the Tang, the Five Dynasties, and the Song) vacillated between that of a distant province and that of a vassal state, we gain a window onto the world of Tang-Song diplomacy from its periphery. Externally, the kings of Dunhuang routinely treated the regimes in North China with reverence, adopted (even in documents on purely domestic matters) the regnal names (*nianhao* 年號) of these regimes, and self-identified as ritually inferior. The urgency and insistence with which the rulers of Dunhuang sought investiture from North China, even during the uncertain times of the Five Dynasties, show the enduring symbolic power of the traditional imperial centers.[39] Internally, however, the rulers of Dunhuang often saw themselves as much more than mere provincial governors or vassals. Many in the tenth century called themselves "great king."[40] The case of Zhang Cheng-feng, who for a short while assumed the title of "Son of Heaven," is only the most extreme example of Dunhuang's attempt to assert its political independence from North China.

In addition to its relation with North China, we have also learned a great deal about how Dunhuang managed its relations with other smaller states in its more immediate vicinity. While the Zhang rulers in the ninth century sometimes tried to subjugate their neighbors through force, the Cao rulers, for more than a century, participated in and helped maintain a stable regional interstate network, particularly with Turfan, Ganzhou, and Khotan. A key institution the Cao rulers exploited was diplomatic marriage, known in the Chinese context as *heqin*. Unlike contemporaneous North China, where such practice was on its way out—the Song emperors never married their princesses to their neighbors—the Cao rulers married widely with the royal families of Khotan, Ganzhou, and other neighbors.[41] Significantly, they not only married their daughters *out* but also solicited wives from non-Chinese states such as Ganzhou and Khotan, thus defying the well-documented unidirectionality of *heqin* marriages, in which the Chinese emperors only married daughters out to foreign rulers but never took a non-Chinese bride.[42] In this case, even though the Cao rulers primarily used Chinese as their bureaucratic language, their practice of diplomacy with non-Chinese neighbors differed from that of a Tang or a Song emperor.

Another departure from standard Tang/Song diplomatic practice is apparent when we compare the two imperial edicts I cite in this book: both the edict from the Tang emperor Ruizong (figure 1.1) and that of the Khotanese king Viśa' Śūra (figure 7.2) bear the gigantic character *chi* that symbolizes imperial power. The heads of the Dunhuang government were the recipients of both imperial letters. Even though Viśa' Śūra's *chi* was executed in a rather clumsy hand and attached to a letter written in Khotanese, the relations embodied by these two letters are similar: in each case, the writer of the edict proclaims his superior status over that of the recipient. Thus, Cao Yuanzhong, the recipient of the second edict, was placed as a clear subordinate to the Khotanese king as if the latter were a Tang emperor. Mirroring this relation revealed by the edicts, in two successive letters to the government of Khotan, Dunhuang envoys referred to the Song as the "Eastern Court" (Dongchao 東朝) and Khotan as the "Western Court" (Xichao 西朝), practically putting the two states on equal diplomatic footing. In these letters, the Dunhuang officials also adopted Khotanese, rather than Song, regnal names as the dating mechanism.[43] Although less well documented, we know that in times of military weakness, the Cao rulers also did not hesitate to elevate the status of other neighboring sovereigns, and sometimes addressed, for instance, the Uyghur khan of Ganzhou as "khaghan, the Son of Heaven."[44] Even though the Tang and Song courts treated all these states (Ganzhou, Dunhuang, Khotan) as similar foreign vassals, in the internal dealings among these states, we often see different sets of hierarchical relations in which the Tang/Song states were not always central.

What is less visible, however, is how non-Chinese states dealt with one another, particularly when Dunhuang was not involved. We have a few tantalizing linguistic clues, such as the use of Uyghur and Tibetan loanwords for diplomatic gifts in Sogdian and Khotanese; the Sogdian loanword *cwn ywzy*, "the bearer of edict," from Chinese; and the appearance of the term *chaoding*—a Kitan word used to describe diplomatic friendship between the Kitan emperor and the Later Tang emperor—in a Dunhuang official report to characterize the friendship between a Dunhuang envoy and a Uyghur envoy in the same mission. In a letter to the king of Dunhuang written in Tibetan, the king of Khotan calls himself "the Great Son of God [*gcen po lha sras*]" and addresses the recipient as "Heavenly Minister [*dang re shang shu*, a combination of the Turkic word *teŋri*, "heaven," and the Chinese title *shangshu* 尚書]."[45] These titles show a curious mixture of Chinese, Tibetan, and Turco-Uyghur kingship terminologies, in a letter issued by an Iranian state. Casting our eyes further west, we also observe that the principles of guest-host relations and gift exchange in the Dunhuang materials seem to correspond to similar practices in the Islamic world as revealed in the *Compendium of the Turkic Dialects* and the records of Marvazī and Tamīm ibn Baḥr.

How should we understand this multilayered diplomatic network observed from the vantage point of medieval Dunhuang? The idea of the "tributary system" is not entirely useless, as the centrality of the Tang and the Song was still sometimes acknowledged and occasionally celebrated in the Dunhuang materials.[46] But such belief was by no means universally held, nor did it align well with most diplomatic practices, especially when Dunhuang dealt with other Inner Asian neighbors.[47] Therefore, I follow Jonathan Skaff's efforts to tell a non-Sinocentric story of diplomacy in Eastern Eurasia and share his skepticism of "the Sinic origins of the ideology and diplomatic praxis."[48] Apart from this Sinocentric tributary system, there were many other ideas from other political and cultural traditions at play in the world of medieval Eurasian diplomacy.[49] More research is needed to develop a necessary set of vocabulary and concepts to describe the interactions among Chinese, Tibetan, Uyghur, pre-Islamic Iranian, and Islamic diplomatic practices in this world of many kings. I hope the examples discussed in this book begin to show how prevalent such interactions were in medieval Eastern Eurasia. As scholars are increasingly viewing the medieval world (especially Eurasia) as an integrated whole, diplomacy promises to be one of the most fertile grounds to explore ideas such as the "global medieval."[50]

But was there any uniting theme in the world of diplomacy described in this book? David Kang has argued that the relative peace in East Asia from 1368 to 1841 hinged on a shared understanding of the hierarchical relations of East Asian states within the tributary system, shared Confucian cultural knowledge, and Sinic writings.[51] None of these shared values were present in the world of Eastern Eurasia from 850 to 1000. Yet such absence did not lead to constant conflict. Instead, from Kaifeng to Khotan, these diplomatic players created a remarkably stable international order that persisted for over a century from the late ninth century to the early eleventh century. Here, I would suggest that, instead of an agreed-upon set of hierarchies or ideologies, it was the common need for a constant influx of luxury goods and political information—

crucial elements in the economic well-being and political legitimation of these kingdoms—that persuaded the kings of Khotan, Turfan, Dunhuang, and Gan-zhou to strive for peace and refrain from war. Such need manifested in diplo-matic letters as an urge to keep the "road" open and secure. The role of the road is also seen in the Kitan khan's letter to the Ghaznavid ruler: the khan ends by saying that the goal of sending the envoy was to "open the road of union and fasten the ties of amity."[52] This alternative rationale for international order transcended linguistic and ideological barriers and deserves further investigation.

Last but not least, my stories center on the diplomatic travelers who actu-ally carried out the policies and wishes of the kings, a group of players gener-ally marginalized in existing scholarship. I explain how envoys moved from one town to the next; how they communicated with the sovereigns; how edicts were composed, transported, and delivered; and how gifts were ex-changed, displayed, and used. The rich Dunhuang documents I use allow me to paint a detailed prosopography of these envoys. In this way, my approach echoes the recent development of a "new diplomatic history" that places more emphasis on the characters conducting diplomatic dealings as opposed to "di-plomacy" itself.[53] My prosopography joins a growing number of works on the lives of these interstate mediators, thus inviting the possibility of future com-parative work.[54]

In recent years, records from Korea, such as the *Yonhaeng-Nok* (燕行錄), have invigorated the study of diplomacy in the Ming and Qing worlds.[55] The Dunhuang materials similarly allow us to see the world of international rela-tions in medieval Eastern Eurasia from the perspective of a relatively minor, peripheral participant. Their lessons should be heeded as we reconsider the history of diplomacy in medieval Eastern Eurasia.

## Chinese History as Eurasian History

One of the main differences between the Silk Road described in this book and that conceptualized by Richthofen concerns geography. None of the envoys discussed in this book traveled the whole length of the road between China and the Mediterranean world. Instead, they were most active in the area between Kaifeng and Khotan. In this book, I call this region "Eastern Eurasia," with the qualification that not all areas of Eastern Eurasia are evenly represented.[56] What does this study of a diplomatic network between Khotan and Kaifeng tell us about other aspects of the history of this *region*?

The histories of Khotan and Kaifeng are rarely told together. Kaifeng, in what is commonly called "North China," belongs to the history of "China," which is traditionally organized around the dynastic units of the Tang (618–907), the Five Dynasties (907–60), and the Northern Song (960–1127). The sources we use to study this period were predominantly composed or edited during the Song. In occupying the heartland of the Tang capitals and conquering much of South and Central China, the Song dynasty powerfully claimed the status of heir to the Tang legacy. Song officials strengthened this claim with historical writings that framed the years between the Tang and the Song as "the Five Dynasties," and with massive compilation projects that filtered historical records through their lens.[57] Some of these projects reflected the will of the emperors, while others were personal endeavors of historians such as Ouyang Xiu (1007–72) and Sima Guang (1019–86). But they shared the objective of positioning the Song as the only legitimate heir to the Tang legacy.[58]

But the Tang and the Song were quite different. While the Tang, at its height before the An Lushan Rebellion, controlled much of Eastern Eurasia, the Northern Song retained only around two-thirds of the Tang domain. Therefore, one consequence of framing Chinese history after the Tang only around Song-dynasty sources is that nearly a third of the old Tang domain, including Dunhuang and its immediate neighboring states, transitions *out* of Chinese history after the An Lushan Rebellion. For instance, in the official *Song History*, Dunhuang, once a Tang province, was placed in the monograph on foreign countries.[59] Therefore, embedded in the historiography of Ouyang Xiu and Sima Guang is a *geographically diminishing view* of "China" in the Middle Period between the Tang and the Song. This view is further reinforced by a widely held belief that the political fragmentation of the ninth and tenth centuries meant decreased connection.[60] If contact with the west was gradually lost, there was no reason to tell the history of "China proper" together with that of places like Dunhuang and Khotan.

Such a geographically diminishing view has direct bearing on how scholars use the Dunhuang materials. In a recent survey of Dunhuang studies published in the authoritative *Chinese Social Sciences*, historian Liu Jinbao summarizes the contribution of the Dunhuang materials to Chinese history.[61] In the early and mid-Tang, the survey contains many examples of how the Dunhuang materials can be used to understand the history of Tang China. But in the ninth and tenth centuries, Liu mentions only the materials' value for the study of "local history in Hexi [Hexi *defangshi* 河西地方史]."[62] Mirroring this view, while the Dunhuang materials are discussed extensively in the

Tang volume of the *Cambridge History of China*, in the more than thousand-page volume that covers the period from 907 to 1279, Dunhuang is not mentioned once. Evidently, historians working with mostly Song sources and their counterparts working with Dunhuang materials have reached an implicit consensus that the Dunhuang materials are largely irrelevant to the broader history of China after the high Tang.

This book challenges such consensus and the geographically diminishing view of Chinese history embedded therein. I show that the Dunhuang materials are meaningful to the broader study of the history of China in the Middle Period in two ways: as evidence of continued connection and interaction, and as an alternative source-base to which developments in North China can be compared.

From this book we know that, after the mid-ninth century, material communications between North China and the northwest never ceased: silk from the Tang and Song capitals continued to invigorate the economy of Dunhuang, while jade from Khotan adorned the bodies of emperors in these capitals. Equally importantly, news of political events and ideas of kingship were communicated by these diplomatic travelers, prompting innovative state-building efforts in the northwest. Because of this open communication channel, key sources for studying the history and culture of the late Tang, the Five Dynasties and the Song, many of which were lost in the transmitted traditions, are preserved in Dunhuang. They include political messages such as letters between the Later Jin and Kitan emperors, social documents such as the copy of a celebratory stela created for new constructions in Chang'an in 963,[63] and literary texts such as the "Lament of Lady Qin" by the late Tang poet Wei Zhuang.[64] Engagement with these documents, as the work of Christopher Nugent on the "Lament of Lady Qin" shows, can invigorate our knowledge, which has traditionally been based on transmitted sources passed through the Song libraries.

As important as these cases of direct connections, the northwest should also be placed in the broader context of post-Tang restructuring, along with the Five Dynasties and the Song. Elsewhere I have argued that the Golden Mountain Kingdom under Zhang Chengfeng in Dunhuang was ideologically very similar to several of the regional states that are conventionally included in the "Five Dynasties and Ten Kingdoms." There is no reason why a political history of China in the tenth century should continue to follow Ouyang Xiu's prescription of Five Dynasties and Ten Kingdoms and exclude places in the northwest like Dunhuang.[65] Similarly, The Song-Liao relation of "Two Sons of Heaven" can be compared to the Dunhuang-Ganzhou relation in the context of the resurgence of northern nomadic powers starting in the eighth century. Both Dunhuang and the Song maintained Sino-centric rhetoric internally, but treated their non-Chinese neighbors (the Liao and Ganzhou) as equals in diplomatic settings.[66] Social developments such as the widespread use of printing, a topic of paramount importance for Song history, can be observed in their incipient stage in the small number of printed texts preserved in the library cave, such as the ones I discussed in chapter 10.[67] Finally, a comprehensive assessment of the Tang legacy is incomplete without considering cases such as the Khotanese kings' claim to be "king of kings of China" and Tang imperial descendants in the early tenth century, a claim observable only in the Dunhuang documents and mural paintings.[68] Indeed, this case challenges our understanding of what was and was not "China."

That is what this book as a whole also intends to do—to challenge existing narratives about "Chinese" history. By recounting numerous cases of connection and interaction, and coupling the Dunhuang materials with Song sources, this book has shown that the Five Dynasties and the Song, often the sole protagonists of Chinese history in the Middle Period, were only parts of a broader world that responded to the decline and fall of the Tang, the Tibetan, and the Uyghur empires, and to one another. Shifting my perspective from the Song historians to the Dunhuang travelers thus allows me to incorporate these changes from the northwest, and to tell "Chinese" history as Eurasian history.

———

The issues I bring up in the conclusion are wide-ranging, and space does not allow me to discuss any of them in detail—even these brief remarks have already rendered this conclusion quite unwieldy. My hope is that my discussion here, and the content of the chapters of this book, will provoke further inquiry, in order that we reach a more textured and open-ended understanding of the histories of the Silk Road, of China, and of Eurasia. The rich stories hidden in the small library cave in Dunhuang will be indispensable in our future telling of these histories.

# NOTES

## Introduction

1. Eliasberg, "Quelques aspects de l'exorcisme"; Ren Wei, "Dunhuang nuo wenhua."

2. P. 3270; for the facsimile, see *Facang* (22.333); for a transcription of the text, see Huang Zheng and Wu's *Dunhuang yuanwen ji* (951). The text of this song: "萬姓歌謠鼓腹, 恰似舜日堯年. 莫愁東路閉塞, 開春天使至前. 進奉盤龍大錦, 綾羅絹彩數般.... 向西直至于闐, 路潤越 於鋪綿. 進奉珍玩白玉, 綿綾雜彩千端. 界內皆唱快活, 同壽彭祖一般." All translations are the author's own unless otherwise noted. P. 3270 is short for Pelliot chinois 3270. In this book, I use the generally accepted shorthand of P. ("Pelliot chinois" items at the Bibliothèque nationale de France), S. ("Stein" items at the British Library), and BD (Beijing [library] Dunhuang collection) in referring to the documents I cite. Using this number, readers can easily locate more information in catalogs such as Shi Pingting's *Dunhuang yishu zongmu*, and (in most cases) images on the International Dunhuang Project website (http://idp.bl.uk/). When I cite compilations of Dunhuang documents, such as "*Shilu*, 1.3," the first number, "1," indicates the number of the printed volume (*ce* 冊 in Chinese) while the second number, "3," indicates the page number. On the other hand, when I cite a traditional source, such as "*Xin Tangshu*, 1.3," the first number indicates the number of the *juan*, while the second number indicates the page number. This distinction is made because the *juan* number is a lot more meaningful in traditional sources (even in their modern editions), whereas in the case of Dunhuang documents, the most convenient way to locate them is to know which physical volumes they are printed in.

3. Zhenping Wang, *Tang China*, 14–20.

4. Golden, *Introduction to the History*, 136–38.

5. See Hoffman, "Early and Medieval Tibet."

6. For the modern "Great Game" between the British and the Russian empires, see Hopkirk's *Great Game*.

7. See Zhang Zhan, "Between China and Tibet."

8. See Wang Xiaofu, *Tang, Tufan, Dashi*, 68–88.

9. Moriyasu, "Toban no Chūō Ajia shinshutsu."

10. Moriyasu, "Qui des Ouïgours."

11. For the claim of the Dunhuang king, see Wen, "Emperor of Dunhuang."

12. Although we do not have a specific date for these songs, scholars generally agree that they were written and performed in the late ninth or the tenth century. Deng Wenkuan dates the song I cite to the mid-880s, while Rong Xinjiang dates the song that follows on the same manuscript to the mid-920s. See Deng Wenkuan, "Zhang Huaishen pingding Ganzhou," 95, and

Rong, *Guiyijun shi yanjiu*, 102, 320. It is important to note that both scholars are talking about the date of the *lyrics* of the songs. The making of the manuscripts should be dated to after the songs were created, possibly the middle of the tenth century.

13. In this book, instead of adhering to terms such as "the Central Plains," which sinologists often use to refer to the heartland of medieval Chinese regimes such as the Tang and the Song, I use the more descriptive term "North China," while being mindful of the changing meaning of the term "China" (which I touch on in chapter 9). This choice is made for the sake of clarity to scholars outside China studies, but also aligns with my sources, which do not always see North China as "central" to their world.

14. Rossabi, introduction to J. Moore and Wendelken, *Teaching the Silk Road*, 3.

15. Sen, *Buddhism, Diplomacy, and Trade*, 212.

16. E.g., Curtin, *Cross-Cultural Trade*, 105; Millward, *Silk Road*, 20. For instance, Janet Abu-Lughad talks about reduced overland connections in the post-Tang-Abbasid period: "Restoration of the land route during the period of Islamic hegemony was continuously threatened by the northern tribes, against whom the Great Wall had originally been built. (These threats were not eliminated until Genghis Khan conquered northern China in the opening decades of the thirteenth century.) Intermittently denied access across the steppes, China was of necessity drawn more to the sea" (*Before European Hegemony*, 303–4). See also Bentley, "Cross-Cultural Interaction."

17. The account is found in Fan's "Dunhuang Daoshi," 43.

18. The dimensions of the chamber are 275 × 473 cm.

19. Van Schaik and Galambos, *Manuscripts and Travellers*.

20. This seemingly straightforward task has not yet been thoroughly performed, primarily for two reasons. First, it took scholars, librarians, and curators almost a century to fully account for and catalogue the Dunhuang documents, and the last major collection was published only in 2009. The publication of these collections, along with the accessibility to manuscripts provided by the International Dunhuang Project website, finally allowed scholars to study the London, Paris, Beijing, Saint Petersburg, Kyoto, and Taipei collections together. Second, the multilingual Dunhuang documents present a more difficult task for scholars than Buddhist and literary texts in the same collection. The social context, institutional backgrounds, and the vernacular languages of these documents all presented obstacles to us in understanding them. My own reading of these documents is based on decades of scholarly effort from all parts of the world.

21. Hansen, *Silk Road*, 195.

22. For an example of such an approach, see Zhenping Wang's *Tang China*.

23. Fairbank, *Chinese World Order*; Kang, *East Asia*.

24. For an excellent example that successfully performs this task in a different context, see Skaff's *Sui-Tang China*.

25. A recent study convincingly shows that this concept was not invented by Richthofen, but had been circulating among German academics for decades. See Mertens, "Did Richthofen Really Coin." But Richthofen remains the first, as far as we know, to give the idea a clear and evidence-based definition.

26. Waugh, "Richthofen's 'Silk Road'"; Marchand, *German Orientalism*.

27. Boulnois, *Silk Road*.

28. Kuzmina, *Prehistory of the Silk Road.*

29. Christian, "Silk Roads or Steppe Roads?"

30. Guan, "Maritime Silk Road."

31. Frankopan, *Silk Roads.*

32. See, for instance, the popular *Silk Road* documentary television series produced by the Nippon Hōsō Kyōkai (Japan Broadcasting Corporation) in 1980.

33. Langenkamp, "Contested Imaginaries."

34. T. Miller, *China's Asian Dream*, 1–92.

35. For a comprehensive criticism, see Levi's *Bukharan Crisis*, 37–69.

36. Ball, *Rome in the East*, 156.

37. Jacobs, "Concept of the Silk Road." See also La Vaissière: "no historical object that might be named 'the Silk Road' has ever been defined with precision" (*Sogdian Traders*, 1).

38. Millward, *Silk Road*, 3–7; Whitfield, *Life along the Silk Road*, 1–2.

39. See Helen Wang and Hansen, "Textiles as Money."

40. See chapter 10.

41. In his monumental nineteen-volume *La nouvelle géographie universelle, la terre et les hommes,* one of the earliest works that helped popularize Ferdinand Freiherr von Richthofen's newly coined term "Silk Roads," Élisée Reclus (1830–1905) described the Silk Road in this manner: "Greek and Chinese merchants met on the Silk Road; Buddhist missionaries, Arab traders, the great Venetian Marco Polo, as well as other European travelers of the Middle Ages all had their stay in the oases of Chinese Turkestan before resuming their difficult march" (7: 104).

42. See the summary of scholarship in Andrea's "Silk Road in World History."

43. Xinru Liu, *Silk Road in World History*, 107. For the dissolution of the Sogdian merchant network, see La Vaissière, *Sogdian Traders*, 291–331.

44. A stylistic choice I made is to use both word "king" and "road" as collective nouns and keep them in the singular. This is mostly done to avoid awkward-looking phrases like "the Kings' Roads." As the book itself makes clear, I am of course talking about many kings, and many roads.

# Chapter 1

1. For a comprehensive survey of the content of the Dunhuang manuscripts, see Rong's *Eighteen Lectures on Dunhuang* (267–426).

2. Hao, *Shishi xiejing*, 1.

3. See, e.g., Dalton and Van Schaik, *Tibetan Tantric Manuscripts.*

4. Ma, "Guangyu Dunhuang cangjingdong."

5. For a representative exposition of this view, see Rong's "Nature of the Dunhuang Library."

6. For a representative exposition of this view, see Fang Guangchang's "Dunhuang Cangjingdong."

7. Van Schaik and Galambos. *Manuscripts and Travellers*, 18–28.

8. There is a long history of the study of the Dunhuang documents. Here I list a few key works that informed my understanding of the collection. For Chinese documents: Ikeda, *Chūgoku kodai sekichō kenkyū*; Ikeda and Yamamoto, *Tun-huang and Turfan documents*; Shilu; Hao, *Yingcang Dunhuang shehui lishi*; Rong, *Guiyijun shi yanjiu*. For Sogdian documents: Sims-Williams

and Hamilton, *Turco-Sogdian Documents*. For Khotanese documents: Emmerick, *Guide to the Literature*; Skjærvø, *Khotanese Manuscripts*. For Uyghur documents: Hamilton, *Manuscrits ouïgours*. For Tibetan documents: Uray, "Emploi du tibétain" and "New Contributions"; Takeu-chi, "Group of Old Tibetan Letters"; Wang Yao and Chen, *Dunhuang Tufan wenxian*.

9. *Shilu*, 3.46–47.

10. *Shilu*, 3.46.

11. P. 3161, *Shilu*, 3.39.

12. See Trombert, *Crédit à Dunhuang*; Sha Zhi, *Dunhuang qiyue wenshu*; Ikeda and Yama-moto, *Tun-huang and Turfan Documents*, vol. 3, *Contracts*.

13. Tuotuo, *Songshi*, 490.14111–12.

14. For an analysis of these military documents, see Chen Juxia's "Xian Fan."

15. Fang Guangchang, "Dunhuang Cangjingdong," 216.

16. Zhu, "Tang jifang kao."

17. My use of the phrase "accidental archive" is informed by the study of another large col-lection of documents, the Cairo Geniza, discovered at the other end of the Afro-Eurasian world. S. D. Goitein, the founder of the study of the Cairo Geniza, realized early on the eclectic nature of the Geniza collection: "It is evident that it is the very opposite of an archive. In an archive one keeps documents in order to use them, if and when necessary. . . . The opposite was the case with the Geniza. Papers were thrown away there only after they had lost all value to their pos-sessors" (*Mediterranean Society*, 1:7). To contrast the Cairo Geniza with an archive, Goitein goes on to point to "its erratic character, the entire absence of selection in the material deposited in it" (9). This view of the Geniza as an "antiarchive" is embraced by many subsequent scholars. See Cohen, *Poverty and Charity*; Rustow, *Heresy*; Goldberg, *Trade and Institutions*. The idea of a group of manuscripts collected haphazardly as an antiarchive helps us understand the nature of the Dunhuang documents. But I am not entirely convinced by the somewhat awkward neolo-gism of "antiarchive," not least because many collections of documents properly considered archives can be messy and disorderly as well. To me, the term "accidental archive" conveys such messiness better without categorically separating collections such as the Dunhuang documents and the Cairo Geniza from other forms of archive.

18. Such abundance of documents from the Buddhist monasteries allows detailed social histories such as Hao's *Tang houqi*.

19. For a comprehensive survey of existing research, see Rong's *Eighteen Lectures on Dun-huang* (205–66).

20. Hansen, *Silk Road*, 167.

21. For a catalog of the contents of the caves, see Dunhuang yanjiuyuan's *Dunhuang shiku neirong zonglu*. For a selection of the paintings, see Dunhuang yanjiuyuan's *Dunhuang shiku yishu quanji*, in twenty-six volumes.

22. Aurel Stein, who discovered many of these documents in his trips to Central Asia, left us with extensive records of these discoveries. See Stein's *Ancient Khotan*, *Serindia*, and *Innermost Asia*.

23. These sources are conveniently collected in Bielenstein's *Diplomacy and Trade*.

24. Xu Song, *Song huiyao jigao*; Li Tao, *Xu zizhi tongjian*.

25. Kāšgarī, *Compendium of the Turkic Dialects*; Ibn Faḍlān, *Journey to Russia*.

26. Liu Xu, *Jiu Tangshu*, 18b.640.

27. Hu Ji and Rong, *Da Tang xishi*, 952–53.

28. See a discussion of these sources in Rong's "Dazhong shinian."

29. For a definition of Eastern Eurasia, see Skaff's *Sui-Tang China* (7).

30. This is a Chinese Buddhist vinaya text. See Rong, *Eighteen Lectures on Dunhuang*, 342–43.

31. See Galambos, *Dunhuang Manuscript Culture*.

32. Ouyang, *Xin Wudai shi*, 74.917–18. The following quotes from Gao's record of his trip can be found here.

33. See my discussion in chapter 4.

34. Standen, "Five Dynasties."

35. Barenghi, "Representations of Descent"; Han, "When Middle Kingdom Was Gone."

36. For the Later Tang's unique attempt at extending its influence to the west beyond North China, see Yang Baoyu and Wu's *Guiyijun zhengquan* (300–334).

37. Lorge, *Reunification of China*.

38. Zhao Zhen, "Wan Tang Wudai Shuofang Hanshi."

39. J. Shi, *Tangut Language and Manuscripts*.

40. Dunnell, "Hsi Hsia."

41. Tang Kaijian, "Guanyu Miluo guo," 18–20.

42. Rong, *Eighteen Lectures on Dunhuang*, 20–21.

43. Rong, *Guiyijun shi yanjiu*, 148–55.

44. This name is usually written in Chinese as 嗢末. There have been many attempts to find the Tibetan "original" of this strange name. The most plausible, yet still by no means confirmed, reconstruction is by Lu Li, who considers it a transcription of *'Bangs Myi on the basis of the correspondence between its meaning of "subjects" with the recorded meaning of this term in Chinese sources. See Lu Li, "Wenmo yinyi kao," 97–102.

45. Rong, "Ganzhou Huihu chengli shilun."

46. Yang Fuxue, *Huihu yu Dunhuang*, 172.

47. Li Jun, "Wan Tang Wudai Suzhou."

48. Rong, "Longjia kao."

49. For more on the 924–26 war, see chapter 10.

50. Tuotuo, *Liaoshi*, 70.1151.

51. Zheng Binglin, "Wan Tang Wudai Dunhuang diqu de Tufan," 41.

52. See Wen, "Emperor of Dunhuang."

53. Rong, *Guiyijun shi yanjiu*.

54. Hamilton, "Le pays des Tchong-yun."

55. Benjamin, *Yuezhi*.

56. Xu Song, *Song huiyao jigao, fanyi* (foreign countries) 4.9777.

57. For a new study of pre-Islamic Khotan, see Hansen's *Silk Road* (199–234). The most complete bibliography of secondary works is found in Zhang Guangda and Rong's *Yutian shi congkao*.

58. For the traces of Kushan rule in Khotan, see Hitch's "Kushan Tarim Domination." The role of the Rouran is only hinted at by Chinese sources, which merely record a message from Khotan asking for military assistance. See Wei Shou, *Weishu*, 102.2263.

59. Skjærvø, "Iranians, Indians, Chinese and Tibetans."

60. Rong and Zhu, *Yutian yu Dunhuang*.

61. Zhang Guangda and Rong, "Concise History."

62. Wittfogel and Feng, *History Of Chinese Society*.

63. See the chapter "Yelü Abaoji zhi si," in Luo Xin's *Heizhan shang de Beiwei huangdi* (96–122).

64. Liu Pujiang, "Liaochao guohao kaoshi."

65. Hongjie Wang, *Power and Politics*.

66. Lorge, *Reunification of China*.

67. Dunnell, "Hsi Hsia."

68. Rong, "Nature of the Dunhuang Library."

69. Ouyang, *Xin Wudai shi*, 74.917. The meaning of the word *nianya* is unclear to me.

70. Wen, "King of Kings of China."

71. Ouyang, *Xin Wudai shi*, 74.918.

72. See chapter 9.

73. Standen, "Five Dynasties," 87–97.

74. Sima, *Zizhi tongjian*, 269.8799.

75. Xue Chen argues that the period between 900 and 1250 should be considered an "Age of Emperors," when more than one emperor existed and emperorship was considered divisible. This characterization does not contradict my suggestion of an "age of kings." Chen is talking about the idea that emperorship can be shared and divided among many emperors, whereas I am concerned about the political reality of smaller regional states, where many who claimed to be emperor were little more than kings in political influence and transregional prestige. However, his assertion about a "Liao World Order" is not directly visible in Dunhuang materials, where the existence of the Song is felt much more strongly than that of the Liao. See X. Chen, "Age of Emperors."

76. See Wilkinson, *Chinese History*, 268–69.

77. See Chen Sanping, "Son of Heaven," 301.

78. Bang and Turner, "Kingship and Elite Formation," 19.

79. For instance, see Hongjie Wang, *Power and Politics*.

80. L. Yang, "'Posthumous Letter.'"

81. The most famous example is a poem, "The Lament of the Lady Qin" by Wei Zhuang (836–910). This poem, which chronicles the life of a woman in the capital Chang'an during the Huang Chao Rebellion, was popular in the tenth century, but was ultimately lost, until several copies were rediscovered in the Dunhuang library cave. See Nugent, *Manifest in Words*.

# Chapter 2

1. For a discussion of this individual, see Kaneko's "Tonkō shutsudo."

2. For other such examples in the Dunhuang documents and the possible impact of non-Chinese writing practice on Chinese manuscripts, see Galambos's "Non-Chinese Influences."

3. For a transcription of the Chinese text, see Zhang Guangda and Rong's *Yutian shi congkao* (91). The Chinese text reads: "壬午年年十二月廿一日, 于闐使張金山幸者, 來取窟頭燃燈來者, 焚香發願, 禮佛慶告者好. 轉經坐禪者, 竟發心造塔, 願以過到來平善者, 再發心造塔, 諸周在世界, 子（只）有沙州人語好者, 又窟更好者, 木石更好, 怎生暫打得者, 幸者. 盡記耳."

This text exhibits some unique syntactic features that are not present in standard Classical Chinese, and might reflect the fact that he was not a native speaker of Chinese.

4. Skjærvø, *Khotanese Manuscripts*, 522–24.

5. Wen, "What's in a Surname?," 81–82.

6. For the Chinese presence in Khotan, see Rong's "Tō Sō jidai Uten shi gaisetsu."

7. Bailey, "Vajrayāna in Gostana-deśa."

8. Bailey, *Indo-Scythian Studies*, 4:1–134. See also Yoeli-Thalim, "Silk Roads as a Model," 51–53. I thank Susan Whitfield for this reference.

9. Bailey, "Itinerary in Khotanese Saka."

10. Skjærvø, *Khotanese Manuscripts*, 524.

11. Kroll, *Student's Dictionary*, 414.

12. See Дх03412+Дх03415 (*Ecang*, 10.289) for the "garrison officer" (*zhenshi*) of Xuanquan.

13. Bailey, *Dictionary of Khotan Saka*, 447. See also Bailey, "Śrī Viśa Śūra," 9.

14. Skjærvø, *Khotanese Manuscripts*, 53; Kumamoto, "Miscellaneous Khotanese Documents," 253.

15. West side line 40, and east side lines 44 and 68. See Li Fang-kuei, "Inscription," 43, 48, 50, 56, 64, and 66.

16. Iwao, "9 seiki no kigigun seiken," 344, 346; Wang Yao and Chen, *Dunhuang Tufan wenxian*, 54.

17. Clauson, *Etymological Dictionary*, 921.

18. Hamilton, *Manuscrits ouïgours*, 85–86, 93–94.

19. Very few people are clearly non-Buddhist in Dunhuang society at this time, so even the nonmonastic figures were probably generally inclined to participate in Buddhist activities as laypeople.

20. This great diversity is seen in the more than thirty thousand personal names from the Dunhuang manuscripts painstakingly collected by Dohi Yoshikazu in *Hasseiki makki jūisseiki shoki Tonkō shizoku jinmei shūsei*.

21. For military officers, see Liang Xingde (P. 3718). For administrative officials, see Dunhuang magistrate Song Zhiyue (P. 3730v, letter 6).

22. For a comprehensive study of his career, see Yang Baoyu and Wu, *Guiyijun zhengquan*, 206–19.

23. This scandal is described in P.3016; see *Shilu*, 4.409–10.

24. P. 2922v. For a detailed study of this document, see Feng Peihong's *Dunhuang de Guiyijun shidai* (320–21).

25. Li Tao, *Xu zizhi tongjian*, 1.167.

26. Zhang Guangda and Rong, *Yutian shi congkao*, 38–47.

27. Rong, *Guiyijun shi yanjiu*, 162–64.

28. A comparable example is the king of Kharashar (Yanqi), who regularly visited and lived in Turfan in the medieval period. See Pei, "Lun 5–8 shiji."

29. Sha Zhi, *Dunhuang qiyue wenshu*.

30. P. 2652, *Shilu*, 2.41.

31. P. 3579v, *Shilu*, 2.308.

32. S. 2786. See Kumamoto, "Khotanese Official Documents," 94, 129.

33. S. 4489v, *Shilu*, 2.307.

34. For a genealogy of the Dunhuang rulers: Rong, *Guiyijun shi yanjiu*, 60–147.

35. Chen Shuangyin, "Dunhuang xieben *Zhushan shengjizhi*."

36. This is clear from the example of a Chinese monk passing through Tibetan regions recorded in a Dunhuang manuscript. See Van Schaik and Galambos, *Manuscripts and Travellers*.

37. P. 3051v, *Shilu*, 2.125.

38. *Shilu*, 1.109–30.

39. I use the category "cultural identity" rather than the more prevalent "ethnic identity" or "ethnicity" because I agree with Naomi Standen's cautious remark that "cultural identity may be felt or ascribed, by individuals or by groups, but it does not become *ethnic* identity until political meaning is ascribed to cultural differences in the context of a struggle for control at the level of the state." See Standen, *Unbounded Loyalty*, 28. Even though, as Yang Shao-Yun has shown ("'Stubbornly Chinese?'"), at least for the ruling class in Dunhuang, cultural difference was sometimes indeed marshaled by the state to exert control, it is uncertain if this use of cultural difference was prevalent in all the states under discussion. Therefore, in order to not muddy the water with the baggage the term "ethnicity" carries, I have opted to use "cultural identity" in this book.

40. I discuss this campaign in detail in chapter 8.

41. Zheng Binglin, *Dunhuang beiming*, 343–51.

42. Zheng Binglin, 343.

43. Xu Song, *Song huiyao jigao*, fanyi 4.9768.

44. Here I need to distinguish between "envoy" and "diplomatic traveler." In my use, an envoy is a person dispatched by the state to conduct official matters with another state, whereas a diplomatic traveler can be anyone who traveled in a diplomatic mission. Diplomatic travelers were not necessarily engaged in the practice of diplomacy, but they were often indispensable parts of it. Once we expand our vision from envoys to the broader world of diplomatic travelers, the role of women becomes much more pronounced.

45. *Shilu*, 4.485.

46. Li Tao, *Xu zizhi tongjian*, 335.8063.

47. There is evidence of marriages beyond these states. For instance, when the prince of Shuofang (Lingzhou) writes "ranījai janavai vīra maira hūśai'na khīvyaina aurga drrūṇ̄ pvais-auma haṣḍā yanai śvahvāṃ raispūra hva pakyāṃ khū tta vaña haysda vī śaika ṣṭāvai" (To the Mother the furen Khī-vyaina in Ratna-janapada with reverence [aurga] I make a report, asking after her health, I the prince of Śvahvāṃ, Hva Pa-kyāṃ) (P. 2958, lines 216–17), it is conceivable that this "mother," who bears a Chinese title ("furen"), could have been married to Khotan and be the actual mother of the prince of Shuofang. However, cases such as these are sporadic and speculative. Therefore, I shall focus on the cases among Shazhou, Khotan, and Ganzhou. See Bailey, "Altun Khan," 98.

48. Kumamoto, "Khotanese in Dunhuang."

49. These paintings appear in, among others, Mogao Caves nos. 61, 98, and 454.

50. Institute of Oriental Manuscripts, Russian Academy of Sciences, Saint Petersburg, Дх.2148(1). *Ecang*, 10.145.

51. Liu Xu, *Jiu Tangshu*, 19.660. For female slaves sold on the Silk Road, see Hansen's *Silk Road* (77–79).

52. P. 2826, *Facang*, 19.9. This text is particularly interesting because it is a letter in actual use with official seals. See Akagi, "Six 10th Century Royal Seals."

53. Xu Song, *Song huiyao jigao*, fanyi 5.9836 ("鑄鐘匠及漢人之善藏珠者").

54. P. 3579v, *Shilu*, 2.308.

55. For an overview of diplomatic missions in Dunhuang: Sakajiri, "Tonkō hantsu kō"; Zhang Guangda, *Xiyu shidi*, 175–87.

56. Xu Song, *Song huiyao jigao*, fanyi 4.9768.

57. For a transcription of this text, see *Shilu* (4.367–69). There is a detailed discussion of the economics of this trip in chapter 8.

58. See the account of the Office of Banquets in Dunhuang preserved in S. 1366 (*Shilu*, 3.281–86).

59. In most documents, the cultural identities of the travelers involved are not explicitly discussed. In these cases, the most convenient way to detect cultural difference, which most scholars adopt, is through the names of travelers mentioned in different types of sources. For instance, a surname An in Chinese is a potential sign that the person under discussion is Sogdian or of Sogdian descent. See Pulleyblank, "Sogdian Colony." But as I have shown elsewhere, names are meaningful yet unreliable indicators of cultural identity in medieval China, as they were one of the most volatile domains of self-representation and were subject to change and manipulation. Therefore, one needs to use the data contained in names cautiously, supplementing it, as much as possible, with information gained from other sources for corroboration. See Wen, "What's in a Surname?"

60. Skjærvø, *Khotanese Manuscripts*, 524.

61. P. 3547, *Shilu*, 4.367.

62. S. 1156, *Shilu*, 4.370–73.

63. Yang Rui, *Huihu shidai*, 72–79.

64. Xu Song, *Song huiyao jigao*, fanyi 4.9767. P. 2155 includes a letter from the lord of Dunhuang to the Uyghur khan in Ganzhou that tells the khan that the fourth month was a good time to travel. It could be a letter used in the organization of such joint diplomatic missions. See *Shilu*, 4.403.

65. The case of the "Shazhou/Dunhuang Uyghurs" in the Song records is likely the result of Song record keepers confusing the envoys from Dunhuang and those from the Uyghur kingdom of Ganzhou.

66. Xu Song, *Song huiyao jigao*, fanyi 4.9827; Yang Rui, *Huihu shidai*, 75.

67. Xu Song, *Song huiyao jigao*, fanyi 7.9940; Yang Rui, *Huihu shidai*, 73. The term I translate as "Persia" is Bosi (波斯). This is the traditional term for the Persian Empire in the Chinese sources. But during the Song, when there was no longer a Persian Empire, it was used to mean various Islamic states in Iran and Central Asia. Because it is often impossible to tell which state it referred to in a particular source, I retain the admittedly vague term "Persia."

68. Wang Qinruo, *Cefu yuangui*, 972.11253. Here *Cefu yuangui* records the name of the Uyghur envoy as 安千想, whereas the Dunhuang document has 安千箱. They are clearly referring to the same person.

69. P. 3016. For a detailed study of this document and this case, see Yang Baoyu and Wu's *Guiyijun zhengquan* (104–18). The text: "不曾歷涉驅馳, 為不諳會國禮."

70. See Wang Qilong and Deng, *Gang Hetai*.

71. Thomas and Konow, "Two Medieval Documents," 122.

72. I thank my friend Zhang Zhan for sharing this information after hunting for the manuscript in the Harvard libraries and museums.

73. Clauson, "Geographical Names"; Bailey, "Staël-Holstein Miscellany"; Pulleyblank, "Date of the Staël-Holstein Roll"; Hamilton, "Autour du manuscrit Staël-Holstein"; Huang Sheng-zhang, "Yutian wen 'Shi Hexi ji.'"

74. Bailey, "Staël-Holstein Miscellany."

75. The use of Tibetan in these reports is not surprising, as Tibetan had become the lingua franca of the diplomatic world of eastern Central Asia. See Uray, "Emploi du tibétain."

76. The use of forensic analysis of Tibetan handwriting has been successfully established. See Dalton, Davis, and Van Schaik, "Beyond Anonymity."

77. These are examples of what I call "bureaucratization of personal names." In a Khotanese mission to Dunhuang, we find envoys with names such as "'Bye Tutu" and "Co Tutu." These names are Tibetan transcriptions of Chinese names, with the "'Bye" and "Co" parts being the surnames. The second part of their names, "Tutu," derives from the Chinese title "military supervisor" (*dudu* 都督). These names are also recorded in Khotanese in the same way (Cām Ttūttū), indicating that the envoys were known by such names on the diplomatic missions. Such bureaucratization of names also crossed linguistic lines. It shows that, for the purpose of their trip as envoys, their given names were not as important as their official titles.

78. Bailey, "Staël-Holstein Miscellany," 44.

79. See my article on the Khotanese official titles: Wen, "Yutian guo guanhao kao."

80. Bailey, "Staël-Holstein Miscellany," 44.

81. Thomas and Konow, "Two Medieval Documents," 128.

82. Thomas and Konow, 128.

83. I discuss this issue extensively in chapter 4.

84. Bailey, "Staël-Holstein Miscellany," 44.

85. Bailey, 45.

86. Thomas and Konow, "Two Medieval Documents," 127–28.

87. 北圖殷字 41, *Shilu*, 2. 38.

88. This text is made up of two fragments of manuscript S. 8702 and S. 8681v. Only the beginning of the contract is extant. See Hao, *Tang houqi*, 104–5.

89. P. 2988v, P. 2909v. Hamilton, *Manuscrits ouïgours*, 83–92.

90. S. 2589, *Shilu*, 4.485–86. See my translation of the text in the appendix of Sims-Williams and Hamilton, *Turco-Sogdian Documents*, 97–98.

91. Bielenstein, *Diplomacy and Trade*, 466–69.

92. Liu Quanbo, "Ganzhou Huihu," 66–67.

93. Yang Rui, *Huihu shidai*, 157.

94. *Shilu*, 4.367–69.

95. "Xizhou waisheng shizi Wang Asilan Han" 西州外生師子王阿廝蘭漢. This new title signifies the renewal of a diplomatic relation in direct imitation of that of the Tang and Uyghur in the eighth and ninth centuries, in which the relation between the Uyghur khan and the Tang emperor was customarily seen as one of nephew and uncle. It also indicates the nature of the Uyghur kingship. As *arslan* in Turkic meant "lion," the two titles "Lion King" and "Arslan Khan"

are essentially identical, with the first spelled out potentially for the convenience of the Song government.

96. Tuotuo, *Songshi*, 14110–13.

97. After these two documents, further writings were copied onto this manuscript after it was turned upside down. This complex manuscript deserves a specialized study to elucidate the process of its making.

98. *Shilu*, 4.404–8. Here I translate the Chinese *zoumashi* 走馬使 as "messenger."

99. I translate *jiu* as wine in this book. It should be pointed out that it is possible, indeed likely, that the term *jiu* was used for more than one kind of alcoholic drink, including wine but also rice- and wheat-based alcohol.

100. P. 3569, *Shilu*, 3.622.

101. Дх2149, *Shilu*, 2.446.

102. P. 3936. See *Facang*, 30.251.

103. See Rong, "Rouran Qaghanate."

# Chapter 3

1. This event is recorded in both *Song huiyao* and *Songshi*, with the latter entry more complete. See Tuotuo, *Songshi*, 490.14107.

2. Schafer, *Golden Peaches of Samarkand*, 82.

3. See the example of elephants who refused to dance for An Lushan: Yao, *An Lushan shiji*, 106.

4. Bailey, "Śrī Viśa' Śūra," 17.

5. For a comprehensive examination of the things that traveled, see Whitfield's *Silk, Slaves, and Stupas*.

6. I borrow this term from Hodder, in *Entangled*. I thank Dr. Daniela Wolin for drawing my attention to this work.

7. Gerritsen and Riello, *Writing Material Culture History*, 7.

8. See the detailed records of the canals and the regulations about their use in P. 3560v, *Shilu*, 1.394–99.

9. This line ("萬頃平田四畔沙" in S. 6234 + P. 5007 + P. 2672) is an impression of Dunhuang from a collection of a traveler's poems. See Xu Jun, *Dunhuang shiji*, 655.

10. See, for instance, the donation of "one plate of rice" to a Buddhist monastery. P. 2837v, *Shilu*, 3.61.

11. Gao, *Tang Wudai Dunhuang yinshi wenhua*, 8–52.

12. This is clear from the wheat and millet marked for use as "road food" in the expenditure account of the Jingtu Monastery (P. 3763v). See *Shilu*, 3.513–20.

13. Gao, *Tang Wudai Dunhuang yinshi wenhua*, 103–35.

14. See, for example, the many references found in the expenditure account of a monastery in P. 4906 (*Shilu*, 3.233–35).

15. The tomb is numbered 72TAM149 by archaeologists. See Xinjiang Weiwu'er zizhiqu bowuguan, *Xinjiang chutu wenwu*, plate 179.

16. Ōmi no Mifune, *Tang Daheshang dong zheng zhuan*, 47.

17. P. 2641. This is a list of the expenditure of the Office of Banquets (Yanshe si) in Dunhuang in 947. See *Shilu*, 3.612.

18. S. 4642v, *Shilu*, 3.547–54.

19. P. 3234v, *Facang*, 22.244.

20. See Wang Dang, *Tang yulin*, 6.556.

21. P. 3672 bis, *Facang*, 26.290

22. S. 4685. This was a letter between Li Nuzi and Li Chou'er. *Yingcang*, 6.235.

23. See Knauer, *Camel's Load*.

24. Many such banquets are recorded in the expenditure account of the Office of Banquets and Hospitality in Dunhuang, such as P. 2641, an account from the sixth month of 947 (*Shilu*, 3.610). Farewell banquets were a regular part of the practices relating to travel in Middle Period China. See C. Zhang, *Transformative Journeys*, 111–29.

25. See S. 1475v, *Yingcang*, 3.74. Judging from the other texts written on the same documents, this text should date to the period when Dunhuang was under Tibetan rule, a few decades before the period this book covers. The text reads: "遠行社: 社內至親兄弟姊妹男女, 遠行迴及亡逝, 人各助借布壹疋吊問. 遠行千里外, 去日, 緣公事送酒壹甕; 迴日軟腳置酒兩甕."

26. See the records of "road food" in many expenditure accounts, such as S. 6330, S. 4642v ("造食送路"), and P. 2040.

27. P. 2049v. See *Shilu*, 3.347–66.

28. P. 2040v. For General Gao: *Facang*, 3.37, 39. For the lord of Dunhuang, who is known as Shangshu in this document: *Facang*, 3.20.

29. Huang Zhengjian, "Dunhuang wenshu."

30. 1 *dou* weighs about 12.5 *jin*, which is around 6.25 kg. According to a Song source, a camel can carry three *shi* of grain (see Li Tao, *Xu zizhi tongjian*, 11211). Therefore, a camel could carry around 375 *jin*, or 187.5 kg, of goods.

31. See the numerous references to fine food ("細供") in P. 2641. See *Facang*, 17.62–63.

32. P.3160: *Facang*, 22.69. The text: "設天使煮肉造食."

33. "灌腸䴑": P. 2641, *Facang*, 17.62–63.

34. S. 1366, *Yingcang*, 2.277–79. I will discuss this issue further in chapter 4.

35. Shi Pingting, "Bensuo cang *jiuzhang*," 142–55. For the provision of wine to envoys, see also P. 3569, *Shilu*, 3.622–23.

36. Ch-2.00269, Skjærvø, *Khotanese Manuscripts*, 512.

37. Minorsky, "Tamīm ibn Baḥr's Journey," 283.

38. This is discussed in chapter 4.

39. P. 5034: "泉有八所, 皆有草, 道險不得夜行, 春秋二時雪潽, 道閉不通." See Li Zhengyu, *Guben Dunhuang xiangtuzhi*, 145.

40. Ouyang, *Xin Wudai shi*, 74.917.

41. P. 2009, *Shilu*, 1.54.

42. Cai, *Tieweishan congtan*, 102. The Chinese text: "于闐國朝貢使每來朝, 必攜其寶鑷以往返. 自國初以來, 迨今如是也. 我主客備見之, 實一鐵鑷爾. 蓋其來入中國, 道涉流沙, 逾三日程無水火, 獨挈其水而行. 攜鑷者投之以水, 頃輒已百沸矣, 用是得不乏, 故寶之."

43. "壹朔鑷壹口, 內有催路." See *Shilu*, 3.40.

44. S. 964. See *Shilu*, 4.447.

45. S. 4191v, *Yingcang*, 5.264.

46. Zhou Qufei, *Lingwai daida*, 6.227.

47. S. 2528. See Zhang and Rong, *Yutian shi congkao* 92. The letter was written on the 25th of the ninth month according to the lunar calendar. The year is unspecified, so I cannot calculate the exact corresponding day in the solar calendar. But some day in late October should be a fair approximation.

48. P. 2786, Kumamoto, "Khotanese Official Documents," 88, 126.

49. IOL Khot. S. 13, Skjærvø, *Khotanese Manuscripts*, 514.

50. S. 2589, *Yingcang*, 4.111. The text: "索漢君等狀: 淮詮郎擬從嗢末使發來, 緣裝束不辦, 發赴不得."

51. P. 3260, *Shilu*, 4.390.

52. P. 3547, *Shilu*, 4.367–69. See my discussion in chapter 8.

53. P. 3718-12, Jiang Boqin, Xiang, and Rong, *Dunhuang miaozhenzan*, 285–86.

54. P. 2613, *Shilu*, 3.9.

55. The Dunhuang government owned a "gilded banner for road god [貼金行路神旗]," which was used for the purpose of sacrificing to god on the road and might have traveled with some of these envoys. See S. 2009, *Yingcang*, 3.192.

56. See, for instance, the images of Xuanzang described in Wong, "Making of a Saint."

57. Xu Song, *Song huiyao jigao*, fanyi 7.9967.

58. In this case, the Song emperor confirms what I discussed in the previous two sections: the accommodation and provision of the envoys were largely provided by the state they encountered on the road, rather than entirely by their home country.

59. The text: "大中祥符二年, 其國黑韓王遣回鶻羅廝溫等以方物來貢. 廝溫跪奏曰: '臣萬里來朝, 獲見天日, 願聖人萬歲, 與遠人作主.' 上詢以在路幾時, 去此幾里. 對曰: '涉道一年, 晝行暮息, 不知里數. 昔時道路嘗有剽掠, 今自瓜沙抵于闐, 道路清謐, 行旅如流. 願遣使安撫遠俗.' 上曰: "路遠命使, 益以勞費爾國. 今降詔書, 汝即貴往, 亦與命使無異也"" (Tuotuo, *Songshi*, 490.14107). It is interesting that the Song emperor thought his sending an envoy would cost "your country," meaning Khotan, rather than the Song. It clearly points to a common understanding of the economic burden diplomatic travelers can impose on hosting states. See chapter 6.

60. IOL Khot. S. 6, Skjærvø, *Khotanese Manuscripts*, 277. The ellipses in this quote represent words whose meanings are unknown.

61. See Or.8212 (89), Sims-Williams and Hamilton, *Turco-Sogdian Documents*, 86.

62. P. 3547. Chinese text: "上四相公啟各一封, 信二角." *Shilu*, 4.368.

63. P. 2992v, *Shilu*, 4.395–96.

64. S. 529, *Shilu*, 5.9.

65. S. 4685, *Yingcang*, 6.235.

66. P. 3672 bis, *Facang*, 26.290.

67. P. 4005 (*Facang*, 30.335) is the letter. P. 5012 (*Facang*, 34.16) is the envelope. For the connection of these two documents, see Wang Shizhen's "Dunhuang yishu," 209.

68. P. 4516v, *Facang*, 31.265.

69. Liu Xu, *Jiu Tangshu*, 660.

70. "沙州僧正會請詣闕, 以延祿表乞賜金字經一藏. 詔益州寫金銀字經一藏賜之." See Xu Song, *Song huiyao jigao*, fanyi 5.9836.

71. P. 4680, *Facang*, 33.78.

72. "lam du rjes ngan dag mthong nas lam gsar pa rtol" in the Staël-Holstein manuscript.

73. For instance, see P. 2031, P. 2741, and P. 2786, discussed in Kumamoto's "Two Khotanese Fragments."

74. S. 2589, *Yingcang*, 4.111. For a transcription of this text, see Hu Yaofei's "Guanyu Huang Chao zhisi."

75. They were similar to Song envoys to the Liao, who kept diaries of their experiences.

76. See Rong, "Tangren shiji."

77. Kumamoto, "Saiiki ryokōsha."

78. S. 367, *Shilu*, 1.39–41.

79. P. 3368, piece 1, *Facang*, 23.357. The text reads: "今於洛營田手內, 得紙五張, 遺瀉烏占者."

80. P. 4640, *Shilu*, 3.253–70.

81. See Tang Geng'ou, *Dunhuang siyuan*.

82. Knauer, *Camel's Load*.

83. Bulliet, *Camel and the Wheel*.

84. The legendary white camel of the Tang Turco-Khotanese general Geshu Han, for instance, is reported to have been able to travel 500 *li* per day. See Zheng Chuhui, *Minghuang zalu*, 54.

85. As E. R. Knauer argues in her comprehensive study of this issue, the earlier, pre-Tang depictions of camels were more realistic than the Tang ones, and the depictions of textiles and objects likely were more realistic than those of the victuals.

86. Knauer, *Camel's Load*, 76–77.

87. See the images in Knauer's *Camel's Load* (45, 49).

88. Yang Rui, *Huihu shidai*, 72–79.

89. Tuotuo, *Songshi*, 490.14116.

90. A horse can carry up to around 100 kg.

91. See Tuotuo, *Songshi*, 490.14110. The text: "次曆茅女王子開道族, 行入六窠沙, 沙深三尺, 馬不能行, 行者皆乘橐駝."

92. The most obvious example is the six named horses whose statues accompany the emperor Taizong of the Tang in his tomb.

93. A famous example is, again, the white camel that belonged to the Tang general Geshu Han.

94. Bailey, "Hvatanica III," 529.

95. From Wang Yande's record about Turfan, where a good horse was valued at one *pi* of silk, while a horse of lower quality (*numa*), which was consumed as food, was valued at one *zhang* of silk. Tuotuo, *Songshi*, 490.14113. The text: "善馬直絹一匹, 其駑馬充食, 才直一丈."

96. P. 2484, *Facang*, 14.262. For similar documents, in which a certain Li Fendui was in charge of camel herds, see 羽 34 and S. 6998a.

97. Tan Chanxue, "Dunhuang ma wenhua," 117.

98. P. 2737, petition no. 4, *Shilu*, 3.602.

99. P. 4525-7v: "呂富定" (*Shilu*, 3.621).

100. P. 2737, petition no. 2, *Shilu*, 3.602. The text: "援于闐去達坦駱駝, 將西州去群上大父駝."

101. S. 2474, *Shilu*, 3.600. The text: "支與于闐使頭, 南山大父駝."

102. P. 3324, *Shilu*, 2.450.

103. Дх02134, *Ecang*, 9.45.

104. 羽 027, Takeda Kagaku Shinkō Zaidan Kyōu Shooku, *Tonkō hikyū*, 1.202; Chen Guocan, "Du *Xingyu shuwu*," 116.

105. *Shilu*, 2.38. For a comprehensive discussion of the camel-hiring contracts, see Gernet's "Location de chameaux."

106. P. 3448v, *Shilu*, 2.39.

107. P. 2652, *Shilu*, 2.41.

108. Five *pi* in P. 2825v (*Shilu*, 2.36) and seven *pi* in P. 3448v (*Shilu*, 2.39).

109. P. 4083, *Shilu*, 2.37.

110. Pelliot sogdien 28, Sims-Williams and Hamilton, *Turco-Sogdian Documents*, 50.

111. IOL Khot., S 13, Skjærvø, *Khotanese Manuscripts*, 509–10.

112. See the record of *fu* (麩; fodder) in P. 2776 (*Facang*, 18.161–62).

113. Wang Qinruo, *Cefu yuangui*, 972.11256.

114. P. 3547, *Shilu*, 4.369.

115. This deity is mentioned in the context of the government's provision of paper for its veneration. See P. 4640, *Shilu*, 3.256, 263. This account mentions only the name of this deity. Its role and relation with travelers cannot be firmly established. However, given the other contexts in which these two animals occur together and their close relation to traveling, I think it is plausible that the "God of Camels and Horses" would have something to do with travel as well.

116. S. 5448, *Shilu*, 1.45.

117. "甘州人教晉使者作馬蹄木澀, 木澀四竅, 馬蹄亦鑿而四竅而綴之, 駝蹄則包以氂皮乃可行." See Ouyang, *Xin Wudai shi*, 74.917.

118. A camel carries three *shi* while a donkey carries one *shi* of grain. See Li Tao, *Xu zizhi tongjian*, 11211.

119. S. 1403, *Shilu*, 2.42.

120. *Shilu*, 2.285.

121. "祭驢文: 教汝托生之処凡有數般: 莫生官人家, 軛馱入長安; 莫生將軍家, 打毬力雖攤須口; 莫生陸路腳家, 終日受皮鞭; 莫生和尚家, 道汝罪彌天," Eliasberg, "Pratiques funéraires animales."

122. "有羊, 尾大而不能走, 尾重者三斤, 小者一斤, 肉如熊白而甚美," Tuotuo, *Songshi*, 490.14111.

123. "大尾白羊," Yang Rui, *Huihu shidai*, 73. Such sheep can still be found today in Xinjiang and Kazakhstan.

124. "以羊皮為囊, 吹氣實之浮於水," Tuotuo, *Songshi*, 490.14110.

125. P. 2958. "In this serpent year I have sent to you as envoys two *ācāryas*, one a Tai-ṣī, and one a Tai-tik, and a report for the rays of light of the (Ratna-)janapada with an address and donation, one monkey" (Bailey, "Altun Khan," 96).

126. "白鶻": Wang Qinruo, *Cefu yuangui*, 972.11255.

127. P. 2741, Bailey, "Khotanese Text concerning the Turks," 32–34.

128. See the winged camel on a Sogdian ewer described in Knauer's *Camel's Load* (71). The most famous case of a horse depicted with a bird is the Han dynasty bronze statuette discovered in Wuwei (*mata feiyan* 馬踏飛燕) where a small, airborne sparrow carries a galloping horse on its back.

129. "野駝峰": see Wang Qinruo, *Cefu yuangui*, 972.11256.

130. P. 2992v-3, *Shilu*, 4.396.

131. Wang Qinruo, *Cefu yuangui*, 972.11257.

132. Wang Qinruo, 972.11257.

133. P. 3547, *Shilu*, 4.367–69.

134. S. 3399, Zhao Heping, *Dunhuang biao zhuang*, 306. The text: "天廷念邊為重, 土不產蠶, 特降絲綿, 兼之錦帛. 此皆尚書功庸所及. 厶乙等忝事旌麾, 下情無任感荷."

135. Whitfield, *Silk, Slaves, and Stupas*, 195–96.

136. Xu Song, *Song huiyao jigao*, fanyi 5.9836.

137. Schafer, *Golden Peaches of Samarkand*, 218.

138. Дх.2148(2)+Дх.6069(1), Zhang Guangda and Rong, *Yutian shi congkao*, 293.

139. Xu Song, *Song huiyao jigao*, fanyi 7.9959.

140. Zhao Feng, *Dunhuang sichou yu Sichou zhilu*, 251.

141. 1848 *pi* of silk would have weighed just over 2000 *jin*, and a camel's load is just under 400 *jin*. See discussion in chapter 8.

142. See Zheng Binglin, "Wan Tang Wudai Dunhuang maoyi," 19–20. One *liang* of silver could purchase 3–4 *shi* of grain, whereas 1 *pi* of silk, which weighed about 11 *liang*, could purchase around 27 *shi* of grain, translating into a rate of 2.45 *shi* per *liang* of silk.

143. Zhao Feng and Wang, *Dunhuang sichou*, 216–25.

144. For that from Persia, see Xue's *Jiu Wudai Shi* (138.1841); for that from Kucha, see Tang Zhangru's *Shanju conggao* (388–98).

145. Zheng Binglin, "Wan Tang Wudai Dunhuang maoyi."

146. Bi, "Gudai Yutian de yizhong zhiwu," 168–69.

147. S. 3565.1, *Shilu*, 3.97.

148. M. Wang, Wen, and Whitfield, "Buddhism and Silk."

149. See Zhao Feng and Wang, *Dunhuang sichou*, 137–203.

150. H. Wang and Hansen, "Textiles as Money."

151. Brown, "Silk Road," 17.

152. This is the *Five Horses* by Li Gonglin. See Harris, *Painting and Private Life*, fig. 10.

153. P. 3458, *Shilu*, 2.119.

154. These road bags (*lu dai* 路袋) appear in the accounting of goods owned by Dunhuang monasteries. See P. 2613 (*Facang*, 16.255), P. 2706 (*Facang*, 17.319), and P. 3432 (*Facang*, 24.183). The bags were made of assorted silk pieces and clothing: I suggest 錯菜 means "randomly patched clothes." See P. 2613 "破错菜經巾." 錯菜 is clearly a variant of 錯彩. In this case, the bags that carried these traveling goods were potentially themselves made of the remnants of other things (silk) that once also traveled.

155. Lattimore, *Desert Road to Turkestan*, 108–15.

156. S. 529, *Shilu*, 5.13. The text: "將緣身衣物, 買得駝兩頭."

# Chapter 4

1. Chin, "Invention of the Silk Road."

2. See, for instance, the maps in Whitfield, *Silk, Slaves, and Stupas*.

3. Williams, "Mapping the Silk Road."

4. Hansen, *Silk Road*, 5.

5. My reading of this document follows the interpretation of Chen Guocan in "Du *Xinyu shuwu*" (118).

6. I consult the research in Chen Tao's "Riben Xingyu shuwu," but do not follow some of his more conjectural identifications.

7. Christian, "Silk Roads or Steppe Roads?"

8. Silverstein, *Postal Systems*; Dang, *Meng Yuan yizhan*; Arakawa, *Yūrashia no kōtsū*.

9. "凡三十里一驛, 天下凡一千六百三十有九所": Li Linfu, *Tang liudian*, 5.163.

10. "凡陸行之程: 馬日七十里, 步及驢五十里, 車三十里": Li Linfu, 3.80.

11. P. 2005, *Shilu*, 1.8.

12. For the postal stops in Chang'an, see Song Minqiu's *Chang'an zhi* (313).

13. See Huili and Yanchong, *Daci'ensi sanzang fashi*, 12.

14. See S. 788v (*Shilu*, 1.42).

15. P. 5034, *Shilu*, 1.30.

16. See *Shilu*, 1.8. The text: "右在州西北一百一十里. 其水鹹苦, 唯泉堪食, 商胡從玉門關道往還居止, 因以為號."

17. Huili and Yanchong, *Daci'ensi sanzang fashi*, 16.

18. This point is noted in the record about this road in *Suishu*. See Wei Zheng, *Suishu*, 83.1847. The text: "四面茫然, 無有蹊徑. 欲往者尋有人畜骸骨而去. 路中或聞歌哭之之聲, 行人尋之, 多至亡失, 蓋魑魅魍魎也."

19. On these days of continuous travel, what they did was similar to how envoys from Khotan described their experience to the Song emperor: "traveling during the day and resting at night [晝行暮息]." See Tuotuo, *Songshi*, 490.14107.

20. For the life of Li Guangli, see Ban Gu's *Hanshu* (61.2699–2704).

21. See the record in *Dunhuang lu* 敦煌錄 (S. 5448, *Shilu*, 1.45).

22. S. 5448, *Shilu*, 1.45.

23. See Jidong Yang, "Transportation, Boarding, Lodging."

24. P. 2005 (*Shilu*, 1.11): "懸泉驛: 右在州東一百卅五里. 舊是山南空谷驛, 唐永淳三年錄奏, 奉敕移就山北, 懸泉驛置. 西去其頭驛八十里, 東去魚泉驛卅里, 同前奉敕移廢."

25. P. 2814 (*Shilu*, 4.495): "走報常樂, 瓜州兩鎮收什(拾)人口, 群牧, □ 備提防訖." P. 2482 (*Shilu*, 4.501–2) also refers to the military situation near Xuanquan.

26. P. 2814, *Shilu*, 4.494.

27. P. 2155v, *Shilu*, 4.401–2.

28. S. 5448, *Shilu*, 1.45.

29. For a similar process in which older Tang towns were reused by later states after the retreat of the Tang, see Fu Ma's *Sichou zhilu* (239–58, 264–79).

30. See the records in the "road" entry in Wang Pu's *Tang huiyao* (86.1573). The text: 開元二十八年正月十三日, 令兩京道路並種果樹, 令殿中侍御史鄭審充使.

31. See *Tang guoshibu* 唐國史補 in Li Fang's *Taiping guangji* (420.3425). "開元末, 西國獻獅子, 至長安西道中, 繫於驛樹, 樹近井, 獅子哮吼, 若不自安. 俄頃風雷大至, 果有龍出井而去."

32. P. 2155(2), *Shilu*, 4.401.

33. P. 2482v, *Shilu*, 4.501

34. Zheng Binglin and Li, *Dunhuang lishi dili*, 79–87.

35. S. 5139, *Yingcang*, 7.25. The petition that contains this reference is preserved in a rough copy. For a corrected transcription, see Rong's "Cao Yijin zheng Ganzhou Huihu" (9).

36. P. 2009, *Shilu*, 1.54–55.

37. P. 2009, *Shilu*, 1.54.

38. See Faxian, *Faxian zhuan jiaozhu*, 6.

39. S. 8702 + S. 8681v, Hao, *Tang houqi*, 104–5.

40. 北圖殷字 41, *Shilu*, 2.38.

41. P. 2741, Bailey, "Khotanese Text concerning the Turks," 29, 33.

42. P. 3016, Rong and Zhu, *Yutian yu Dunhuang*, 130–31.

43. S. 383, *Shilu*, 1.78.

44. See Li Jifu, *Yuanhe junxian tuzhi*, 40.1026. Entry on Dunhuang has: "北至伊州七百里."

45. Or. 8212.162, Skjærvø, *Khotanese Manuscripts*, 53.

46. Ni, Kamiya, and Ding, *Cities Network*, 123.

47. Millward, *Silk Road*, 20.

48. For the social life of this kingdom prior to its destruction, see Atwood's "Third–Fourth Century Cadh'ota."

49. Mischke et. al., "Earliest Aral-Sea Type Disaster."

50. P. 2962, Wang Zhongmin, *Dunhuang bianwen ji*, 116.

51. For details, see chapter 5.

52. P. 2992v-2, *Shilu*, 4.393–94.

53. P. 4640, *Shilu*, 3.268.

54. See Rong, "Rouran Qaghanate." I discussed this document in chapter 2.

55. P. 2155, *Shilu*, 4.401–2.

56. P. 2695 (*Shilu*, 1.24–26) and S. 2593v (*Shilu*, 1.1) are examples. S. 2593v is written on the verso side of a Prajnaparamita sutra. Both are likely Guiyijun-period copies because the texts were tightly clustered together, no doubt to save paper. The tightness of the writing poses a clear contrast to earlier, much more loosely (and lavishly) written copies, such as P. 5034 (*Shilu*, 1.27–37).

57. S. 5448, which carries the title "A Record on Dunhuang," is copied on a small codex, along with "the panegyric of the portrait of Hun Ziying," a famed local general and diplomat. This text does not include practical information about the locations of different military and governmental establishments. Instead, it tells readers about sites of interest in Dunhuang, including the Mogao caves and the "Singing Sand Mountain," first listing the names of these places and then relating an anecdote about them. Both the Mogao caves and the Singing Sand Mountain are still major tourist attractions in Dunhuang today. In this way, the manual works as a guide for visitors of Dunhuang to fully appreciate its sites of cultural significance. Li Zhengyu, *Guben Dunhuang xiangtuzhi*, 299–325.

58. The *Shouchang xian dijing* 壽昌縣地境 lists only places in Shouchang county to the southwest of Dunhuang. But because many of the towns between Dunhuang and Khotan were nominally under the jurisdiction of Shouchang county, this treatise effectively could serve as a guide to places leading up from the western border of Dunhuang to the eastern border of the kingdom of Khotan. The colophon of this text tells us that it was copied by a scholar at the Prefectural School for the county head of Shouchang, indicating a transmission of geographical knowledge from Dunhuang to the counties under its rule.

59. See La Vaissière, *Sogdian Traders*, 123–24.

60. Li Zhengyu, *Guben Dunhuang xiangtuzhi*, 145.

61. S. 383, *Shilu*, 1.78.

62. Van Schaik and Galambos, *Manuscripts and Travellers*, 161–62.

63. Minorsky, *Hudūd Al-ʿĀlam*, 83–86. Minorsky notes that "the source utilized by our author was chiefly acquinted with the Tarim basin and Kan-su, inclusive of the road leading to the Tang capital Chang-an" (228). For a general view of the interaction between Chinese and Islamic geographies, see Park's *Mapping the Chinese*.

64. For the special place of Lingzhou: Maeda Masana, *Kasei no rekishi chiri*; Zhao Zhen, *Guiyijun shishi kaolun*.

65. P. 2748. This letter is partially preserved because a slice of it was cut and pasted to support the Confucian text. See *Facang*, 18.67. The image from the International Dunhuang Project website ("Pelliot chinois 2748," International Dunhuang Project, http://idp.bl.uk/database/oo _scroll_h.a4d?uid=7094268637;recnum=59904;index=6) is clearer in showing this process.

66. The text in this section reads as follows: "tcarrvą dvīpvą nama tsalaka jabvī dvīpa baida rāauysanauda ranījai janavai vīra maistyai caiga rauda vara tta haṣḍa yanai ñaśa prravai śvahvąṃ raispūra hva pakyau ñaśa . . . ttąhtta-vadą pada narrvai ttąṣṭa janavai vīrąṣṭa hąysa tsai ttu dvī-sa śaca hai'ra tha śa ttąṣṭa hąysa buḍai ttąṣṭa ttą janavai vīrąṣṭa tsamadai hvai na yai ca ttą rrvī va tcainahū haṣḍą yanīna." For a translation, see Bailey's "Altun Khan" (97–98).

67. S. 529, *Shilu*, 5.9.

68. *Shilu*, 1.39–41.

69. P. 3322, *Facang*, 23.185. The text: "庚辰年正月十七日學生張大慶書記之也."

70. P. 3485v, *Facang*, 24.312–15.

71. See the transformation text of Zhang Huaishen: Wang Zhongmin, *Dunhuang bianwen ji*, 125.

72. P. 2741. Bailey, "Khotanese Text concerning the Turks," 31. Late Khotanese regularly abbreviates nasals, resulting in a "corrupt" transcription of the Chinese.

73. Emmerick, "Cā tteya khī."

74. Li Tao, *Xu zizhi tongjian*, 335.8063.

75. Thomas and Konow, "Two Medieval Documents."

76. P. 3532. The text: "君恨西蕃遠, 余嗟東路長." See Lopez, *Hyecho's Journey*, 32. My translation departs a little from that of Donald Lopez. See also Kuwayama, *Echō*.

77. Rong, "Tangren shiji."

78. "假官向張掖." Xu Jun, *Dunhuang shiji*, 660.

79. Xu Jun, 654.

80. Xu Jun, 653.

81. Xu Jun, 655.

82. Xu Jun, 654.

83. The text: "鐵門關外東西道, 過盡前朝多少人. 客舍丘墟存舊跡, 山川猶自疊魚鱗." Xu, *Dunhuang shiji*, 659.

84. Cen Sen's famous poem reads "鐵關天西涯, 極目少行客. 關門一小吏, 終日對石壁. 橋跨千仞危, 路盤兩崖窄. 試登西樓望, 一望頭欲白" (Peng Dingqiu, *Quan Tangshi*, 198.2046).

85. Tuotuo, *Songshi*, 490.14113.

86. Xuanzang famously invoked the Bodhisattva Avalokiteśvara (*guanyin*) during his trek in the desert between Dunhuang and Turfan. See Huili and Yancong, *Daci'ensi sanzang fashi*, 17.

## Chapter 5

1. This practice of hosting a banquet for diplomats at the polo court was also seen in Dunhuang itself.

2. The Mongolia Itinerary uses language such as they "arrived" (*zhi* 至) somewhere and "stayed overnight" (*su* 宿). See Chen Guocan, "Du *Xingyu shuwu*," 6. Wang Yande's record, on the other hand, talks about how they "passed" (*li* 歷) certain places.

3. P. 2641, *Shilu*, 3.610–13.

4. See the now-lost *Geography of Shouchang* 壽昌縣地境, *Shilu*, 1.52–53.

5. Bailey, "Staël-Holstein Miscellany," 2.

6. Yang Sen, "Wudai Song shiqi Yutian taizi."

7. See the case of one such Khotanese prince in Zhang Guangda and Rong's *Yutian shi congkao* (38–47).

8. This proximity to the river is made clear by the existence of a dam at Maquankou. See P. 2005 in *Shilu*, 1.6.

9. "西行過馬圈, 北望近陽關. 回首見城郭, 黯然林樹間" (Xu Jun, *Dunhuang shiji*, 705).

10. "廿二日, 使出馬圈口, 酒壹甕." See the wine expenditure in *Shilu*, 3.273.

11. The standard term for this practice is "suburban welcome" 郊迎. Cong Zhang also notes that "traveling for some distance and waiting for the arrival of superiors on the roadside appear to have been standard administrative practice" (*Transformative Journeys*, 137).

12. P. 2926, *Facang*, 16.362. The text: "三日, 城西莊刘麥酒壹甕, 面前看于闐使酒壹斗."

13. S. 2474 talks about envoys staying in the gardens in the southern and eastern suburbs of the city. *Shilu*, 3.278.

14. Rong, *Eighteen Lectures on Dunhuang*, 119.

15. For an example, see the mission of the monk Wuzhen in Chang'an: Fu Junlian, "Tangdai Dunhuang gaoseng Wuzhen."

16. See Shi Pingting, "Bensuo cang *jiuzhang*."

17. Shi Pingting, 148. The text reads "先報消息來回鶻."

18. See Sakajiri, "Tonkō hantsu kō," 182–83.

19. The Suspended Spring Garrison generally served as a place to welcome incoming envoys from the east for the Dunhuang government.

20. Skjærvø, *Khotanese Manuscripts*, 512.

21. Ouyang, *Xin Wudai shi*, 74.918.

22. Li Jifu, *Yuanhe junxian tuzhi*, 4.93.

23. See, for instance, the shift of the Tang border discussed in Rong and Wen's "Semantic Shift of 'Western Region.'"

24. P. 2992v (2), B. Yang and Wu, *Guiyijun zhengquan*, 119–32.

25. For the claim to a Chinese identity in Dunhuang, see Yang Shao-Yun's "'Stubbornly Chinese?'"

26. P. 2741, Bailey, "Khotanese Text concerning the Turks," 29, 33.

27. Wang mentions that when he arrived only the uncle of the khan was there. After sending him an initial message, the uncle waited for "several more days" before meeting him. Then he spent at least thirteen days on the road to the north, where he waited for at least seven more days before meeting the khan.

28. "其王遣人來言, 擇日以見使者, 願無訝其淹久" (Tuotuo, *Songshi*, 490.14112).

29. See P. 3547, *Shilu*, 4.367–69.

30. P. 2741, Bailey, "Khotanese Text concerning the Turks," 29–34.

31. See P. 3547, *Shilu*, 4.368.

32. I will discuss this in more detail in the next chapter.

33. Tuotuo, *Songshi*, 490.14113.

34. P. 2741. Bailey, "Khotanese Text concerning the Turks," 33.

35. The original text has *daqiu* 打毬 and *she* 設, which mean "playing polo" and "offering banquet." It is unclear how these two things are related. It is possible, as some Dunhuang documents show, that the banquet happened at the polo field.

36. Canepa, *Two Eyes of the Earth*, 180.

37. Zhou Tianyou, *Zhanghuai taizi mu*, 30–39.

38. For how the dead would have experienced their tombs in the Tang, see Hay's "Seeing through Dead Eyes."

39. James Liu, "Polo and Cultural Change," 222–23.

40. Tan Chanxue, "Dunhuang ma wenhua," 118–19.

41. P. 3451, Wang Zhongmin, *Dunhuang bianwen ji*, 124. The text: "毬場宣詔諭."

42. S. 5636, *Yingcang*, 8.197.

43. P. 3773v, *Facang*, 28.9. The title is "凡節度使新受旌節儀."

44. P. 3945, *Shilu*, 3.587.

45. P. 3451, Wang Zhongmin, *Dunhuang bianwen ji*, 123. The text: "羅列球場, 萬人稱賀."

46. Tuotuo, *Songshi*, 490.14113.

47. Zhang Guangda and Rong, *Yutian shi congkao*, 91.

48. Bailey, "Staël-Holstein Miscellany," 44.

49. Sha Wutian, "Dunhuang shiku."

50. Tuotuo, *Songshi*, 490.14113.

51. P. 3016, Rong and Zhu, *Yutian yu Dunhuang*, 130–31.

52. See Shi Pingting, "Bensuo cang jiuzhang," 142–55.

53. Zhang Guangda and Rong, *Yutian shi congkao*, 46.

54. Xu Song, *Song huiyao jigao*, fanyi 7.9958, 9961.

55. Sowerby, "Early Modern Diplomatic History," 441.

56. For records of the wine provided as "road goods," see Shi Pingting's "Bensuo cang *jiuzhang*" (144). For the situation in the Song, see C. Zhang's *Transformative Journeys* (111–29).

57. See the record of the masses (*dazhong*, likely meaning Buddhists) who participated in the sending off of the lord of Dunhuang himself to the east in P. 2049v (*Shilu*, 3.380).

58. Skaff, *Sui-Tang China*, 167.

59. P. 4525-9, *Shilu*, 4.305.

60. P. 2155v, *Shilu*, 4.401–2.

61. For the role of Xuanquan as a point of border management for the Dunhuang government, see P. 2814v (*Shilu*, 4.494) and Дх03412+Дх03415 (*Ecang*, 10.289).

62. P. 2155v, *Shilu*, 4.401.

63. P. 3272, *Shilu*, 4.411.

64. For a discussion of this mission, see Yang Baoyu and Wu's *Guiyijun zhengquan* (133–45).

65. P. 3718, Jiang Boqin, Xiang, and Rong, *Dunhuang miaozhenzan*, 285–86.

66. P. 3564, Yang Baoyu and Wu, *Guiyijun zhengquan*, 137.

67. See Hamilton, *Ouïghours*, 143–44.

68. Skjærvø, *Khotanese Manuscripts*, 512–13.

69. Xue, *Jiu Wudai shi*, 138.1842.

70. P. 3016v, Yang Baoyu and Wu, *Guiyijun zhengquan*, 104–18.

71. P. 3016, *Facang*, 21.61–62. For a transcription, see Rong and Zhu's *Yutian yu Dunhuang* (131). The original text reads: "於陸月貳拾壹日出於本道, 沿途雖逢奸危賊殺, 上下一行並無折欠, 其於國朝信物亦無遺失, 於柒月貳拾三日得達西朝."

72. Rong, "Dazhong shinian."

73. Hu Ji and Rong, *Da Tang xishi*, 952–53.

74. S. 5949, 下女夫詞, *Yingcang*, 9.221. The text: "賊來須打, 客來須看."

75. This story appears in the chapter on the "evil friend" 惡友品 of the *Bao'en jing* 報恩經 (Takakusu and Watanabe, *Taishō shinshū daizōkyō*, 3.142–47) and the chapter on Prince Virtuous's trip to the sea (善事太子入海品) of the *Xian yujing* 賢愚經 (Takakusu and Watanabe, 4.410–15).

76. Hamilton, *Conte bouddhique*.

77. MacKenzie, *Sūtra of the Causes*.

78. *mDo mdzangs blun*; see Pelliot tibétain 943. For an edition of this text in Tibetan, see Terjék's "Fragments of the Tibetan Sutra."

79. For instance, mural paintings based on this text are found in Cave 85. See Dunhuang yanjiuyuan, *Dunhuang shiku neirong zonglu*, 34.

80. Moule and Pelliot, *Description of the World*, 1:154.

81. Kāšgarī, *Compendium of the Turkic Dialects*, 95.

82. The idea of a guest-friend is common among early Indo-European societies. See Herman, *Ritualised Friendship*; C. Watkins, *How to Kill a Dragon*, 71–72; see also Benveniste, *Vocabulaire des institutions indo-européennes*.

83. Kāšgarī, *Compendium of Turkic Dialects*, 232.

84. Bailey, "Khotanese Text concerning the Turks." Bailey translates this as "blame or praise."

85. Skjærvø, *Khotanese Manuscripts*, 55.

86. Van Schaik and Galambos, *Manuscripts and Travellers*, 161–62.

87. Zhang Xiuqing, "Dunhuang xiejuan S.526 kao."

88. S. 526. The Chinese text reads: "弟子夫人別有少事上告尊慈, 幸望甫垂聽念. 前者東去之時, 弟子情多戀切, 意極思深, 盡力接待, 竭心侍足. 如斯邀勒, 不可聽留. 便是前行, 違背迷士. 已後諸官人口說: 和尚去時於阿郎極有唱說不是. 阿郎尋自知聞, 轉甚煩惱. 只為和尚在此之日, 小來如兄如弟, 似水似魚, 遞互謙恭, 不聞別事. 今者為甚不知唱說惡名, 左右人聞, 名價不善. 倍多羅塞, 欲得和尚再要迴來, 要知腹事. 弟子如今渴仰法慈, 請歸上府, 即為滿願矣" (Hao, *Yingcang Dunhuang shehui lishi* 3.21–23).

89. P. 3691, *Facang*, 26.321. The text reads: "謝所到州供給: 厶乙等庸賤, 奉本使驅馳, 幸過貴土. 伏蒙訟 (沿) 路管界州鎮特賜供備倍常. 厶乙等下情無任感恩惶懼."

## Chapter 6

1. Mauss, *Gift*.

2. Davis, *Gift in Sixteenth-Century France*, 4.

3. Trombert notes, for instance, that in the monastic community in Dunhuang, silk was predominantly used as gifts and rewards, but not as money. Trombert, "Demise of Silk," 329.

4. See S. 6981v, *she*-community circular about marriage gifts, *Yingcang*, 12.12.

5. Hao, *Tang houqi*, 241–53.

6. Kāshgarī, *Compendium of the Turkic Dialects*, 138.

7. Kāshgarī, 162.

8. Kāshgarī, 295.

9. Sims-Williams and Hamilton, *Turco-Sogdian Documents*, 49–50.

10. Scholars who study Chinese letters have noticed the close connection between letters and gifts. See X. Tian, "Material and Symbolic Economies."

11. Pelliot tibétain 1129, Yamaguchi, *Tonkō Kogo bunken*, 511–12.

12. Pelliot ouïgour 12, Hamilton, *Manuscrits ouïgours*, 137–38.

13. Zhang Xiaoyan, *Dunhuang shuyi yuyan yanjiu*, 365–72.

14. Or. 8212 (89), Sims-Williams and Hamilton, *Turco-Sogdian Documents*, 76–78.

15. According to Sims-Williams, "it would seem that this epistolary formula was in origin Chinese, that it was first borrowed by Turkish in an abridged form, and that subsequently it was translated directly from Turkish into Sogdian. Clearly, the formula indicates that a letter is accompanied by a gift showing that the sender is not 'empty' or 'devoid' of warm feelings towards the addressee" (Sims-Williams and Hamilton, 89).

16. Pelliot sogdien 28, Sims-Williams and Hamilton, 49–50.

17. Pelliot ouïgour 6, Uygur text in Hamilton, *Manuscrits ouïgours*, 154. The text: "menämä sügčuda erür men anın beläk ıtu umatım."

18. Pelliot tibétain 1129, Wang Yao and Chen, *Dunhuang Tufan wenshu lunwenji*, 198.

19. Other gifts not from sovereigns were also transferred by envoys. Because of the lack of a postal system, envoys often served as messengers, and the messages invariably carried gifts with them. In a particularly well documented case, the monastic chief of Turfan wrote to his counterparts in Dunhuang to report his recent promotion. He also complained that "Since we parted, it has been several years. There was no lack of envoys traveling back and forth, yet I have not received a word of greeting. The human feeling [you have shown] is extremely slim." This letter he sent also was carried by an envoy, as it states that "I am sending the letter of greeting, now, with the departing envoy." The gifts to Dunhuang that accompanied the letter were three locally produced watermelons. See P. 3672 bis, *Facang*, 26.290.

20. *Shilu*, 4.367–69.

21. P. 2741, Bailey, "Khotanese Text concerning the Turks," 33. I have revised the translation.

22. See the discussion in chapter 5.

23. Skjærvø, *Khotanese Manuscripts*, 513–14. See also Skjærvø, "Perils of Ambassadors."

24. Speaking of the Byzantine Empire and its contact with Turkic envoys, Jonathan Skaff points out that "Even though the two powers lacked previous contacts, their meetings went smoothly in part because they shared some ideas about diplomatic protocol, particularly gifts

and correspondence exchanges" (Skaff, *Sui-Tang China*, 149). The combination of gifts and letters was the common practice among medieval Eurasian states.

25. Xu Song, *Song huiyao jigao*, fanyi 4.9775.

26. P. 5538: "viña ttā tteyi hvāṃ' vaski tvā buri mu'śdā' pastāṃdū hajsāṃde, paḍauysä myậnī ịrä śau dvāritcihaisä kīṇa u śe' vasve īrä dasau kīṇa u dịdä īrä haṣṭi kīṇa hālai drai mậṇḍi īrä hamye kṣạ'ṣṭä kīṇi hālai u kaṃgīnai baṃgāṃ śau u ṣvīnā daśṭậnya byaṣṭi līka mārsalä śä u byaṣṭi līkä parạṣä' śau u bārai śau u kūsä śau."

27. The difference in status between these two sovereigns is a result of the Khotanese king's claim to be king of kings of China. See Wen, "King of Kings of China."

28. P. 2992v-3, *Shilu*, 4.396.

29. The calculation is based on Zheng Binglin's "Wan Tang Wudai Dunhuang maoyi."

30. This is based on Huang Zhengjian, "Dunhuang wenshu," 271.

31. Laufer, *Jade*, 24.

32. Each *jin* in the Tang is about 650 g, so eight *jin* is therefore 5.2 kg.

33. See my discussion in chapter 2.

34. Tuotuo, *Songshi*, 490.14107.

35. For asafetida, or *awei*, see: Laufer, *Sino-Iranica*, 353–62; Schafer, *Golden Peaches of Samarkand*, 188–89.

36. Xu Song, *Song huiyao jigao*, fanyi 5.9836. The text: "且言本州僧惠藏乞賜師號，龍興，靈圖二寺修像，計金十萬箔，願賜之。又乞鑄鐘匠及漢人之善藏珠者，至當道傳授其術。"

37. Rong and Zhu, "Yizu fanying 10 shiji," 101.

38. P. 3016, *Facang*, 21.61–63. Rong and Zhu, *Yutian yu Dunhuang*, 130.

39. Minorsky, *Marvazī on China*, 20.

40. Hansen, "International Gifting," 288–91.

41. P. 2642, *Shilu*, 3.209.

42. Reischauer, *Ennin's Diary*, 367–68.

43. P. 3931, lines 116–19, Zhao Heping, *Dunhuang biao zhuang*, 236. The text: "謝馬書，右伏蒙恩私，特此寵賜。遠路既難於辭讓，逸蹤莫匪於權奇。收受之時，兢兢銘倍切。謹專修狀陳謝。伏惟照察。謹狀。"

44. The social context that enabled such an apparently unidirectional offer of favor was the often-delayed guest-host reciprocity, which was discussed in chapter 5.

45. See my discussion in chapter 3.

46. For example: P. 2032v (*Shilu*, 3.455–512), P. 2040v (*Shilu*, 3.401–36), P. 2049v (*Shilu*, 3.347–66, 369–89), P. 2629 (Shi Pingting, "Bensuo cang *jiuzhang*"), P. 3234v (*Shilu*, 3.438–54).

47. P. 2032v-9, *Shilu*, 3.472.

48. P. 2040v, *Shilu*, 3. 416, 418.

49. P. 2049v, *Shilu*, 3.347–66, 369–89.

50. P. 3763v (for officials; *Shilu*, 3.515, 519), P. 4697 (for a mason; *Facang*, 33.113), P. 4906 (for shepherds; *Facang*, 33.257).

51. *Shilu*, 4.9.

52. Galambos, "She Association Circulars."

53. S. 6537v, *Shilu*, 1.282. The text: "若有東西出使遠行，一般去送來迎，各自總有。"

54. I discuss the economic roles of these road goods in detail in chapter 8.

55. S. 5636, *Yingcang*, 8.197. The text: "送客下擔橫過使: 絁壹匹, 綾壹匹等色目. 右前件物謹令馳送, 聊充翌日草料當直. 多慙寡鮮, 用表衷誠. 伏惟不責輕觸, 俯賜領納. 何要進發, 專侯留行, 郊外奉送, 謹狀." Translation of "*shi* silk" from Zhao Feng and Wang, "Glossary of Textile Terminology," 354.

56. S. 1366, *Shilu*, 3.281–86.

57. P. 3569, *Shilu*, 3.622–23.

58. P. 4640, *Shilu*, 3.253–70.

59. See my discussion of an envoy's economic life in chapter 8.

60. 1 *pi* = 40 *chi* = about 12 meters.

61. I discuss the economic consequences to the society of Dunhuang in chapter 8.

62. S. 5636, *Yingcang*, 8.197. The text: "偶因營運, 得達名邦, 思慕故流, 幸窺顏色, 未施織許, 悚惕尤增. 蒙賜主請, 豈敢當此. 欲趨高第, 面謝丘恩, 轉應饗煩, 專侯展訴下宣, 謹狀."

63. P. 3691, *Facang*, 26.321. The text: "謝下擔: 厶乙等庸賤, 奉本使驅馳, 幸達貴土, 未蒙伏拜. 特賜下擔羊, 酒. 厶乙等無任感恩戰懼."

64. S. 5713, *Yingcang*, 9.94.

65. P. 3438, *Facang*, 24.206–8.

66. S. 5981, *Yingcang*, 10.11.

67. Chinese text: "智嚴回日發願: 將此凡身, 於五臺山供養大聖文殊師利菩薩. 焚燒此身, 用酬往來道途護衛之恩" (*Yingcang*, 10.11). More information about this person can be found in a colophon (Shangbo 48) now preserved at the Shanghai museum.

68. Benn, *Burning for the Buddha*, 60.

69. Skaff, *Sui-Tang China*, 266.

70. S. 1920 ("Treatise on a Hundred Conducts" 百行章), no. 51, *Yingcang*, 3.180, emphasis added. The text: "蒙人引接, 至死銜恩; 受祿居寵, 滅身非謝.... 是以寧人負己, 而莫己負人."

71. India Office Library, Khotanese collection, S. 22, Skjærvø, *Khotanese Manuscripts*, 527–28.

72. Such as the Moka exchange. See Strathern, *Rope of Moka*.

73. Mauss, *Gift*, 35.

74. Sahlins, *Stone Age Economics*, 186.

75. P. 3931, Zhao Heping, *Dunhuang biao zhuang*, 240. The text: "國家稍籍其聲光, 部族不妨於貿易."

## Chapter 7

1. The most original account of this record is in Cai Tao's *Tieweishan congtan* (1.8–9). Cai was at the meeting where Wang Anzhong related the letter from the king of Khotan, and his account should be considered the original one. Later accounts of the same incident, such as the one in the Southern Song collection *Qingbo zazhi* 清波雜誌 (6.250), have a few variants in the content of the letter. My translation of this passage is based on Cai Tao's version, and differs from that of Dilnoza Duturaeva, who bases her reading on the *Qingbo zazhi* version. See Duturaeva "Qarakhanid Envoys to Song China," 188.

2. This story is included in Ming and Qing dynasty texts. See Feng Menglong, *Gujin tangai*, 166; Duyiwo tuishi, *Xiaoxiao lu*, 2.11a–b.

3. The Chinese text reads: "日出東方, 赫赫大光, 照見西方, 五百國中條貫主, 阿舅黑汗王. 表上日出東方, 赫赫大光, 照見四天下, 四天下條貫主,  阿舅大官家: 你前時要那玉, 自家然是用心. 只被難得似你那尺寸底, 我已令人尋討, 如是得似你那尺寸底, 我便送去也."

4. Jiang Lansheng and Cao, *Tangdai yuyan cidian*, 146–47.

5. Cai, *Tieweishan congtan*, 1.9.

6. See Beckwith, *Tibetan Empire in Central Asia*.

7. Zhang Zhan, "Between China and Tibet." See also Rong and Wen, "Chinese-Khotanese Bilingual Tallies"; Yoshida, *Kōtan shutsudo*.

8. Rong, *Eighteen Lectures on Dunhuang*, 38–40.

9. Rong, 315–40; Takata, "Multilingualism in Tun-huang."

10. See the website of Turfan Forschung at the Berlin Brandenburgische Akademie der Wissenschaften, http://turfan.bbaw.de/projekt/#4. See also Durkin-Meisterernst, *Turfan Revisited*.

11. Millward, *Silk Road*, 29.

12. Sinor, "Languages and Cultural Interchange," 4.

13. La Vaissière, *Sogdian Traders*, 324.

14. Lu Qingfu, "Tang Song jian."

15. Uray, "Emploi du tibétain."

16. Uray, "New Contributions"; Takeuchi, "Group of Old Tibetan Letters."

17. Hansen, *Silk Road*, 187; Kapstein, "Treaty Temple," 56.

18. Takeuchi, "Sociolinguistic Implications," 343.

19. See chapter 2.

20. S. 5448–42, Jiang Boqin, Xiang, and Rong, *Dunhuang miaozhenzan*, 245–46. Hun's biography is copied in the same booklet as a geography of Dunhuang. See *Yingcang*, 7.91–97.

21. Zhang Yanqing, "Zhang Yichao yu Tubo wenhua."

22. Tuotuo, *Songshi*, 277.9425.

23. An Lushan is said to have been able to speak "six barbarian languages." See Liu Xu, *Jiu Tangshu*, 200a.5367. For another person of Sogdian descent who served as an interpreter in the Tang, see the epitaph of Shi Hetan 史訶耽 in Luo Feng's *Huhan zhijian* (483–85). Larner, *Marco Polo*, 64–65.

24. "His tongue is refined and his are lips sweet, and in translating the barbarian languages, the barbarian Hun [Tuyuhun] people marvel at the beauty [of his words]" (Zheng Binglin, *Dunhuang beiming*, 343).

25. P. 2786, lines 172 to 250.

26. The Khotanese text reads: "ca jsā caigą hvailā ttai ṣa' jsā auna aspaura caigau bauttai na jsā hvaṇau bauttai na." See Kumamoto, "Khotanese Official Documents," 131.

27. See chapter 1.

28. Xu Song, *Song huiyao jigao*, fanyi 4.9768.

29. Tuotuo, *Songshi*, 490.14116–17.

30. In this way, the khan behaved in much the same way as the lord of Dunhuang did toward the Khotanese envoys. See chapter 5.

31. Ouyang, *Xin Wudai shi*, 74.917–18.

32. The twelfth month of the seventh year of Tianfu reign (942).

33. P. 5535, *Facang*, 34.207. The signature reads: "大寶于闐国進奉使司空劉再昇." *Sikong* is a high, but by then archaic, Chinese title originally meaning "minister of works."

34. Kaneko, "Pelliot 2782 monjo."

35. Pelliot tibétain 1256. For a study of this document, see Rong and Zhu, "Yizu fanying 10 shiji," 103–5.

36. This was first noticed by Takao Moriyasu; see his "Isumaru ka izen no Chūō Ajia-shi" (66).

37. Rong and Zhu, "Yizu fanying 10 shiji," 104.

38. P. 4525-9, *Shilu*, 4.305.

39. This method of certification is widely used in contracts. See the contract from Turfan dated to 475 in Rong, Li, and Meng, *Xinhuo Tulufan chutu wenxian*, 125–26, item no. 97TSYM1:5.

40. P. 4044, Rong, *Guiyijun shi yanjiu*, 223. The text: "汝甘州充使, 亦要結耗（好）和同, 所過砦, 堡, 州, 城, 各需存其禮法. 但取使頭言教, 不得亂話是非. 沿路比此回還, 仍須守自本分. 如有拗束掀西, 兼浪言狂語者, 使頭記名, 將來到州, 重有刑法者."

41. P. 3016, Yang Baoyu and Wu, *Guiyijun zhengquan*, 105.

42. Xu Song, *Song huiyao jigao, zhiguan* (governmental offices) 36.3923–24.

43. Li Jinxiu, "Tangdai de fanshu yiyu zhiguan," 39.

44. Xu Song, *Song huiyao jigao*, zhiguan 36.3905

45. Shi Pingting, "Bensuo cang *jiuzhang*," 145.

46. Shi Pingting, 145.

47. Shi Pingting has already noticed this point (152–53).

48. Several of these are preserved in Wang Qinruo's *Cefu Yuangui* (999.11557–60).

49. I have counted over fifty letters exchanged between heads of states among the Dunhuang documents. See my dissertation "Kingly Exchange" (136–38). This is no doubt an incomplete list.

50. For similar type of "conspicuous consumption" in edict writing, see the Fatimid decrees discussed in Rustow's *Lost Archive* (312–18).

51. This document was discussed in detail in chapter 6.

52. See Bischoff and Hartman, "Padmasambhava's Invention of the Phur-bu."

53. This is first pointed out in Takeuchi's "Sociolinguistic Implications."

54. This observation was made with the help of Dr. Sakamoto Shouji when we worked on the Pelliot collection together in the summer of 2013.

55. See also the nine paper flowers that were on display at the Victoria and Albert Museum on loan from the Government of India and the Archaeological Survey of India: "The Stein Collection: Paper Flowers; 7th Century to 10th Century (Made)," Victorian and Albert Museum, accessed May 20, 2022, https://collections.vam.ac.uk/item/O85719/the-stein-collection-paper-flowers-unknown/.

56. P. 3111, *Shilu*, 3.99.

57. The text: 凡書信去, 請看二印: 一大玉印, 一小玉印, 更無別印也.

58. Takeda Kagaku Shinkō Zaidan Kyōu Shooku, *Tonkō hikyū*, 9.65.

59. Uray, "New Contributions," 520–21.

60. Takeuchi, "Sociolinguistic Implications," 342.

61. The Khotanese prince Congde, for instance, became King Viśa' Śūra after his assumption of the throne in 967. Given his childhood visit to Dunhuang, his later extended stay in Dunhuang (at least one year), and his long journey to the Song, it is very likely that he had mastered

Chinese, if he had not been brought up speaking it, when he became king. See Zhang Guangda and Rong, *Yutian shi congkao*, 46.

62. For the different stages of the envoy-host interaction, see chapter 5.

63. Most of them are in the Paris collection. See the catalogue in Zhang Guangda and Rong's *Yutian shi congkao* (118–48).

64. The Tibetan messages: Bailey, "Staël-Holstein Miscellany." The Chinese letter: S. 2528. See my discussion in chapter 3.

65. See Takata, "Multilingualism in Tun-huang."

66. Wen, "King of Kings of China."

67. Sims-Williams and Hamilton, *Turco-Sogdian Documents*, 35.

68. Sims-Williams and Hamilton, 83–85.

69. P. 3016, Yang Baoyu and Wu, *Guiyijun zhengquan*, 105.

70. Yang Baoyu and Wu, 115–16, Sima, *Zizhi tongjian*, 275.8989.

71. P. 2992v, *Shilu*, 4.395–96.

72. See Yang Baoyu and Wu, *Guiyijun zhengquan*, 125–27.

73. P. 2992v is not an "original" letter because it lacks seals and other official apparatus. Instead, it has been copied along with two other diplomatic letters, and on the back one finds a Buddhist text. I cannot conclusively determine the order of writing, but the assemblage of three different letters written at different times on the same paper seems to suggest an intentional act of record keeping.

74. The identification of these two names was suggested by Luo Tonghua in "Guiyijun qi Dunhuang siyuan" (203). I agree with her suggestion.

75. Cheng Minsheng, "Songdai de fanyi," 64. The text: "本所大小通事, 傳語, 指使, 使臣等, 遇人使到關, 引接使, 副, 三節人從. 殿庭並在驛抄札聽審語錄, 押送吃食, 酒, 果等, 及入位承領傳語計會公事, 輪差奉使, 接送伴覺察祗應."

76. Tuotuo, *Songshi*, 298.9921–22.

77. S. 1000, S. 2736, and S. 5212. See Iwao, Van Schaik, and Takeuchi, *Old Tibetan Texts*.

78. Or. 8210/S. 5212 and Or. 8212.162, Skjærvø, *Khotanese Manuscripts*, 35–36, 44–45.

79. The Turco-Khotanese phrasebook is at P. 2892, lines 157–85.

80. Thomas and Giles, "Tibeto-Chinese"; Kumamoto, "Saiiki ryokōsha."

81. Skjærvø, *Khotanese Manuscripts*, 44–55.

82. Skjærvø, 53.

83. See Bailey, "Hvatanica III."

84. Skjærvø, *Khotanese Manuscripts*, 36, 44.

85. Skjærvø, 35.

86. Skjærvø, 44.

87. Tuotuo, *Songshi*, 490.14107.

88. Tuotuo, 490.14109.

89. Tuotuo, 490.14119. The text: "引對於崇政殿, 譯者代奏云."

90. Bailey, "Hvatanica III," 528–29.

91. Sinor, "Interpreters in Medieval Inner Asia."

92. Takeuchi, "Sociolinguistic Implications," 343.

93. Yūsuf, *Wisdom of Royal Glory*, 1–3. I owe this invaluable reference to Dilnoza Duturaeva, who also discussed this passage but in the context of Qarakhanid diplomacy. See *Qarakhanid*

*Roads to China*, 38–39. Yūsuf used the same word for envoy (*yala:vaç*) as Uyghur documents from Dunhuang.

94. Yūsuf, *Wisdom of Royal Glory*, 125.

95. Yūsuf, 126–27.

# Chapter 8

1. S. 4359v, *Yingcang*, 6.43. The text: "關于闐, 綿綾家家總滿. 奉戲生龍及玉碗, 將來百姓看. 尚書座客典, 四塞休征罷戰. 但阿郎千秋歲, 甘州他自離亂." See Zhang Guangda and Rong, *Yutian shi congkao*, 85.

2. On the office of the Bureau of Guests, see Li Linfu's *Tang liudian* (18.506–7).

3. P. 3270, Huang Zheng and Wu, *Dunhuang yuanwen ji*, 951.

4. For a discussion of this trip, see Hansen's *Silk Road* (191–92).

5. Hansen mentions that "the documents do not specify what kind" of cloth was given to the envoys (*Silk Road*, 191). In fact, the document does specify that "the price of camel and horse" was paid in silk (*juan* 絹, line 40). As for the first group of return gifts, the document first summarizes that they come in three categories: "*jin-cai* [錦綵] silk, silverware, and clothing" (lines 23–24). It then lists the specific amount each person received in each category. The three generals (*yaya*), for instance, each received "15 *pi*, one silver bowl, and one set of cotton [*mian* 綿] clothing." It is quite clear that, because of the correspondence of the categories, the "15 *pi*" refers to the "*jin-cai* silk" of the first category. There is some confusion regarding the type of clothes involved, partly because of a mistranscription that confused cotton (綿) for *jin*-silk (錦; see *Shilu*, 4.368). For a transcription and analysis of this document, see Wu Zhen's *Wu Zhen Dunhuang Tulufan* (107–15).

6. See my discussion in chapter 5.

7. Дх06031v 沙州上都進奏院狀, *Ecang*, 12.323.

8. Zheng Binglin and Xue, "Du *Ecang Dunhuang wenxian* di 12 ce," 82–83.

9. Bailey, "Staël-Holstein Miscellany," 44.

10. Xu Song, *Song huiyao jigao*, fanyi 4.9767.

11. Xu Song, fanyi 4.9767.

12. Li Delong, "Dunhuang yishu S.8444 hao yanjiu." For a comprehensive study of this document, see Dohi's "Tonkō hakken Tō-Kaikotsu."

13. Li Delong, "Dunhuang yishu S.8444 hao yanjiu," 39.

14. Huang Chunyan, *Songdai chaogong*, 402–4.

15. Rong, *Guiyijun shi yanjiu*, 188.

16. 北圖殷字41, *Shilu*, 2.38.

17. The exact meaning of this term, *dali* (大例), is unclear.

18. S. 4120, *Shilu*, 3.213.

19. S. 6452.1, *Shilu*, 3.222.

20. P. 3627, *Shilu*, 3.121.

21. Ning Xin, "Tangdai Dunhuang diqu shuili."

22. Liu Jinbao, *Tang Song zhiji Guiyijun jingjishi*, 7–18.

23. Liu Jinbao, 21–28.

24. See Hua Linfu, "Tang mu kao."

25. P. 3236 + 4528, Liu Jinbao, *Tang Song zhiji Guiyijun jingjishi*, 87.

26. S. 3877, Liu Jinbao, 53.

27. For an example, see S.6062. *Shilu*, 2.28.

28. Liu Jinbao, *Tang Song zhiji Guiyijun jingjishi*, 88.

29. *Ecang*, 10.140. The math of this document is slightly off. By adding the six pieces together, Suo's family owned 50 rather than 48 *mu* (49.5 *mu* of land and 0.5 *mu* of garden).

30. Yang Jiping, "Tangdai chi bu," 41.

31. A small issue that requires a bit clarification here is the pronunciation of the character 石 when it is used as a unit of measurement. There is a common belief that it should be pronounced *dan*. But this is a later development. In the Tang and the Song, the term likely was still pronounced as *shi*. Therefore, I transcribe it as *shi* in this book.

32. Liu Jinbao, *Tang Song zhiji Guiyijun jingjishi*, 179.

33. Liu Jinbao, *Tang Song zhiji Guiyijun jingjishi*, 179–80.

34. Huang Zhengjian, "Dunhuang wenshu," 271.

35. Trombert, "Demise of Silk."

36. See Trombert, *Crédit à Dunhuang*.

37. See the collection of Dunhuang contracts in Sha Zhi's *Dunhuang qiyue wenshu*.

38. S. 3877, *Shilu*, 2.5–6.

39. S. 1285, *Shilu*, 2.9.

40. P. 4083, *Shilu*, 2.37.

41. S. 6341, *Shilu*, 2.40.

42. This rate is found, for example, in S. 3877, S. 3011, S. 6452, S. 1897, S. 5578. See Zheng Binglin, "Wan Tang Wudai Dunhuang maoyi."

43. S. 5509, Zheng Binglin, 30.

44. S. 3877, *Shilu*, 2.47.

45. S. 1946, *Shilu*, 2.49.

46. P. 3150, *Shilu*, 2.51.

47. See P. 2825v, *Shilu*, 2.36; P. 3448v, *Shilu*, 2.39.

48. This description of the "Silk Road" economy is inspired by Paul and Laura Bohannan's conceptualization of the economy of the Tiv people in eastern Nigeria. They show that there were three "spheres of economy" in this society. The first sphere, the subsistence sphere, consisted of everyday necessities, and these goods were bartered in local markets. The second sphere consisted of goods of high prestige that did not circulate on the market. The third sphere consisted of people like women and children who could be exchanged. These spheres of exchange were generally separated from one another. But, occasionally, certain goods like brass rods, which were usually regarded as belonging to the second sphere, could be used in the subsistence sphere. See L. Bohannan and Bohannan, *Tiv of Central Nigeria*; P. Bohannan, "Impact of Money." As Trombert pointed out, the use of silk in ninth- and tenth-century Dunhuang was largely restricted to either gift exchange or contracts drawn prior to a diplomatic trip ("Demise of Silk"). Therefore, we can similarly view the world of diplomacy and gift exchange in Dunhuang as constituting a sphere of economy quite distinct from the daily transactions centered on agriculture. Broadly speaking, the sphere of the diplomatic economy involved silk, while the other sphere did not.

49. P. 3579v, *Shilu*, 2.308.

50. P. 2155v, *Shilu*, 4.401–2.

51. Yang Baoyu and Wu, *Guiyijun zhengquan*, 104–18.

52. S. 2059, Yang Baoyu and Wu, 181–82.

53. P. 2642, *Shilu*, 3.209.

54. P. 2453, *Shilu*, 2.120.

55. See Trombert, *Crédit à Dunhuang*, 150–52.

56. Дх03863, Mie Xiaohong, *Ecang Dunhuang qiyue*, 107.

57. The text is missing here, and only an "8" is left. So the amount of the grain could be 8 *shi*, 18 *shi*, 28 *shi*, or even larger numbers that end with "8."

58. P. 3556-12, *Shilu*, 2.304.

59. P. 2786. I have generally followed the translation of Kumamoto in "Khotanese Official Documents" (128).

60. P. 3458, *Shilu*, 2.119.

61. Luo Tonghua, "Guiyijun qi Dunhuang siyuan," 200.

62. P. 3440, *Shilu*, 4.16–17.

63. The first wedding list is S. 4700 + P. 4121 + P. 4643 (*Shilu*, 4.10–13); the second is P. 3942 (*Shilu*, 4.14–15). The other list is S. 1153 (*Yingcang*, 2.240).

64. Liu Zaicong, "Cong Dunhuang *Rongqin kemu* wenshu," 58.

65. P. 3985, *Shilu*, 4.9.

66. P. 3579, *Shilu*, 4.18.

67. See Hao, *Zhonggu shiqi sheyi yanjiu*; Meng, *Dunhuang minjian jieshe yanjiu*.

68. S. 1475, *Yingcang*, 3.74. A thousand *li* is about five hundred kilometers, which would have included journeys to Dunhuang's closest neighbors, such as Khotan, Turfan, and Ganzhou.

69. P. 2704, *Shilu*, 3.85–88. The Chinese text: "請大眾轉經一七日, 設齋一千五百人供, 度僧尼一七人, 紫盤龍綾襖子壹領, 紅宮錦暖子壹領, 大紫綾半臂壹領, 白獨窠綾袴壹腰. 布壹拾陸疋, 細緤壹疋, 緤壹疋. 右件設齋轉經度僧捨施, 所申意者, 先奉為龍天八部, 調瑞氣於五涼; 梵釋四王, 發祥風於一郡. 當今聖主, 帝業長隆. 三京息戰而投臻, 五府輸誠而向化. 大王受寵, 台星永曜而長春. 功播日新, 福壽共延於海岳. 天公主抱喜, 日陳忠直之謀. 夫人陳歡, 永闡高風之訓. 司空助治, 紹倅職於龍沙. 諸幼郎君, 負良才而奉國. 小娘子姊妹, 恆保寵榮. 合宅宮人, 同霑餘慶. 然後燉煌境內, 千祥並降於王庭; 蓮府域中, 萬瑞咸來而自現. 東朝奉使, 早拜天顏; 于闐使人, 往來無滯. 今日大眾, 親詣道場, 渴仰慈門, 幸希迴向."

70. Zheng Binglin "Wan Tang Wudai Dunhuang diqu renkou."

71. *Shilu*, 3.85.

72. This is suggested by Rong and Zhu in *Yutian yu Dunhuang* (154).

73. P. 3750. See Wang Shizhen, "Liangjian Dunhuang shuzha qianshi."

74. This observation is made by Wang Shizhen in "Dunhuang yishu," (195).

75. P. 4518-28, *Shilu*, 4.8.

76. "C'est même la seule rason qui soit donnée de manière explicite dans les contrats" (Trombert, *Crédit à Dunhuang*, 103).

77. S. 4445, *Shilu*, 2.118. See Trombert, *Crédit à Dunhuang*, 106.

## Chapter 9

1. Cai Tao, *Tieweishan congtan*, 3. Cai also recorded the story about the funny Khotanese diplomatic message that I discussed at the beginning of chapter 7.

2. For the unique importance of the precedence of the first emperors in the history of the Northern Song, see Deng Xiaonan's *Zuzong zhifa*.

3. Laufer, *Jade*, 24; J. Lin, "Khotan Jades."

4. Huizong's use of jade objects likely also has something to do with his Daoist beliefs. See Ebrey, *Emperor Huizong*, 281–82.

5. For a comparative case in the Mongol Empire, see Arnold's *Princely Gifts*.

6. Shang and Cheng, "Tang Daying ku yu Qionglin ku."

7. Ge Chengyong, *Tangdai guoku zhidu*.

8. Lu Zhi, *Lu Zhi Ji*, 14.421.

9. Ge Chengyong, *Tangdai guoku zhidu*, 141.

10. Dong, *Quan Tangwen*, 45.496.

11. B. Wang, "Tang Tax Textiles." For a succinct summary of the role of silk and other textiles in the Tang taxation and economy, see Chen Bu-Yun's *Empire of Silk* (15–45).

12. The fact that gold- and silverware were stored in the Qionglin treasury is made clear from an edict in 866. See Song, *Tang dazhaoling ji*, 86.489.

13. The name of the treasury shows the legacy of the Tang local administration, as the Dunhuang government was modeled on that of a Tang military garrison.

14. Feng Peihong, "Tang Wudai Guiyijun junziku chutan."

15. P. 4061v, *Shilu*, 3.617. This request was made in the twelfth intercalary month in a Renwu year (922 or 982), in the dead of winter—like the Khotanese envoys I discussed earlier (chapter 3), the Tatar envoys also requested new winter clothes from the lord of Dunhuang.

16. Feng Peihong, "Kesi."

17. Ouyang and Song, *Xin Tangshu*, 221a.6236. The text: "初, 德宗即位, 遣內給事朱如玉之安西, 求玉於于闐, 得圭一, 珂佩五, 枕一, 帶胯三百, 簪四十, 奩三十, 釧十, 杵三, 瑟瑟百斤, 並它寶等. 及還, 詐言假道回紇為所奪. 久之事泄, 得所市, 流死恩州."

18. Wang Qinruo, *Cefu yuangui*, 168.1868. The text: "朕所重惟穀, 所寶惟賢. 不作無益之費, 不貴遠方之物. 故錦繡珠玉, 焚於殿庭; 車渠瑪瑙, 總賜蕃國."

19. Torbert, *Ch'ing Imperial Household Department*, 122.

20. Bayly, "'Archaic' and 'Modern' Globalization," 51.

21. Zhao Feng and Wang, *Dunhuang sichou*, 184–85.

22. See the four prayer texts copied on P. 2704 (*Shilu*, 3.85–88). I discuss these texts in detail in chapter 10.

23. For the connection between these two sets of documents, see Hao, *Tang houqi*, 289.

24. P. 2638, *Shilu*, 3.391–95.

25. See Rong and Zhu, *Yutian yu Dunhuang*, ch. 7.

26. Ouyang and Song, *Xin Tangshu*, 221b.6261.

27. Khotanese jade, for instance, even decorated the emperor's tomb. See Tuotuo, *Songshi*, 122.2848–49.

28. Schafer, *Golden Peaches of Samarkand*, 74.

29. Schafer, 89–90.

30. Xu Song, *Song huiyao jigao*, fanyi 7.9950. "Tears of the wutong tree" should be the same as "tears of the hutong tree" (see below).

31. Schafer, *Golden Peaches of Samarkand*, 170–71.

32. This type of cloth was even used in the Kucha kingdom as a medium of exchange. See Tuotuo, *Songshi*, 490.14123.

33. See Ouyang and Song, *Xin Tangshu*, 40.1045. Earlier records of "the tears of the hutong tree" indicate that they were from Loulan. See Yan Shigu's note in Ban's *Hanshu* (96a.3876).

34. This note was added by Ouyang as a commentary to a poem. The relevant line of the poem reads "my sick bones, withering, are conveniently warmed by pistil-patterned [cloth] [病骨瘦便花蕊暖]" (*Ouyang Xiu quanji*, 14.237).

35. For descriptions of the "jade chariot" of the emperors, see Ouyang and Song's *Xin Tangshu* (24.511) and Tuotuo et al.'s *Songshi* (149.3479).

36. See Deng Shupin, "Tang Song yuce."

37. Liu Xu, *Jiu Tangshu*, 45.1937; Ouyang and Song, *Xin Tangshu*, 24.529.

38. Tuotuo, *Songshi*, 143.3378. The text: "儀衛志: 金銅甲二人, 兜鍪, 甲衫, 錦臂衣, 執金銅鉞斧."

39. Xiao, *Dai Tō kaigenrei*, 4.38–44. See also Wechler, *Offerings of Jade and Silk*, 118–20.

40. Zhang Shinan, *Youhuan jiwen*, 5.46. The text: "國朝禮器, 及乘輿服御, 多是于闐玉."

41. Tuotuo, *Songshi*, 490.14107–8.

42. Rong and Zhu, *Yutian yu Dunhuang*, 200.

43. Tuotuo, *Songshi*, 490.14114.

44. Neimonggu wenwu kaogu yanjiusuo, "Liao Chenguo gongzhu."

45. See, for instance, the record in Ye's *Qidan guozhi* (21.230). See Hansen, "International Gifting," 293–99.

46. Tuotuo, *Liaoshi*, 14.541. The *Liaoshi* misrecords the name of the king as "Cao Shou." I use "Tajik" to translate the term *Dashi* (大食), which generally denoted the Muslim state based in Arabia in Chinese sources. It is possible that this particular "Tajik" could mean other Muslim states in Central Asia. See Duturaeva, *Qarakhanid Roads to China*, 50–55.

47. Zhao Feng and Wang, *Dunhuang sichou*, 183–203.

48. Wang Qinruo et al., *Cefu yuangui*, 46.501. The text: "朕嘗聞, 前時內庫有兩領錦褾子, 其上飾以金鳥."

49. P. 2704. See Zhao Feng and Wang, *Dunhuang sichou*, 189.

50. Purple was a recognizably royal color. Reinhold, *History of Purple*.

51. See Dunhuang yanjiuyuan, *Yulin ku*, 84–85.

52. Guoli Gugong bowuguan, *Gugong shuhua lu*, 4.13–14, 23.

53. See the description of the dress of emperors in Tuotuo's *Songshi* (151.3530).

54. See Tuotuo, 490.14108.

55. For the image of Lady Zhai, I have referred to the line reproduction made by the famous painter Zhang Daqian, which shows details not easily discernable in direct reproductions of the mural painting.

56. For the Uyghur donors, see Russell-Smith's *Uygur Patronage in Dunhuang* (25).

57. See Sha Wutian, "Wudai Song Dunhuang," 79. Sha identifies the non-Han style of Cao Yanlu's dress, but attributes it to his supposed Sogdian origin. But according to this logic, shouldn't Cao Yuanzhong just to the left be dressed in like manner? I see this image as a conscious attempt to dress in a way that departed from Han male expectations, in order to elevate Cao Yanlu above the Han commoners his family ruled over.

58. Dunhuang yanjiuyuan, *Dunhuang Mogaoku gongyangren tiji*, 219.

59. Q. Ning, "Imperial Portraiture."

60. Li Tao, *Xu zizhi tongjian*, 71.1598. Another similar conversation between Khotanese envoys and Emperor Shenzong in 1083 is at 335.8061.

61. Tuotuo, *Songshi*, 490.14109.

62. Tackett, *Origins of the Chinese Nation*, 246–75.

63. S. 2589, *Shilu*, 4.485–86. See my translation of the text in the appendix of Sims-Williams and Hamilton's *Turco-Sogdian Documents* (97–98).

64. See my discussion of this text in chapter 2.

65. Hu Yaofei, "Guanyu Huang Chao zhisi."

66. P. 2696. The title of the text is: "唐僖宗中和五年三月車駕還京師大赦詔書." See *Shilu*, 4.263–67.

67. For a transcription of these texts, see *Shilu* (4.337–53).

68. See Wu Liyu, *Tangli zhiyi*, 151–56.

69. For a biographical account, see Xue's *Jiu Wudai shi* (108.1419–22).

70. Xue, 108.1420–21.

71. Shi Pingting, *Dunhuang yishu zongmu*, 139; *Shilu*, 4.337–53.

72. Papers from this period generally are rectangular in shape, about 25–30 centimeters high and 35–45 centimeters wide. See Drège, "Papiers de Dunhuang."

73. This process has already been pointed out by Wang Shizhen in "Dunhuang yishu" (103).

74. L. Yang, "'Posthumous Letter.'"

75. Bailey, "Śrī Viśa' Śūra," 19. I have revised Bailey's translation.

76. P. 2992v-3, *Shilu*, 4.395.

77. P. 2786. Skjærvø, "Perils of Ambassadors."

78. For placement on the leading horse, see the case of the Khotanese envoys discussed in chapter 3. For storage in specially designated houses, see the case of Turfan discussed in chapter 1.

79. Good examples include the Shu kingdom in Sichuan and the Southern Han kingdom in Guangzhou. See Kurz, "Problematische Zeiten."

80. This sequence of events is expertly elucidated in Yang Baoyu and Wu in *Guiyijun zhengquan* (42–58).

81. Wen, "Emperor of Dunhuang," 44.

82. The standard treatment of this subject is Gu's "Wude zhongshishuo." See also Chan, *Legitimation in Imperial China*.

83. See Yu Xin, "Furui yu difang zhengquan," 349–56.

84. P. 2594 + P. 2864. This poem is transcribed in Yan Tingliang's "*Baiquege* xinjiao bing xu."

85. In "Problematische Zeiten," Johannes Kurz already noticed the similarities between Former Shu and Southern Han, and their difference from the other "Ten Kingdoms." He called these two states empires (*Kaiserreiche*). I would add Dunhuang to this list and point out that there are important differences between this type of local empire and other empires in the core areas of early Chinese empires.

86. Bailey, "Staël-Holstein Miscellany," 2–3; *Indo-Scythian Studies*, 123.

87. Lions appear frequently, either accompanying the king or serving as his throne, in Kushan arts. See Verardi, "Kuṣāṇa Emperors."

88. The Khotanese reads: "theyna tcūnä sūhye bāḍi pūhye kṣuāṇä pasa sälya ttaujjrä māṣṭä hāḍūsạmye haḍai nadạva kūṣḍvī āṇä dā rāysạnāṃdi baudhasạttu vīśa' śūrä caiga rāṃdānä rrādi."

Skjærvø, *Khotanese Manuscripts*, 551–53. This text (IOL Khot. S 47) is a Buddhist Vajrayāna text composed by Zhang Jinshan, the envoy we met in chapter 2. The quoted section comes at the end of the text, as a way of dating.

89. The story might give the false impression of a clear development from Viśa' Saṃbhava's claim to Viśa' Śūra's claim. But it is important to note that since I am dealing with a fairly small number of texts, and these texts are in no way comprehensive in their coverage of the self-image of the kingdom of Khotan, it could very well be the case that Viśa' Saṃbhava already claimed to be the "king of kings of China" but did not leave any documents in Dunhuang that explicitly state this. Judging from the extant documents from him, it is indeed more likely than not that he would have made such a claim.

90. P. 2826, *Facang*, 19.9. For a study of this and other Khotanese seals, see Akagi's "Six 10th Century Royal Seals."

91. Chen Sanping, "Son of Heaven."

92. See Wen, "King of Kings of China."

93. See P. 2786, Kumamoto, "Khotanese Official Documents," 92.

94. So, *Tang Song fazhishi yanjiu*, 1–38. See also Li Quande, *Tang Song biangeqi shumiyuan yanjiu*.

95. P. 4065. For a transcription of the text, see Rong and Zhu's *Yutian yu Dunhuang* (332–33).

96. Russell-Smith, "Wives and Patrons," 409.

97. Shao, "Dunhuang Cao Yijin di 98 ku yanjiu," 1–2.

98. Dunhuang yanjiuyuan, *Dunhuang shiku neirong zonglu*, 38.

99. These relations are described in detail in Feng Peihong's *Dunhuang de Guiyijun shidai* (309–23, 333–49).

100. It is important to note that these paintings in the cave were not all created at the same time. The portraits of the king and the queen of Khotan were repainted between the late 930s and early 940s, likely over a portrait of the Uyghur khan. So visitors who viewed the cave when it was first built in the 920s would have seen a different foreign sovereign than did later visitors. But the visibility of diplomacy in Cao Yijin's display of power remained constant. For the repainting of the cave, see Dunhuang yanjiuyuan's *Dunhuang Mogaoku gongyangren tiji* (219).

101. P. 3781. See Zheng Yinan and Zheng, "Dunhuang Caoshi Guiyijun shiqi xugongdeji," 2–3.

102. One might even compare these cases to what Jonathan Skaff (following Pamela Crossley) has termed "simultaneous kingship." See Skaff, "Ideological Interweaving."

103. Bayly, "'Archaic' and 'Modern' Globalization," 52.

104. Brown, "Silk Road," 20.

# Chapter 10

1. The biographical accounts are collected in Jiang Boqin, Xiang, and Rong's *Dunhuang miaozhenzan*.

2. See *Shilu*, 4.307–415.

3. See Huang Zheng and Wu, *Dunhuang yuanwen ji*.

4. See the documents I translated in Sims-Williams and Hamilton's *Turco-Sogdian Documents* (97–101).

5. Rong, *Guiyijun shi yanjiu*, 214–30. Here, I use the term "emperor" to translate *huangdi* in the context of Dunhuang with full awareness of the irony, and of the fact that one can claim to be an emperor without one's state being in any way imperial. For a fuller discussion, see my "Emperor of Dunhuang."

6. For a history of the "Five Liangs": Qi Chenjun, Lu, and Guo, *Wuliang shilue*.

7. "繼五涼之中興, 擁八州之勝地": Yan Tingliang, "*Baiquege* xinjiao bing xu," 63.

8. "打却甘州坐五涼": Yan Tingliang, "*Longquan shenjiange*," 109.

9. See Wen, "Emperor of Dunhuang."

10. P. 3633v. For an edition of the text, see Yan Tingliang's "*Shazhou baixing yiwanren*." See also *Shilu*, 4.377–80.

11. *Shilu*, 4.377. The text reads: "至大中三年, 本使太保, 起燉煌甲□, □卻吐蕃, 再有收復.... 子孫便鎮西門, 已至今□. 中間遇天可汗居住張掖, 事同一家, 更無貳心. 東路開通, 天使不絕."

12. The text reads: "天子一時間懍々發心, 百姓都來未肯."

13. Rong, "Cao Yijin zheng Ganzhou Huihu."

14. See S. 5448, Jiang Boqin, Xiang, and Rong, *Dunhuang miaozhenzan*, 246.

15. See chapter 2 for his career as an envoy.

16. P. 3270, Huang Zheng and Wu, *Dunhuang yuanwen ji*, 951. For this genre of poem, see Eliasberg's "Expression *eul-lang wei*."

17. See Ren Wei, "Dunhuang nuo wenhua."

18. Huang Zheng and Wu, *Dunhuang yuanwen ji*, 952. The text: "河西是漢家舊地, 中臨獫狁安居. 數年閉塞東路, 恰似小水之魚."

19. On the issue of the alleged Han identity in Dunhuang, see S. Yang, "'Stubbornly Chinese?'"

20. Huang Zheng and Wu, *Dunhuang yuanwen ji*, 952. The text: "今遇明王利化, 再開河隴道衢. 太保神威發憤, 遂便點緝兵衣."

21. Huang Zheng and Wu, 952. The text: "已後勿愁東路, 便是舜日堯時. 內使新降西塞, 天子慰曲名師. 向西直至于闐, 納貢獻玉琉璃."

22. S. 5139v, Rong, "Cao Yijin zheng Ganzhou Huihu," 9. The Chinese text: "河西道路安泰."

23. See Hamilton, *Ouïghours*.

24. S. 5139v. The text: "開以河西老道."

25. For Yin Shanxiong's portrait elegy: P. 2970, Jiang Boqin, Xiang, and Rong, *Dunhuang miaozhenzan*, 301–3. For that of Hun Ziying: S. 5448, Jiang Boqin, Xiang, and Rong, 245–46.

26. P. 3718-1, Jiang Boqin, Xiang, and Rong, 250.

27. For this group and its connection to the Wenmo and other Tibetan descendants, see Lu Li's "Guanyu Dunhuang.'"

28. See the chapter "The looting from Nanshan on the Guiyijun" in Feng Peihong's *Dunhuang de Guiyijun shidai* (364–77).

29. P. 3718-1, Jiang Boqin, Xiang, and Rong, *Dunhuang miaozhenzan*, 250.

30. P. 4525-12v, *Facang*, 31.372.

31. P. 3257, *Shilu*, 2.295.

32. P. 3835v, *Facang*, 28.308–9. This document was cut into thin slices.

33. S. 5750v (*Yingcang*, 9.116) and S. 2578 (*Yingcang*, 4.103).

34. See Feng Peihong, *Dunhuang de Guiyijun shidai*, 267–391.

35. For this incident, See Yang Baoyu and Wu's *Guiyijun zhengquan* (133–45). There are many different attempts to interpret this incident, and I find Yang and Wu's reading of the sequence of events most plausible. However, they might be a bit contrarian in alleging that Liang died of natural causes and was not murdered. On this point, I follow the conventional wisdom.

36. P. 3718-12, Jiang Boqin, Xiang, and Rong, *Dunhuang miaozhenzan*, 285–86.

37. P. 2992v-1, *Shilu*, 4.391–92. The text: "衆宰相念以兩地社稷無二, 途路一家, 人使到日, 允許西迴, 即是恩幸. 伏且朝庭路次甘州, 兩地豈不是此件行使, 久後亦要往來? 其天使般次, 希垂放過西來. 近見遠聞, 豈不是痛熱之名? 幸矣! 今遣釋門僧政慶福, 都頭王通信等一行, 結歡通好. 衆宰相各附白花綿綾壹拾疋, 白㲲壹疋, 以充父大王留念. 到日檢領. 況衆宰相先以(與)大王結爲父子之分, 今者縱然大王奄世, 痛熱情義, 不可斷絶. 善容申可汗天子, 所有世界之事, 並令允就, 即是衆宰相周旋之力, 不宣謹狀." The text we have now is not the original document, but a later copy.

38. For this incident, see Yang Baoyu and Wu's *Guiyijun zhengquan* (104–18).

39. P. 3016v, Yang Baoyu and Wu, 106. The text: "此為小瑕, 不可斷于萬年之道路. 死者已歿, 難再復生, 昆季交通, 千載莫絕."

40. For a thorough study of this letter and related documents, see Kumamoto's "Khotanese Official Documents."

41. The text: "pātca ttä cvāväja māśtä draisamyai haḍai tcyauvä ammäga āstamna haḍa tsvāmda pajsä : ttakyau gauśtä jsä hā kamącū vāṣṭä pīḍaką hajsāda ḍīkau tta tta sä : ca magāra ạmanā ttura[~ ttara]-u pā ạ na kūśū na pvaisūm khvai śaikä bāḍa kṣamīyai cai ttä būnā hvạṇḍä īdai be'śqvä vāṣṭä paśą śau ttä sä na a'haijä : ttī jsä caiga-kṣīrāṣṭä padä prrahājä" (Kumamoto, 81, 122–23).

42. Rong, "Ganzhou Huihu yu Caoshi Guiyijun," 69–70.

43. Rong, 70.

44. P. 3272, *Shilu*, 4.411.

45. Pelliot tibétain 1189r. The text: "yar sha cab phyogs su di ring phan cad // rta mgo myi bstan sgra myi rgyug par bgyis // gang zhig rkog nas song 'am / snga rgyugs byas te rta sga bstad de / sha cu phyogs jag byi pa yod na / bu byas na pha bsad par bgyis // nu bo song na pho bo bsad par bgyis //" For this document, see Ren Xiaobo's "Tang Song zhiji Hexi diqu."

46. See Forte, *Political Propaganda and Ideology*.

47. Robert Hymes suggested that this phrase can be read as similar to the expression "don't show your face around here," which seems likely to me.

48. P. 3931, Zhao Heping, *Dunhuang biao zhuang*, 228–65.

49. For a comprehensive study of this manuscript, see Yang Baoyu and Wu's *Guiyijun zhengquan* (220–99).

50. Yang Baoyu and Wu, *Guiyijun zhengquan*, 245.

51. *Analects*, 13.7.

52. P. 2992-1, *Shilu*, 4.391. The text: "社稷無二, 途路一家."

53. P. 2155v, *Shilu*, 4.402. The text: "道途開泰, 共保一家."

54. P. 3931-16, Zhao Heping, *Dunhuang biao zhuang*, 240. The text: "道路雖遙於千里, 恩知豈異於一家?"

55. These texts are among the very rare examples of printed texts in the Dunhuang collection. The earliest printed text from Dunhuang is the famous 868 Diamond Sutra. But not many more

prints followed this glorious early example. The other sporadic cases of printing in Dunhuang all date to the tenth century, and are most likely imported from elsewhere, in particular the Sichuan region. Cao Yuanzhong is the only local ruler known to have made extensive use of printing.

56. Shu Xue, "Dunhuang hanwen yishu," 281–85.

57. Teiser, *Ghost Festival*, 4.

58. P. 4514-1. See the copies reprinted in *Facang*, 31.228–31. The text: "國安人泰, 社稷恆昌, 道路和平, 普天安樂."

59. P. 4514-4. See the copies reprinted in *Facang*, 31.244–46. The text: "城隍安泰, 闔郡康寧, 東西之道路開通, 南北之凶渠順化."

60. Dorothy Wong connects these two prints to the mural painting of Mount Wutai in Cave 61 of Dunhuang: "In the mural the two figures closest to the Central Peak and leading the heavenly assembly are Avalokiteśvara and Vaiśravaṇa. The prints therefore confirm the political meaning that the mural represented for Cao" (Wong, *"Representation of Mt. Wutai,"* 41).

61. BD 06412 v1, Huang Zheng and Wu, *Dunhuang yuanwen ji*, 275. The text: "亦願觀音引路, 萬里無危; 四大天王, 雙雙圍繞; 人馬平善, 早達天庭; 舞喜階前, □願滿足; 四路奉使, 往來不滯於關山."

62. P. 2341, Huang Zheng and Wu, 661. The text: "今為王事, 欲涉長途. 道路懸遠, 關山峻阻. 欲祈告達, 仰托三尊, 敬捨珍財, 應保清通. 惟願伐折羅大將引道, 所向皆通; 毗沙門天王密扶, 往來安泰." The Three Worthies can mean any number of combinations of a Buddha and two Bodhisattvas.

63. P. 2704, *Shilu*, 3.85–88. The text: "東朝奉使, 早拜天顏; 于闐使人, 往來無滯."

64. P. 2812, *Facang*, 18.350. The text: "一行長幼, 沿路□泰而無危; 兩國通流, 平善早臨於桑梓."

65. S. 4536, Huang Zheng and Wu, *Dunhuang yuanwen ji*, 312–12. The text: "道路開泰, 五穀豐盈; 四路伏首, 八表傾心; 東西路泰, 使人不滯於關山."

66. P. 3564. See Zheng Binglin and Liang, *"Liang Xingde miaozhenzan."*

67. The reference to Vaiśravaṇa in the prayer text makes it clear that the original plan included Vaiśravaṇa and Nāga kings. But the former must have been painted over in later reconstructions.

68. S. 4601. See Ikeda, *Chūgoku kodai shahon shikigo*, 528.

69. The text: "國安人泰, 社稷恆昌; 四路通和, 八方歸伏."

70. Cf. the text on the print: "國安人泰, 社稷恆昌, 道路和平, 普天安樂."

71. Huang Zheng and Wu, *Dunhuang yuanwen ji*, 372. The text: "城隍安泰, 道路無危."

72. There are two copies of this text, P. 3935 and BD 14925. Huang Zheng and Wu, *Dunhuang yuanwen ji*, 848. This text dates to a much earlier period.

73. P. 3500. See Rong, "Cao Yijin zheng Ganzhou Huihu," 10–11.

74. Junping Liu and Huang, "Evolution of Tianxia Cosmology."

75. The meaning of the line about being sturdy without falling is not entirely clear to me. Tentatively, I think it is referring to the physical health of these royal members of Cao Yijin's family.

76. Chen Sanping, *Multicultural China*, 103.

77. See my discussion of this poem in chapter 8.

78. According to Hou Xudong's calculation, the most common non-Buddhist themes covered in these prayers are the fortunes of the state and the longevity of the emperor (151 cases).

Next most popular are wishes to "gain fortune" (得福; 64 cases), live a long life (62), maintain stability (42), have peace for all under heaven (58), have personal peace (30), be promoted quickly (17), have good health (23), be freed from disease (14), have numerous sons and grandsons (12), gain intelligence (9), come into wealth (9), and to have good luck (8). See Hou, *Wuliu shiji beifang minzhong*, 211–17.

79. For instance, the Zhang family, still considering themselves Han Chinese, saw the Uyghurs in Ganzhou as barbarians not worthy of diplomatic friendship. The fictive family ties formed over the shared road in the tenth century under the Cao family were not evident in Dunhuang under the Zhang family.

## Conclusion

1. P. 3270, *Facang*, 22.333 (facsimile); Huang Zheng and Wu, *Dunhuang yuanwen ji*, 951 (transcription).

2. See Bell, "This Is what Happens."

3. Xinru Liu, *Silk Road in World History*.

4. For example, I have noticed that papers from Khotan tend to be wider than papers produced locally in Dunhuang. But how many more manuscripts were produced outside of Dunhuang? This is a question that nobody can answer with any certainty now. A comprehensive examination of the Dunhuang manuscripts of extraneous origin, which should include not only the study of the texts but also the microscopic analysis of paper, ink, and mounting materials, would lead to a more nuanced appreciation of the nature of the Dunhuang manuscript collection.

5. See Zeder et al., "Documenting Domestication"; Kuzmina, *Prehistory of the Silk Road*.

6. In the Belitung shipwreck, dated to around 830, there were sixty thousand pieces of porcelain, which has a much lower value/weight ratio than aromatics or silk, whereas records of contemporary travelers on land-based roads never mention them carrying porcelain. See Chong and Murphy, *Tang Shipwreck*.

7. A shipwreck from the Goryeo period (918–1392) off the Korean coast contains, in addition to porcelain vessels, several different kinds of grain in large quantity. See M. Kim and Moon, "Tracking 800-Year-Old Shipments." In the Mediterranean world, grain, wine, and pottery were also common cargos on ships. See Horden and Purcell, *Corrupting Sea*, 368–72. None of these things, one should note, was prominent in the human-thing symbiosis I describe in this book.

8. Schivelbusch, *Railway Journey*.

9. Beckwith, *Empires of the Silk Road*; Frankopan, *Silk Roads*.

10. See my explanation of the terms used in chapter 2 (for "envoys") and chapter 6 (for "gifts").

11. S. 1475, *Yingcang*, 3.74.

12. Xinru Liu, *Silk Road in World History*, 1–19.

13. Ibn Faḍlān, *Journey to Russia*.

14. Meng, "Qu Wendai yu Xuanzang."

15. Vogel, *Marco Polo* Was in China, 80–84. See also Guzman, "European Clerical Envoys."

16. Jidong Yang, "Transportation, Boarding, Lodging," 426.

17. See the study of this document in Rong's "Rouran Qaghanate."

18. A recent volume of *Cambridge World History* that deals with the world between 500 and 1500 sees courtly cultures as important forms of "Eurasian commonalities." See Geary et al., "Courtly Cultures."

19. Marshak, "Programme iconographique"; Grenet, "What Was the Afrasiab Painting." For an interactive reconstruction of the paintings, see Markus Mode's website "Court Art of Sogdian Samarqand in the 7th Century AD" (Seminar für Orientalische Archäologie und Kunstgeschichte, Universität Halle, May 7, 2002, http://www.orientarch.uni-halle.de/ca/afras/index .htm).

20. Works in this area are too many to list. See, e.g., Mintz, *Sweetness and Power*; Beckert, *Empire of Cotton*.

21. Brown, "Silk Road," 20.

22. La Vaissière, *Sogdian Traders*, 43–70.

23. See those discussed in Skaff, "Sogdian Trade Diaspora."

24. For instance, the contract (S. 4445) where a resident of Dunhuang, He Yuande, possibly of Sogdian descent judging by his surname, borrowed cotton cloth for "doing business [*maimai* 買賣]" in the Southern Mountains. See *Shilu*, 2.118.

25. For a definition of the Silk Road as a "network of transcontinental commercial routes," see Boulnois's *Silk Road* (16). Most popular works and many scholarly ones, sometimes implicitly, follow this definition.

26. I will offer one example to show the willingness to read commerce into very thin evidence. In 1959, construction workers building a dam near a village to the west of Hohhot in Inner Mongolia discovered a corpse wearing a golden plaque (21 cm long) and two well-preserved gold finger rings with jewels. Near the corpse archaeologists also recovered toothpicks, a scabbard, bronze rings, silver cups, and one golden coin of Leo I (457–74). Because this corpse was not found in a coffin, the original archaeological report makes a claim that the dead man "might have been a merchant from a caravan who died suddenly on the road and was roughly buried" (Neimenggu Wenwu Gongzuodui and Neimenggu Bowuguan, "Huhehaote shi fujin chutu de waiguo jinyinbi," 183). According to this claim, we are expected to imagine a scenario in which a merchant from a caravan was wearing the goods that he was supposedly trading, died suddenly while traveling on the road, and was buried by his companions still wearing the gold plaque and rings and carrying the gold coin. There are a few problems with this scenario. First, gold and silver objects such as rings and coins were never the mainstay of commerce on the Silk Road. But even were we to accept these goods as commodities, why would a merchant be *wearing* them while traveling to sell them? And after this supposed sudden death, why would the companions bury this merchant with these luxury goods? Each step of this story, frankly speaking, defies credibility. To me, a much more likely scenario is that the person was buried, just as many medieval elites in North China were, with gold and silver burial goods, and the tomb was disrupted later, either by robbers or by the very same construction workers who made the discovery.

Nonetheless, this discovery has been picked up by many scholars as evidence of commerce on the Silk Road. Samuel Lieu summarizes the discovery in this way: "The body of one such itinerant trader who died of natural causes while travelling through Inner Mongolia was not even buried, showing that he had no travelling companion" (*Manichaeism*, 222). Perhaps sensing that it was improbable for his supposed caravan companions to leave the dead man with all his luxuries, Lieu suggests that he was in fact traveling by himself, and apparently perished while still wearing a gold plaque and rings and holding silver cups. In his retelling, it is already taken for granted that the dead man was a "trader." Following Lieu, Étienne de la Vaissière, in his study of Sogdian traders, describes the corpse as the "abandoned body of a merchant," and suggests that "this merchant was traveling by himself and died alone, without being robbed" (*Sogdian Traders*, 207). Importantly, he also suggests the possibility that the dead man was not only a merchant but a *Sogdian* merchant on the basis of the coin and luxury goods. Yoshida Yutaka, in his recent entry "The Sogdian Merchant Network" in the *Oxford Research Encyclopedia*, goes one step further and argues that "another route reaching Mongolia from China started from Taiyuan via modern Huhehot. That Sogdians also followed this route is inferred from what seems to have been left by a Sogdian peddler who lost his way and died alone with precious merchandise including silver cups and a Byzantine gold coin of Leo (r. 457–474)." Here, the suggestion of Étienne de la Vaissière is presented as a fact ("Sogdian peddler"), and a starting point (Taiyuan) and end point (Mongolia) of a route followed by Sogdians (plural!) are given. In this way, after an academic relay, a fifth-century branch of the Sogdian merchant network from Taiyuan to Mongolia is reconstructed.

We have to accept several improbable assumptions, one predicating on another, before we can arrive at the suggestion of a route on the Sogdian merchant network. I have devoted some space to following this chain of argument because it is a good example, and far from the only one, of scholars' eagerness to read Silk Road commerce in general—and Sogdian people in particular—into places where, to me at least, the evidence is not strong enough to support it.

27. For a criticism of the uncritical invocation of trade as a way of explaining connection in a different context, see Grierson's "Commerce in the Dark Ages." I thank Patrick Geary for pointing this source out to me.

28. Lattimore, *Pivot of Asia*, 171.

29. For a recent claim of merchants "pretending" to be diplomatic travelers, see Li Yun's "Wan Tang gongci de gouzao."

30. The story scholars often cite to prove this point is from *Hanshu* (96a.3886), where envoys from Jibin (modern Kashmir) were described as "lowly merchants" who were trying to conduct commerce but came claiming to offer tributes. It is important to note, however, that this story comes from the petition of a Han dynasty official who had a clear agenda of denigrating the king of Jibin by discrediting his envoys. It is not surprising, and should not be taken at face value, that he accused them of "really" being merchants of low status.

31. These letters talk about making "profit," something that is absent from the rhetoric of diplomatic documents. They also show a network of postal and personnel exchange that exclusively served Sogdian merchants (La Vaissière, *Sogdian Traders*, 47). When in distress, they did not seek help from the local government but wrote to distant relatives and other Sogdian people. Unlike the diplomatic network I describe in this book, the Sogdian merchant network was largely based on family connections. The material exchange found in these letters was also of a commercial nature, and distinct from the gift exchange discussed in chapter 6. See, in particular, Sims-Williams, "Sogdian Ancient Letters II."

32. Pei Chengguo, in his meticulous study of Turfan's economy from the fifth to the early seventh century, comments on the Turfan government's provision of food to travelers: "unlike envoys who figure in the provisioning records discussed above, these Sogdian merchants do

not appear in such records. They were private caravanners, not official emissaries, and thus presumably had to arrange accommodation at their own expense" ("Silk Road," 52). Unlike Dunhuang in the ninth and tenth centuries, we have ample evidence of the existence of Sogdian merchants in Turfan in this earlier period. Yet, the provisions of the Turfan government, like those of the Dunhuang government discussed in this book, were reserved for envoys and excluded private Sogdian merchants.

33. An additional objection: to suggest that many of the envoys we observe in our sources were "in fact" merchants pretending to be envoys is to assume a level of gullibility on the part of the receiving governments that is hard to believe, and in any case not supported by enough evidence.

34. Curtin, *Cross-Cultural Trade*, 105. This view finds support with other global historians. For instance, Janet Abu-Lughod talks about reduced overland connections in the post–Tang-Abbasid period: "Restoration of the land route during the period of Islamic hegemony was continuously threatened by the northern tribes, against whom the Great Wall had originally been built. (These threats were not eliminated until Genghis Khan conquered northern China in the opening decades of the thirteenth century.) Intermittently denied access across the steppes, China was of necessity drawn more to the sea" (*Before European Hegemony*, 303–4).

35. Bentley, "Cross-Cultural Interaction."

36. James Millward, for instance, argues that "the eras of the most intense silk-road communications were those when not only the sedentary states of the Eurasian rim but also the nomadic confederations on the Eurasian steppe were relatively centralized. Centralized states and confederations promoted trade and diplomacy, and invested in communications and economic infrastructure (secure roads, water depots, inns, reliable coinage, standard weights and measures). They assessed taxes and tributes from travelers and subjects, but it was easier and safer to pay a few larger powers for safe passage than to risk a shakedown or worse from numerous bandit gangs along the way" (*Silk Road*, 20).

37. For this leg of Xuanzang's trip, see Huili and Yancong's *Daci'ensi sanzang fashi* (11–29).

38. This book is focused on the ninth and tenth centuries. But, as Dilnoza Duturaeva convincingly demonstrated in a work that makes extensive use of Chinese and Islamic sources, the diplomatic connection between China and Central Asia continued to flourish in the eleventh and twelfth centuries. See *Qarakhanid Roads to China*.

39. Wen, "Emperor of Dunhuang," 46–50.

40. Rong, *Guiyijun shi yanjiu*, 103–7, 121–22, 126–27.

41. I describe this network of diplomatic marriages in detail in my dissertation: "Kingly Exchange," 127–35.

42. For the unidirectionality of *heqin* marriages in the Tang, see Skaff's *Sui-Tang China* (238–39). Skaff calls this a "one way traffic in brides" (238). See also Pan, "Marriage Alliances."

43. P. 3016, Rong and Zhu, *Yutian yu Dunhuang*, 130–31.

44. P. 2992v, *Shilu*, 4.395.

45. Uray, "New Contributions," 520–21.

46. For the classic description of the tributary system, see Fairbank's *Chinese World Order* (1–19). It is important to note that, unlike the way certain scholarship has characterized him, Fairbank in fact did not paint a picture of an unchanging system of diplomacy with China at the

center, but saw the "order" as flexible. Many of the articles included in that volume already demonstrate such flexibility.

47. In this sense, Perdue's criticism of the tributary system of the late imperial period largely applies here too. See Perdue, "Tenacious Tributary System."

48. Skaff, *Sui-Tang China*, 7.

49. An important example is the widely shared belief that the world was ruled by four "great kings." See Pelliot, "Quatre Fils du Ciel"; see also Canepa, "Distant Displays of Power."

50. My thinking is inspired by, but differs from that of, Robert I. Moore, who sees intensification of various types as the defining feature of a possible global Middle Ages ("Global Middle Ages?"). See also the report of an Oxford-led initiative—Holmes and Standen, "Defining the Global Middle Ages." For efforts to find more direct connections, see Hansen's *Year 1000*.

51. Kang, *East Asia*.

52. Minorsky, *Marvazī on China*, 20.

53. Neumann, "To Be a Diplomat"; J. Watkins, "Toward a New Diplomatic History"; Harrison, *Perils of Interpreting*.

54. For a comparable case of Northern Song envoys to the Liao and their policy and intellectual impacts on the Song court, see Tackett's *Origins of the Chinese Nation* (31–73). For a later case that mirrors many of the issues I discuss in chapter 7, see Harrison's *Perils of Interpreting*.

55. See Ge Zhaoguang, *Xiangxiang yiyu*; Yuanchong Wang, *Remaking the Chinese Empire*.

56. One example is the lack of reference to the Kitans in the Dunhuang materials. The lack of Kitan language documents and Chinese texts from the Liao state in the Dunhuang manuscript collection might be explained as coincidental. But it is important to consider that, while prayers by lords and commoners of Dunhuang routinely mention states in North China (the Tang, the Five Dynasties, and the Northern Song), the Liao emperor never once appears in these texts. People in Dunhuang also never used the regnal names of Liao emperors. Such systemic absence of the Liao in our story becomes more conspicuous if we consider the fact that, from the Liao sources, Dunhuang envoys regularly visited the Liao court. At this moment, I am unable to explain such absence.

57. Kurz, "Consolidation of Official Historiography"; Hartman, *Making of Song Dynasty History*.

58. This traditional Tang–Five Dynasties–Song genealogy is bolstered in modern scholarship by the "Tang-Song transition" first conceived by Naitō Konan (1866–1934). The Naitō thesis maintains that between the Tang (618–907) and the Song dynasties (960–1276), the Chinese world underwent a series of dramatic cultural and political changes that marked a major turning point in its history. The beginning of the turning point is widely regarded as the An Lushan Rebellion (755–63), when the Tang central authority succumbed irrevocably to regionalism. Scholars disagree as to the specific timing of the end of this transitional period, but few now doubt the basic wisdom of Naitō's observation. The exploration of this thesis provides the backbone for the current understanding of Chinese history between the sixth and the fourteenth centuries. By framing this era as a transition from the Tang to the Song, the Naitō thesis tallies with the vision of the Song historians. See Naitō, "Gaikatsuteki Tō Sō jidaikan"; Miyakawa, "Outline of the Naito Hypothesis."

59. *Songshi*, 490.14123–24.

60. Rossabi, introduction to J. Moore and Wendelken, *Teaching the Silk Road*, 3. I have already mentioned this point in the introduction.

61. Liu Jinbao, "Dunhuang xue."

62. See Also Zheng Xuemeng's synthesis of Dunhuang and Turfan materials for the study of the Tang, "Dunhuang Tulufan wenshu." It is notable that there are very few comparable works that discuss the connection between the Dunhuang materials and the history of the Five Dynasties or the Song.

63. Tian Weiwei, "Dunhuang xieben."

64. Nugent, *Manifest in Words*.

65. Wen, "Emperor of Dunhuang."

66. See Tao, *Two Sons of Heaven*; G. Wang, "Rhetoric of a Lesser Empire." The comparable cases in Dunhuang are particularly numerous during the reign of the Cao family rulers and with their relation to Ganzhou. See Feng Peihong, *Dunhuang de Guiyijun shidai*, 307–91.

67. Shu Xue, "Dunhuang hanwen yishu"; Su Bai, *Tang Song shiqi*.

68. Wen, "King of Kings of China."

# BIBLIOGRAPHY

## Abbreviatons

*Ecang*: Eluosi kexueyuan dongfang yanjiusuo Sheng bidebao fensuo 俄羅斯科學院東方研究所聖彼得堡分所, Eluosi kexue chubanshe dongfang wenxue bu 俄羅斯科學出版社東方文學部, and Shanghai guji chubanshe 上海古籍出版社, eds. *Eluosi kexueyuan dongfang yanjiusuo Sheng bidebao fensuo cang Dunhuang wenxian* 俄羅斯科學院東方研究所聖彼得堡分所藏敦煌文獻 [Dunhuang manuscripts in the Saint Petersburg branch of the Oriental Institution of the Russian Academy of Sciences]. 17 vols. Shanghai: Shanghai guji chubanshe, 1992–2001.

*Facang*: Shanghai guji chubanshe 上海古籍出版社 and Faguo guojia tushuguan 法國國家圖書館編, eds. *Faguo guojia tushuguan cang Dunhuang Xiyu wen xian* 法國國家圖書館藏敦煌西域文獻 [Dunhuang manuscripts in the Bibliothèque nationale de France]. 34 vols. Shanghai: Shanghai guji chubanshe, 1995–2003.

*Shilu*: Tang Geng'ou 唐耕耦 and Lu Hongji 陸宏基, eds. *Dunhuang shehui jingji wenxian zhenji shilu* 敦煌社會經濟文献真蹟釋錄 [Transcriptions and photographs of social and economic documents from Dunhuang]. 5 vols. Beijing: Shumu wenxian chubanshe, 1986–90.

*Yingcang*: Zhongguo shehui kexueyuan lishi yanjiu suo 中國社會科學院歷史研究所, ed. *Yingcang Dunhuang wen xian (hanwen fojing yiwai bufen)* 英藏敦煌文獻 (漢文佛經以外部份) [Dunhuang manuscripts in the British Library (documents excluding Chinese Buddhist texts)]. 15 vols. Chengdu: Sichuan renmin chubanshe, 1990–2009.

## Online Databases

"Digital Dunhuang." Dunhuang Academy. Last modified 2020. https://www.e-dunhuang.com/. In Chinese. (Showing images of some of the caves.)

"International Dunhuang Project." Last modified September 2016. http://idp.bl.uk/.

"Old Tibetan Documents Online." Research Institute for Languages and Cultures of Asia and Africa, Tokyo University of Foreign Studies. Last modified January 24, 2022. https://otdo.aa-ken.jp/.

"Thesaurus Indogermanischer Text- und Sprachmaterialien" (Thesaurus of Indo-European text and language materials; TITUS). Johann Wolfgang Goethe-Universität Frankfurt am Main. Last modified January 2016. https://titus.fkidg1.uni-frankfurt.de/framee.htm?/index.htm.

## Other Sources

Abu-Lughod, Janet L. *Before European Hegemony: The World System A.D. 1250–1350*. New York: Oxford University Press, 1989.

Akagi, Takatoshi. "Six 10th Century Royal Seals of the Khotan Kingdom." In *New Studies of the Old Tibetan Documents: Philology, History and Religion*, edited by Yoshiro Imaeda, Matthew Kapstein, and Tsuguhito Takeuchi, 217–29. Tokyo: Tokyo University of Foreign Studies, 2011.

Andrea, Alfred. "The Silk Road in World History: A Review Essay." *Asian Review of World Histories* 2, no. 1 (2014): 105–27.

Arakawa Masaharu 荒川正晴. *Yūrashia no kōtsū, kōeki to Tō Teikoku* ユーラシアの交通・交易と唐帝国 [Eurasian transportation and trade and the Tang Empire]. Nagoya, Japan: Nagoya Daigaku Shuppankai, 2010.

Arnold, Lauren. *Princely Gifts and Papal Treasure: The Franciscan Mission to China and Its Influence on the Art of the West, 1250–1350*. San Francisco: Desiderata Press Art, 1999.

Atwood, Christopher. "Life in Third–Fourth Century Cadh'ota: A Survey of Information Gathered from the Prakrit Documents Found North of Minfeng (Niyä)." *Central Asiatic Journal* 35 (1991): 161–99.

Bailey, Harold Walter. "Altun Khan." *Bulletin of the School of Oriental and African Studies* 30, no. 1 (1967): 95–104.

———. *Dictionary of Khotan Saka*. Cambridge: Cambridge University Press, 1979.

———. "Hvatanica III." *Bulletin of the School of Oriental Studies* 9, no. 3 (1938): 521–43.

———, trans. and ed. *Indo-Scythian Studies: Being Khotanese Texts*. Vol. 4. Cambridge: Cambridge University Press, 1961.

———. "An Itinerary in Khotanese Saka." *Acta Orientalia* 14 (1936): 258–67.

———. "A Khotanese Text concerning the Turks in Kanṭsou." *Asia Major*, n.s., 1, no. 1 (1949): 28–52.

———. "Śrī Viśa Śūra and the Ta-uang." *Asia Major*, n.s., 11, no. 1 (1964): 1–26.

———. "The Staël-Holstein Miscellany." *Asia Major*, n.s., 2, no. 1 (1951): 1–45.

———. "Vajrayāna in Gostana-deśa." *Journal of the International Association of Buddhist Studies* 1, no. 1 (1978): 53–56.

Ball, Warwick. *Rome in the East: The Transformation of an Empire*. 2nd ed. London: Routledge, 2016.

Ban Gu 班固. *Hanshu* 漢書 [Han history]. Bejing: Zhonghua shuju, 1962.

Bang, Peter Fibiger, and Karen Turner. "Kingship and Elite Formation." In *State Power in Ancient China and Rome*, edited by Walter Scheidel, 11–38. Oxford: Oxford University Press, 2015.

Barenghi, Maddalena. "Representations of Descent: Origin and Migration Stories of the Ninth- and Tenth-Century Turkic Shatuo." *Asia Major*, 3rd ser., 32, no. 1 (2019): 53–86.

Bayly, Christopher. "'Archaic' and 'Modern' Globalization in the Eurasian and African Arena c.1750–1850." In *Globalization in World History*, edited by A. G. Hopkins, 47–93. London: Pimlico, 2002.

Beckert, Sven. *Empire of Cotton: A Global History*. New York: Alfred A. Knopf, 2014.

Beckwith, Christopher I. *Empires of the Silk Road: A History of Central Eurasia from the Bronze Age to the Present*. Princeton, NJ: Princeton University Press, 2011.

———. *The Tibetan Empire in Central Asia: A History of the Struggle for Great Power among Tibetans, Turks, Arabs, and Chinese during the Early Middle Ages.* Princeton, NJ: Princeton University Press, 1993.

Bell, David. "This Is What Happens When Historians Overuse the Idea of the Network." *New Republic*, October 25, 2013. https://newrepublic.com/article/114709/world-connecting -reviewed-historians-overuse-network-metaphor.

Benjamin, Craig G. R. *The Yuezhi: Origins, Migration and the Conquest of Northern Bactria.* Turnhout, Belgium: Brepols, 2007.

Benn, James. *Burning for the Buddha: Self-Immolation in Chinese Buddhism.* Honolulu: University of Hawaiʻi Press, 2007.

Bentley, Jerry. "Cross-Cultural Interaction and Periodization in World History." *American Historical Review* 101, no. 3 (1999): 749–70.

Benveniste, Emile. *Le vocabulaire des institutions indo-européennes.* Vol. 1, *Economie, parenté, société.* Paris: Éditions de Minuit, 1969.

Bi Bo 畢波. "Gudai Yutian de yizhong zhiwu: Baidie" 古代于闐的一種織物：白氎 [A textile from ancient Khotan: White cotton]. *Zhongguo jingji shi yanjiu* 2018, no. 3: 162–70.

Bielenstein, Hans. *Diplomacy and Trade in the Chinese World, 589–1276.* Leiden: Brill, 2005.

Bischoff, F. A., and Charles Hartman. "Padmasambhava's Invention of the Phur-bu: Ms. Pelliot tibétain 44." In *Études tibétaines dédiées à la mémoire de Marcelle Lalou*, edited by Ariane Macdonald, 11–28. Paris: Adrien-Maisonneuve, 1971.

Bohannan, Laura, and Paul Bohannan. *The Tiv of Central Nigeria.* London: International African Institute, 1953.

Bohannan, Paul. "The Impact of Money on an African Subsistence Economy." *Journal of Economic History* 19, no. 4 (1959): 491–503.

Boulnois, Luce. *Silk Road: Monks, Warriors and Merchants on the Silk Road.* Hong Kong: Odyssey Books and Guides, 2012.

Brown, Peter. "The Silk Road in Late Antiquity." In *Reconfiguring the Silk Road: New Research on East-West Exchange in Antiquity*, edited by Victor H. Mair, 15–22. Philadelphia: University of Pennsylvania Press, 2014.

Bulliet, Richard W. *The Camel and the Wheel.* New York: Columbia University Press, 1990.

Cai Tao 蔡絛. *Tieweishan congtan* 鐵圍山叢談 [Assorted conversations in Tiewei Mountain]. Beijing: Zhonghua shuju, 1983.

Canepa, Matthew P. "Distant Displays of Power: Understanding Cross-Cultural Interaction among the Elites of Rome, Sasanian Iran, and Sui-Tang China." *Ars Orientalis* 38 (2010): 121–54.

———. *The Two Eyes of the Earth: Art and Ritual of Kingship between Rome and Sasanian Iran.* Berkeley: University of California Press, 2009.

Chan, Hok-lam. *Legitimation in Imperial China: Discussions under the Jurchen–Chin Dynasty (1115–1234).* Seattle: University of Washington Press, 1984.

Chen Bu-Yun. *Empire of Silk: Silk and Fashion in Tang China.* Seattle: University of Washington Press, 2019.

Chen Guocan 陳國燦. "Du *Xinyu shuwu cang Dunhuang miji* zhaji" 讀《杏雨書屋藏敦煌秘笈》札記 [Notes on reading *Tonkō hikyū: Kyōu Shooku zō*]. *Shixueshi yanjiu* 149, no. 1 (2013): 113–22.

Chen Juxia 陳菊霞. "Xian Fan qian de Dunhuang wenshu: S.11287 xintan" 陷蕃前的敦煌文書：S.11287 新探 [Dunhuang documents before its fall to Tibetan rule: New investigations into S. 11287]. *Dunhuang tulufan yanjiu* 13 (2013): 183–96.

Chen Sanping. *Multicultural China in the Early Middle Ages*. Philadelphia: University of Pennsylvania Press, 2012.

———. "Son of Heaven and Son of God: Interactions among Ancient Asiatic Cultures regarding Sacral Kingship and Theophoric Names." *Journal of the Royal Asiatic Society*, 3rd ser., 12, no. 3 (2002): 289–325.

Chen Shuangyin 陳雙印. "Dunhuang xieben *Zhushan shengjizhi* jiaoshi yu yanjiu" 敦煌寫本《諸山聖跡志》校釋與研究 [An edition and study of the Dunhuang manuscript *Sacred Places on Various Mountains*]. PhD dissertation, Lanzhou University, 2007.

Chen Tao 陳濤. "Riben Xingyu shuwu cang Dunhuang ben *yicheng ji* diming ji niandai kao" 日本杏雨書屋藏敦煌本《驛程記》地名及年代考 [The place names and date of the Dunhuang manuscript *Yicheng ji* preserved in Kyōu Shooku in Japan]. *Nandu xuetan* 34, no. 5 (2014): 28–31.

Chen, Xue. "Age of Emperors: Divisible Imperial Authority and the Formation of a 'Liao World Order' in Continental East Asia, 900–1250." *Journal of Song-Yuan Studies* 49 (2020): 45–83.

Cheng Minsheng 程民生. "Songdai de fanyi" 宋代的翻譯 [Translators in the Song dynasty]. *Beijing shifan daxue xuebao* 2013, no. 2: 62–70.

Chin, Tamara T. "The Invention of the Silk Road, 1877." *Critical Inquiries* 40, no. 1 (2013): 194–219.

Chong, Alan, and Stephen A. Murphy, eds. *The Tang Shipwreck: Art and Exchange in the 9th Century*. Singapore: Asian Civilisations Museum, 2017.

Christian, David. "Silk Roads or Steppe Roads? The Silk Roads in World History." *Journal of World History* 11, no. 1 (2000): 1–26.

Clauson, Gerard. *An Etymological Dictionary of Pre-thirteenth-Century Turkish*. Oxford: Clarendon, 1972.

———. "The Geographical Names in the Staël-Holstein Scroll." *Journal of the Royal Asiatic Society* 2 (1931): 297–309.

Cohen, Mark R. *Poverty and Charity in the Jewish Community of Medieval Egypt*. Princeton, NJ: Princeton University Press, 2005.

Curtin, Philip D. *Cross-Cultural Trade in World History*. Cambridge: Cambridge University Press, 1984.

Dalton, Jacob, Tom Davis, and Sam van Schaik. "Beyond Anonymity: Palaeographic Analyses of the Dunhuang Manuscripts." *Journal of the International Association of Tibetan Studies* 3 (2007): 1–23.

Dalton, Jacob, and Sam van Schaik. *Tibetan Tantric Manuscripts from Dunhuang: A Descriptive Catalogue of the Stein Collection at the British Library*. Leiden: Brill, 2006.

Dang Baohai 黨寶海. *Meng Yuan yizhan jiaotong yanjiu* 蒙元驛站交通研究 [A study of postal stations in the Mongol and Yuan periods]. Beijing: Kunlun chubanshe, 2006.

Davis, Natalie Zemon. *The Gift in Sixteenth-Century France*. Madison: University of Wisconsin Press, 2000.

Deng Shupin 鄧淑蘋. "Tang Song yuce jiqi guangguan wenti" 唐宋玉冊及其相關問題 [The jade plates in the Tang and the Song dynasties and related issues]. *Gugong wenwu yuekan* 9, no. 10 (1992): 12–25.

Deng Wenkuan 鄧文寬. "Zhang Huaishen pingding Ganzhou Huihu shishi gouchen" 張淮深平定甘州回鶻史事鉤沉 [An investigation into Zhang Huaishen's victory over the Ganzhou Uyghur kingdom]. *Beijing daxue xuebao* 1986, no. 5: 86–98.

Deng Xiaonan 鄧小南. *Zuzong zhifa: Beisong qianqi zhengzhi shulue* 祖宗之法：北宋前期政治述略 [Invoking imperial ancestors' instructions in early Northern Song politics]. Beijing: Sanlian shudian, 2006.

Dohi Yoshikazu 土肥義和. *Hasseiki makki jūisseiki shoki Tonkō shizoku jinmei shūsei: Shizoku jinmeihen jinmeihen* 八世紀末期—十一世紀初期燉煌氏族人名集成: 氏族人名篇, 人名篇 [A collection of lineages and names in Dunhuang from the end of the eighth century to the beginning of the eleventh century: Names of certain lineages]. Tokyo: Kyūko shoin, 2015.

———. "Tonkō hakken Tō-Kaikotsu kan kōeki kankei kanbun monjo dankan kō" 燉煌発見唐・回鶻間交易関係漢文文書断簡考 [A study of a Chinese manuscript fragment of Tang-Uyghur trade from Dunhuang]. In *Chūgoku kodao no hō to shakai: Kurihara Masuo sensei koki kinen ronshū*, 399–436. Tokyo: Kyūko shoin, 1988.

Dong Hao 董浩, ed. *Quan Tangwen* 全唐文 [Complete Tang essays]. Beijing: Zhonghua shuju, 1983.

Drège, Jean-Pierre. "L'analyse fibreuse des papiers et la datation des manuscrits de Dunhuang." *Journal Asiatique* 274, nos. 3–4 (1986): 403–15.

———. "Papiers de Dunhuang: Essai d'analyse morphologique des manuscrits chinois datés." *T'oung Pao* 67, nos. 3–5 (1981): 305–60.

Dunhuang yanjiuyuan 敦煌研究院, ed. *Dunhuang Mogaoku gongyangren tiji* 敦煌莫高窟供養人題記 [Donor colophons in the Mogao caves of Dunhuang]. Beijing: Wenwu chubanshe, 1986.

———. *Dunhuang shiku neirong zonglu* 敦煌石窟內容總錄 [Complete records of the Dunhuang caves]. Beijing: Wenwu chubanshe, 1996.

———, ed. *Dunhuang shiku yishu quanji* 敦煌石窟藝術全集 [Complete collection of Dunhuang cave art]. 26 vols. Shanghai: Tongji daxue chubanshe, 2015.

———, ed. *Yulin ku: Zhongguo shiku yishu* 榆林窟：中國石窟藝術 [Yulin Caves: Cave art in China]. Nanjing: Jiangsu meishu chubanshe, 2014.

Dunnell, Ruth. "The hsi Hsia." In *The Cambridge History of China*, vol. 6, *Alien Regimes and Border States*, edited by Herbert Franke and Dennis Twitchett, 154–214. Cambridge: Cambridge University Press, 1994.

Durkin-Meistererernst, Desmond, ed. *Turfan Revisited: The First Century of Research into the Arts and Cultures of the Silk Road*. Berlin: Reimer, 2004.

Duturaeva, Dilnoza. "Qarakhanid Envoys to Song China." *Journal of Asian History* 52, no. 2 (2018): 179–208.

———. *Qarakhanid Roads to China: A History of Sino-Turkic Relations*. Leiden: Brill, 2022.

Duyiwo tuishi 獨逸窩退士. *Xiaoxiao lu* 笑笑錄 [A record of jokes]. Shanghai: Shenbao guan, 1879.

Ebrey, Patricia Buckley. *Emperor Huizong*. Cambridge, MA: Harvard University Press, 2014.

Eliasberg, Danielle. "L'expression *eul-lang wei* dans certains manuscrits de Touen-houang." In *Nouvelles contributions aux études de Touen-houang*, edited by Michel Soymié, 261–71. Geneva: Droz, 1981.

———. "Pratiques funéraires animales en Chine ancienne et médiévale." *Journal Asiatique* 280, nos. 1–2 (1992): 115–44.

———. "Quelques aspects de l'exorcisme no à Touen-houang." In *Contributions aux études de Touen-houang*, vol. 3, edited by Michel Soymié, 237–53. Paris: l'Ecole française d'Extrême-Orient, 1984.

Emmerick, Ronald E. "Cã tteya khī in the Musée Guimet." *Studia Iranica* 13, no. 2 (1984): 251–52, plate 16.

———. *A Guide to the Literature of Khotan*. 2nd ed. Tokyo: International Institute for Buddhist Studies, 1992.

Fairbank, John King, ed. *The Chinese World Order: Traditional China's Foreign Relations*. Cambridge, MA: Harvard University Press, 1968.

Fan Guangchun 樊光春. "Dunhuang Daoshi Wang Yuanlu pingzhuan" 敦煌道士王圓籙評傳 [A biography of the Dunhuang Daoist monk Wang Yuanlu]. *Zhongguo Daojiao* 5 (2008): 43–47.

Fang Guangchang 方廣錩. "Dunhuang Canjingdong fengbi yuanyin zhi wojian" 敦煌藏經洞封閉原因之我見 [My view on the reason for the sealing of the library cave in Dunhuang]. *Zhongguo shehui kexue* 5 (1991): 213–23.

Faxian 法顯. *Faxian zhuan jiaozhu* 法顯傳校註 [Annotated biography of Faxian]. Edited by Zhang Xun 章巽. Shanghai: Shanghai guji chubanshe, 1985.

Feng Menglong 馮夢龍. *Gujin tangai* 古今譚概 [A survey of anecdotes from antiquity to the present]. In *Feng Menglong quanji* 馮夢龍全集 [Complete collected works of Feng Menglong], edited by Wei Tongxian 魏同賢, vol. 6. Nanjing: Fenghuang chubanshe, 2007.

Feng Peihong 馮培紅. *Dunhuang de Guiyijun shidai* 敦煌的歸義軍時代 [Dunhuang's Guiyijun period]. Lanzhou: Gansu jiaoyu chubanshe, 2013.

———. "Kesi yu Guiyiju de waijiao huodong" 客司與歸義軍的外交活動 [The Office of Hospitality and the diplomatic activities of the Guiyijun]. *Dunhuang xue jikan* 1999, no. 1: 72–84.

———. "Tang Wudai Guiyijun junziku chutan" 唐五代歸義軍軍資庫司初探 [A preliminary study of the military treasury of the Guiyijun in the Tang and the Five Dynasties periods]. *Dunhuang xue jikan* 1998, no. 1: 31–38.

Forte, Antonino. *Political Propaganda and Ideology in China at the End of the Seventh Century: Inquiry into the Nature, Authors and Function of the Dunhuang Document S.6502*. 2nd ed. Kyoto: Scuola Italiana di Studi sull'Asia Orientale, 2005.

Frankopan, Peter. *The Silk Roads: A New History of the World*. New York: Alfred A. Knopf, 2016.

Fu Junlian 伏俊璉. "Tangdai Dunhuang gaoseng Wuzhen ru Chang'an shi kaolue" 唐代敦煌高僧悟真入長安事考略 [A study of Wuzheng, an eminent monk from Dunhuang in the Tang dynasty, and his trip to Chang'an]. *Dunhuang yanjiu* 2010, no. 3: 70–77.

Fu Ma 付馬. *Sichou zhilu shang de Xizhou Huihu wangchao: 9–13 shiji Zhongya dongbu lishi yanjiu* 絲綢之路上的西州回鶻王朝：9–13世紀中亞東部歷史研究 [The Xizhou Uyghur regime on the Silk Road: A study of the history of eastern Central Asia from the ninth to the thirteenth century]. Beijing: Shehui kexue wenxian chubanshe, 2019.

Galambos, Imre. *Dunhuang Manuscript Culture: End of the First Millennium*. Berlin: De Gruyter, 2020.

———. "Non-Chinese Influences in Medieval Chinese Manuscript Culture." In *Frontiers and Boundaries: Encounters on China's Margins*, edited by Zsombor Rajkai and Ildikó Bellér-Hann, 71–86. Wiesbaden, Germany: Harrassowitz, 2012.

———. "She Association Circulars from Dunhuang." In *A History of Chinese Letters and Episto-lary Culture*, edited by Antje Richter, 853–77. Leiden: Brill, 2015.

Gao Qi'an 高啟安. *Tang Wudai Dunhuang yinshi wenhua yanjiu* 唐五代敦煌飲食文化研究 [The culinary culture of Dunhuang during the Tang and the Five Dynasties periods]. Bei-jing: Minzu chubanshe, 2004.

Ge Chengyong 葛承雍. *Tangdai guoku zhidu* 唐代國庫制度 [The national treasuries of the Tang dynasty]. Xi'an: Sanqin chubanshe, 1990.

Ge Zhaoguang 葛兆光. *Xiangxiang yiyu: Du Lichao Chaoxian Hanwen yanxinglu wenxian zhaji* 想象異域：讀朝鮮李朝漢文燕行文獻札記 [Imagining a foreign land: Notes on reading the Korean Yi dynasty's Beijing journals in classical Chinese]. Beijing: Zhonghua shuju, 2014.

———. *Zhaizi Zhongguo: Chongjian youguan "Zhongguo" de lishi lunshu* 宅茲中國：重建有關"中國"的歷史論述 [Residing in this Zhongguo: Reconstructing historical narratives regarding "Zhongguo"]. Beijing: Zhonghua shuju, 2011.

Geary, Patrick, Daud Ali, Paul S. Atkins, Michael Cooperson, Rita Costa Gomes, Paul Dutton, Gert Melville, et al. "Courtly Cultures: Western Europe, Byzantium, the Islamic world, India, China, and Japan." In *Cambridge World History*, vol. 5, *Expanding Webs of Exchange and Conflict, 500CE–1500CE*, edited by Benjamin Z. Kedar and Merry E. Wiesner-Hanks, 170–205. Cambridge: Cambridge University Press, 2015.

Gernet, Jacques. *Les aspects économiques du bouddhisme dans la société chinoise du Ve au Xe siècle*. Paris: Ecole française d'Extrême-Orient, 1956.

———. "Location de chameaux pour des voyages, à Touen-huang." In *Mélanges de sinologie offerts à Monsieur Paul Demiéville*, 1:41–51. Paris: Institut des hautes études chinoises, 1966.

Gerritsen, Anne, and Giorgio Riello, *Writing Material Culture History*. London: Bloomsbury Academic, 2015.

Goitein, S. D. *A Mediterranean Society: The Jewish Communities of the Arab World as Portrayed in the Documents of the Cairo Geniza*. 6 vols. Berkeley: University of California Press, 1967–93.

Goldberg, Jessica. *Trade and Institutions in the Medieval Mediterranean: The Geniza Merchants and Their Business World*. Cambridge: Cambridge University Press, 2012.

Golden, Peter B. *An Introduction to the History of the Turkic Peoples: Ethnogenesis and State-Formation in Medieval and Early Modern Eurasia and the Middle East*. Wiesbaden, Germany: Harrassowitz, 1992.

Grenet, Frantz. "What Was the Afrasiab Painting About?" *Rivista degli studi orientali* 78 (2005): 43–58.

Grierson, Philip. "Commerce in the Dark Ages: A Critique of the Evidence." *Transactions of the Royal Historical Society* 9 (1959): 123–40.

Gu Jiegang 顧頡剛. "Wude zhongshishuo xia de zhengzhi he lishi" 五德終始說下的政治與歷史 [Politics and history in the context of the five-elements theory]. In *Gushi bian*, vol. 5, edited by Gu Jiegang, 404–617. Reprint. Shanghai: Shanghai guji chubanshe, 1982.

Guan, Kwa Chong. "The Maritime Silk Road: History of an Idea." Nalanda-Sriwijaya Centre Working Paper Series no. 23, 2016. https://www.iseas.edu.sg/images/pdf/nscwps23.pdf.

Guoli Gugong bowuyuan 國立故宮博物院. *Gugong shuhua lu* 故宮書畫錄 [A catalogue of works of calligrapy and paintings in the Palace Museum]. 4 vols. Taipei: Gugong bowuyuan, 1965.

Guzman, Gregory G. "European Clerical Envoys to the Mongols: Reports of Western Merchants in Eastern Europe and Central Asia, 1231–1255." *Journal of Medieval History* 12 (1996): 53–67.

Hamilton, James Russell. "Autour du manuscrit Staël-Holstein." *T'oung Pao* 46, nos. 1–2 (1958): 115–53.

———. *Le conte bouddhique du Bon et du Mauvais Prince en version ouigoure: Manuscrits ouigours de Touen-houang*. Paris: Klincksieck, 1971.

———. *Manuscrits ouïgours du IXe–Xe siècle de Touen-houang*. Paris: Peeters, 1986.

———. *Les Ouïghours à l'époque des cinq dynasties d'après les documents chinois*. Bibliothèque de l'Institut des hautes études chinoises, v. 10. Paris: Collège de France, Institut des hautes études chinoises, 1988.

———. "Le pays des Tchong-yun: Čungul, on Cumuǧa au Xe siècle." *Journal asiatique* 265 (1977): 351–79.

Han, Soojung. "When Middle Kingdom Was Gone: Identities and States of the Shatuo Turks." PhD dissertation, Princeton University, 2022.

Hansen, Valerie. "The Impact of the Silk Road Trade on a Local Community: The Turfan Oasis, 500–800." In *Les sogdiens en Chine*, edited by Eric Trombert and Etienne de la Vaissière, 283–310. Paris: Ecole française d'Extrême-Orient, 2005.

———. "International Gifting and the Kitan World, 907–1125." *Journal of Song-Yuan Studies* 43 (2013): 273–302.

———. *The Silk Road: A New History*. Oxford: Oxford University Press, 2012.

———. "The Tribute Trade with Khotan in Light of Materials Found at the Dunhuang Library Cave." *Bulletin of the Asia Institute* 19 (2005): 37–46.

———. *The Year 1000: When Explorers Connected the World—and Globalization Began*. New York: Scribner, 2020.

Hao Chunwen 郝春文. *Shishi xiejing: Dunhuang yishu* 石室寫經：敦煌遺書 [Sutras from a stone cave: Dunhuang manuscripts]. Lanzhou: Gansu renmin chubanshe, 2007.

———. *Tang houqi Wudai Song chu Dunhuang seng-ni de shehui shenghuo* 唐後期五代宋初敦煌僧尼的社會生活 [The social life of monks and nuns in Dunhuang during the late Tang, Five Dynasties, and the early Song periods]. Beijing: Zhongguo shehui kexue chubanshe, 1998.

———, ed. *Yingcang Dunhuang shehui lishi wenxian shilu* 英藏敦煌社會歷史文獻釋錄 [Transcriptions of social and economic documents from Dunhuang in the British Library]. 17 vols. Beijing: Shehui kexue wenxian chubanshe, 2001–21.

———. *Zhonggu shiqi sheyi yanjiu* 中古時期社邑研究 [Local communities in the medieval time]. Taipei: Xinwenfeng chuban gongsi, 2006.

Harris, Robert E. *Painting and Private Life in Eleventh-Century China: "Mountain Villa" by Li Gonglin*. Princeton, NJ: Princeton University Press, 1988.

Harrison, Henrietta. *The Perils of Interpreting: The Extraordinary Lives of Two Translators between Qing China and the British Empire*. Princeton, NJ: Princeton University Press, 2021.

Hartman, Charles. *The Making of Song Dynasty History: Sources and Narratives, 960–1279 CE*. Cambridge: Cambridge University Press, 2021.

Hay, Jonathan. "Seeing through Dead Eyes: How Early Tang Tombs Staged the Afterlife." *Res: Anthropology and Aesthetics* 57–58 (2010): 16–54.

Hedin, Sven. *The Silk Road*. Translated from Swedish by F. H. Iyon. London: George Routledge, 1938.

Henning, Walter B. "The Date of the Sogdian Ancient Letters." *Bulletin of the School of Oriental and African Studies* 12, no. 3 (1948): 601–15.

Herman, Gabriel. *Ritualised Friendship and the Greek City*. Cambridge: Cambridge University Press, 1987.

Hitch, D. A. "Kushan Tarim Domination." *Central Asiatic Journal* 32, nos. 3–4 (1988): 170–92.

Hodder, Ian. *Entangled: An Archaeology of the Relationships between Humans and Things*. Malden, MA: Wiley-Blackwell, 2012.

Hoffman, Helmut. "Early and Medieval Tibet." In *The Cambridge History of Early Inner Asia*, edited by Denis Sinor, 371–99. Cambridge: Cambridge University Press, 1990.

Holmes, Catherine, and Naomi Standen. "Defining the Global Middle Ages." *Medieval Worlds* 1 (2015): 106–17.

Hopkirk, Peter. *The Great Game: The Struggle for Empire in Central Asia*. New York: Kodansha International, 1992.

Horden, Peregrine, and Nicholas Purcell. *The Corrupting Sea: A Study of Mediterranean History*. Oxford: Blackwell, 2000.

Hou Xudong 侯旭東. *Wuliu shiji beifang minzhong Fojiao xinyang* 五六世紀北方民眾佛教信仰 [Popular Buddhist beliefs in North China during the fifth and the sixth centuries]. Beijing: Zhongguo shehui kexue chubanshe, 1998.

Hu Ji 胡戟 and Rong Xinjiang 榮新江. *Da Tang xishi bowuguan cang muzhi* 大唐西市博物館藏墓誌 [Tomb epitaphs in the collection of the Museum of the Western Market of the Great Tang]. 3 vols. Beijing: Beijing daxue chubanshe, 2012.

Hu Yaofei 胡耀飞. "Guanyu Huang Chao zhisi de shiliao shengcheng: Cong Dunhuang S.2589 hao wenshu chufa de tantao" 關於黃巢之死的史料生成——從敦煌 S.2589 號文書出發的探討 [The making of the historical sources about the death of Huang Chao: Starting the discussion with Dunhuang document S. 2589]. *Sichou zhilu yanjiu jikan* 3 (2019): 224–37.

Hua Linfu 華林甫. "Tang mu kao" 唐畝考 [A study of the *mu* in the Tang dynasty]. *Nongye kaogu* 1991, no. 3: 152–54.

Huang Chunyan 黃純艷. *Songdai chaogong tixi yanjiu* 宋代朝貢體系研究 [A study of the tributary system in the Song dynasty]. Beijing: Shangwu yinshuguan, 2014.

Huang Shengzhang 黃盛璋. "Yutian wen 'Shi Hexi ji' de lishi dili yanjiu" 于闐文使河西記的歷史地理研究 [A historical and geographical study of the Khotanese text *A Journey to Hexi*]. *Dunhuang xue jikan* 1986, no. 2: 1–18.

Huang Zheng 黃征 and Wu Wei 吳偉. *Dunhuang yuanwen ji* 敦煌願文集 [Prayers from Dunhuang]. Changsha: Yuelu shushe, 1995.

Huang Zhengjian 黃正建. "Dunhuang wenshu yu Tang Wudai beifang diqu de yinshi shenghuo" 敦煌文書與唐五代北方地區的飲食生活 [Dunhuang documents and the culinary life of North China during the Tang and the Five Dynasties periods]. *Weijin Nanbeichao Suitang shi ziliao* 11 (1991): 263–73.

Huili 慧立 and Yancong 彥悰. *Daci'ensi sanzang fashi zhuan* 大慈恩寺三藏法師傳 [The biography of the Tripiṭaka-master of the Great Ci'en Monastery]. Edited by Sun Yutang 孫毓棠 and Xie Fang 謝方. Beijing: Zhonghua shuju, 1983.

Ibn Faḍlān, Aḥmad. *Ibn Fadlan's Journey to Russia: A Tenth-Century Traveler from Baghdad to the Volga River*. Translated by Richard N. Frye. Princeton, NJ: Markus Wiener, 2005.

Ikeda On 池田温. *Chūgoku kodai sekichō kenkyū: Gaikan, rokubun* 中國古代籍帳研究: 概觀、錄文 [A study of ancient Chinese household registers: Overview and transcribed texts]. Tokyo: Tōkyō daigaku Tōyō bunka kenkyūjo, 1979.

———. *Chūgoku kodai shahon shikigo shūroku* 中國古代寫本識語集錄 [Collected colophons of ancient Chinese manuscripts]. Tokyo: Tōkyō daigaku Tōyō bunka kenkyūjo, 1990.

Ikeda On and Tatsuro Yamamoto. *Tun-huang and Turfan Documents Concerning Social and Economic History*. 3 vols. Tokyo: Committee for the Studies of the Tun-huang Manuscripts, The Toyo Bunko, 1978–87.

Iwao Kazushi 岩尾一史. "9 seiki no kigigun seiken to ishu" 9世紀の帰義軍政権と伊州 [The Guiyijun state and Yizhou in the ninth century]. *Tonkō shahon kenkyū nenpō* 2016, no. 10: 341–56.

Iwao Kazushi, Sam van Schaik, and Takeuchi Tsuguhito. *Old Tibetan Texts in the Stein Collection Or.8210*. Tokyo: Tōyō Bunko, 2012.

Jacobs, Justin. "The Concept of the Silk Road in the 19th and 20th Centuries." In *Oxford Research Encyclopedia of Asian History*, edited by David Ludden. New York: Oxford University Press, 2020. https://oxfordre.com/asianhistory/view/10.1093/acrefore/9780190277727.001.0001/acrefore-9780190277727-e-164.

Jiang, Boqin 姜伯勤. *Dunhuang Tulufan wenshu yu Sichou zhi lu* 敦煌吐魯番文書與絲綢之路 [Dunhuang and Turfan documents and the Silk Road]. Beijing: Wenwu chubanshe, 1994.

Jiang Boqin, Xiang Chu 項楚, and Rong Xinjiang 榮新江. *Dunhuang miaozhenzan jiaolu bing yanjiu* 敦煌邈真讚校錄并研究 [Elegies of portraits from Dunhuang: Transcriptions and studies]. Taipei: Xinwenfeng chuban gongsi, 1994.

Jiang Lansheng 江藍生 and Cao Guangshun 曹廣順, eds. *Tangdai yuyan cidian* 唐代語言詞典 [A dictionary of Chinese in the Tang dynasty]. Shanghai: Shanghai jiaoyu chubanshe, 1997.

Kaneko Ryōtai 金子良太. "Pelliot 2782 monjo shoken no Dyau Tceyi-śīnä" Pelliot 2782 文書所見の Dyau Tceyi-śīnä [Dyau Tceyi-śīnä seen in the Dunhuang document Pelliot 2782]. *Buzan gakuhō* 22 (1977): 125–30.

———. "Tonkō shutsudo Chō kinzan kankei monjo" 敦煌出土張金山關係文書 [Dunhuang documents concerning Zhang Jinshan]. *Buzan gakuhō* 19 (1974): 109–118.

Kang, David. *East Asia before the West: Five Centuries of Trade and Tribute*. New York: Columbia University Press, 2010.

Kapstein, Matthew. "The Treaty Temple of the Turquoise Grove." In *Buddhism between Tibet and China*, edited by Matthew Kapstein, 21–72. Boston, MA: Wisdom, 2009.

Kāshgarī, Maḥmūd al-. *Compendium of the Turkic Dialects (Dīwān Lughāt at-Turk)*. Edited and translated by Robert Dankoff and James Kelly. 3 vols. Duxbury, MA: Harvard University Printing Office, 1982.

Kim, Minkoo, and Whan Suk Moon. "Tracking 800-Year-Old Shipments: An Archaeological Investigation of the Mado Shipwreck Cargo, Taean, Korea." *Journal of Maritime Archaeology* 6, no. 2 (2011): 129–49.

Knauer, Elfriede Regina. *The Camel's Load in Life and Death: Iconography and Ideology of Chinese Pottery Figurines from Han to Tang and Their Relevance to Trade along the Silk Road*. Zurich: Akanthus, Verlag für Archäologie, 1998.

Kroll, Paul W. *A Student's Dictionary of Classical and Medieval Chinese*. Leiden: Brill, 2015.

Kumamoto Hiroshi 熊本裕. "The Khotanese in Dunhuang." In *Cina e Iran: Da Alessandro Magno alla dinastia Tang*, 79–101. Florence: Casa Editrice Leo S. Olschki, 1996.

———. "Khotanese Official Documents in the Tenth Century A.D." PhD dissertation, University of Pennsylvania, 1982.

———. "Miscellaneous Khotanese Documents from the Pelliot Collection." *Tokyo University Linguistics Papers* 14 (1994): 229–57.

———. "Saiiki ryokōsha yō Sansukuritto-Kōtango kaiwa renshūchō" 西域旅行者用サンスクリット＝コータン語會話練習帳 [Sanskrit-Khotanese phrasebooks used by travelers in the western regions]. *Sinan-Azia Kenkyu* 28 (1988): 53–82.

———. "Two Khotanese Fragments concerning Thyai Padä-tsā." *Tokyo University Linguistics Papers* 11 (1991): 101–20.

Kurz, Johannes L. "The Consolidation of Official Historiography during the Early Northern Song Dynasty." *Journal of Asian History* 46, no. 1 (2012): 13–35.

———. "Problematische Zeiten: Die Fünf Dynastien und Zehn Staaten in Chinas 10. Jahrhundert." In *Zeitenwenden: Historische Brüche in asiatischen und afrikanischen Gesellschaften*, edited by Sven Sellmer and Horst Brinkhaus, 273–90. Hamburg: E. B. Verlag, 2002.

Kuwayama Shoshin 桑山正進, ed. *Echō ōgo Tenjikukoku den kenkyū* 慧超往五天竺國傳研究 [A study of the journey to India by Hyecho]. Kyoto: Institute for Research in Humanities, Kyoto University, 1992.

Kuzmina, Elena E. *The Prehistory of the Silk Road*. Philadelphia: University of Pennsylvania Press, 2008.

Langenkamp, Harm. "Contested Imaginaries of Collective Harmony: The Poetics and Politics of 'Silk Road' Nostalgia in China and the West." In *China and the West: Music, Representation, and Reception*, edited by Yang Hon-Lun and Michael Saffle, 243–64. Ann Arbor: University of Michigan Press, 2017.

Larner, John. *Marco Polo and the Discovery of the World*. New Haven, CT: Yale University Press, 1999.

Lattimore, Owen. *The Desert Road to Turkestan*. Boston: Little, Brown, 1929.

———. *Pivot of Asia: Sinkiang and the Inner Asian Frontiers of China and Russia*. Boston: Little, Brown, 1950.

Laufer, Berthold. *Jade: A Study in Chinese Archaeology and Religion*. Chicago: Field Museum of Natural History, 1912.

———. *Sino-Iranica: Chinese Contributions to the History of Civilization in Ancient Iran, with Special Reference to the History of Cultivated Plants and Products*. Chicago: Field Museum of Natural History, 1919.

La Vaissière, Étienne de. *Sogdian Traders: A History*. Translated by James Ward. Leiden: Brill, 2005.

Levi, Scott. *The Bukharan Crisis: A Connected History of 18th Century Central Asia*. Pittsburgh: University of Pittsburgh Press, 2020.

Li Delong 李德龍. "Dunhuang yishu S.8444 hao yanjiu: Jianlun Tang mo Huihu yu Tang de chaogong maoyi" 敦煌遗书 S.8444 号研究——兼论唐末回鹘与唐的朝贡贸易 [A study of Dunhuang document S. 8444, with a discussion of the tribute trade between the Uyghurs and the Tang in the late Tang period]. *Zhongyang minzu daxue xuebao* 1994, no. 3: 35–39.

Li Fang 李昉. *Taiping guangji* 太平廣記 [Extensive records assembled in the Taiping era]. Beijing: Zhonghua shuju, 1961.

Li Fang-kuei. "The Inscription of the Sino-Tibetan Treaty of 821–822." *T'oung Pao* 44, nos. 1–3 (1956): 1–99.

Li Jifu 李吉甫. *Yuanhe junxian tuzhi* 元和郡縣圖志 [Maps and gazetteers of provinces and counties in the Yuanhe era]. Beijing: Zhonghua shuju, 1983.

Li Jinxiu 李錦繡. "Tangdai de fanshu yiyu zhiguan: Cong Shi Hedan muzhi tanqi" 唐代的翻書譯語直官–從史訶耽墓誌談起 [The official interpreters of the Tang: Starting the discussion from the epitaph of She Hedan]. *Jinyang xuekan* 2016, no. 5: 35–57, 131.

Li Jun 李軍. "Wan Tang Wudai Suzhou xiangguan shishi kaoshu" 晚唐五代肅州相關史實考述 [Examination of the history of Suzhou in the late Tang and the Five Dynasties]. *Dunhuang xue jikan* 2005, no. 3: 90–100.

Li Linfu 李林甫. *Tang liudian* 唐六典 [Compendium of administrative law of the six divisions of the Tang government]. Beijing: Zhonghua shuju, 1992.

Li Quande 李全德. *Tang Song biangeqi shumiyuan yanjiu* 唐宋變革期樞密院研究 [The *Shumi yuan* during the Tang-Song transition]. Beijing: Guojia tushuguan chubanshe, 2009.

Li Tao 李燾. *Xu zizhi tongjian changbian* 續資治通鑒長編 [The long draft continuation of the comprehensive mirror that aids governance]. Beijing: Zhonghua shuju, 2004.

Li Yun 李昀. "Wan Tang gongci de gouzao: Yi Ganzhou Huihu he Shazhou Guiyijun de gongci bijiao wei zhongxin" 晚唐貢賜的構造——以甘州迴鶻和沙州歸義軍的貢賜比價爲中心 [The construction of late Tang tributes: Centering on the tribute and endowment ration in the cases of the Ganzhou Uyghur and Shazhou Guiyijun states]. *Tang Yanjiu* 22 (2016): 245–68.

Li Zhengyu 李正宇. *Guben Dunhuang xiangtuzhi bazhong jianzheng* 古本敦煌鄉土志八種箋證 [Annotations on eight ancient local geographies of Dunhuang]. Taipei: Xinwenfeng chuban gongsi, 1998.

Lieu, Samuel. *Manichaeism in the Later Roman Empire and Medieval China*. 2nd ed. Tübingen, Germany: J.C.B. Mohr, 1992.

Lin, James. "Khotan Jades in the Fitzwilliam Museum Collection." *Journal of Inner Asian Art and Archaeology* 2 (2007): 117–22.

Liu, James T. C. "Polo and Cultural Change: From T'ang to Sung China." *Harvard Journal of Asiatic Studies* 38 (1978): 203–24.

Liu Jinbao 劉進寶. "Dunhuang xue dui zhonggu shidi yanjiu de xin gongxian" 敦煌學對中古史地研究的新貢獻 [The contribution of Dunhuang studies to the study of the history and geography of the medieval era]. *Zhongguo shehui kexue* 2012, no. 8: 128–39.

———. *Tang Song zhiji Guiyijun jingjishi yanjiu* 唐宋之際歸義軍經濟史研究 [The economic history of the Guiyijun in the Tang-Song transition period]. Beijing: Zhongguo shehui kexue chubanshe, 2007.

Liu, Junping, and Deyuan Huang. "The Evolution of Tianxia Cosmology and Its Philosophical Implications." *Frontiers of Philosophy in China* 1, no. 4 (2006): 517–38.

Liu Pujiang 劉浦江. "Liaochao guohao kaoshi" 遼朝國號考釋 [A study of the state name of the Liao dynasty]. *Lishi yanjiu* 2001, no. 6: 30–44.

Liu Quanbo 劉全波. "Ganzhou Huihu chaogong zhongyuan wangchao shishi kaolüe" 甘州回鶻朝貢中原王朝史實考略 [A brief study of the tribute missions to Central China from the Ganzhou Uyghurs]. *Xixia yanjiu* 2017, no. 2: 64–73.

Liu, Xinru. *Ancient India and Ancient China: Trade and Religious Exchanges, A.D. 1–600*. Delhi: Oxford University Press, 1988.

———. *Silk and Religion: An Exploration of Material Life and the Thought of People, AD 600–1200*. Delhi: Oxford University Press, 1996.

———. *The Silk Road in World History*. Oxford: Oxford University Press, 2010.

Liu Xu 劉昫. *Jiu Tangshu* 舊唐書 [Old Tang history]. Beijing: Zhonghua shuju, 1975.

Liu Zaicong 劉再聰. "Cong Dunhuang *Rongqin kemu* wenshu kan Tang-Song hunsu zhong de tianxiang xisu" 從敦煌《榮親客目》文書看唐宋婚俗中的「添箱」習俗 [The *Tianxiang* custom in marriage rituals in the Tang and the Song as seen in the wedding guest lists from Dunhuang]. *Xibei shida xuebao* 50, no. 4 (2013): 54–62.

Lopez, Donald, Jr. *Hyecho's Journey: The World of Buddhism*. Chicago: University of Chicago Press, 2017.

Lorge, Peter Allan. *Five Dynasties and Ten Kingdoms*. Hong Kong: Chinese University Press, 2011.

———. *The Reunification of China: Peace through War under the Song Dynasty*. Cambridge: Cambridge University Press, 2015.

Lu Li 陸離. "Guanyu Dunhuang wenshu zhong de 'Lho bal' (Manmo) yu 'Nanbo,' 'Nanshan'" 關於敦煌文書中的 "Lho bal"（蠻貊）與 "南波" "南山" [On the Lho bal, (Manmo), Nanbo, and Nanshan in Dunhuang documents]. *Dunhuang xue jikan* 2010, no. 3: 28–39.

———. "Wenmo yinyi kao" 嗢末音義考 [A study on the pronunciation and meaning of "Wenmo"]. *Dunhuang yanjiu* 2009, no. 4: 97–102.

Lu Qingfu 陸慶夫. "Tang Song jian Dunhuang Suteren zhi Hanhua" 唐宋間敦煌粟特人之漢化 [The Sinicization of Sogdians in the Tang-Song time]. *Lishi yanjiu* 1996, no. 6: 25–34.

Lu Zhi 陸贄. *Lu Zhi ji* 陸贄集 [Collected works of Lu Zhi]. Edited by Wang Su 王素. Beijing: Zhonghua shuju, 2006.

Luo Feng 羅豐. *Huhan zhijian: Cizhou zhilu yu xibei kaogu* 胡漢之間：絲綢之路與西北考古 [Between the Hu and the Han: The Silk Road and the archaeology of northwest China]. Beijing: Wenwu chubanshe, 2004.

Luo Tonghua 羅彤華. "Guiyijun qi Dunhuang siyuan de yingsong zhichu" 歸義軍期敦煌寺院的迎送支出 [The expenses from receiving guests in Dunhuang monasteries during the Guiyijun period]. *Hanxue yanjiu* 21, no. 1 (2003): 193–224.

Luo Xin 羅新. *Heizhan shang de Beiwei huangdi* 黑氈上的北魏皇帝 [Northern Wei emperors on the black felt carpets]. Beijing: Haitun chubanshe, 2014.

Ma Shichang 馬世長. "Guangyu Dunhuang cangjingdong de jige wenti" 關於敦煌藏經洞的幾個問題 [Several issues regarding the library cave in Dunhuang]. *Wenwu* 1978, no. 12: 21–33.

MacKenzie, D. N. *The 'Sūtra of the Causes and Effects of Actions' in Sogdian*. Oxford: Oxford University Press, 1970.

Maeda Masana 前田正名. *Kasei no rekishi chiri gakuteki kenkyū* 河西の歷史地理学的研究 [A historical and geographical study of the Hexi region]. Tokyo: Yoshikawa Kōbunkan, 1964.

Marchand, Suzanne L. *German Orientalism in the Age of Empire: Religion, Race, and Scholarship*. New York: Cambridge University Press, 2009.

Marshak, B. I. "Le programme iconographique des peintures de la 'Salle des ambassadeurs' à Afrasiab (Samarkand)." *Arts Asiatiques* 49 (1994): 5–20.

Mauss, Marcel. *The Gift: Forms and Functions of Exchange in Archaic Societies*. Translated by Ian Cunnison. New York: Norton, 1967.

Meng Xianshi 孟憲實. *Dunhuang minjian jieshe yanjiu* 敦煌民間結社研究 [Local communities in Dunhuang]. Beijing: Beijing daxue chubanshe, 2009.

———. "Qu Wendai yu Xuanzang" 麴文泰與玄奘 [Qu Wentai and Xuanzang]. *Dunhuang Tulufan yanjiu* 4 (1999): 89–101.

Mertens, Matthias. "Did Richthofen Really Coin 'the Silk Road'?" *Silk Road* 17 (2019): 1–9.

Mie Xiaohong 乜小红. *Ecang Dunhuang qiyue wenshu yanjiu* 俄藏敦煌契約文書研究 [A study of Dunhuang contracts in the Russian collection]. Shanghai: Shanghai guji chubanshe, 2009.

Miller, Tom. *China's Asian Dream: Empire Building along the New Silk Road*. London: Zed Books, 2017.

Millward, James. *The Silk Road: A Very Short Introduction*. Oxford: Oxford University Press, 2013.

Minorsky, Vladimir, trans. *Hudūd al-'Ālam*. London: Luzac, 1937.

———, trans. *Sharaf al-Zamān Ṭāhir Marvazī on China, the Turks, and India*. London: Royal Asiatic Society, 1942.

———. "Tamīm ibn Baḥr' s Journey to the Uyghurs." *Bulletin of the School of Oriental and African Studies* 12, no. 2 (1948): 275–305.

Mintz, Sidney. *Sweetness and Power: The Place of Sugar in Modern History*. New York: Penguin Books, 1986.

Mischke, Steffen, Chenglin Liu, Jiafu Zhang, Chengjun Zhang, Hua Zhang, Pengcheng Jiao, and Birgit Plessen. "The World's Earliest Aral-Sea Type Disaster: The Decline of the Loulan Kingdom in the Tarim Basin." *Scientific Reports* 7 (2017): 43102. https://doi.org/10.1038/srep43102.

Miyakawa Hisayuki. "An Outline of the Naito Hypothesis and Its Effect on Japanese Studies of China." *Far Eastern Quarterly* 14, no. 4 (1955): 533–52.

Moore, Jacqueline M., and Rebecca Woodward Wendelken, eds. *Teaching the Silk Road: A Guide for College Teachers*. Albany: State University of New York Press, 2010.

Moore, Robert I. "A Global Middle Ages?" In *The Prospect of Global History*, edited by James Belich, John Darwin, Margret Frenz, and Chris Wickham, 80–92. Oxford: Oxford University Press, 2016.

Moriyasu Takao 森安孝夫. "Isumaru ka izen no Chūō Ajia-shi kenkyū no genkyō ni tsuite" イスラム化以前の中央アジア史研究の現況について [Regarding the current research on the history of pre-Islamic Central Asia]. *Shigaku zasshi* 89, no. 10 (1980): 50–71.

———. "Qui des Ouïghours ou des Tibétains ont gagné en 789–92 à Be͡-Balïq?" *Journal Asiatique* 269, nos. 1–2 (1981): 193–205.

———. "Toban no Chūō Ajia shinshutsu" 吐蕃の中央アジア進出 [Tibet's entry into and exit from Central Asia]. *Kanazawa daigaku bungakubu ronshū, Shigakuka hen* 4 (1984): 1–85.

Moule, A. C., and Paul Pelliot, trans. *The Description of the World*. 2 vols. London: Routledge, 1938.

Naitō Konan 內藤湖南. "Gaikatsuteki Tō Sō jidaikan" 概括的唐宋時代觀 [A general view of the Tang and the Song dynasties]. *Rekishi to chiri* 9, no. 5 (1922): 1–12.

Neimenggu wenwu gongzuodui 內蒙古文物工作隊 and Neimenggu Bowuguan 內蒙古博物館. "Huhehaote shi fujin chutu de waiguo jinyinbi" 呼和浩特市附近出土的外國金銀幣 [Foreign gold and silver coins excavated near Hohhot]. *Kaogu* 1975, no. 3: 182–85.

Neimonggu wenwu kaogu yanjiusuo 內蒙古文物考古研究所. "Liao Chenguo gongzhu fuma hezang mu fajue jianbao" 遼陳國公主駙馬合葬墓發掘簡報 [A brief report on the excavation of Princess Chenguo and her husband of the Liao dynasty]. *Wenwu* 1987, no. 11: 4–24.

Neumann, I. B. "What Does It Mean to be a Diplomat?" *International Studies Perspectives* 6, no. 1 (2005): 72–93.

Ni, Pengfei, Marco Kamiya, and Ruxi Ding. *Cities Network along the Silk Road: The Global Urban Competitiveness Report 2017*. Singapore: Springer Singapore, 2017.

Ning, Qiang. *Art, Religion, and Politics in Medieval China: The Dunhuang Cave of the Zhai Family*. Honolulu: University of Hawai'i Press, 2004.

———. "Imperial Portraiture as Symbol of Political Legitimacy: A New Study in the Portraits of Successive Emperors." *Ars Orientalis* 35 (2008): 97–128.

Ning Xin 寧欣. "Tangdai Dunhuang diqu shuili wenti chutan" 唐代敦煌地區水利問題初探 [A preliminary study of irrigation in the Dunhuang region during the Tang dynasty]. *Dunhuang Tulufan wenxian yanjiu lunji* 3 (1986): 467–541.

Nugent, Christopher. *Manifest in Words, Written on Paper: Producing and Circulating Poetry in Tang Dynasty China*. Cambridge, MA: Harvard University Asia Center, 2010.

Ōmi no Mifune 淡海三船. *Tang Daheshang dong zheng zhuan* 唐大和上東征傳 [Record of the eastward expedition of the great Tang monk]. Edited by Wang Xiangrong 汪向榮. Beijing: Zhonghua shuju, 1979.

Ouyang Xiu 歐陽脩. *Ouyang Xiu quanji* 歐陽脩全集 [Complete collected works of Ouyang Xiu]. Edited by Li Yi'an 李逸安. Beijing: Zhonghua shuju, 2001.

———. *Xin Wudai shi* 新五代史 [New history of the Five Dynasties]. Beijing: Zhonghua shuju, 1974.

Ouyang Xiu and Song Qi 宋祁. *Xin Tangshu* 新唐書 [New Tang history]. Beijing: Zhonghua shuju, 1975.

Pan, Yihong. "Marriage Alliances and Chinese Princesses in International Politics from Han through T'ang." *Asia Major*, 3rd ser., 10, nos. 1–2 (1997): 95–131.

Park, Hyunhee. *Mapping the Chinese and Islamic Worlds: Cross-Cultural Exchange in Pre-modern Asia*. Cambridge: Cambridge University Press, 2012.

Pei Chengguo 裴成國. "Lun 5–8 shiji Tulufan yu Yanqi de guanxi" 論 5–8 世紀吐魯番與焉耆的關係 [On the relation between Turfan and Yanqi from the fifth to the eighth century]. *Xinjiang shifan daxue xuebao* 2016, no. 3: 127–32.

———. "The Silk Road and the Economy of Gaochang: Evidence on the Circulation of Silver Coins." *Silk Road* 15 (2017): 39–58.

Pelliot, Paul. "Une bibliothèque médiévale retrouvée au Kan-sou." *Bulletin de l'École française d'Extrême-Orient* 8 (1908): 501–29.

———. "La théorie des quatre Fils du Ciel." *T'oung Pao* 22, no. 2 (1923): 97–125.

Peng Dingqiu 彭定求, ed. *Quan Tangshi* 全唐詩 [Complete Tang poetry]. Beijing: Zhonghua shuju, 1960.

Perdue, Peter. "The Tenacious Tributary System." *Journal of Contemporary China* 24, no. 96 (2015): 1002–14.

Pulleyblank, Edwin G. "The Date of the Staël-Holstein Roll." *Asia Major*, n.s., 4, no. 1 (1954): 90–97.

———. "A Sogdian Colony in Inner Mongolia." *T'oung Pao* 41, no. 4/5 (1952): 317–56.

Qi Chenjun 齊陳駿, Lu Qingfu 陸慶夫, and Guo Feng 郭鋒. *Wuliang shilue* 五涼史略 [A brief history of the Five Liang dynasties]. Lanzhou: Gansu renmin chubanshe, 1988.

Reclus, Elisée. *La nouvelle géographie universelle, la terre et les hommes*. 19 vols. Paris: Librairie Hachette, 1882.

Reinhold, Meyer. *History of Purple as a Status Symbol in Antiquity*. Brussels: Collection Latomus, 1970.

Reischauer, Edwin O., trans. *Ennin's Diary: The Record of a Pilgrimage to China in Search of the Law*. New York: Ronald, 1955.

Ren Wei 任伟. "Dunhuang nuo wenhua yanjiu" 敦煌傩文化研究 [A study of the Nuo culture in Dunhuang]. PhD dissertation, Lanzhou University, 2017.

Ren Xiaobo 任小波. "Tang Song zhiji Hexi diqu de buzu guanxi yu huguo xinyang" 唐宋之際河西地區的部族關係與護國信仰 [Intertribal relations and state-protection faith in Hexi region in the Tang and Song dynasties]. *Xiyu lishi yuyan yanjiu jikan* 7 (2014): 107–16.

Rong Xinjiang 榮新江. "Cao Yijin zheng Ganzhou Huihu shishi biaowei" 曹議金征甘州回鶻史事表微 [New light on Cao Yijin's campaign against the Ganzhou Uyghurs]. *Dunhuang Yanjiu* 1991, no. 2: 10–11.

———. "Dazhong shinian Tangchao qianshi celi Huihu shishi xinzheng" 大中十年唐朝遣使冊立回鶻史事新證 [New evidence for the Tang diplomatic mission to the Uyghurs in the tenth year of the Dazhong reign]. *Dunhuang yanjiu* 2013, no. 139: 128–32.

———. *Eighteen Lectures on Dunhuang*. Translated by Imre Galambos. Leiden: Brill, 2013.

———. "Ganzhou Huihu chengli shilun" 甘州回鶻成立史論 [The formation of the Ganzhou Uyghur state]. *Lishi yanjiu* 1993, no. 5: 32–39.

———. "Ganzhou Huihu yu Caoshi Guiyijun" 甘州回鶻與曹氏歸義軍 [Ganzhou Uyghur kingdom and Guiyijun under the Cao family rule]. *Xibei minzu yanjiu* 1993, no. 2: 60–72.

———. *Guiyijun shi yanjiu: Tang Song shidai Dunhuang lishi kaosuo* 歸義軍史研究：唐宋時代敦煌歷史考索 [A study of Guiyijun history: Investigating the history of Dunhuang in the Tang and the Song dynasties]. Shanghai: Shanghai guji chubanshe, 1996.

———. "Khotanese Felt and Sogdian Silver: Foreign Gifts to Buddhist Monasteries in Ninth- and Tenth-Century Dunhuang." *Asia Major*, 3rd ser., 17, no. 1 (2014): 15–34.

———. "Longjia kao" 龍家考 [A study on Longjia]. *Zhongya xuekan* 4 (1995): 144–61.

———. "The Nature of the Dunhuang Library Cave and the Reasons of Its Sealing." Translated by Valerie Hansen. *Cahiers d'Extreme-Asie* 11 (1999–2000): 247–75.

———. "The Rouran Qaghanate and the Western Regions during the Second Half of the Fifth Century Based on a Chinese Document Newly Found in Turfan." In *Great Journeys across the Pamir Mountains: A Festschrift in Honor of Zhang Guangda on His Eighty-Fifth Birthday*, edited by Chen Huaiyu and Rong Xinjiang, 59–82. Leiden: Brill, 2018.

———. "Tangren shiji de chaoben xingtai yu zuozhe lice: Dunhuang xieben S.6234+P.5007, P.2672 zongkao" 唐人詩集的鈔本型態與作者蠡測——敦煌寫本S.6234+ P.5007、P.2672 綜考 [The state of the manuscript and the author of Tang poetry anthologies: A comprehensive study of the Dunhuang manuscripts S. 6234 + P. 5007, P. 2672]. In *Xiang Chu xiansheng xinkai bazhi songshou wenji* 項楚先生欣開八秩頌壽文集, edited by Sichuan daxue Zhongguo su wenhua yanjiusuo 四川大學中國俗文化研究所, 141–58. Beijing: Zhonghua shuju, 2012.

————. "Tō Sō jidai Uten shi gaisetsu" 唐宋時代于闐史概説 [An overview of the history of Khotan in the Tang-Song period]. Translated by Kida Tomoo. *Ryukoku shidan* 97 (1991): 28–38.

Rong Xinjiang, Li Xiao 李肖, and Meng Xiaoshi 孟憲實, eds. *Xinhuo Tulufan chutu wenxian* 新獲吐魯番出土文獻 [Newly discovered Turfan documents]. 2 vols. Beijing: Zhonghua shuju, 2008.

Rong Xinjiang and Wen Xin. "Newly Discovered Chinese-Khotanese Bilingual Tallies." *Journal of Inner Asian Art and Archaeology* 3 (2010): 99–118.

————. "The Semantic Shift of 'Western Region' and the Westward Extension of the 'Border' in the Tang Dynasty." *Eurasian Studies* 3 (2015): 321–34.

Rong Xinjiang and Zhu Lishuang 朱麗雙. "Yizu fanying 10 shiji Yutian yu Dunhuang guanxi de Zangwen wenshu yanjiu" 一組反映10世紀于闐與敦煌關係的藏文文書研究 [A study of a group of Tibetan documents concerning the Khotan-Dunhuang relation in the tenth century]. *Xiyu lishi yuyan yanjiu jikan* 5 (2012): 87–111.

————. *Yutian yu Dunhuang* 于闐與敦煌 [Khotan and Dunhuang]. Lanzhou: Gansu jiaoyu chubanshe, 2013.

Rossabi, Morris, ed. *China among Equals: The Middle Kingdom and Its Neighbors, 10th–14th Centuries*. Berkeley: University of California Press, 1983.

————. Introduction to J. Moore and Wendelken, *Teaching the Silk Road*, 1–11.

Russell-Smith, Lilla. *Uygur Patronage in Dunhuang*. Leiden: Brill, 2005.

————. "Wives and Patrons: Uyghur Political and Artistic Influence in Tenth-Century Dunhuang." *Acta Orientalia Academiae Scientiarum Hungaricae* 56, nos. 2–4 (2003): 401–28.

Rustow, Marina. *Heresy and the Politics of Community: The Jews of the Fatimid Caliphate*. Ithaca, NY: Cornell University Press, 2008.

————. *The Lost Archive: Traces of a Caliphate in a Cairo Synagogue*. Princeton, NJ: Princeton University Press, 2020.

Sahlins, Marshall. *Stone Age Economics*. Chicago: Aldine-Atherton, 1972.

Sakajiri Akihiro 坂尻彰宏. "Tonkō hantsu kō" 敦煌般次考 [Diplomatic missions of Dunhuang]. *Nairiku Ajia gengo no kenkyū* 30 (2015): 173–97.

Schafer, Edward H. *The Golden Peaches of Samarkand: A Study of T'ang Exotics*. Berkeley: University of California Press, 1963.

Schivelbusch, Wolfgang. *The Railway Journey: The Industrialization of Time and Space in the Nineteenth Century*. Berkeley: University of California Press, 2014.

Sen, Tansen. *Buddhism, Diplomacy, and Trade: The Realignment of Sino-Indian Relations, 600–1400*. Honolulu: University of Hawai'i Press, 2003.

Sha Wutian 沙武田. "Dunhuang shiku Yutian guowang huaxiang yanjiu" 敦煌石窟于闐國王畫像研究 [A study of the portraits of the Khotanese kings in the Dunhuang caves]. *Xinjiang shifandaxue xuebao* 27, no. 4 (2006): 22–30.

————. "Wudai Song Dunhuang shiku huihuzhuang nügongyang xiang yu Cao shi Guiyijun de minzu texing" 五代宋敦煌石窟回鶻裝女供養像與曹氏歸義軍的民族特性 [The female donor images in Uyghur attire in the Dunhuang caves during the Five Dynasties and the Song period and the ethnic nature of the Guiyijun under Cao family rule]. *Dunhuang yanjiu* 2013, no. 2: 74–83.

Sha Zhi 沙知. *Dunhuang qiyue wenshu jijiao* 敦煌契約文書輯校 [An edition of Dunhuang contracts]. Nanjing: Jiangsu guji chubanshe, 1998.

Shang Minjie 尚民傑 and Cheng Linquan 程林泉. "Tang Daying ku yu Qionglin ku" 唐大盈庫與瓊林庫 [The Daying and Qionglin treasuries of the Tang]. *Kaogu yu wenwu* 2004, no. 6: 81–85.

Shao Qiangjun 邵強軍. "Dunhuang Cao Yijin di 98 ku yanjiu" 敦煌曹議金第 98 窟研究 [A study of cave 98 by Cao Yijin in Dunhuang]. PhD dissertation, Lanzhou University, 2017.

Shi, Jinbo. *Tangut Language and Manuscripts: An Introduction.* Leiden: Brill, 2020.

Shi Pingting 施娉婷. "Bensuo cang *jiuzhang* yanjiu" 本所藏《酒帳》研究 [A study of the wine expenditure account in Dunhuang Academy]. *Dunhuang yanjiu* 1 (1983): 142–55.

———. *Dunhuang yishu zongmu suoyin xinbian* 敦煌遺書總目索引新編 [A new complete catalogue of Dunhuang manuscripts]. Beijing: Zhonghua shuju, 2000.

Shu Xue 舒學. "Dunhuang hanwen yishu zhong diaoban yinshua ziliao zongshu" 敦煌漢文遺書中雕版印刷資料綜述 [Data on woodblock printing in Chinese manuscripts from Dunhuang]. In *Dunhuang yuyan wenxue yanjiu*, edited by Zhongguo Dunhuang Tulufan xuehui yuyan wenxue fenhui, 280–99. Beijing: Beijing daxue chubanshe, 1998.

Silverstein, Adam J. *Postal Systems in the Pre-modern Islamic World.* Cambridge: Cambridge University Press, 2007.

Sima, Guang, 司馬光. *Zizhi tongjian* 資治通鑑 [The comprehensive mirror that aids governance]. Beijing: Zhonghua shuju, 1956.

Sims-Williams, Nicolas. "Sogdian Ancient Letters II." In *Philologica et linguistica: Historia, pluralitas, universitas; Festschrift für Helmut Humbach zum 80. Geburtstag am 4. Dezember 2001*, edited by M. G. Schmidt and W. Bisang, 267–80. Trier: Wissenschaftlicher Verlag, 2001.

Sims-Williams, Nicholas, and James Hamilton. *Turco-Sogdian Documents from 9th–10th Century Dunhuang.* Translated by Nicholas Sims-Williams, with an appendix by Wen Xin. London: School of Oriental and African Studies, 2015.

Sinor, Denis. "Interpreters in Medieval Inner Asia." *Asian and African Studies: Journal of the Israel Oriental Society* 16 (1982): 293–320.

———. "Languages and Cultural Interchange along the Silk Roads." *Diogenes* 43, no. 3 (1995): 1–13.

Skaff, Jonathan Karam. "Ideological Interweaving in Eastern Eurasia: Simultaneous Kingship and Its Origins." In *Empires and Exchanges in Eurasian Late Antiquity: Rome, China, Iran, and the Steppe, ca. 250–750*, edited by Nicola Di Cosmo and Michael Maas, 386–99. Cambridge: Cambridge University Press, 2018.

———. "The Sogdian Trade Diaspora in East Turkestan during the Seventh and Eighth Centuries." *Journal of the Economic and Social History of the Orient* 46, no. 4 (2003): 475–524.

———. *Sui-Tang China and Its Turko-Mongol Neighbors: Culture, Power and Connections, 580–800.* Oxford: Oxford University Press, 2012.

Skjærvø, Prods O. "Iranians, Indians, Chinese and Tibetans: The Rulers and Ruled of Khotan in the First Millennium." In *The Silk Road: Trade, Travel, War and Faith*, edited by Susan Whitfield and Ursula Sims-Williams, 34–42. Chicago: Serindia, 2004.

———. *Khotanese Manuscripts from Chinese Turkestan in the British Library: A Complete Catalogue with Texts and Translations.* With a contribution by U. Sims-Williams. London: British Library, 2003.

———. "Perils of Ambassadors and Official Messengers." Unpublished manuscript. Microsoft Word file, 2011.

———. "Turks (Uighurs) and Turkic in the Khotanese Texts from Khotan and Dunhuang." In *Turks and Iranians: Interactions in Language and History*, edited by Éva Á. Csató, Lars Johanson, András Róna-Tas, and Bo Utas, 22–26. Wiesbaden, Germany: Harrassowitz, 2016.

So, Billy Kee-long 蘇基朗. *Tang Song fazhishi yanjiu* 唐宋法制史研究 [Studies on the legal history of the Tang-Song period]. Hong Kong: Chinese University of Hong Kong Press, 1995.

Song Minqiu 宋敏求. *Chang'an zhi* 長安志 [A gazetteer of Chang'an]. Edited by Xin Deyong 辛德勇 and Lang Jie 郎潔. Xi'an: Sanqin chubanshe, 2013.

———, ed. *Tang dazhaoling ji* 唐大詔令集 [A collection of Tang edicts]. Beijing: Zhonghua shuju, 2008.

Sowerby, Tracey A. "Early Modern Diplomatic History." *History Compass* 14, no. 9 (2016): 441–56.

Standen, Naomi. "The Five Dynasties." In *The Cambridge History of China*, vol. 5, *The Sung Dynasty and Its Precursors, 907–1279*, pt. 1, edited by Denis Twitchett and Paul Jakov Smith, 38–132. Cambridge: Cambridge University Press, 2009.

———. *Unbounded Loyalty: Frontier Crossings in Liao China*. Honolulu: University of Hawai'i Press, 2006.

Stein, Aurel. *Ancient Khotan: Detailed Report of Archaeological Explorations in Chinese Turkestan*. 2 vols. Oxford: Claredon, 1907.

———. *Innermost Asia: Detailed Report of Explorations in Central Asia, Kan-su and Eastern Iran*. 4 vols. Oxford: Clarendon, 1928.

———. *Serindia: Detailed Report of Explorations in Central Asia and Westermost China*. 5 vols. Oxford: Clarendon, 1921.

Strathern, Andrew. *The Rope of Moka: Big-Men and Ceremonial Exchange in Mount Hagen New Guinea*. Cambridge: Cambridge University Press, 1971.

Su Bai 宿白. *Tang Song shiqi de tiaoban yinshua* 唐宋時期的雕版印刷 [Woodblock printing in the Tang-Song period]. Beijing: Wenwu chubanshe, 1999.

Tackett, Nicolas. *The Origins of the Chinese Nation: Song China and the Forging of an East Asian World Order*. Cambridge: Cambridge University Press, 2017.

Takakusu Junjirō 高楠順次郎 and Watanabe Kaigyoku 渡邊海旭, eds. *Taishō shinshū daizōkyō* 大正新脩大藏經 [The Tripiṭaka newly edited in the Taishō reign]. Tokyo: Taishō issaikyō kankōkai, 1924–32.

Takata Tokio. "Multilingualism in Tun-huang." *Acta Asiatica* 78 (2000): 49–70.

Takeda Kagaku Shinkō Zaidan Kyōu Shooku 武田科学振興財団杏雨書屋, ed. *Tonkō hikyū: Kyōu Shooku zō* 敦煌秘笈: 杏雨書屋藏 [Secret treasures from Dunhuang in the Kyōu Shooku Collection]. 9 vols. Osaka: Takeda Kagaku Shinkō Zaidan, 2009.

Takeuchi Tsuguhito. "A Group of Old Tibetan Letters Written under Kuei-I-Chun: A Preliminary Study for the Classification of Old Tibetan Letters." *Acta Orientalia Academiae Scientiarum Hungaricae* 44, nos. 1–2 (1990): 175–90.

———. "Sociolinguistic Implications of the Use of Tibetan in East Turkestan from the End of Tibetan Domination through the Tangut Period (9th–12th c.)." In *Turfan Revisited*, edited by D. Durkin-Meistererernst, Simone-Christine Raschmann, Jens Wilkens, Marianne Yaldiz, and Peter Zieme, 341–48. Berlin: Reimer, 2004.

Tan Chanxue 譚蟬雪. "Dunhuang ma wenhua" 敦煌馬文化 [Horse culture in Dunhuang]. *Dunhuang yanjiu* 1996, no. 1: 111–20.

Tan Qixiang 譚其驤, ed. *Zhongguo lishi ditu ji* 中國歷史地圖集 [A historical atalas of China]. 8 vols. Beijing: Zhongguo ditu chubanshe, 1982–87.

Tang Geng'ou 唐耕耦. *Dunhuang siyuan kuaiji wenshu yanjiu* 敦煌寺院會計文書研究 [A study of accounting documents from Dunhuang monasteries]. Taipei: Xinwenfeng chuban gongsi, 1997.

Tang Kaijian 湯開建. "Guanyu Miluo guo, Miyao, Hexi dangxiang ji Tanggu zhu wenti de kaobian" 關於彌羅國、彌藥、河西党項及唐古諸問題的考辨 [An investigation of issues involving Miluo, Miyao, the Dangxiang in Hexi and Tanggu]. *Xibei di'er minzu xueyuan xuebao* 43, no. 1 (2000): 15–23.

Tang Zhangru 唐長孺. *Shanju conggao* 山居叢稿 [A collection of essays from a mountain dwelling]. Beijing: Zhonghua shuju, 1989.

Tao, Jing-shen. *Two Sons of Heaven: Studies in Sung-Liao Relations.* Tucson: University of Arizona Press, 1988.

Teiser, Stephen F. *The Ghost Festival in Medieval China.* Princeton, NJ: Princeton University Press, 1988.

Terjék, József. "Fragments of the Tibetan Sutra of 'The Wise and the Fool' from Tun-huang." *Acta Orientalia Academiae Scientiarum Hungaricae* 22–23 (1970): 289–334.

Thomas, F. W., and Lionel Giles. "A Tibeto-Chinese Word-and-Phrase Book." *Bulletin of the School of Oriental and African Studies* 12, nos. 2–3 (1948): 753–69.

Thomas, F. W., and S. Konow. "Two Medieval Documents from Tun-huang." *Oslo Ethnografiske Museums skrifter* 3, no. 3 (1929): 121–60.

Tian Weiwei 田衛衛. "Dunhuang xieben Beisong 'Chongxiu Kaiyuansi xinglang gongdebei bingxu' xishu kao" 敦煌寫本北宋《重修開元寺行廊功德碑並序》習書考 [A study of the Dunhuang version of the practice writing of the *Inscription Created for the Restoration of the Hallways of the Kaiyuan Monastery and a Preface* from the Northern Song]. *Wenshi* 2016, no. 1: 117–32.

Tian, Xiaofei. "Material and Symbolic Economies: Letters and Gifts in Early Medieval China." In *A History of Chinese Letters and Epistolary Culture*, edited by Antje Richter, 135–86. Leiden: Brill, 2015.

Torbet, Preston. *The Ch'ing Imperial Household Department: A Study of Its Organization and Principal Functions, 1662–1796.* Cambridge, MA: Harvard University Press, 1977.

Trombert, Eric. *Le crédit à Dunhuang: Vie matérielle et société en Chine médiévale.* Paris: Collège de France, 1995.

———. "The Demise of Silk on the Silk Road: Textiles as Money at Dunhuang from the Late Eighth Century to the Thirteenth Century." In H. Wang and Hansen, "Textiles as Money," 327–47.

Tuotuo 脫脫. *Liaoshi* 遼史 [Liao history]. Beijing: Zhonghua shuju, 1974.

———. *Songshi* 宋史 [Song history]. Beijing: Zhonghua shuju, 1985.

Uray Geza. "L'emploi du tibétain dans les chancelleries des Etats du Kan-sou et du Khotan posterieurs à la domination tibétaine." *Journal Asiatique* 269 (1981): 81–90.

———. "New Contributions to Tibetan Documents from the Post-Tibetan Tun-huang." In *Tibetan Studies: Proceedings of the 4th Seminar of the International Association for Tibetan Studies, Schloss Hohenkammer—Munich, 1985*, edited by Helga Uebach and Jampa L. Panglung, 514–28. Munich: Kommission für Zentralasiatische Studien Bayerische Akademie der Wissenschaften, 1988.

Van Schaik, Sam, and Imre Galambos. *Manuscripts and Travellers: The Sino-Tibetan Documents of a Tenth-Century Buddhist Pilgrim*. Berlin: De Gruyter, 2012.

Verardi, Giovani. "The Kuṣāṇa Emperors as Cakravartins, Dynastic Art and Cults in India and Central Asia: History of a Theory, Clarifications and Refutations." *East and West* 33, no. 1/4 (1983): 225–94.

Vogel, Hans Ulrich. *Marco Polo Was in China: New Evidence from Currencies, Salts and Revenues*. Leiden: Brill, 2013.

Wang, Binghua. "A Study of the Tang Tax Textiles (Youdiao Bu) from Turfan." Translated by Helen Wang. In H. Wang and Hansen, "Textiles as Money," 263–80.

Wang Dang 王讜. *Tang yulin jiaozheng* 唐語林 [Forest of sayings from the Tang]. Edited by Zhou Xunchu 周勛初. Beijing: Zhonghua shuju, 2008.

Wang, Gungwu. "The Rhetoric of a Lesser Empire: Early Sung Relations with Its Neighbors." In *China among Equals: The Middle Kingdom and Its Neighbors, 10th–14th Centuries*, edited by Morris Rossabi, 47–65. Berkeley: University of California Press, 1983.

Wang, Helen. *Money on the Silk Road: The Evidence from Eastern Central Asia to c. AD 800*. London: British Museum Press, 2004.

———. "Textiles as Money on the Silk Road?" In H. Wang and Hansen, "Textiles as Money," 165–74.

Wang, Helen, and Valerie Hansen, eds. "Textiles as Money on the Silk Road." Special issue, *Journal of the Royal Asiatic Society*, 3rd ser., 23, no. 2 (2013).

Wang, Hongjie. *Power and Politics in Tenth-Century China: The Former Shu Regime*. Amherst, NY: Cambria, 2011.

Wang, Michelle, Xin Wen, and Susan Whitfield. "Buddhism and Silk: Reassessing a Painted Banner from Medieval Central Asia in the Metropolitan Museum of Art." *Metropolitan Museum Journal* 55 (2020): 8–25.

Wang Pu 王溥. *Tang huiyao* 唐會要 [Essential documents and regulations of the Tang]. Beijing: Zhonghua shuju, 1960.

Wang Qilong 王啟龍 and Deng Xiaoyong 鄧小詠. *Gang Hetai (Staël-Holstein) xueshu pingzhuan* 鋼和泰學術評傳 [A biography of Alexander von Staël-Holstein, with a focus on his scholarship]. Beijing: Beijing daxue chubanshe, 2009.

Wang Qinruo 王欽若. *Cefu yuangui* 冊府元龜 [Outstanding models from the storehouse of literature]. Nanjing: Fenghuang chubanshe, 2006.

Wang Shizhen 王使臻. "Dunhuang yishu zhong de Tang Song chidu yanjiu" 敦煌遺書中的唐宋尺牘研究 [A study of Tang and Song letters in the Dunhuang manuscripts]. PhD dissertation, Lanzhou University, 2012.

———. "Liangjian Dunhuang shuzha qianshi" 兩件敦煌書札淺釋 [A brief explanation of two Dunhuang letters]. *Lishi dang'an* 2011, no. 2: 129–32.

Wang Xiaofu 王小甫. *Tang, Tufan, Dashi zhengzhi guanxi shi* 唐、吐蕃、大食政治關係史 [The political relations between the Tang and the Tibetan and Arabic Empires]. Beijing: Beijing daxue chubanshe, 1992.

Wang Yao 王堯 and Chen Jian 陳踐. *Dunhuang Tufan wenshu lunwenji* 敦煌吐蕃文書論文集 [A collection of essays on Tibetan documents from Dunhuang]. Chengdu: Sichuan minzu chubanshe, 1988.

———. *Dunhuang Tufan wenxian xuan* 敦煌吐蕃文献選 [A selection of old Tibetan texts]. Chengdu: Sichuan minzu chubanshe, 1983.

Wang, Yuanchong. *Remaking the Chinese Empire: Manchu-Korean Relations, 1616–1911*. Ithaca, NY: Cornell University Press, 2018.

Wang, Zhenping. *Ambassadors from the Islands of Immortals: China-Japan Relations in the Han-Tang Period*. Honolulu: Association for Asian Studies and University of Hawai'i Press, 2005.

———. *Tang China in Multi-polar Asia: A History of Diplomacy and War*. Honolulu: University of Hawai'i Press, 2013.

Wang Zhongmin 王重民. *Dunhuang bianwen ji* 敦煌變文集 [Collection of Dunhuang transformation texts]. Beijing: Renmin wenxue chubanshe, 1957.

Watkins, Calvert. *How to Kill a Dragon: Aspects of Indo-European Poetics*. New York: Oxford University Press, 2001.

Watkins, John. "Toward a New Diplomatic History of Medieval and Early Modern Europe." *Journal of Medieval and Early Modern Studies* 38, no. 1 (2008): 1–14.

Waugh, Daniel. "Richthofen's 'Silk Road': Toward the Archaeology of a Concept." *Silk Road* 5, no. 1 (2007): 1–10.

Wechler, Howard J. *Offerings of Jade and Silk: Ritual and Symbol in the Legitimation of the T'ang Dynasty*. New Haven, CT: Yale University Press, 1985.

Wei Shou 魏收. *Weishu* 魏書 [Wei history]. Beijing: Zhonghua shuju. 1974.

Wei Zheng 魏徵. *Suishu* 隋書 [Sui history]. Beijing: Zhonghua shuju, 1973.

Wen Xin 文欣. "The Emperor of Dunhuang: Rethinking Political Regionalism in Tenth Century China." *Journal of Chinese History* 6, no. 1 (2022): 43–68.

———. "Kingly Exchange: The Silk Road and the East Eurasian World in the Age of Fragmentation (850–1000)." PhD dissertation, Harvard University, 2017.

———. "King of Kings of China: Central Asian Political Imagination after the Fall of the Tang." *Harvard Journal of Asiatic Studies* (forthcoming).

———. "What's in a Surname? Central Asian Participation in the Culture of Naming in Medieval China." *T'ang Studies* 34 (2016): 73–98.

———. "Yutian guo guanhao kao" 于闐國官號考 [A study of Khotanese official titles]. *Dunhuang Tulufan yanjiu* 11 (2009): 121–46.

Whitfield, Susan. *Life along the Silk Road*. Berkeley: University of California Press, 2001.

———. *Silk, Slaves, and Stupas: Material Culture of the Silk Road*. Berkeley: University of California Press, 2018.

Wilkinson, Endymion. *Chinese History, a New Manual*. 4th ed. Cambridge, MA: Harvard University Asia Center, 2015.

Williams, Tim. "Mapping the Silk Road." In *The Silk Road: Interwoven History*, edited by Mariko Namba Walter and James P. Ito-Adler, 1–42. Cambridge, MA: Cambridge Institute Press, 2015.

Wittfogel, Karl, and Feng Chia-Sheng. *History of Chinese Society Liao (907–1125)*. Philadelphia: American Philosophical Society, 1949.

Wong, Dorothy. "The Making of a Saint: Images of Xuanzang in East Asia." *Early Medieval China* 8 (2002): 43–95.

———. "A Reassessment of the *Representation of Mt. Wutai* from Dunhuang Cave 61." *Archives of Asian Art* 46 (1993): 27–52.

Wu Liyu 吳麗娛. *Tangli zhiyi: Zhonggu shuyi yanjiu* 唐禮摭遺: 中古書儀研究 [Remnants of Tang rites: A study of medieval letter models]. Beijing: Shangwu yinshu guan, 2002.

Wu Zhen 吳震. *Wu Zhen Dunhuang Tulufan wenshu yanjiu lunji* 敦煌吐魯番文書研究論集 [Collected articles on Dunhuang and Turfan studies by Wu Zhen]. Shanghai: Shanghai guji chubanshe, 2009.

Xiao Song 蕭嵩. *Dai Tō kaigenrei, tsuketari Dai Tō kōshiroku* 大唐開元禮, 附大唐郊祀錄 [The ritual of the Great Tang in the Kaiyuan era, with an appendix: The record of the suburban sacrifice in the Great Tang]. Tokyo: Kyūko shoin, 1972.

Xinjiang Weiwu'er zizhiqu bowuguan 新疆維吾爾自治區博物館, ed. *Xinjiang chutu wenwu* 新疆出土文物 [Excavated documents from Xinjiang]. Urumchi: Xinjiang renmin chubanshe, 1975.

Xu Jun 徐俊. *Dunhuang shiji canjuan jikao* 敦煌詩集殘卷輯考 [An edition and study of fragments of collections of Dunhuang poetry]. Beijing: Zhonghua shuju, 2000.

Xu Song 徐松, comp. *Song huiyao jigao* 宋會要輯稿 [The recovered draft of the collected essential documents of the Song]. 16 vols. Edited by Liu Lin 劉琳, Diao Zhongmin 刁忠民, Shu Dagang 舒大剛, and Yin Bo 尹波. Shanghai: Shanghai guji chubanshe, 2014.

Xue Juzheng 薛居正. *Jiu Wudai shi* 舊五代史 [Old history of the Five Dynasties]. Beijing: Zhonghua shuju, 1976.

Yamaguchi Zuiho 山口瑞鳳, ed. *Tonkō Kogo bunken* 敦煌胡語文獻 [Non-Chinese manuscripts from Dunhuang]. Tokyo: Daitō Shuppansha, 1985.

Yan Tingliang 顏廷亮. "*Baiquege* xinjiao bing xu" 《白雀歌》新校並序 [A new edition of the *Song of the White Sparrow*]. *Dunhuang xue jikan* 16, no. 2 (1989): 60–69.

———. "*Longquan shenjiange* xinjiao bing xu" 《龍泉神劍歌》新校並序 [A new edition of the *Song of the Divine Sword of the Dragon Fountain*]. *Gansu shehui kexue* 1994, no. 4: 108–12.

———. "*Shazhou baixing yiwanren shang Huihu Tiankehan zhuang* xinjiao bingxu" 《沙州百姓一萬人上回鶻天可汗狀》新校並序 [A new edition of the *Petition from the Ten-Thousand Shazhou Commoners to the Heavenly Khagan of the Uyghurs*]. *Lanzhou jiaoyu xueyuan xuebao* 1994, no. 1: 3–9.

Yang Baoyu 楊寶玉 and Wu Liyu 吳麗娛. *Guiyijun zhengquan yu zhongyang guanxi yanjiu: Yi ruzou huodong wei zhongxin* 歸義軍政權與中央關係研究: 以入奏活動為中心 [A study of the relation between the Guiyijun state and the central government: Focusing on tribute-paying activities]. Beijing: Zhongguo shehui kexue chubanshe, 2015.

Yang Fuxue 楊富學. *Huihu yu Dunhuang* 回鶻與敦煌 [The Uyghur state and Dunhuang]. Lanzhou: Gansu jiaoyu chubanshe, 2013.

Yang, Jidong. "Transportation, Boarding, Lodging, and Trade along the Early Silk Road: A Preliminary Study of the Xuanquan Manuscripts." *Journal of the American Oriental Society* 135, no. 3 (2015): 421–32.

Yang Jiping 楊繼平. "Tangdai chi bu, muzhi, muchan xiaoyi" 唐代尺步、畝制、畝產小議 [A brief discussion of the *chi*, *bu*, *mu*-system and agricultural production in the Tang]. *Zhongguo shehui jingji shi yanjiu* 中國社會經濟史研究 1996, no. 2: 32–44.

Yang, Lien-sheng. "A 'Posthumous Letter' from the Chin Emperor to the Khitan Emperor in 942." *Harvard Journal of Asiatic Studies* 10 (1947): 418–28.

Yang Rui 楊蕤. *Sichouzhilu de Huihu shidai* 絲綢之路的回鶻時代 [The Uyghur age on the Silk Road]. Beijing: Zhongguo shehui kexue chubanshe, 2015.

Yang Sen 楊森. "Wudai Song shiqi Yutian taizi zai Dunhuang de taizi zhuang" 五代宋時期于闐太子在敦煌的太子莊 [The Khotanese crown princes and their estates in Dunhuang during the Five Dynasties and the Song dynasty]. *Dunhuang yanjiu* 2013, no. 4: 40–44.

Yang, Shao-Yun. "'Stubbornly Chinese?' Clothing Styles and the Question of Tang Loyalism in Ninth-Century Dunhuang." *International Journal of Eurasian Studies* 5 (2016): 152–87.

Yao Runeng 姚汝能. *An Lushan shiji* 安祿山事跡 [The life of An Lushan]. Beijing: Zhonghua shuju, 2006.

Ye Longli 葉隆禮. *Qidan guozhi* 契丹國志 [A treatise on the Kitan state]. Beijing: Zhonghua shuju, 2014.

Yoeli-Thalim, Ronit. "The Silk Roads as a Model for Exploring Eurasian Transmission of Medical Knowledge: Views from the Tibetan Medical Manuscripts of Dunhuang." In *Entangled Itineraries: Materials, Practices, and Knowledges across Eurasia*, edited by Pamela H. Smith, 47–62. Pittsburgh, PA: University of Pittsburgh Press, 2019.

Yoshida Yutaka 吉田豊. *Kōtan shutsudo 8–9 seiki no Kōtango sezoku monjo ni kansuru oboe gaki* コータン出土 8 — 9 世紀のコータン語世俗文書に關する覺え書き [A note on the secular Khotanese documents from the eighth and ninth centuries discovered in Khotan]. Kobe, Japan: Kobe City University of Foreign Studies, 2006.

———. "The Sogdian Merchant Network." In *Oxford Research Encyclopedia of Asian History*, edited by David Ludden. New York: Oxford University Press, 2020. https://oxfordre.com/asianhistory/view/10.1093/acrefore/9780190277727.001.0001/acrefore-9780190277727-e-491.

Yu Xin 余欣. "Furui yu difang zhengquan de hefaxing goujian: Guiyijun shiqi Dunhuang ruiying kao" 符瑞與地方政權的合法性構建：歸義軍時期敦煌瑞應考 [Omens and the construction of political legitimacy in a regional state: A study of the auspicious omens in Dunhuang during the Guiyijun period]. *Zhonghua wenshi luncong* 100, no. 4 (2010): 325–78.

Yūsuf Khāṣṣ Ḥājib. *Wisdom of Royal Rlory: A Turko-Islamic Mirror for Princes (Kutadgu bilig)*. Translated by Robert Dankoff. Chicago: University of Chicago Press, 1983.

Zeder, Melinda A., Eve Emshwiller, Bruce D. Smith, and Daniel G. Bradley. "Documenting Domestication: The Intersection of Genetics and Archaeology." *Trends in Genetics* 22, no. 3 (2006): 139–55.

Zhang, Cong Ellen. *Transformative Journeys: Travel and Culture in Song China*. Honolulu: University of Hawai'i Press, 2011.

Zhang Guangda 張廣達. *Xiyu shidi conggao chubian* 西域史地叢稿初編 [A first collection of writings on the history and geography of the western regions]. Shanghai: Shanghai guji chubanshe, 1995.

Zhang Guangda and Rong Xinjiang. "A Concise History of the Turfan Oasis and Its Exploration." *Asia Major*, 3rd ser., 11, no. 2 (1998): 13–36.

———. *Yutian shi congkao* 于闐史叢考 [A collection of essays on the history of Khotan]. 2nd ed. Beijing: Zhongguo renmin daxue chubanshe, 2008.

Zhang Shinan 張世南. *Youhuan jiwen* 遊宦紀聞 [Tales heard in a life in bureaucracy]. Beijing: Zhonghua shuju, 1981.

Zhang Xiaoyan 張小艷. *Dunhuang shuyi yuyan yanjiu* 敦煌書儀語言研究 [A study of the language of letter models from Dunhuang]. Beijing: Shangwu yinshuguan, 2007.

Zhang Xiuqing 張秀清. "Dunhuang xiejuan S.526 kao." 敦煌寫卷 S.526 考 [An investigation of the Dunhuang manuscript S. 526]. *Zhongguo wenhua yanjiu* 2008, no. 3: 166–75.

Zhang Yanqing 張延清. "Zhang Yichao yu Tubo wenhua" 張議潮與吐蕃文化 [Zhang Yichao and Tibetan culture]. *Dunhuang yanjiu* 91, no. 3 (2005): 87–92.

Zhang Zhan. "Between China and Tibet: A Documentary History of Khotan in the Late Eighth and Early Ninth Century." PhD dissertation, Harvard University, 2016.

Zhao Feng 趙豐. *Dunhuang sichou yu Sichou zhilu* 敦煌絲綢與絲綢之路 [Dunhuang silk and the Silk Road]. Beijing: Zhonghua shuju, 2009.

Zhao Feng 趙豐 and Wang Le 王樂. *Dunhuang sichou* 敦煌絲綢 [Dunhuang silk]. Lanzhou: Gansu jiaoyu chubanshe, 2013.

———. "Glossary of Textile Terminology (Based on the Documents from Dunhuang and Tufan)." In H. Wang and Hansen, "Textiles as Money," 349–87.

Zhao Heping 趙和平. *Dunhuang biao zhuang jian qi shuyi jijiao* 敦煌表狀箋啓書儀輯校 [An edition of epistolary texts from Dunhuang]. Nanjing: Jiangsu guji chubanshe, 1997.

Zhao Zhen 趙貞. *Guiyijun shishi kaolun* 歸義軍史事考論 [Discussions of the history of the Guiyijun state]. Beijing: Beijing shifan daxue chubanshe, 2010.

———. "Wan Tang Wudai Shuofang Hanshi shiji lueshuo" 晚唐五代朔方韓氏事跡略說 [A brief history of the Han family in Shuofang during the late Tang and the Five Dynasties]. *Qinghai minzu xueyuan xuebao* 35, no. 1 (2009): 61–65, 144.

Zheng Binglin 鄭炳林. *Dunhuang beiming zan jishi* 敦煌碑銘讚輯釋 [Collection and explanation of inscriptions, epitaphs, and elegies from Dunhuang]. Lanzhou: Gansu jiaoyu chubanshe, 1992.

———. "Wan Tang Wudai Dunhuang diqu de Tufan jumin chutan" 晚唐五代敦煌地區的吐蕃居民初探 [A preliminary inquiry into the Tibetan residents in Dunhuang during the late Tang and the Five Dynasties period]. *Zhongguo zangxue* 2005, no. 2: 40–45.

———. "Wan Tang Wudai Dunhuang diqu renkou bianhua yanjiu" 晚唐五代敦煌地區人口變化研究 [A study of population change in the Dunhuang region during the late Tang and the Five Dynasties period]. *Jiangxi shehui kexue* 2014, no. 12: 20–30.

———. "Wan Tang Wudai Dunhuang maoyi shichang de wujia" 晚唐五代敦煌貿易市場的物價 [The price of commodities in Dunhuang markets in the late Tang and the Five Dynasties period]. *Dunhuang xue jikan* 1997, no. 3: 14–32.

Zheng Binglin and Li Jun 李軍. *Dunhuang lishi dili* 敦煌歷史地理 [The historical geography of Dunhuang]. Lanzhou: Gansu renmin chubanshe, 2013.

Zheng Binglin and Liang Zhisheng 梁志勝. "*Liang Xingde miaozhenzan* yu Liang Yuanqing *Mogaoku gongde ji*" 《梁幸德邈真讚》與梁願清《莫高窟功德記》 [The portrait elegy of Liang Xingde and Liang Yuanqing's record on the merit for building the Mogao ku]. *Dunhuang yanjiu* 1992, no. 2: 62–70.

Zheng Binglin and Xue Xiaoli 徐曉麗. "Du *Ecang Dunhuang wenxian* di 12 ce jijian fei fojing wenxian zhaji" 讀俄藏敦煌文獻第 12 冊幾件非佛經文獻札記 [Notes on several secular documents from volume 12 of *Ecang Dunhuang wenxian*]. *Dunhuang yanjiu* 80, no. 4 (2003): 81–89.

Zheng Chuhui 鄭處誨. *Minghuang zalu* 明皇雜錄 [Miscellaneous records of Emperor Xuanzong of the Tang]. Beijing: Zhonghua shuju, 1994.

Zheng Xuemeng 鄭學檬. "Dunhuang Tulufan wenshu yu Tangshi yanjiu" 敦煌吐魯番文書與唐史研究 [Dunhuang and Turfan documents and the study of Tang history]. *Xingda lishi xuebao* 13 (2002): 199–206.

Zheng Yinan 鄭怡楠 and Zheng Binglin. "Dunhuang Caoshi Guiyijun shiqi xugongdeji wenti de yanbian" 敦煌曹氏歸義軍時期修功德記文體的演變 [The transformation of the *Records of Merits* from Dunhuang during the Cao family period]. *Dunhuang xue jikan* 2014, no. 1: 1–11.

Zhou Qufei 周去非. *Lingwai daidai jiaozhu* 嶺外代答校注 [Annotated answers to questions from the land beyond the pass]. Edited by Yang Wuquan 楊武泉. Beijing: Zhonghua shuju, 1999.

Zhou Tianyou 周天遊, ed. *Zhanghuai taizi mu bihua* 章懷太子墓壁畫 [Mural paintings from the tomb of Crown Prince Zhanghuai]. Beijing: Wenwu chubanshe, 2002.

Zhu Lei 朱雷. "Tang jifang kao" 唐籍坊考 [A study of the office of household registers in the Tang]. *Wuhan daxue xuebao* 1983, no. 5: 114–19.

# INDEX

Page numbers in *italics* refer to figures and tables.

# A NOTE ON THE TYPE

This book has been composed in Arno, an Old-style serif typeface in the classic Venetian tradition, designed by Robert Slimbach at Adobe.